K R Taylor
01/12/2024
Americus, GA

THE WORLDLY YEARS

THE WORLDLY YEARS

THE LIFE OF LESTER PEARSON

VOLUME II: 1949-1972

JOHN ENGLISH

ALFRED A. KNOPF CANADA

PUBLISHED BY ALFRED A. KNOPF CANADA

Copyright © 1992 by John English.
All rights reserved under International and
Pan-American Copyright Conventions.

Distributed by Random House of Canada Limited, Toronto.

FIRST EDITION

Canadian Cataloguing in Publication Data

English, John, 1945—
The worldly years

Continues the author's: Shadow of heaven.
Includes bibliographical references and index.
ISBN 0-394-22729-8

1. Pearson, Lester B., 1897-1972. 2. Canada — Politics and government —
1963-1968.* 3. Canada — Politics and government — 1957-1963.*
4. Canada — Politics and government — 1935-1957.* 5. Prime ministers —
Canada —Biography. I. Title. II. Title: Shadow of heaven.

FC621.P43E5 1992   971.064'3'092   C92-095088-4
F1034.3.P43E5 1992

Printed and bound in Canada.

New York, Toronto, London, Sydney, Auckland

To Jonathan

CONTENTS

PREFACE

IN LONDON in wartime, the Canadian diplomat Charles Ritchie recalled Canada in the years between the wars and declared: "I cannot imagine going back to the old small town Canada with its narrow, intense local interests and sitting down under it again." Lester "Mike" Pearson, Ritchie's colleague at the Canadian High Commission in London during the early war years, felt equally uncomfortable with the Canada of the 1930s, with its anti-Semitic school texts, small-town puritanism, and isolationist ways.

In 1946 Mike Pearson returned to Canada to stay, but it was by then a different country from the one that he had served since 1928 as an officer in Canada's department of External Affairs. The war had cleared out the debris from the Canadian economy's arteries, and the hopes that had shrivelled during the long depression now swelled once more. The economic resurgence and the Allied victory brought a new self-confidence to Canada that not even the Cold War's chill could erase. In these better times, Mike Pearson became emblematic of a Canada that was rapidly shedding its tattered and drab garments and donning a post-war "new look" that was neither staid nor small-town, but a well cut and neatly tailored fashion that caught the world's eye.

Mike Pearson had spent most of his adult life outside of Canada, fighting its wars and trying as a diplomat to keep it at peace, but he fitted comfortably into the more cosmopolitan Canada that he encountered upon his return. He was forty-nine years old when he became under-secretary of state for External Affairs in 1946. To the frequent dismay of Prime Minister Mackenzie King, Pearson and Louis St. Laurent, who became External Affairs minister in 1946, placed Canada in the swirl of global politics in Palestine, Europe, and Korea. Pearson's successes in international diplomacy — and they seemed many — became his nation's. King recognized their value as a political currency, and when it was finally time for that politically shrewdest prime minister to leave, he made St. Laurent his own successor and persuaded Pearson to replace St. Laurent at External Affairs. Mike was, the Conservative *Ottawa Journal* claimed, the Liberal's "golden boy", whose greatest victories lay ahead. The lustre would eventually dim, but in those days, as a nation long bashful left its North American corner to take its place at the centre of the ring, Mike Pearson won the crowd's cheers. In 1949, when this second volume of his biography begins, the cheers were the loudest.

CHAPTER ONE

THE
GOOD YEAR

...Thus we signed the North Atlantic Treaty on that pleasant spring day in Washington while the band of the U.S. Marines played soft music, including two selections from *Porgy and Bess*: "I got plenty of nothing" and "It ain't necessarily so."

— Lester Pearson on the signing of the
North Atlantic Treaty on April 4, 1949[1]

SPRING came early to Ottawa in 1949. The ice broke in the rivers in April, and the unloosed logs swirled down the swollen Gatineau River to the mills not far from Parliament Hill. In the valley below the city, along the Rideau River, the villagers and farmers, in the fashion of their Irish and French ancestors, tilled their gardens after the last frost on May 7. The city had swollen beyond the boundaries of its Victorian centre during the war years, but the centre looked much the same as, in its Sandy Hill district, beneath winter-naked trees the residents cleared away the last traces of winter and planted the seeds for the glorious summer that was soon to follow.[2]

Mike and Maryon Pearson, now middle-aged, would spend the rest of their life together in the small Canadian capital. In 1945, they had sold the Rockcliffe home they adored, and in 1946, on their return from Washington, had moved into an older house on Augusta Street in Sandy Hill. The house, a British reporter condescendingly but accurately wrote, was an "old villa with clumsy gables and early Edwardian plumbing in a district of decaying gentility".[3] The house was rented, for Mike and Maryon knew that political life could be short and so nasty that long-term planning was foolish. Its furniture was solid yet ordinary — what one would expect in the home of a retired diplomat whose peripatetic life prevented the accumulation of either delicate or bulky treasures. The "decaying gentility" of the district was deceptive, for many of the city's more prosperous residents, including Mackenzie King, had not moved to Rockcliffe with its recent imitations of English country manors and its sylvan isolation from mid-century urban life.

Ottawa was now a city of 200,000 people, compared with only 125,000 when the Pearsons had moved there in the late 1920s.[4] Unlike London, however, it remained too small to allow diplomatic life to be swallowed up in it. Maryon, whose candour was unusual in a politician's wife in those days, told the British reporter that she much preferred London where it was possible to have "a life of your own".[5] Such a life of one's own was no longer an option for the Pearsons in Canada's capital. Mike's ruddy Irish face, still handsome at fifty-two, was recognized on Parliament Hill, along Sandy Hill's tree-lined streets, and sometimes even in the small French shops of the lower town. He had been Canada's best-known civil servant, and his eminence in that profession, whose status was never so high as it then was, had carried him onto the front bench of the Liberal government of Louis St. Laurent. Even though St. Laurent had barely taken the reins from Mackenzie King, there was already speculation that the new "golden boy", Mike Pearson, would some day be his successor.[6]

Mike's political charm derived not only from a broad "smile which softened hard faces" but also from his reputation as the diplomat who led Canada away from its pre-war isolation towards an active participation in world councils — a role that had come, rather surprisingly, to define for many Canadians what post-war Canada was. He wore his eminence lightly, shunning self-importance with a quick wit that he usually directed at his own foibles and frailties. He was Maryon's most frequent target, too, as she regaled dinner parties with tales of Mike's ineptitude in replacing lightbulbs and driving cars, and his difficulty in remembering to take along his money. And Annie, his mother, retained a Methodist mother's sense that worldly honours meant little in the sight of God. When she attended the Honourable Lester B. Pearson's swearing-in ceremony, she turned to her son's new colleagues and reportedly said, a bit too loudly but with a wry smile, "Do you think he's up to it?"[7]

He was certainly "up to it" in 1949. The young academic who in 1928 had seemed, to those who hired him at External Affairs, "curiously loose-jointed and sloppy" in his "mental makeup" and physical bearing had passed into department mythology. Now, Mike seemed very much a person in touch with his times, those post-war years when North America, freed from the deprivations of the Depression and the sacrifices of wartime, began to unbutton its waistcoat, loosen its tie, and stride (and unfortunately in some cases strut) among the world of nations. Instead of the depression that followed the First World War, the years following the Second World War brought a sudden gust of material prosperity and a new willingness to savour it. The most popular book of those years was Dr. Benjamin Spock's *Common Sense Book of Baby and Child Care*, which advised the astonishing number of new parents to "comfort and love" their offspring as their "repressive" parents had not done. Two years after the appearance of Spock's book, Alfred Kinsey's *Sexual Behaviour in the Human Male* (1948) revealed that the parents had not been as "repressed" as many thought them to be. What these books reflected was the sense that North Americans had an unprecedented freedom of choice and that the formality of a more restrictive society could and should end. A Gallup editor surveying his post-war polling results thought that North Americans had become "a little giddy", as visions of new bungalows, crammed refrigerators, and Raymond Loewy's daring Studebakers danced in their heads. "Mike" — a splendid nickname in the age of "Rocket" Richard, "Toe" Blake, and "Bogie" — symbolized for

3

many Canadians, especially young, middle-class English Canadians, the more confident and open face that post-war Canada wanted to possess. His manner was easy, his wit gentle and increasingly self-deprecating, and he exuded an apparent candour, a quality that was increasingly prized in political life.[8]

Mike was certainly not giddy, and the candour cleverly concealed a private self, yet he did feel comfortable as a Canadian public figure in the late 1940s. Maryon, however, was not always so comfortable with the times or with public life. Photographs of her taken on her first appearances as a politician's wife show her wearing a veil over her face. The veil was fashionable in the post-war years and Maryon had a keen sense of fashion, but one wonders if the veil was not a symbol of her desire to conceal a self that resented the public's intrusion. Later, when veils were not fashionable, she wore sun-glasses on public occasions. She had spent two weeks on the campaign trail with Mike in Algoma East in 1948, "a trim figure in a grey tailored ensemble with matching hat and wine accessories". She sipped coffee and chewed rubbery doughnuts with miners, farmers, and Indians in small towns scattered along the rail line on the great Laurentian Shield. She told a reporter that she was enjoying herself and "would do [her] best" in her "role" as a politician's wife. Her frustrations, however, sometimes broke through that pose. "How does it feel to be back in the West?" a reporter asked. "Not very good," she snapped.[9]

Nothing irritated her more than reporters who asked her what a "wife's view" was. In her opinion, "women are as intelligent as men, surely, and just as capable of forming sensible opinions on any subject."[10] Expressing these opinions, however, was not so easy. She became nervous when meeting the eminent persons who crossed the Pearsons' path. When one of her husband's colleagues noticed her trembling beside him just before they were to meet the American secretary of state, Dean Acheson, and the United Nations secretary general, Trygve Lie, she told him that she was always nervous on such occasions: "I never know how I'm going to face up to all these people until I get there."[11] But she did face up to them, even if

4

she sometimes used silence and a sardonic wit as a protective shield. She accompanied Mike on trips more frequently now that the children, Geoffrey and Patsy, were away at the University of Toronto. The children's student lives she shared by an effort of imagination, piecing together the evidence from scraps in their letters, pauses in their too-infrequent chats, and her own memories of those days at Victoria College, when Cromwell was her greatest annoyance and Mike, her British history teacher, her fascination. Maryon was typical of all parents in believing that her past was more sedate than it actually was.

Time and circumstances had dashed her collegian dreams of "being together [with Mike] and doing and thinking together" while doing "some mental work" herself. By 1949, Mike and Maryon had "settled down" — to use the term she so dreaded in her early twenties — and his world of public life defined most of hers. She chafed against the restrictions and the protocol of public life. But, as her friend Mary MacKeen observed, she really did accept that restrictions and protocol should exist. Her ambivalence, which was also characteristic of the times, was later noted by Dean Acheson, when he sarcastically but perceptively wrote to his wife after Mike won the general election of 1963 that Marion disliked being in office as much as being out.[12] She resented the sacrifice of private moments and was uncomfortable with the contemporary view expressed by the psychiatrist Helene Deutsch, and even by Dr. Spock, that "normal femininity" meant identifying with a husband as a means of relating to the outside world.[13] Mme. St. Laurent completely shunned the political world. Maryon Pearson accepted it, but her spirited response to it revealed her belief that it was misshapen. Still, for all its shortcomings, it could be fun, and the Pearsons had a good time.

When the Ottawa "season" began in the fall, the Pearsons' days were crammed with dinners, cocktail parties, ambassadors' receptions, and gatherings of friends. Taking two weeks randomly from Maryon's date book, one can see how their lives were intertwined and dependent.

		Afternoon	*Evening*
Mon.	Jan. 5	2:30 bridge	6-8 Cocktails – Beaudry
Tues.	Jan. 6		
Wed.	Jan. 7		6 Cocktails – Towers/concert
Thurs.	Jan. 8		6 Norman Smiths
Fri.	Jan. 9	4:30 Tea	
Sat.	Jan. 10	4:00 Parliament	6 McTavishes for Ritchie
Sun.	Jan. 11		6 Heeneys for Ritchie
Mon.	Apr. 5	1:00 lunch – Chesters	6:00 Garners
		4:00 Mme Basdevant calling	
Tues.	Apr. 6	3:00 bridge – Verse's	6-8:00 U.S. Army – Lansdowne
			6:00 Reception – Earnscliffe
Wed.	Apr. 7		8:00 Dinner – Italians
			6:30 Drink –K. Walker
Thurs.	Apr. 8	10:15 French	6-8 Garners
Fri.	Apr. 9	9:30 Hair	Dance Club
		12:00 Lunch – 3 women	
			7:45 dinner Heeneys
Sat.	Apr. 10		6:00 Cocktails Heeneys
Sun.	Apr. 11	Lunch – Bruces	7:30 Supper – Gerry Riddell
		Heeneys at	
		Country Club	Marrs for Tea

This was the way they lived through the post-war years except for the brief but hot Ottawa summers, when so many of their crowd migrated to the cool lakes of the Gatineau Hills, and social life in the capital died. Their "crowd", some members of which are named in Maryon's datebook entries above, was a mixture of old and new friends: the "season" was a blend of private and public functions. The cocktails on January 5 were for Laurent Beaudry, who was retiring after a long career that had lacked much distinction — an embarrassment, since Beaudry had been the first and most senior francophone in the department. The "Towers" were Graham and Mollie Towers, who looked every bit a distinguished governor of the Bank of Canada and a banker's wife, but who, after hours, enlivened and lengthened every party. The Pearsons had become friends with Graham and Mollie in the thirties, and their friendship was nurtured by shared views, quick wit, and good Scotch. In the summers, the Pearsons usually went down to "Steepways", the Towers' summer home at fashionable Murray Bay. "Steepways" offered a splendid view of the St. Lawrence, breakfast in bed delivered by a maid to any guest who asked for it, and the company of other friends, such as Bill and Ethel Harris, who also vacationed there. As the years passed, however, Mike tended increasingly to remain in Ottawa at the office, or in New York at the United Nations, while Maryon continued the trek to Murray Bay. Mike lost his taste for the parties. Graham's off-colour jokes told in mixed company embarrassed the parson's son. He preferred to "nurse" drinks, when the others around him did not, and his nocturnal ways had long ago disappeared. Moreover, his personal relationship with Graham had cooled. But the Towers' "crowd", with its wit, wealth, and bonhomie, made Maryon feel comfortable. As the years passed, Graham became a confidant, and one of her best friends.

In her fascinating study of prime ministers' wives and "other women", Heather Robertson claims that "Maryon's affection for Graham created scandalous rumours in Ottawa that swirl around to this day …". They swirl but do not settle, for the evidence of the closeness of the relationship is mere fragments in Maryon's sporadic and cryptic diary and Towers' appointment book. "Drove to M. Bay in am w. Graham," she wrote on June 22, 1967. She despaired when his health failed later. Towers liked alcohol, parties, barbed comments, gossip, and flirting, and so did Maryon. The style, content, and tone are distinctly London society in the age of Diana Cooper, the Duke of Windsor, and Lord Beaverbrook. The "Beaver", like Towers, delighted in astonishing his Caribbean guests by inviting Henry Luce with his mistress and in shocking his innocent fellow-Canadians with risqué tales of the amours and intrigues of the mighty of the day. It was a style that Maryon and Graham and Mike knew and enjoyed, but that Ottawa in the forties and fifties did not. We cannot say that Maryon and Graham were lovers, but we can be quite certain that Maryon delighted in making others speculate on the question as we have.[14]

Maryon adored Charles Ritchie, as did most men and, seemingly, all women who knew him. The receptions in Maryon's January calendar honoured his impending wedding, an event greeted with warm approval mingled with wistful regret that the saga of Ritchie's amorous complications — a source of delight to the Canada House staff in London when Charles and Mike served there during the blitz — would have no more chapters. Ritchie had returned from Paris for Christmas leave. The Garners — Saville (or, more popularly, "Joe") and his wife, Margaret — were returning to London after his stint as the United Kingdom's deputy high commissioner in Ottawa. Mike had known "Joe" from London in the 1930s. He had known Fraser Bruce, the vice-president of Alcan and its future president, since Mike had coached the football team at the University of Toronto in 1927. He had met Arnold Heeney in the late 1930s when Heeney came to Ottawa as Prime Minister King's personal secretary. King was a friend of Heeney's father, Bertal, an Anglican priest. Despite a Tory background, Bertal had found, most remarkably, in Mackenzie King, "a simple and beautiful mind set in guiding people and the country along the path of Truth". Like King, Bertal condemned "cocktail parties, women's lipstick and frivolous life". And it must be said that Bertal's son, an exemplary public servant, was not so comfortable when he surveyed what his poetic fellow-Montrealer Frank Scott (also a friend of Mike's from the early thirties) dubbed "the latex tintex kotex cutex" quality of post-war North American life.[15] Not surprisingly, Arnold did not like Maryon, who enjoyed parties, wore lipstick, drank Scotch, and was outspoken. "I can't stand Maryon Pearson," he confided to his diary after one unpleasant dinner party in the fifties.[16] Nevertheless, he and Mike got on well, and Mike asked him to become his under-secretary of state for External Affairs when Mike left that position to become minister in 1948. The appointment of the extraordinarily capable administrator, who, like Mike, had studied under W.C. Costin at Oxford, was a decision that Mike, whose own administrative skills were not much admired, never regretted.[17] Neither did those who worked for them.

Former students, students of the same tutor, sons of Mackenzie King's friends, companions in peacetime and wartime London, blood and tradition were all around Ottawa, and sometimes they could become oppressive. The Ottawa élite was small with few French, too much Oxbridge, and too many closed windows. The "dance club" on Maryon's calendar had been organized by her when Mike became under-secretary to bring together the younger diplomats with Ottawa's young women. Maryon would invariably "break the ice" by asking some poor junior diplomat to start off the Paul Jones with her. More than one recalls with terror treading on the toes of the under-secretary's wife. She always forgave them, especially if they laughed or gave her Scotch at Christmas.

For all Maryon's regrets about having no life of her own and Mike's preoccupation with public life, they did laugh a lot in those days, particularly when the family came home or when favourite nephews and nieces visited, especially Pam and Freddy from Boston. Their family photographs of the time are full of gaiety. Freddy, who looked so much like Mike, had survived the war and was richly enjoying the peace. Geoffrey and Patsy had passed successfully through the dangerous years of adolescence, without war service, disease, or any other natural or unnatural disasters, and their futures seemed more secure than Mike's had been when he was their age. Both Mike and Maryon had good health, which some of their friends, among them Hume Wrong and Norman Robertson, unfortunately did not. Although many of their friends were wealthier than they, the Pearsons could still afford to send their children to private schools and to university, to travel, and to enjoy good books and good food, although neither became a gourmet. Certainly Maryon thought that her life was much to be preferred to one as the wife of a history professor — the "tranquil life on a university campus" that Mike later and disingenuously claimed had been her goal.*

If Ottawa was a capital whose corridors of power brimmed with old friends and acquaintances, so were London and Washington, where young diplomats Mike had come to know in the 1930s and early 1940s had risen to positions of influence and eminence. When Mike went to Washington to sign the NATO treaty in April 1949, he took his place beside the U.S. secretary of state, Dean Acheson, whom he had known since the 1930s and with whom he had jousted and joked in wartime Washington. When Acheson was appointed in January 1949 by Harry Truman, Mike had asked the Canadian Embassy in Washington to tell Acheson that Mike and Maryon were "delighted personally, officially, internationally and alcoholically".[18] When, shortly thereafter, the Senate Committee on Foreign Relations quizzed Acheson about Alger Hiss, who had been charged with involvement in a Communist cell, and Acheson attacked the notion of guilt by association, Mike was moved to telephone Acheson at his home "to give him my personal congratulations on the fine statement that he made on the Hiss affair ... [Pearson] said it would be heartening and encouraging to anyone who read it and believed in liberal principles..."[19]

Pearson's confidence in Acheson sprang also from his knowledge of the close relationship between Acheson and Canada's ambassador, Hume Wrong, a friendship forged in early New Deal Washington when the two acerbic public servants gloomily dissected the foolish and pompous of the day. Mike sometimes joined them at their male parties in wartime Washington, and he knew the spirit of

---

* The ordeal of Mike's former University of Toronto colleague George Brown, a distinguished historian and the university librarian, in trying to scrape together $4,500 to have a short leave in 1947 contrasts starkly with Mike's situation. His salary was almost three times as much; travel was frequent; and offers (such as the presidency of the Rockefeller Foundation) came often. Academic salaries decreased considerably in real terms from the twenties to the fifties. George Brown Papers, University of Toronto Archives, and Vincent Bladen, *Bladen on Bladen: Memoirs of a Political Economist* (Toronto: Privately printed, 1978).

those gatherings. When he learned from Wrong that such a party was to be held at Felix Frankfurter's home in Washington on January 22 to honour Acheson's appointment as secretary of state, he sent the following "most urgent, most secret, most personal" telegram to Wrong, in which, after teasing Acheson about his "red" tinge and Canadian ancestors, he concluded:

> If at the party the Secretary of State appears to be in any condition to understand any of this, a highly improbable assumption, you may tell him that the job of looking after the foreign relations of a country is an easy one when a country has a consistent, wise and understandable policy. He will probably have a hell of a time. On the other hand, you may point out, if the Secretary is not by this time unconscious, how lucky he is in having to be confirmed only by a Senate in Washington and not elected by a lot of hardboiled trappers and lumberjacks in Algoma East who are not so easily fooled. You may finally tell Mr. Acheson that if he makes a botch of his new post, and there is an acute division of opinion in Ottawa as to whether this is bound to happen or not, we will give him a job as Canadian consul at one of the American bases which are now sullying our fair country.

The telegram, Wrong reported, was the "highlight of the evening" at which, remarkably, Donald Hiss was one of the six guests. Dean was a new person, certainly not the one Wrong had seen only a few weeks before at an intimate dinner when Wrong and Acheson's wife, Alice, became "really quite worried because of the malice and cruelty of his attacks on almost everybody".[20] The bad mood soon returned, however; Mike's humour lost its charm; and when Acheson years later came to write his memoirs, only the intervention of a close mutual friend, the journalist Bruce Hutchison, saved Mike from a scathing attack.[21]

Their problems came early with the final stages of the negotiations for the North Atlantic treaty. Canadians have sometimes credited themselves with the idea for the treaty that would serve to stiffen European resolve to resist the advance of Soviet Communism. Escott Reid, who was second-in-command to Mike in External in the summer of 1947 and who later wrote the best account of the origins of the North Atlantic Treaty Organization (NATO), traces Canada's catalytic role to a speech that he gave and Mike cleared in August 1947. Reid called for a regional security organization that would pool its economic and political resources to confront Soviet expansionism. Louis St. Laurent, then the secretary of state for External Affairs, brought forward the notion in a speech at the United Nations General Assembly on September 18, 1947. Americans and Britons, who were also frustrated with a U.N. Security Council that had become, in words that Mike wrote and St. Laurent spoke, "frozen in futility and divided by dissension", simultaneously began to think of a mutual security pact that would supplement the ineffective United Nations.[22] These speeches would probably have meant little had not the Soviets been so difficult at the Council of Foreign Ministers' conference in London in late November and early December of 1947. The problem, as always, was Germany, its future and its past. The Soviets were incorrigible, seeking preposterous reparations and making, at least in Western eyes, outrageous assertions about Western intentions.

Nineteen forty-eight brought more evidence of how fragile European democracy was. Mackenzie King had been startled in London in November 1947 when Winston Churchill, "his eyes ... bulging out of the side of his head", told him that war was imminent unless the United States stood up to "Russia's effort to communize the balance of Europe and ... America." King quickly agreed in March 1948 to accept an invitation from Clement Attlee to join in discussions that would lead to a regional security pact. King's fears mirrored his cabinet's, which agreed unanimously that Canada should participate in exploratory talks with the Americans and the British that would lead to a regional security pact under Article 51 of the United Nations charter. King, his colleagues, and even the opposition party leaders were shocked by the death of Jan Masaryk, sceptical of Soviet claims that Masaryk's fall from the window of the

Czech foreign office was suicide, and profoundly shaken by the rumours that a general European collapse would follow that of Czechoslovakia. They therefore did not resist the urgings of Louis St. Laurent, the secretary of state for External Affairs, and Mike, his deputy, that Canada should actively press the Americans to commit themselves fully and openly to the defence of Western Europe.[23]

Following the cabinet decision and the signing of the Treaty of Brussels on March 17, 1948, by Britain, France, and the Benelux countries, King and St. Laurent authorized Mike to go to Washington to explore how the Brussels Treaty might be strengthened by the Anglo-Saxon North Atlantic triangle. King had no hesitations about Canada's participation in the talks, but he did not possess the enthusiasm with which Mike approached his tasks. When Mike suggested on March 18, 1948, that a conference to discuss the proposed pact might be held in Ottawa, King spent a restless night. "It would be a mistake," he wrote in his diary in the morning, "to make Canada a sort of apex to a movement which would be linking together United States and United Kingdom and other nations in a project that is intended to offset the possibility of immediate war with Russia." The notion was typical of Pearson, "one of the dangers of having Pearson take too sudden a lead in any matters of the kind. He can get us much more deeply involved with world situations than we ever should be. He likes keeping Canada at the head of everything, in the forefront in connection with United Nations affairs." King's complaints reflected an old leader's reluctance to give way, as well as his traditional aversion to taking risks or declaring intentions. Still, King's acute political antennae had rightly sensed that in the spring of 1948 Mike Pearson was willing to push Canada beyond its customary boundaries of international activity into arenas where it had previously feared to tread.[24]

Fearful of an American return to isolationism and shocked by the "fall" of Czechoslovakia, Mike was a troubled and determined builder that spring, eager to place new mortar between the apparently crumbling bricks of what he called "the tradition of democratic liberty". He privately compared the "fall of Czechoslovakia" with Munich in 1938 and prodded his American and British counterparts in Washington to accept a broader definition of the North Atlantic security pact. As in the aftermath of Munich, Mike in 1948 thought that Canada's wisest course was to cling even more to its closest allies and thereby gain influence in their capitals that would be employed to steel their nerves in confronting the dictators — Hitler earlier, Stalin now. King, and some later historians, are correct in suggesting that Mike worried little about the dangers of "Big Powers ... using" Canada. The events of the 1930s and the devastating war that followed had weakened for him the arguments of those who fretted about the loss of sovereignty, whether to the British Empire or to the United States. His sense of what the West meant was stronger than it had ever been, and his belief that its unity must be preserved and strengthened was deeply rooted in personal conviction, experience, and, perhaps, ambition. National sovereignty was of secondary importance to him, and he deeply believed that it must be so for embattled Europe. Union brought strength; with division and lack of vision, the peoples of the West would perish.[25]

This was, then, one of those rare opportunities when, in Hotspur's metaphor that Mike frequently quoted, the flower, safety, might be plucked from the nettle, danger. He went to Washington in the first days of spring 1948, passing through a kitchen door into the bowels of the Pentagon where, along with three other Canadians, he met with the British representatives, including his old friend Gladwyn Jebb, and the American representatives, including two old friends, Jack Hickerson and Ted Achilles. The secrecy was extraordinary: as a cover, Mike concocted a story that he was visiting New York. It was also quite unnecessary: one of the five British representatives at these meetings in the Pentagon's bowels was the Soviet spy Donald Maclean, who almost certainly passed on the details of what happened to Moscow. What Stalin learned was that the Anglo-American democracies were not plotting a war against Communism but were showing a resolve to link U.S. military potential with a more united Europe.[26] Stalin would also have learned that, when

Lester Pearson spoke for Canada at the "Security Conversations", Canada was strongest in support of an "Atlantic pact on a broad political basis" rather than simply a unilateral military guarantee to Europe. In summarizing the talks for Mackenzie King, Mike concluded: "In the discussions as to what else might be included in the Security Pact, I stated more than once that the document should not be exclusively military in character and that there were economic and even spiritual defences against attack which should not be overlooked.... Otherwise, it would be considered as merely another old fashioned military alliance."[27]

"Old fashioned military alliances" did not please Mike Pearson or Mackenzie King or, both thought, most Canadians. King had been suspicious of bilateral alliances with Britain in the past and, latterly, with the United States. But the North Atlantic proposals offered something more, what Norman Robertson in London called "a providential solution for so many of [Canada's] problems" — how to assure American commitment to European defence, how to avoid a bilateral Canadian-American commitment, and how to escape being "orphaned" by a purely American-European entente.[28] For Mike, for his second-in-command, Escott Reid, and for the diplomat Arnold Smith, then at Canada's National Defence College, the North Atlantic proposals offered a historically unique opportunity, in Mike's words as embodied in the first draft of the security pact, "to promote the economic well being of their peoples, and to achieve social justice, thereby creating an overwhelming superiority of moral, material, and military force on the side of peace and progress."[29]

The ideas that these words represent flow directly from the Protestant missionary tradition, strengthened by the despair of the Depression and the liberalizing experience of the Second World War, that came to be embodied in the welfare state. The political scientist Denis Smith, who criticizes Canada's ambitious role in the founding of NATO and the willingness of Reid and others to use fear of the Soviet Union to fulfil a much broader agenda, suggests that "Reid and Smith [he might have added Pearson] were both, at heart, romantics who believed in the secular mission of the West, the ultimate challenge of the evil empire to the East, and the mellowing or collapse of Soviet power when confronted with the preponderant strength of the West."[30] The term "romantic" is too dismissive, but Smith captures correctly the sense that Reid, a social democrat, and Arnold Smith, a liberal idealist, believed that western liberal values, strengthened by a more equal and prosperous society through an interventionist welfare state, would ultimately assure the collapse of Communism. Their voices found echoes in the United States, as New Deal liberals adjusted to the post-war years by emphasizing the "vital center". This phrase formed the title of an extraordinary influential 1949 book by Arthur Schlesinger that argued for the essential similarity of Fascism and Communism and for a combination of economic reconstruction and military containment to defeat Communism. Mike may not have read Schlesinger that busy year, but at Lake Couchiching in August he, like Schlesinger, extolled the virtues of travelling in "the middle of the road".

> When the middle of the road is no longer occupied firmly by stable and progressive groups in the community it is turned into a parade ground for those extremist forces who would substitute goose-stepping for walking. All others are driven to hide, disconsolate and powerless, in the hedges, ditches, and culverts.[31]

There were also echoes in Europe, especially among social democrats like Mike's old friend Philip Noel-Baker, then a minister in Britain's Labour government, and Barbara Ward, who was later to become, perhaps, the major influence upon Mike's thoughts about international development. In 1948 Ward wrote, in six weeks, a remarkable book, *The West at Bay*, in which she argued that the West might one day thank the Communists for giving it the "strength" to unite to fulfil "the promise inherent yet still unrealized within it of creating a free, good and just society." She derided those, including social democrats, who, when they spoke of Western civilization and the proposed "Western Union", thought of "no more than international steel, a European electricity grid and the spread through Western Europe of Joint Production Councils." Western unity, she argued, "will remain, as in Ezekiel's vision, a valley of dry bones unless there is a spirit to inform them and bring them together...".[32]

It was such a spirit that animated Pearson's approach to Atlantic unity. Noel-Baker of Britain, Paul-Henri Spaak of Belgium, Ted Achilles and Jack Hickerson of the United States, and Canada's Escott Reid were also infected with this spirit; but others seemed immune, among them Gladwyn Jebb of Britain, State Department officials Charles Bohlen and George Kennan, and Canada's ambassador to the United States, Hume Wrong. To Kennan and Bohlen, the talk of a broader alliance was provocative and too much of a departure from a realistic approach to "containing" the Soviet Union. A far better solution in their eyes was a unilateral military guarantee to Europe to parallel Marshall Plan economic assistance. Kennan argued that such a solution would avoid giving Stalin the impression that he was being encircled by capitalist enemies. Kennan, then and later, distrusted "entangling alliances", especially ones that over-extended U.S. economic and political resources and limited American freedom of action. He had little patience with the Canadians' peculiar attitudes as they expressed it to him in the spring of 1948. He told the secretary of state, General Marshall, on his return from an Ottawa visit, about

[the Canadians'] adherence to the multilateral principle in the determination of policy on these mattes. This, incidentally, is part of the whole general pattern of their attitude with respect to ourselves, which is one of reluctance to do things in company with us alone but of readiness to do them if we get a number of other countries, either in the UN, to join us. This is a very real factor in the Canadian psychology and one which I am afraid we shall have to take into account, as a reality, even though we may not agree with the reasons for it.[33]

Pearson sent Wrong to try to persuade Kennan of the arguments for a multilateral pact, but Kennan remained a sceptic.[34]

The beginning of the Berlin blockade on April Fool's Day, 1948, just after the end of the Washington security talks, made the need for an alliance more urgent, and the Senate responded with the passage of the historic Vandenberg resolution through which the Senate, by a vote of 60 to 4, supported American association in a regional collective security organization. Senator Vandenberg's chief aide, Francis Wilcox, realized that most of the senators "don't know what they're voting on".[35] But they did know that it was an election year and that the Gallup polls were supporting American assistance to Europe. Nevertheless, the election campaign in which "Give 'em hell" Harry Truman lambasted the "do-nothing" Congress acted as an anaesthetic upon the movement towards a North Atlantic pact. Mike fretted as he waited for the American election, and for Mackenzie King to leave, so that he could move from the office of the under-secretary to that of the minister. The government, he believed, was losing momentum, and the spirit of Western unity was flagging. He feared for the future and was not optimistic. King's scuttling of the free-trade negotiations with the United States at the same time as the North Atlantic pact was being drafted upset Pearson. He told Norman Robertson on April 22 that, "I cannot help but feel that a very great opportunity has been missed". In his view, a free-trade agreement "might have had a decisive strengthening effect on the whole economy of the country against the day when such strength is bound to be needed". His hopes that the trade talks might be resumed after "a satisfactory North Atlantic Security Pact" was signed were dashed in May when King demanded that Wrong tell the U.S. undersecretary of state, Robert Lovett, that free trade was forever dead.[36]

Nor could Mike's arguments that Canada "would be implicated in any conflict which might result" from the Berlin crisis overcome King's refusal to become involved. When Wrong wrote to Pearson in September reporting that Kennan and Bohlen, the State Department's leading experts on the Soviet Union, had told Wrong that the Soviet regime "had passed its zenith", Mike refused to share such optimistic thoughts.

> There are not ... [he wrote to Wrong] any conclusive signs [of Soviet decline] yet. While the Western powers are holding their own in Europe, the position of the West in Asia has been weakened. I should think that the Russians, looking at the world from Moscow, might still be confident that in another three years or so the balance which is now tipping against them may begin to be redressed as a result of instability in France, a serious economic recession in the United States and continued political and economic instability in Asia.[37]

There were administrative problems and personality differences that affected the debate about what form the treaty should take and whether the statements on economic and social matters should be preserved. The British, like some Americans, did not think much of the references to co-operation in economic, social, and cultural affairs. In the United States, General Marshall, with tumours on both kidneys and profound doubts that Harry Truman would win the election, gave no leadership, although Hickerson and Achilles had managed to outflank Kennan and Bohlen, their superiors, to convince Undersecretary of State Robert Lovett that their arguments for an Atlantic pact made the most sense. And the French, as always, were difficult, even though, in Mike's view, they had the most to lose if the Atlantic pact crumbled.[38]

In September, the by-election campaign took him to Algoma East, where he spent every day between his nomination meeting on September 24 and election day, October 25, shaking hands in small post offices, church basements, and town halls on the great Laurentian Shield and spending nights in roadside inns and frame homes of local Liberals. The win was expected, but the margin (1,236) was the lowest for a Liberal candidate since Tom Farquhar first took the seat from the Conservatives in 1935 with a margin of 8,275. A greater surprise was Harry Truman's electoral success in early November. The

19

victory reassured Mike, who had some doubts about Truman's skills in foreign policy but none about his courage.

After the by-election, Mike went almost immediately to Paris for the United Nations General Assembly. He reported to St. Laurent that they were not accomplishing very much in Paris: "The hours are too long and the results not encouraging enough to justify them." Later, he told a private meeting of the Canadian Institute of International Affairs that the Paris session had been "frustrating, disappointing and discouraging." The Soviets, he added, deserved nearly all the blame for their "irritating and fatiguing" tirades.[39] He did take the opportunity of his presence in Europe to talk with Jean Désy and Pierre Dupuy about the possibility that either one of them might return to become his under-secretary. Dupuy claimed, rather curiously, that "health problems" made his return impossible. Désy wanted more money and an official residence for the post, terms that a frugal St. Laurent, who himself was renting a fairly modest Ottawa apartment, could not accept.[40] The attempt to find a francophone under-secretary is interesting, first, because it reveals Pearson's and St. Laurent's sensitivity to the overly anglophone character of the Department of External Affairs, and secondly, because neither Robertson nor Wrong was appointed to the under-secretary's post, even though both had served in their posts in London and Washington for three years, a normal length for a posting.*

In the end, Pearson and St. Laurent decided, as we have seen,

---

*Despite their long association, Pearson and Robertson were thought by some of their closest colleagues to be uneasy with each other. Some suggested that the Mackenzie King's choice of Robertson to be under-secretary when O.D. Skelton died caused a lasting jealousy. Others pointed to a difference in their personal styles, with Pearson being bored by long explanations and historical perspectives. Robertson, in contrast, would place the Cold War in the context of the European wars of religion and spice his conversation with literary allusions. Robertson prided himself on obscure references to Baudelaire; Pearson's talk was replete with the latest Reston column in the *New York Times* or with arcane references to earned-run averages. Interviews with John Holmes, George Ignatieff, and Charles Ritchie, and confidential interviews.

that Arnold Heeney should become his under-secretary. Robertson returned from London to take Heeney's place as clerk of the privy council. "Arnold," Mike wrote to Robertson on January 22, 1949, "should be just the person to provide that emphasis on organization and administration in the Department which his predecessors at times tended to overlook."[41] Certainly Escott Reid had not provided that emphasis when he had been acting under-secretary, for his energies were absorbed in the conflict with Wrong about what the Atlantic alliance should be. Early in October 1948, the Canadian cabinet formally agreed that Canada should negotiate a North Atlantic treaty. Reid was to draft the instructions for the Canadian negotiators in Washington; Wrong was to handle the negotiations. Their views, alas, were incompatible. Wrong, with some assistance from Robertson in London and in the spirit of a severe Oxbridge tutor, picked apart Reid's drafts. "Put the ideology of the treaty in the preamble where it belongs," he pointedly rebuked Reid, "and let the rest be put in as direct language as we can find, without frills or use of phrases such as North Atlantic Community, North Atlantic Assembly, or free world in capitals." For Wrong, Canada should stick to "the central purpose in these negotiations, which is, put bluntly, the creation of a military alliance encircling the North Atlantic".

But that was not Reid's view of the central purpose; nor, for that matter, was it Achilles' or Hickerson's. Nor was it Mike Pearson's. Now the minister had to adjudicate between Reid and Wrong, and it was difficult. He had always found Wrong's intellect intimidating and knew how intolerant he could be when he encountered what he thought were fools or knaves. Mike had no desire to be thought either. Reid, by his own later admission, had become "feverish" in his commitment to a broader Atlantic pact, and he swamped Mike with memoranda and telegrams in Mike's first months in office.[42] In reading Reid's own account of the episode much later, Gladwyn Jebb, who participated in the negotiations for the British, felt sorry for Mike, "that hard-worked and competent politician, busy presiding over the General Assembly of the United Nations, being confronted by an admirably argued, if perhaps rather long, disquisition on the exact significance of Article 2 demanding an immediate reply".[43]

The fight between Reid and Wrong over Article 2 came after Acheson was appointed secretary of state in January 1949. Article 2 flowed directly out of Mike's contribution to the original recommendation emanating from the March "security conversations". Between February 3 and 5, 1949, Acheson met with senators Vandenberg and Connally, who shared his view that "the Canadian proposal of Article 2, which got us into cultural, economic, and social cooperation", should be scrapped because it was politically dangerous. Mike gave his maiden speech in the House of Commons on February 4 in between these meetings, and his view of the political dangers was completely different. For him, the Atlantic pact must not be "an instrument of unimaginative militarism". It should have "a deeper meaning and deeper roots" and, for that reason, he attached "great importance to the part which the pact" would play "in the encouragement of peacetime co-operation ... in the economic, social and cultural fields". Four days later, Mike told Wrong that rather than working for a compromise, he should work to strengthen Article 2, and that such an article was politically necessary for the Liberals in Canada. Wrong warned him the instructions would be difficult to carry out.[44]

Certainly Wrong's heart was not in the battle, but he fought bravely nonetheless. He emphasized the political appeal of Article 2 in Canada, especially the needs of Quebec with its anti-military traditions. When St. Laurent met with Truman in early February, he too asked the president for understanding of the political importance in Canada of Article 2. (He also told Truman that it was important for the United States that the Liberals win.) The Canadians thought they gained presidential agreement; the American record, however, states that the discussion was general and "called for no commitments."[45] In the meantime, Ottawa rallied European support, which was forthcoming, albeit with little British enthusiasm. In Washington, Wrong met stern resistance from Acheson and finally asked whether Pearson and Reid could accept a compromise.

They would not. Once again Pearson stiffened Wrong's resolve, warning him that Canada might not be able to sign the treaty if Article 2 were omitted or seriously weakened. Wrong, who had certainly not expected to do battle with his close friend Acheson so soon after his appointment, had to persist. Fortunately, Hickerson and Achilles were themselves sympathetic to Article 2's spirit, if Wrong was not. They were astonished when Wrong told them that Canada's signature might hang upon Article 2. Together with Wrong, they drew up a compromise that they thought might satisfy Acheson, and on a Sunday morning trotted over to Acheson's home where the secretary of state lay in bed, ill with influenza. In Hickerson's words, Wrong and he "beat the poor sick man over the head" until he gave up. There was a further skirmish when Wrong, backed by the Europeans, suggested another sentence that referred to the need to work for higher living standards and social justice; but Acheson, now recovered, would not budge. This time Pearson agreed. The Canadians had got enough. Article 2 became, deservedly, the "Canadian article" in NATO lore. Acheson and Pearson fired their last shots at each other in their memoirs. Acheson claimed in 1969 that Article 2 "has continued to bedevil NATO" and that "Lester Pearson has continually urged the council to set up committees of 'wise men' to find a use for it, which the 'wise men' continually have failed to do." Mike had the last word, but his reply was oblique. Some years later, he wrote, "to my surprise I read in Dean Acheson's [memoirs] how he had 'defused' the Canadian draft of Article 2 by redrafting it to bring it into line with United States' objectives. In diplomacy, it is a good result when your victory is also felt by the other side to be a success." He was gracious to Wrong both in his memoirs and at the time, praising the "magnificent work" that he had done and telling Wrong that the treaty marked "another stage in our joint progress from the days when we used to put our initials, together, on first year pass-papers in history at U of T".[46]

All was forgiven, if not forgotten, when the foreign ministers gathered in Washington to sign the NATO treaty that bright spring day in 1949. Mike was in a splendid mood. When Acheson asked what languages the foreign ministers would speak in order that translators could be arranged, Mike replied that he would speak "North American English with a French accent".[47] His speech reflected the spirit of his work on NATO and contained rhetorical flourishes that embellished his sincere commitment to what was being done that day. NATO, Mike declared, was "a forward move in man's progress from the wasteland of his postwar world, to a better, safer ground. But as we reach distant pastures, we see greener ones far on. As we reach the summit of a lofty peak, higher ones loom up beyond. We are forever climbing the ever mounting slope and must not rest until we reach the last objective of a sane and moral world."[48] Acheson's rhetoric was appropriate but empty, like that of an Anglican priest presiding at the obsequies of one whom he barely knew and cared for little. He noted slyly that the Marine band selections from *Porgy and Bess*, "I've Got Plenty of Nothin'" and "It Ain't Necessarily So", were appropriate. Acheson, two biographers write, "knew full well that NATO was an empty shell"[49] and had to be filled with realistic tanks, airplanes, and soldiers to give it meaning. That would soon happen. But Mike's vision of a new Atlantic community, one that broadened the sides and enriched the interior of the North Atlantic triangle in which Canada had felt most comfortable, was not to be. NATO remained for Mike one of the greatest accomplishments of his public life; but in some ways, like a brilliant child who never fulfils his early promise, it profoundly disappointed.

The euphoric mood in Washington was matched in Ottawa in early spring as Newfoundland joined Confederation. Mike had been one of the covert suitors who had worked to persuade Newfoundlanders to cast their lot with Confederation, and he shared the exhilaration that, in Ottawa if not everywhere in St. John's, accompanied the marriage vows.[50] St. Laurent took advantage of the mood to call a general election for June 27. The Conservatives did not have a chance. Two issues "captured the public imagination", Newfoundland and NATO, and by the end of the campaign St. Laurent himself had captured the public's imagination, as he was transformed into the wise and understanding "Uncle Louis", who spoke ill of no one, not even his Conservative opponent, George Drew. Like St. Laurent, Mike moved quickly to the non-partisan terrain of foreign policy, where he emphasized that even the Tories had supported his policies. In his opening parliamentary speech he had made a bad error by taking a partisan jibe at the Tory failure to endorse the Atlantic Pact before the text was published, and he was effectively rebuked by Gordon Graydon, an old personal friend and an experienced parliamentarian. In those kinder and gentler parliamentary times, Graydon simply said he expected better from Pearson, and Mike quickly agreed. He took a lesson from the experience: his political skills were not those of the partisan joust. He therefore fought on the terrain where he was comfortable, foreign policy, where his listeners expected him to be "more impressive and knowledgeable".[51]

Mike once again moved easily through the villages and hamlets of Algoma East. From his Methodist minister father he knew that the voters, like Ed's parishioners, wanted to feel part of a higher purpose, however homely their own station might be. He soon became aware that, like Christianity, political Liberalism required good works as well as faith. Early in the campaign, he visited a village store on Manitoulin Island where he "held forth" on the grand ceremony in Washington when the NATO treaty was signed. One elderly farmer who had listened thoughtfully drawled: "Yes, that was a fine thing you did down there in Washington, a fine thing for Canada, but it won't help you much around here if you don't get us a new post office." They likely got it, as did many other villages in Algoma East. His Conservative opponent in 1949, Grant Turner, had deep local roots and was a successful businessman, but his party lacked the power to provide post offices, clocks, and mail routes. Mike's major position in the governing Liberal Party brought not only prestige but also patronage. On June 27, Mike increased his margin from 1,236 to 3,276, even though he and Maryon, his brother Duke, and Duke's wife, Connie, from Boston, spent a nervous evening together at Beauchamp's Inn in Massey awaiting the final results from a constituency that was larger than all of Ireland.[52]

The Liberals won an overwhelming victory, capturing 190 out of 262 seats in the House of Commons. The Conservatives won only 41 seats, 25 of them in Ontario; the Co-operative Commonwealth Federation, suffering from the disrepute into which socialism had fallen, took only 13. During the campaign, Heeney had written to Mike to give him some information about what was happening in the department. As expected, Heeney had established an orderly system of administration that had been able to cope with the flow of business. Half-jokingly, he indicated to Mike that his absence had done a good deal to help in defining the limits of Mike's authority. He added: "Indeed on your return (which you assured me will not be before Labour Day!) you will probably find that practically nothing is referred to the Minister under the new conventions and practices which have been established since March."[53] The remark was not a jest. Heeney had decided just after he accepted the post of under-secretary that he had to protect Mike. He had written a private and confidential letter to Robertson on February 16, 1949, suggesting that Robertson return from London as soon as possible. Mike he found "very tired and (what was more disturbing) really quite nervous". His condition troubled Heeney: "He is, of course, under a new set of strains in the political arena and while he is adjusting himself to them with his accustomed facility, there is, I think, no doubt that he is finding it hard to maintain his normal buoyancy."[54]

Over the next three years, Heeney succeeded in keeping Mike buoyant in very troubled international seas. The flotsam and jetsam were his and his deputies' concern, and they were cleared away from the path of the minister. Escott Reid remained in Ottawa to assist in navigating the more intellectually treacherous shoals and in seeking new directions, and Gerry Riddell adapted his thoughts so closely to Pearson's own that the many speeches he wrote for the minister were indistinguishable from Mike's. Most important, however, was Mary Macdonald, a sprightly and extraordinarily engaging young woman who left the Canadian army to become, in Mike's own words, "the bulwark of [his] political life".[55] With these companions, Mike had unusual freedom to pursue his ambitions beyond Parliament Hill and outside Canada.

The end of the election campaign signalled no respite — nor did Mike seek one. The last half of 1949 brought a cascade of international turmoil that swept him up in its flow. Contrary to his plans, he returned to Ottawa in late June, distressed by the growing indications of yet another serious British financial crisis that threatened the possibilities of economic co-operation that the Atlantic pact promised.[56] Attempts to stitch together a co-operative framework over the summer failed, and the British were forced to devalue the pound from $4.03 to $2.80, a step that all Canadians knew had historic meaning for Canada and for Anglo-American relations. The well-informed journalist Bruce Hutchison reported that the result of the summer's talks and the devaluation was that "Britain has joined the American Empire". All knew, however, that there was, in this empire, no equality of status.[57] Mike had attended the Commonwealth Conference in April and had watched as the British Commonwealth of Nations became simply the Commonwealth of Nations, with "only self-interest" to hold it together. He had been surprisingly taciturn as Nehru brilliantly dominated the conference's proceedings, although his skills as a draftsman were called upon at the last moment for the final statement. Silence, perhaps, did not mean so much consent as acceptance of a new world where the verities of his childhood — imperial anthems, Kipling's stories, and Ed Pearson's loyal sermons — were passing as if in a dream.[58]

On November 16, 1949, Mike gave his first review of international affairs in the House of Commons. He had been away since Parliament opened in September, and the speech was the centrepiece of the first major debate on foreign policy in eighteen months, a fact that testified to the Cold War consensus on foreign policy. He had spent the fall in New York where he had chaired the Canadian U.N. delegation and also the U.N.'s Political and Security Committee. Its work concentrated on atomic control, a response to the Soviet testing of an atomic bomb in September. The Soviets, as always, infuriated Mike and little was accomplished. In his speech, Mike gave much attention not to the United Nations but rather to the Commonwealth. His nervousness showed. When John Diefenbaker interrupted him to ask why he had used the term "Commonwealth" rather than "British Commonwealth", Mike found it difficult, as King George had at the Commonwealth Conference's closing ceremony, to admit that the change of wording had significance. Not for the last time, Mike simply evaded Diefenbaker's rhetorical question.[59]

What captured attention in Washington and London, however, was not the exchange with Diefenbaker but his comments on Canadian-American relations. Neither country, he said, should "take their relations with each other too much for granted". The United States must lead the Western Democratic powers, but Canada had its own contribution to make which it could do "most effectively as a co-operating partner but not as a camp follower".[60] The United States, once so coy in its approach to the international stage, had gained much confidence in the first act of the post-war play, but now that confidence threatened to become an enthusiasm that demanded all other players follow its step. For Canada, now so closely tied to the leader, the next act would be more difficult. And Mike Pearson, who had moved so deftly through his first political year, would be much more closely watched for signs that he could act and not merely follow.

CHAPTER TWO

BECOMING ADULT

On the official level, in our contacts with Canadian officials in London, we notice a difference between them and any other Commonwealth officials. Though the South Africans are also sensible, they, like the New Zealanders, are a little ill-informed and parochial. The Australians are politically immature and always looking for fancied insults, however good one's personal relations are. The Canadians are admirable colleagues, a little cautious, but un-selfconscious and assured. They are in fact, as Mr. Pearson claims, adult.
— British official R.H. Scott commenting
on Pearson speech of April 10, 1951[1]

Oₙₑ ᴅᴀʏ during the Korean War, Lieutenant Chris Snider of the Canadian Brigade in Korea complained to a Korean visitor that one of the Koreans in his platoon had often fallen asleep while on duty. Snider awoke the next morning to learn that the visitor, along with a senior Korean non-commissioned officer, had taken out the sleepy soldier, ordered him to dig a hole, shot him, and buried him in the hole before the astonished Canadians could stop them. The Canadian platoon was "traumatized" by the incident. Most Canadians who fought in Korea suffered similar traumas, fighting to defend a country where human life seemed cheap, whose president, Syngman Rhee, mocked the values of democracy and liberty, and whose people, in Lieutenant Snider's view, "so plainly didn't want us there". South Korean troops turned back refugees, battered beggars with sticks, and shot suspects on sight. In Lieutenant Snider's words, "the whole country seemed to have become a quag-mire" where "everything had been beaten down to the lowest level".[2] The battlefield was strange and distant, the people's values dramatically different, and the Korean government extremely venal, but the war in which Lieutenant Snider and about 20,000 other Canadians took part in Korea was probably the most popular war Canada ever fought.

In part, of course, the absence of conscription, which divided the country in the two world wars, explains the lack of overt opposition. Nevertheless, the Korean War evoked none of the vigorous political dissent that marked the Boer War and the two world wars. When the Korean People's Army stormed across the thirty-eighth parallel on the first weekend of the Canadian summer, Mike and his acting under-secretary were at their cottages in the Gatineau Hills, and the prime minister was at his summer home at St. Patrice in Quebec. Neither Reid nor Pearson had a telephone at the cottage. Mary Macdonald, Mike's assistant, heard the news on the CBC's 2:00 p.m. Sunday report, took a rowboat to tell Reid, who was in the middle of a lake, and then drove to tell Mike. Once informed, Mike had Macdonald drive him to the nearest general store that had a pay phone, on which he called the prime minister. Both agreed that the Western response must come through the United Nations and that Canada must work to assure a United Nations role.[3]

When, in 1936, the League of Nations had crumbled after the sanctions against Italy failed, Pearson had blamed the failure partly on the fact that the League had a "bad client", Abyssinia. This time the client was no better, but Pearson's experience in the 1930s made him see the Korean case in a different light. The client's character was unimportant; the principle of collective security, which had been jettisoned in the 1930s, had to be upheld in the 1950s when the test came. South Korea was distant, its government corrupt, and the test peculiar, but for Pearson the war was not fought for that flawed country but rather for collective security and the United Nations and, equally important, against an expansionist Communist state.

If the principle was important, its application was to prove difficult, not least because the terrain was so unfamiliar and the step of Westerners so unsure. Mike was troubled about the shift of the Cold War towards Asia that had followed Mao Tse-tung's passage into the Heavenly City in 1949. Writing to Hume Wrong three months before the Korean War began, Mike lamented the obsession of the American right with blaming other Americans for "the loss" of China. Although he had much sympathy for Dean Acheson, who was the victim of the attacks by Richard Nixon and others in Congress, he wondered about Acheson's own growing interest in Asia. Acheson, perhaps in response to the baiting from the American right, had seemed "to draw the line of western defence firmly across the southern borders of China" and had hinted that a Pacific pact should be signed to protect Asian nations, as NATO now shielded Western Europe. Mike had "very grave doubts" about such an alliance: "The North Atlantic Treaty is not a fair parallel, for in that case we drew our line around an area of relative stability, within which there was a genuine community of interest, political, economic and cultural." He told Wrong that he would need "a lot of convincing that we were not simply being asked to repeat in South East Asia, through an international instrument, policies which the United States had followed with such unhappy consequences in China; and which are not working out too well in Korea".[4]

In fact, during Mike Pearson's lifetime, nothing ever worked out too well in the West's efforts to contain Communism in Asia. There is much irony and some tragedy in the fact that, after 1949, Mike's diplomatic skills, which had been so sharply honed in the work of the North Atlantic triangle of Britain, the United States, and Canada, were tested so often in an area whose history he barely knew and whose diplomats were mostly nameless faces at international gatherings. After NATO froze European boundaries, the Cold War's skirmishes came mainly in Asia, and Canada, through the American alliance, was caught up in them. Canada's non-recognition of China, its doubts about American military intentions in the Korean War,

Canadian membership on the international control commissions in Indochina, and the worries about American brinkmanship in the defence of the Chinese offshore islands Quemoy and Matsu were the result of this involvement. As well, the American military build-up in Vietnam, culminating in a vicious war of dubious legitimacy, bedevilled Mike Pearson's prime ministership in the mid-1960s and undermined that sense of Western purpose he had worked so long to create. The experience, in short, was unpleasant.

Mike's background and education had prepared him very well for dealing with Europe and America. With Asia, the background was much different. His early life as a child of a Methodist manse made him very familiar with the missionary mind as it was being applied to the Asian challenge. At the age of nine, Mike saw a freshly ordained cousin proceed, much honoured, to the exotic mission field of Ren-Shon in Szechuan province.[5] And the tales of the China mission spun out by the returned missionary broke the monotony of Methodist Sunday afternoons. They brought forth the flavour of Kipling and Henty, who were so much to young Mike's taste. At Victoria College in the early 1920s, he watched as some friends, such as James Endicott and his wife, Mary Austin, who had caught Mike's eye in the pews of his father's Methodist Church in Chatham, went off as missionaries to China, and he listened to Jim and Mary's counsel about Chinese events in the 1940s as the Communists and Nationalists battled to gain control over one-quarter of humanity.[6]

Even though Asia remained a concern of Mike's, he found it difficult to understand those Westerners who became fascinated with it, whether it be the Endicotts, who took up the cause of Mao's Communists, or John Foster Dulles and Henry Luce, who championed Chiang Kai-shek. Mike's artistic interest was not keen, and his reaction to a 1936 exhibition that featured Oriental art was notably philistine: "I fear I was not in an 'arty' mood, as I had dined most successfully at the Services Club.... Hence I insisted on treating the priceless Mings, Changs and Tons with unseemly indifference and at times unbecoming frivolity."[7] Pearson approached Asia with a Eurocentric vision, and it affected deeply the way he saw the dramatic events in East Asia in the 1940s. In August 1942, he attended his first meeting of the Pacific Council at the White House. In his report, he admitted that he was "as much interested in the appearance and personality of the President" as he was in the discussions, about whose substance he said nothing.[8] Yet the Japanese War was very much the Americans' war, and Mike's posting in Washington between 1942 and 1946 alerted him to the significance that East Asia would have in American post-war diplomacy. He was an early member of the Far Eastern Advisory Commission that supervised the peace that followed the dropping of the atomic bombs on Hiroshima and Nagasaki. As a member of that commission, he soon became troubled by the American tendency to claim a special expertise that entitled them to special rights and interests in the Pacific. It was a tendency that found full-blown expression in Henry Luce's *Time* magazine. Influenced by Herbert Norman, Pearson's successor on the Far Eastern commission, and by Endicott and Chester Ronning, a missionaries' son who had been brought into External in the war years, Mike trusted neither Luce's views nor his influence.[9]

When Mike returned to Ottawa in 1946, he argued strongly against powerful cabinet minister C.D. Howe that Canada should not grant a $60 million Mutual Aid Credit to Chiang Kai-shek's Kuomintang because he believed, like Ronning and a young External officer, Arthur Menzies, that Canada should not take sides in the Chinese civil war.[10] Yet he was willing to enter where Mackenzie King feared to tread when Canada was proposed for a position on the U.N. Temporary Commission on Korea*. And when Mao proclaimed the new China on October 1, 1949, Mike took a stand by hesitating to recognize the new government. Chester Ronning, Canada's chargé d'affaires in Nanking, waited in vain in the Canadian mission in Nanking for the telegram to come granting recognition to the new People's Republic of China. In the House of

---

* See Volume I (*Shadow of Heaven: The Life of Lester Pearson, 1897-1948*), 326.

Commons, Mike assured his listeners that "no pressure of any kind from any quarter has been brought to bear on the Canadian government to recognize or not to recognize" the Communist government, but, in fact, the American decision not to recognize had created a strong pressure to maintain a common front.[11] When the choice was between the United States and China, there was, by late 1949, no room for an independent Asian policy for Canada.

Pearson's hesitations reflected his puzzlement, a state he hoped to alleviate by his first visit to Asia in January 1950, three months after the proclamation of the People's Republic of China. The occasion was a Commonwealth Foreign Ministers' Conference that was held in Ceylon (now Sri Lanka) from January 9 to 15, 1950. Since Ceylon was half way around the world, Mike and Maryon took the opportunity for their first "around the world" trip. The journey seemed exotic to the Pearsons and to those they left behind. It was not only the Pearsons' first round-the-world trip but also the first for the Royal Canadian Air Force. To mark the occasion, fifty dignitaries came to the airport to cheer on the Pearson party as it was piped into the plane by Pipe Major A.R. Mitchell of the RCAF Pipe Band. Mary Macdonald reported to Mike in Colombo that "everyone" was following the Pearsons' progress as they moved from Europe, through the Middle East, and then to the Near East.* They had been "lost in Baghdad" but turned up again in Karachi. In the typically jaunty tone that Macdonald used in reporting to the "Boss", she added that "in your honour the new technicolour

---

* From the time Mike entered politics until he left it, Mary Macdonald took care of the rest of the Pearsons' lives when they were away. In the case of the Colombo trip, she took photographs at the airport, sent them on to Patsy and Geoffrey, reported on the riding, making sure that "the Children's Aid Society can have a room at the Post Office building at Gore Bay", sent on *Maclean's* magazine and the treasured *New Yorker*, checked with the housekeeper, and paid the family bills. She was, quite simply, indispensable, and Mike Pearson's success without her would seem to any biographer of him inconceivable. In a later day, she would have been a senator, a deputy minister, or even a minister. Her political judgement was shrewd, her personality strikingly warm, but Ottawa, then, was, in the worst sense, a man's town.

movie 'Baghdad' arrived at the Odeon today and other pictures in town feature such songs as 'The Road to Mandalay'".[12]

Although historians have suggested that the purpose of the Commonwealth Conference was the creation of the Colombo Plan, the first significant non-European foreign-aid program, the Colombo Plan was not the major focus of Canada's interest at the time. While it was certainly an important part of the conference agenda, learning what the Asians thought of the events in Southeast Asia made the long journey worthwhile for Mike. He reported to Heeney shortly after the conference's end that "on the whole" the conference was a success. With further faint praise, Mike noted that the conference "in general ... accomplished what I had considered to be its main objective — providing the non-Asian members of the Commonwealth with an opportunity to gain a better understanding of the points of view of the Asian members on some of the main questions of foreign policy, especially those relating to South-East Asia." As Canada's marriage to the British Empire moved from the monogamy of colonial status to the polygamy of the modern Commonwealth, new jealousies and differences abounded, and Mike watched warily as the British tried to deal with their imperial legacy. Part of that legacy was the sterling bloc, of which Canada, alone among Commonwealth nations, was not a member; its interest was therefore less. Australia and New Zealand clung to their British (and Caucasian) tradition as a means of separating them from their Pacific neighbours. Their foreign ministers spoke harshly of Japan and urged its continuing isolation, and their views were similar on the question of the treatment of Communist China. In fact, Mike regarded them as antique: at the beginning of the conference, the New Zealand foreign minister, F.W. Doidge, actually talked about New Zealand as "a daughter in her mother's house but mistress of her own". No other representative, Mike told Heeney, so echoed Victorian times.[13]

Mike spoke little, and Canada and South Africa spoke last, in recognition of the fact that they were least affected by Asian issues. Mike told Heeney that in the formal sessions there was no discus-

sion of such "delicate" issues as the Indian-Pakistani dispute over
Kashmir or South Africa's treatment of Indians. There was also no
mention of parts of Canada's past, such as the refusal to allow the
Komagata Maru, with its Indian passengers, to land at British
Columbia in 1914, or the stern attempts to halt Asian immigration to
Canada, or the total exclusion of Chinese immigrants from Canada
between 1943 and 1947. There was a practical air to the gathering: the
wealthier and white Commonwealth, with the exception of South
Africa, seemed to recognize that there was a need to expiate their
past, through technical and financial assistance and through respectful attention when the new members spoke. The new members,
then (if not later, when decolonization issues dominated Commonwealth meetings), were polite in not mentioning old colonial
wounds and in agreeing that Communism represented a threat to
Asia. Indeed, in opening the conference, Prime Minister D.S.
Senanagaki of Ceylon proved to be keenly aware of the interests of
the guests. "World politics," he claimed, were "at present dominated by the attitude and actions of the Soviet Union." NATO had
checked the "advance of Communism in the West", but now its
malevolent energies that were being unleashed upon Asia must be
countered.[14]

Ernest Bevin, the bluff British foreign secretary, one of the
Labour Party's true labourers, who had memorably challenged his
Soviet Communist counterpart, Molotov, to match the calluses on
his hands, welcomed the Ceylonese prime minister's attitude. Bevin
and Jawaharlal Nehru of India, whose hands were not callused,
whose accent was Oxonian, and who knew British jails as well as
British drawing rooms, formed an unlikely couple that gave leadership to the conference. Mike marvelled at Bevin's fractured
grammar and working-class accent, neither of which impaired his
ability to make points most effectively. The silk-jacketed brahmin
Nehru, of course, was more complex, his arguments impressive in
their sinuosity and elegance. The poet-diplomat Doug LePan, who
was part of the Canadian delegation, marvelled at "Nehru at the
conference table ... impassive, reflective, smoking cigarettes in a

long black holder and blowing the smoke through his nostrils"
while combining in his own person "at least as wide a knowledge of
the range of western civilization as any of his Western colleagues...."
Nehru went out of his way to pay attention to the Canadians, especially Mike, but it must be said that Nehru made Mike uneasy. So
much seemed familiar — the Oxbridge accent and the grace — but
they were cloaked in an exotic garb that disoriented Mike. In part, it
was because, as Escott Reid says, Mike never "took" to India as Reid
and, later, Geoffrey Pearson did. The contradictions baffled him. In
his memoirs, he wrote of Nehru that he "was one of the most subtle
and difficult men whom I had ever met, an extraordinary combination of a Hindu god, and an Eton-Oxbridge type of Englishman".
Like a Bloomsbury Englishman, he delighted in conversation that
shocked. Once when chatting with Mike about Gandhi, he
remarked upon what a great actor Gandhi was, how clever he was
with the British, how he cultivated a "simple mystic character"
because that would appeal to them. "You know," Nehru said, "he
was really an awful old hypocrite." The remark shocked Mike, and
in his mind it symbolized the constant contradictions he saw in
India — the magnificent viceroy's palace with its "gnome-like" governor general who wore little more than a loincloth; the profound
aura of a passive spirituality amidst the legacy of recent violence; and
the stunning poverty close by an astonishing artistic richness.[15]

Unlike Harry Truman and Acheson, who loathed Nehru and
thought him a dreadful hypocrite and poseur, Mike marvelled at his
political skill and intelligence.[16] He was perhaps its unwitting victim
when, during his visit, he tried to persuade Nehru to accept the
efforts of the United Nations and its appointed mediator, the Canadian general A.G.L. McNaughton, in the India-Pakistan dispute
over Kashmir. The British and the Americans were impressed with
the Pakistani case and viewed the Indians as intransigent. Acheson
had proposed that Bevin take a "hard line" when he met with Nehru
at Colombo, and the British proposed that Pearson do the same.
For his part, Mike thought that Acheson himself had not been firm
enough with the Indians and that McNaughton's mediatory role

was unusual and probably unproductive, since Canada had left the U.N. Security Council in January 1950. Mike did meet with Nehru about Kashmir on January 13 for an hour and a half. The British thought Nehru had charmed him; certainly the wily Nehru persuaded Pearson that McNaughton's mediation was not worth continuing. A senior British Foreign Office official privately denounced Pearson's meeting with Nehru as "a most unfortunate development" that "played right into Indian hands". Mike's "defeatism" led to the end of the mediatory effort, and to irritated allies and the return of a grumpy McNaughton to Ottawa. Mike, however, was wary of involvement where success seemed remote and when the possibility of fraying the still delicate threads that were linking Canada to India through the Commonwealth was great. The wariness about Kashmir was reflected in his cautious welcome to the proposals for what later became the Colombo Plan. The terrain was new, the perils everywhere, and the future path unclear.[17]

Despite Mike's reluctance to allow the use of McNaughton, his work and presence evidently impressed the British and Bevin. Bevin's biographer, in fact, claims that Mike, Nehru, and Bevin were the "leading figures" at Colombo. It is an odd claim, given Mike's laconic performance and his lack of success with Nehru on Kashmir, but it may derive from Mike's sole major presentation to the conference, where he told Bevin, whom he addressed in the most flattering terms, that he should not hesitate to become involved in movements leading to European co-operation because of fears about the future of the Commonwealth. But Mike also insisted that Britain's historic ties and position should be respected. It was precisely what Bevin wanted to hear, and it is not what he heard from others, notably the Australians and New Zealanders.[18] If Bevin enjoyed hearing Mike, he equally appreciated seeing Maryon. At the end of the Colombo meetings, Bevin decided to visit Kandy where, in his honour, the Ceylonese had agreed to open the sacred shrine of the Temple of the Tooth in which one of Buddha's teeth was preserved. The tooth, it was said, had remarkable healing powers, which Bevin certainly needed. Along with Bevin came Dr. Alec

McCall, his constant companion and medical nag, who when he first examined the hard-drinking, obese, and heavy-smoking Bevin in 1943 declared that he could not find a sound organ in his body, apart from his feet. Bevin retaliated against McCall's prohibitions by introducing him "This is Alec. 'E treats me be'ind like a dart-board."[19]

The tale of the sacred tooth had also lured Maryon to Kandy. Bevin spotted her lunching by herself at a hotel as he and his angry doctor quarrelled about his plan to mount the long stairs that led to the tooth at the top of the temple. Roger Makins, a dashing British diplomat who had known Maryon since 1930, took Bevin to her table where he promptly asked the startled Canadian to accompany him on his journey to the tooth. They left the hotel for the temple. Both took off their shoes, Bevin thereby revealing a hole in the heel of one of his socks, and slowly began the upward trek. "Alec" insisted that Bevin be lifted by chair, but the presence of journalists fortified his determination to use his still-healthy feet. Puffing and groaning he finally made it, and saw the tooth. No miracle occurred, and he had to be helped down. As the exhausted Bevin was being assisted into his car, he suddenly revived and said, "Where's my lady?" He invited Maryon to join him for the journey back to Colombo. The first words he said to her were, "I thought that it had finally done me in." It didn't, and he survived to write her a gracious note recalling their quest for the holy tooth that hot afternoon in Kandy.[20]

Mike and Maryon went on from Colombo to Pakistan, and then to India, where they stayed in New Delhi's magnificent Government House, its splendid gardens in glorious full bloom. They attended a state dinner to mark the end of the Raj and the inauguration of the new republic. Mike, alas, had to sit, much honoured of course, beside the "Queen of Nepal, who did not know or speak any language that I knew anything about, and the lady on my right was Queen of some other Himalayan country, familiar no doubt with many tongues, but with none familiar to me."[21] It was, perhaps, wise in a larger sense to remain silent and simply watch the spectacle as it developed. Mike knew his Kipling well and knew that the Westerner who tried to "hustle the East" was the fool. He left the Indian sub-continent wary about its future when its various peoples so bitterly resented each other and spent most of their budgets not on the alleviation of the horrible poverty but on the means of war. Burma, which he visited next, appalled him more. It was a country "down at the heel", where a visit to the foreign minister meant being accompanied by a convoy of machine-gun-toting soldiers through barbed-wire entanglements outside the foreign ministry. The romance of the road to Mandalay remained a faded imperial memory, and Burma's future seemed bleak. Singapore and Malaya followed and brought the welcome sight of Malcolm MacDonald, a very old friend of Mike's from London and Ottawa days. There were rebels nearby who would disrupt the Malay peninsula for several more years, but there was also a strong spirit of optimism, which the future would bear out. After a brief stop in Hong Kong, the Pearsons arrived in Tokyo, where Mike had an audience with Douglas MacArthur, the supreme commander of allied forces in the Pacific, the greatest American proconsul, one of its greatest generals, and, soon, one of its greatest problems.

Mike knew that Colombo had been a wake for the British Raj. Its monuments were still everywhere, but both its virtues and its flaws were studiously ignored as the new Commonwealth family came together for the occasion. It was odd how the past touched upon the present, and the West upon the East. The Indian Nehru spoke the best English, Escott Reid said. The British foreign secretary, the heir to the tradition of Castlereagh and Grey, probably spoke the worst. In the afternoons, they broke for tea. At the state dinner, they toasted the King and only then began to smoke. Their discussions followed British parliamentary rules, and the decorum contrasted sharply with the U.N., where debates on procedure were endless. And yet they were so different: Muslims, Buddhists, Hindus, Christians, atheists and believers, rich and poor. The experience overwhelmed Mike, as all first contacts with Asia do. Mike and most Canadians of the day came to see value in the curious legacy of the

Empire, an antidote to pervasive Americanism. Escott Reid, who then began a romance with India that deeply affected him, said much later that he realized in Colombo how Ottawa "could be helped to a less distorted view of the world by seeing it through the eyes of nations with different traditions from ours, different concepts of national interest, different emotional reactions to world events, different views". It was an early lesson; in the aftermath of Colombo there would be many others.[22]

If Colombo harked back to a familiar past, Tokyo and MacArthur pointed to a troubled future. There had been no Japanese peace treaty following the war, and the American occupation under MacArthur had prevailed. Historians now debate about MacArthur's and the occupation's influence upon Japan, but in 1950 Mike and his company had no doubts about MacArthur's power. Indeed, the call upon the Japanese prime minister seemed incidental when compared with the two audiences Mike had with MacArthur.[23] MacArthur wore the proconsul's mantle with ease. At the luncheon he gave for an amazed Mike and Maryon, his entrance bore more resemblance to a scene from Rodgers and Hammerstein's *The King and I* than to anything one encountered in Harry Truman's democratic White House. Mrs. MacArthur first took her place; then aides came forward to announce "the arrival" in breathless fifteen-second bulletins. Finally, the General was near, the crowd lined up, the doors flew open, and MacArthur, resplendent in his medals and uniform, strode through. Mike's instinct was to "fall down and worship". But he did not.[24]

The head of the British Liaison Mission, Sir Alvary Gascoigne, reported to Bevin that he felt that Mike "had not succumbed" to MacArthur's personality. Indeed, he emphasized Mike's belief that it was "a pity that the Supreme Commander did not get about more". As it was, he was "completely out of touch with the people" and had to rely on staff reports. MacArthur did tell Mike that he favoured a Japanese peace treaty, unlike the American Joint Chiefs of Staff then visiting him. Equally surprising were his refusal to become "alarmist" about the spread of Communism on the mainland and his unwillingness to consider Korea "vital" to the security of the United States. The latter view was, in fact, not so surprising. MacArthur had expressed it earlier, and in early January 1950 Dean Acheson had given a speech along the same lines in Washington, but Mike had probably failed to notice Acheson's statement, which had brought an immediate protest from the South Korean ambassador. The visits in Tokyo seem to have reassured Mike about events in East Asia, and he told "Joe" Gascoigne "very confidentially" that he was thinking of taking the initiative in the recognition of "Red China".[25]

The hopeful tone at Tokyo gave way quickly to a hardening of attitudes on both sides in the mid-winter of 1950. The Communist victory in China in the fall created an aftershock in January in Washington. The Truman administration responded to the events in China with the publication of a "White Paper" that essentially expressed a policy of caution, one in which the United States did not actively espouse the cause of Chiang Kai-shek's nationalists who had taken refuge on Formosa. The White Paper almost immediately became an object of scorn by the Republican right wing and the so-called China lobby. Who "lost" China? became their rhetorical and inflammatory question, and Dean Acheson's "soft" policies their ready target. In January, just as the "loss" of China had inflamed the Republican right and just after Alger Hiss, an old friend and colleague of Acheson's, was convicted of perjury for denying that he gave classified documents to Soviet agent Whittaker Chambers, Acheson held a press conference. There, with the tailoring of Savile Row, the moustache of a guardsman, and the accent of Groton, Acheson seemed to defend Hiss, a fellow Democrat patrician who represented everything the Republican right loathed: "I should like to make it clear to you that, whatever the outcome of any appeal which Mr. Hiss or his lawyer may take in this case, I do not intend to turn my back on Alger Hiss." Richard Nixon declared the remark disgusting; William Knowland moved to withhold State Department appropriations; and not a Democrat rose in Congress to defend Acheson. The remark was politically catastrophic.[26]

Hume Wrong, however, rallied quickly to the defence of his close friend. He told Mike that Senator James Eastland's comment attacking Acheson and praising Whittaker Chambers was "the most deplorable utterance that has come to my notice this year". Pearson himself called Acheson at home on a Saturday afternoon to tell him that his statement to the Senate appropriations committee on Alger Hiss was "the finest and most heartening thing he had read for years".[27] By early March 1950, Acheson had become the object of vicious personal attacks from Senator Joseph McCarthy, who, in Wheeling, West Virginia, on Lincoln's birthday, February 9, began his vitriolic and demagogic attack on the State Department and Acheson, "this pompous diplomat in striped pants with a phony British accent". To Mike the "persecution" of Acheson was "certainly dangerous and irresponsible", but it was not surprising. Nor did it surprise Wrong, who had warned two years before that the United States might resort to "dangerously noisy and provocative methods" to slow the supposed Soviet influence. In summarizing Wrong's views for Mackenzie King, Pearson concluded that the "consciousness" of Americans "of their responsibilities in the world community depends too greatly on their dislike and fear of the Soviet Union and Communist ideology". Although Mike welcomed American leadership and had come to admire American "liberals" and identify with them, he and Wrong retained a traditional Anglo-Canadian disdain for the excesses of American democracy as represented by McCarthy, who dealt in simplicities and conspiracies, black and white, ghosts and goblins, and who dwelt in the world of the *National Enquirer,* not the *New Yorker.* Mike had said in the thirties that middle courses were "notoriously difficult for intoxicated nations ... to follow. And the United States is often intoxicated." And so it was again.[28]

The search for scapegoats and conspiracies came at a moment when, ironically, Acheson and the Truman administration were preparing to take a much harder line against the Soviet Union. The Canadians sensed the change and themselves began a review of their relationship with the United States and their role in the Cold

War. In the United States, the famous debate between George Kennan, the head of the State Department's policy planning section, and Paul Nitze, Kennan's deputy, about whether the United States should begin work on a "superbomb" — the hydrogen bomb — was resolved in favour of Nitze and the bomb on January 31, 1950. Kennan's voice was silenced, and the author of the famous article on containment that had so deeply shaped American policies took early refuge on Princeton's campus and fretted about what he might have wrought. Nitze was placed in charge of writing the major re-evaluation of American strategy that came to be known as NSC-68. In contrast to Kennan, who had argued for "drastic measures to reduce the exorbitant cost of national defence", Nitze and his committee called for a large military build-up and a recognition that the Soviet threat was world-wide and that free institutions everywhere must therefore be defended.[29] Acheson and Truman came down firmly on his side. So did Wrong, who dismissed Kennan's ideas as an "oddment".

Mike, however, was not so sure. While he understood "the reluctance of responsible people like [Acheson] and Rusk to acquiesce" in demands for negotiations, he was concerned about Acheson's tactics. He questioned Acheson's growing commitment to stop Communism in Asia, and he thought that Acheson's dismissal of any approach to the Soviet Union was misguided.* Writing on March 24, 1950, he accepted that Dean Rusk, the State Department official responsible for Asia, and Acheson had reason to be sceptical about the current proposals, which seemed to be activity for its own sake, but he still wondered

---

* When rumours of Mike's desire to approach Moscow leaked out, he received a stern letter from a member of the British-Israel-World Federation warning that "Anglo-Saxondom is Modern Israel and that she is bound by the injunction given to Israel of old with regard to alliance with non-Israel peoples, namely, 'Thou shalt make no Covenant with them nor with their Gods'". Mike sent on this letter to the prime minister of the Canadian portion of Anglo-Saxondom, Louis St. Laurent. St. Laurent Papers, v. 89, National Archives.

if we need conclude that any renewed initiative will necessarily and inevitably be ill-considered and therefore abortive. Is there no chance that, by careful consultation amongst ourselves (by ourselves I mean the United States, the United Kingdom, Canada and possibly France) we could not work out in advance some agreed programme for an approach to the Russians, either on a broad front or in some particular field, that would enable us to get a wedge into the encircling wall of frustration?

Unless we put an oar in the water, Mike warned, we were in danger of being "carried over Niagara Falls in something a great deal less secure than a barrel".[30]

Wrong set up a meeting between Pearson and himself and Rusk and Philip Jessup, both of whom Mike knew well from U.N. times. The meeting was shrouded in secrecy; Mike's cover was an invitation to speak to the Council on Foreign Relations in New York on April 2. He feared that the press would suspect that the meeting was a prelude to Canadian recognition of Communist China, and that was, in fact, one reason for the meeting. Mike had recommended to cabinet on February 25, 1950, that China be recognized. The talks disappointed him. Earlier American consideration of recognition of China had ended; Rusk and Jessup wanted to isolate China, encourage its opponents, and prevent Chinese admission to the U.N. as long as possible. The hands-off policy towards Taiwan and Chiang was being replaced by an embrace of the China lobby. Ho Chi Minh was not regarded as a significant factor: he had "no capital city or administrative centre", and was not "getting much help from the Chinese". He might have to flee the country. The United States, therefore, was placing its bets on the French choice, Bao Dai. A month later Acheson announced that the United States would provide aid to the Bao Dai government. The first fateful step towards American involvement in Vietnam had been taken.[31]

Mike told St. Laurent after the meeting that Rusk did not accept his point that it was a "fiction" to maintain that Formosa was China. He and his colleagues remained "anxious to use all possible means for encouraging the anti-Communist forces on which their policy depends". Seeing the strength of American opinion caused Mike to become nervous again about recognizing China. It was to remain unrecognized for a generation. Even in the view of Rusk's official biographer, Rusk erred on the day he spoke with Pearson and Wrong. What Rusk and his superiors had done was adopt the Republican policy towards China "virtually intact".[32]

> In the first few years of the postwar period the United States fought not only the Cold War with the Soviets but also a hot war with the Chinese. If the former was inevitable, the latter was not. The error was compounded when … the small window of opportunity to right our policy with China that had opened with the White Paper slammed shut. With it, the possibility of peace in Asia also disappeared, almost for a generation.

The events of the winter of 1950 — the Hiss trial and its aftermath, the H-bomb decision, the embrace of Chiang — made the American decision to support South Korea almost inevitable. On Sunday evening, June 25, 1950, with intelligence reports telling them that South Koreans would be overwhelmed and that the North Korean attack must be "considered a Soviet move", Rusk and Jessup joined eleven other top American officials who met with Truman in the Blair House dining-room and decided, in General Omar Bradley's words, that the line had to be drawn in Korea.[33]

Mike did not know of the American decision when he returned from his Quebec cottage to Parliament's East Block on Sunday evening. Events had moved more quickly than he. By a vote of 9 to 0, with the Soviet Union still absent as a protest against the refusal to seat Mao's China, the Security Council had passed a resolution calling upon the North Koreans to halt their aggression. Neither Stalin nor Mike thought the United Nations or the United States would intervene. On Monday, Mike gave a briefing to Canadian journalists — a favourite practice of his — in which he gave his confidential opinion that "the North Koreans would be allowed to complete their operations relatively unopposed".[34] But soon the Americans were committing naval and air power to Korea and the Seventh Fleet to the Strait of Formosa. Although Mike was surprised, he did not dissent. It might have been better to await a Security Council authorization for military action rather than to stretch the June 25 resolution to justify the military commitments, but this disagreement was minor. After his Sunday dinner meeting, Truman had asked Jack Hickerson to stay for some bourbon. Inspired by the drink they both cherished, Truman told Hickerson that the decision to go to war was hard but he had done it "for the United Nations". He added: "If a collective system under the UN can work, it must be made to work and *now* is the time to call their bluff."[35] In the House of Commons on June 28, three days later, Mike commended Truman's action. There was to be no U.N. police force, as the U.N. Charter had envisaged and as Mike had hoped. The only solution was for the United States to take the lead, and he lauded the United States for recognizing "a special responsibility which it [had] discharged with admirable dispatch and decisiveness".[36]

If both Truman and Mike rallied to support the U.N., it was not because of what it had accomplished by 1950 but because both believed that it had largely failed. Mike and the Americans shared the belief that its secretary general, Trygve Lie, had been, as a biographer has recently said, "the wrong man, in the wrong place, at the wrong time".[37] The North Americans thought that Lie had been too easy upon the Soviets, too willing to appease their destructive demands.* In the spring of 1950 he had embarked on a fruitless "peace mission" to Moscow that had failed to bring the Soviets back

---

* Lie was nevertheless reappointed in 1950 because the alternatives were impossible. He was finally reappointed for three years. Mike's name was raised as an alternative, but he recognized that too many interests were against him to encourage a movement in his cause. It does seem, however, that he would have accepted the position had it been available. Dean Rusk was Mike's strongest supporter. See Wrong to Pearson, Dec. 22, 1949, MG26 N1, v. 4 (NAC); and Pearson to Wrong, Dec. 29, 1949, *ibid.* For a full account, see James Barros, *Trygve Lie and the Cold War* (DeKalb, Ill.: Northern Illinois University Press, 1989), 250-73.

to the Security Council and had heightened the doubts of the West. No one could have anticipated his vigorous response to the North Korean attack, but his frustration with the Soviets, his memories of the German attack on his native Norway, and his quick conclusion that Korea represented an opportunity to breathe life into the United Nations made him react strongly. Working closely with the Americans, he had put flesh upon the skeletal plans that Truman and his officials had sketched out on June 25. On June 27, the Security Council passed a resolution authorizing the U.N. to render whatever assistance "may be necessary to repel the armed attack and to restore international peace and security in the area".[38]

Mike's prediction of June 26 that neither the United States nor the U.N. would intervene directly lay in tatters by late June. The phrase "peace and security in the area" troubled him, because the area might be interpreted to include Formosa and China, and it could mean that the U.S.-U.N. response would not merely "hold the line" at the thirty-eighth parallel but would carry the war into North Korea. But the Canadian objection was ignored.[39] For the next few months, the Canadians scrambled to learn what was happening and to decide what they should do. The parliamentary opposition placed no apparent limits upon what could be done. When the eccentric and lonely isolationist Liberal Jean-François Pouliot rose in the House to criticize Mike for offering support to South Korea, asking, in the fashion of Mackenzie King, what interest Canada had in Korea, he was firmly rebuked by a Liberal Quebec colleague, who announced that the House should know that those from Quebec "will be like brothers with those from other provinces" in supporting the government and the U.N. cause. From the Conservatives came even stronger urging of support, and the leftist Co-operative Commonwealth Federation (CCF) did not dissent. Indeed, on July 27, 1950, the CCF convention overwhelmingly supported the U.N. action and urged that Canada commit ground forces to the battle, which was then going badly. On the same day, leading cabinet ministers returned to Ottawa from the burial of Mackenzie King in Toronto and reached agreement in St. Laurent's private car that

Canada should send a ground force to Korea, although the announcement of the contribution and its exact nature were delayed. Much of Mackenzie King's Canada had died with him.[40]

Mike's freedom as External Affairs minister must strike his successors as remarkable. The greatest asset was St. Laurent, who placed so much trust in his foreign minister. Like his colleague Defence minister Brooke Claxton, who said at the time, "with this prime minister we can do anything", Mike did not fret about what the Quebec reaction might be. There was the expected opposition from Quebec nationalists.* *Le Devoir* raised the arguments against war that it had raised in every war and at each threat of war since 1911. The first Gallup poll on Korea, published on August 3, 1950, indicated that only 21 per cent of Quebec respondents would approve of sending ground forces to Korea.[41] But public opinion was not newspaper opinion, and it was not parliamentary opinion. Four days after the poll appeared, the process of recruiting a Canadian brigade for Korea began, and with the small U.N. force and the South Koreans being pushed into the sea by the rapidly advancing North Koreans, open dissent melted as heated editorials called for Canadians to join the battle as soon as possible. By the time a full Canadian brigade entered the battle, almost a year had passed since the war began. With it had passed much of the amity and unity among the Western allies that had marked the war's first weeks.

Mike had hoped for an effort in which the U.N. played a central role and for a military structure that would be the embryo for an international force that could be used "for other United Nations duties in the future".[42] But this notion of a U.N. "foreign legion" died as the military crisis heightened. To Acheson, the United Nations was, in the circumstances of 1950, a useful device to employ

---

* Claxton and St. Laurent were much less disposed than Pearson to commit Canadian forces to the Korean War. That they did so is testimony to their respect for Pearson's judgement and the influence he had within the cabinet and caucus. The disagreement is discussed in David Bercuson's forthcoming biography of Brooke Claxton.

to further the paramount American and Western interest: the crushing of Communism. Korea, he told Mike in the earliest days of the war, was not important in itself; its significance lay in the opportunity it gave the "free world" to call a halt to Communist aggression. Like Mike, he was an "Atlantic man", one who believed that the West's strategic interest lay in Europe; but, unlike Mike, he "cared little for Asia or Africa and had no desire to worry about them".[43] He also rarely, and then only perfunctorily, mentioned the U.N. This attitude troubled Mike in mid-summer 1950. He had recently returned from Asia and had acquired a better understanding of the complexities of the Cold War there. Acheson, who cared too little for Asia, and MacArthur, who cared too much, lent an erratic character to American Asian policy, one that could be dangerous.

The Soviets returned to the Security Council on August 1, 1950, and General MacArthur made a highly publicized trip to Formosa, where he embraced Chiang and declared that the defence of Formosa was the defence of free peoples everywhere.[44] MacArthur's actions frightened Mike (and angered Truman), and the return of Soviet U.N. ambassador Jacob Malik to the Security Council made diplomatic skills more important. On August 7, Mike expressed his first strong doubts about the direction the United States was taking. In a despatch to Wrong that Gerry Riddell drafted but that Mike rewrote much more than he usually did, Pearson expressed concern that the United States was lurching towards war with China. Such a war over Formosa would be a disaster "from which only the Soviet Union would profit". It would drain off resources needed in Europe and would strain the anti-Communist coalition forming to repel North Korea. In the longer run, "it would postpone indefinitely the day when the now latent tensions which exist between China and the USSR would begin to make themselves felt" and, Mike added to the original draft, "it would reinforce the doubts about US policy in [the] area already held by area govts and by leaders like Nehru".[45]

On August 15, with the U.N.-U.S. forces clinging perilously to the toehold of Pusan, within fifteen miles of defeat, Mike wrote to Acheson to "get things off [his] chest". He wrote a personal letter because it would "be easier for you in reply (if you care to reply) to tell me I am off the beam and to stop bothering you". In careful prose, he suggested that there appeared "to be a real danger" that war might expand beyond Korea and that expansion would not command "the same measure of support" as the Korea action had. He "wondered" whether nationalist Chinese actions and MacArthur's visit had not raised the likelihood of a broader conflict. A conflict with China would benefit only the Soviets, and the distinction between a unilateral U.S. action and a U.N. action would be lost on public opinion and other national leaders. (He was wise enough not to mention Nehru, whom Acheson loathed.) Perhaps there was an argument for deterring China from attacking Formosa, but surely, Mike continued, "the political results of armed conflict between the United States and Communist China would be disastrous". Might it not be wise to allow U.N. representation to Communist China to undermine the Soviet propaganda arguments, so effective in Asia, that the United States was the "villain". The provocative suggestion he coated in sugar: "You will probably reply that it might contribute also to the upsetting of Mr. Acheson!" It undoubtedly did.

Acheson, it is said, did not suffer fools gladly. Mike was no fool, but, in Acheson's view, he listened to them too often. Acheson's reply was delayed. It was written on September 8, more than three weeks after he received Mike's letter. He did not even bother to comment upon Mike's remarks about MacArthur's provocativeness. He responded to Mike's comments about Chinese U.N. representation as a Groton headmaster might rebuke a bright but naughty student. There could be no seat for the Chinese Communists at the U.N. "I think you are fully aware of our reason for this," Acheson archly wrote. He concluded with a wish that he hoped Mike would continue "to let me have the benefit of your comments and suggestions". He made it clear in his letter, however, that he would be discussing these broad questions with British foreign minister Bevin and French foreign minister Schuman prior to the meeting of the U.N. General Assembly. Mike was not invited.[46]

That fall things went badly wrong for the U.N. intervention, for Canadian-American relations, and for Mike Pearson. In September, MacArthur's brilliant landing at Inchon trapped the North Korean army and decisively turned likely defeat into apparent victory. As the U.N. troops approached the thirty-eighth parallel, Mike, who was at the U.N. General Assembly, urged the Americans that the U.N. should declare a victory and set the terms for the peace. Mike thought he had a promise that the Americans would permit some time for a halt in the advance past the old boundary. Expecting that American U.N. ambassador Warren Austin would make such an announcement, Mike listened in "amazement and disquiet" as Austin instead moved a resolution that authorized MacArthur to go into North Korea. Then, a junior aide to Austin came across the Assembly floor to tell Mike that "he understood that I wished to see Senator Austin about something connected with the Korean resolution. I told him that I did not want to see Senator Austin about anything, but I understood that he wished to see me in an attempt to explain why the United States had withdrawn from the arrangements previously agreed on." Mike called Wrong, who had Acheson call him to apologize, which he did, although his explanation of the course of events, then and later, was disingenuous. The Americans stormed across the thirty-eighth parallel, to Acheson's satisfaction, and by the end of October were approaching the Yalu River, where hundreds of thousands of Chinese troops waited on the other side.[47]

The first Chinese appeared on November 5; by the end of November, they were a human flood crossing the Yalu, overwhelming the U.N. forces and ending the "victory" of a month earlier. The Indians had warned the world that the attack might happen. Acheson had not trusted the messenger. Mike had, but it did not matter.[48]

Ensconced at New York's elegant Biltmore hotel, Mike tried to argue for restraint. His position was difficult. He valued his contacts with the Americans. He profoundly approved of the reinvigoration of the United Nations that Korea had brought. He looked forward to the vice-presidency and later the presidency of the U.N. General

Assembly, and he wanted those positions and appreciated and needed American support. From Ottawa, where the pressures of New York were absent, came advice that favoured a harder line against U.S. militancy. Yet even though angered by Austin's "doublecross" on October 7, Mike voted for the American resolution approving a war in the north. He told Norman Robertson in Ottawa, who had urged him to oppose it, that Robertson had "no idea what the pressure is like here. I can't possibly oppose the resolution."[49] Again, he tried in vain to halt an American resolution, declaring China an aggressor, which passed on February 1 and which contributed, in Mike's view, to the prolongation of the conflict.[50] Despite Mike's doubts and those of his government, Canada also voted for the resolution condemning China.

Both votes distressed Canadians, who thought the Americans too dominant in the Korean campaign and too militant in their approach. When A.R.M. Lower complained about Canada's apparent silence, Mike responded to the distinguished historian and "national gadfly" (as Carl Berger termed him) in a long letter on Biltmore Hotel stationery that crystallized his approach to the problem. He told Lower that the answers he would give "if we were discussing the matter personally, might not be exactly the same" as those which he would give publicly. "That is not," he hoped, "because I say one thing in public and believe something else in private, but merely because it is not ... wise, with the international situation as it is today, to wash our democratic dirty linen in public in a way which would give aid and comfort to an 'enemy' which is trying to make it dirtier." In private, he expressed his anxieties to his "American friends", but in public he would not be so frank. We could be thankful that the United States had stepped forward "to assume the leadership and exercise the power that formerly lay in Western Europe". But while there was much to admire in the United States, "there are also currents of immaturity, indecision, roughness and lack of comprehension of the problems of other peoples which perplex and frighten" Canadians. Canada, therefore, was "constantly faced with the problem of trying to influence

United States policy in a manner which will protect both our interests and our conception of what is good for the world," but that would not involve Canada in a fight with its neighbour. And Lower should not think that Mike believed, as many Americans did, that victory would only come in Korea when that benighted land was "blessed" with "Western capitalism or free enterprise". If Mike did not always express this view publicly, Lower could "put that down to my natural timidity and the innate caution of the politician!"[51]

This letter defined what later came to be called — and was sometimes condemned as — quiet diplomacy. It describes what Denis Stairs in his excellent study of Canada's diplomacy during the Korean War called "the diplomacy of constraint", whereby initiatives were taken on a multilateral basis through the United Nations "with a view to moderating the exercise of American power …".[52] Mike attempted to constrain U.S. actions throughout the summer and fall of 1950. In December, he worked with the British to gain assurance that the United States would not use atomic weapons after an offhand Truman comment suggested they might. He was part of a three-person U.N. Cease-Fire Committee that tried to establish principles for a peace, though with little success. When Mike thought he saw a kernel of hope, he had St. Laurent write to Nehru asking him to approach China in the cause of peace. The Americans, in Mike's own words, "felt that [the commission] were dealing behind their back".[53] In a sense they were, and one result was probably stronger Canadian backing for the U.S. resolution that deemed China an "aggressor".

In his diary, Mike took credit for "some measure of success" in getting the United States to modify the resolution and to agree to a more flexible interpretation of it.[54] He had worked, in traditional Canadian fashion, to concert his behaviour with the British. His old friend Roger Makins, whose wife, Alice, the daughter of the wealthy American Dwight Davis of Davis Cup fame, had been his frequent doubles partner in the 1930s, had indicated to him that the British supported his work for a cease-fire proposal and argued that the "Asiatics" not be left out. They were left out:

Pearson's Indian colleague on the cease-fire commission, Sir Benegal Rau, angrily denounced the United States for pressing forward its resolution condemning China as an aggressor. After Canada supported the American resolution* and abstained on an Asian counter-resolution, Pearson had St. Laurent write to Nehru suggesting how important it was that their ties be continued and indicating they should continue to work together. And often they did, although the deepening chill of the Cold War made their co-operation increasingly difficult.[55]

The Cold War was never so chilly as in the winter of 1951. Lacking the "moles" that Stalin had in London and Washington, the Western nations believed that the Soviets would take advantage of the widening of the Korean conflict to expand their control in Europe. In Ottawa, the Chiefs of Staff Committee warned the cabinet in November 1950 that the Soviet Union was ready to wage a "major war". Moreover, if the Soviet Union waited "more than twelve months, they [would] lose part of their superiority on land and their advantage at sea may be reduced by allied countermeasures". The chiefs of staff thus concluded that there was "an increased danger within the immediate future of the Soviet Union precipitating a major war". A later report said the Soviets would reach the English Channel in sixty days, the Spanish frontier in sixty-five. The danger was real. Stalin was old, his paranoia deep, his distrust profound — even of reassuring news that came from his spies. At the NATO council meeting in mid-December 1950, the decision was made to form an integrated defence force and to create the office of Supreme Allied Commander, Europe, to which the American war hero Dwight Eisenhower was immediately appointed. In February 1951, Defence minister Brooke Claxton announced a massive defence build-up costing $5 billion over three

---

* Escott Reid later argued that Canada should have abstained on this vote. Had it done so it would have joined Afghanistan, Egypt, Indonesia, Pakistan, Sweden, Syria, Yemen, and Yugoslavia. All NATO members voted for it, and Canada's abstention in February 1951 would have been politically and diplomatically impossible.

years and the return of Canadian armed forces to Europe.[56]

Mike supported the decision; he shared the fears. In mid-January, he wrote to Geoffrey at Oxford and told him "to concentrate on Beowulf or Chaucer" and not "let the alarums and excursions in the outer world worry you too much". But, the worried father added, "if everything blows up" and he had to abandon Oxford "at least for a time, for other less worthy activities, you will know about it and will know what to do".[57] Mike knew that the West would fight and that his twenty-three-year-old son would have to join the battle, as he had himself so long before. The Soviets' will-power and Stalin's madness frightened Mike, but the U.S. response to the Soviet threat became increasingly troubling to him in the winter of 1951. He told Geoffrey in late January that he had "attempted and failed" to moderate the United States' desire to isolate China. "Emotionalism," he complained, "has become the basis of their policy. But we have certainly let them know here that we profoundly suspect that policy and will not follow them in its pursuit beyond the strict interpretation of our obligation under the Charter."[58] A few days later he wrote to Hume Wrong complaining about the "outbursts of impatience and tactlessness, and the absence of any clear-cut sense of direction, both of the forming and carrying out" of U.S. policy in Asia.[59] He asked Wrong to discover what the Americans were thinking and planning. Wrong saw Dean Rusk, who told him that the United States would not deal with the Communist government and that American intelligence suggested that the Communists in China would be overthrown.* Considering that American intelligence had failed so dismally in predicting the Chinese intervention in the war, Rusk's claim was breathtaking in its boldness. It was also tailored to fit Canada's needs. It satisfied Wrong more than Mike, who had the Department of External

---

* American intelligence may have been correct in this case. A letter from Mao to Stalin, written in 1950 but released in 1992, indicates that the Chinese entered the war because Mao feared popular uprisings against his rule. See the *New York Times*, June 23, 1992.

Affairs begin a study of the overall state of Canada's relations with the Americans.[60]

This review spanned a variety of issues, ranging from the St. Lawrence Seaway project, which American sectional interests were imperilling, through the obtuseness and domineering tactics of American representatives on the International Monetary Fund, to American Asian policy. Escott Reid co-ordinated the review while Mike and Maryon took a break at Ste. Adèle in Quebec, a break on which Maryon made him swear that he would not "read a newspaper, or a magazine or a book that have anything to do with international affairs".[61] The review was to provide background for a major speech that Mike was to give in Toronto on April 10. If Mike read nothing at Ste. Adèle, he certainly caught up with events upon his return, as Reid presented him with a thick wad of memoranda.

Their tone was surprisingly angry. The most bitter memorandum came from the pen of R.L. Rogers, a young officer responsible for Asian affairs.* In Rogers' view:

(a) The United States does not apprehend the nature of the alliance of which it is the principal member;
(b) The United States follows a rapidly changing, almost mercurial, policy;
(c) The United States is often intolerant of any line of thought or action which does not coincide with its own;
(d) The United States is at times unduly hasty in its diplomacy; and
(e) There is a lack of confidence in United States Far Eastern policy and leadership.

Assessments of economic problems were not so harsh, but even they were laments about arrogance and lack of co-operation. A.F.W. Plumptre, who supervised the economic papers, tried to put

---

* Rogers had married June Wrong, Hume's daughter, in 1949. Following the rules of the day, Mike as under-secretary gave Rogers permission to marry, which he did in a humorous letter that mocked the rules.

forward a bright face when he summed up their sentiment as "the Americans are still their usual mixture of high minded inefficiency and exasperating generosity."[62]

The memorandum betrays the angry mood of the times that the External Affairs officers shared. The war dragged on in Asia; a worse one threatened in Europe. The shrill tones of McCarthyism and the erratic leadership of MacArthur shook Canadian confidence in the United States. Canada, and Mike personally, were drawn into the American search for subversion when the FBI asked the RCMP for information about Herbert Norman in the fall of 1950. Norman was recalled from Tokyo and interviewed by Heeney and Robertson, and his file sent to Washington. Mike was at the U.N. General Assembly, and when he heard of the American request he asked that the file not be sent. It was too late. Nevertheless, Norman was cleared — temporarily — and Mike tweaked the anti-Communist eagle's beak by appointing Norman as head of the American and Far East Division.[63] It was, as we shall see, a mistake.*

A personal tragedy also struck Mike in March. Gerry Riddell, who had drafted so many of Mike's memos and who had worked late into countless nights in New York at the U.N., died suddenly of a heart attack. Mike wrote to Geoffrey three days after Riddell's death telling him of his "great sorrow", and, perhaps with some guilt, added that he died "of exhaustion and overtaxing his strength". He was a "close friend" whom Mike would miss "terribly".[64]

With sad memories and troubled thoughts, Mike spoke to the Canadian Bar Association on March 31 about the course of the Korean War. He lamented the tendency of Americans to reject "constructive criticism" from their friends and, without naming MacArthur, rebuked his controversial pronouncements. The British Foreign Office thought it a good speech and one that reflected traditional Canadian concern that the primacy of Europe should not

---

* See Chapter 5.

be forgotten. A Wall Street banker, however, had warned C.D. Howe in March that Mike was undermining Canadian-American friendship. Howe rose to his colleague's defence and said Mike was "less excitable" than Warren Austin, the U.S. ambassador to the U.N.[65]

Fortified by the lack of hostile reactions to his bar-association speech and by the strong tone of the External Affairs study, and deeply troubled by MacArthur's apparent insubordination towards President Truman, Mike went to Toronto to speak to the joint meeting of the Canadian and Empire clubs on April 10. Drawing on his memoranda but using mostly his own words, he said that the U.N. must not be the "instrument of any one country"; that country, of course, was the United States. Canada had a right to criticize American actions "if we feel it necessary". Then, in a sentence that is often cited, Mike stated his belief that "the days of relatively easy and automatic political relations with our neighbour are, I think, over". Canada's concern was no longer "*whether* the United States will discharge her international responsibilities, but how she will do it and whether the rest of us will be involved".

In his memoirs, Mike said that commentators ignored those parts of his speech that spoke of collective security and the United Nations and focused on the last part that dealt with the United States. He also claimed that it was not so much the speech that caused controversy as the fact that Truman fired MacArthur that evening, thus drawing attention to Pearson's critical remarks. This rather apologetic tone was not reflected in a letter to Geoffrey written within a week of the speech in which Mike said that, despite the controversy, "the main thing is that I said what I honestly feel should be said and for an honest purpose". His words, moreover, echoed the sentiments of his colleagues. His "outburst" was deliberate; its effect unpredictable.[66]

The reaction was quick and, from the American administration, harsh. The American ambassador sent a hasty despatch the evening of the speech, *before* MacArthur's firing, that spoke of the "declaration of independence" aspects of the speech, certainly an emotionally charged description coming from an American. *Le Devoir*, the American consul in Montreal reported, "seized Mr. Pearson's remark, with delight that was bounded only by its reluctance to agree with anything" a Liberal minister might say.[67] C.D. Howe's American friend whom Howe had rebuked in March wrote again asking Howe to look at Mike's speech. This time Howe did not defend his colleague: "I agree with your letter to the extent that I can see no good reason for Pearson having made his Toronto speech. The relations between our two countries are excellent, and will, in my opinion, continue so, regardless of speeches by members of the Cabinet. Certainly my best efforts will be directed to that end." The reply was unwise, but Howe was often blunt and rash.[68] More troubling was Hume Wrong's response. He was not happy.

Wrong, of course, had to bear the direct heat of the eruption that came from the State Department. He rightly objected to the failure of the Department of External Affairs to show him the speech before it was delivered. But Mike had been warning Wrong of his concerns about American policy for some time, and Wrong had reassured him. He had also reassured the Americans. When the Canadian government asked Wrong to complain about some particular American action, the American reports of his meetings with American officials suggest that he presented these protests rather reluctantly.[69] He had become close to Acheson, sharing his friend's fears and, more importantly, his prejudices. He had been in Washington a long time, and "localitis" is a virus that affects many diplomats who serve so long in foreign capitals. Perhaps he had come to see the American viewpoint too easily and that of his own capital with too much difficulty. He did let Mike know that he was annoyed with the speech. He also did not hide his sentiments from American friends.

He told Americans that he was not consulted in advance and that the speech was made for "domestic consumption" (a tactic Mike used, too, as a justification), and gave, in the words of a State Department report, "the general impression" that he did not approve of the speech. Indeed, another State Department report written by the young historian Mason Wade, who had recently been appointed cultural attaché to Ottawa, described a conversation at an embassy party in which Wrong claimed that too much was made of the Pearson speech. Wade thought the embassy was "much embarrassed by the Pearson speech", although he did not detect "the reported professional jealousy" between Pearson and Wrong. Significantly, at the end of the conversation, Wrong said that "perhaps he had been in Washington too long, that it was time he went either home or elsewhere".[70]

Probably he had been there too long. A brilliant analyst who could identify the strengths and weaknesses of policy, Wrong had come to share many of the premises of Acheson about what American leadership meant. When Wrong first came to Washington as a young diplomat in the later 1920s, he noted that among the qualities a Washington diplomat required were "a good head for liquor" and a "cynicism about governments and pessimism about human nature, with both of which I am amply provided". So was Acheson, and they quickly became friends who bird-watched on long walks and lamented the state of the world. Mike, Acheson, and Wrong shared a profound distrust of emotionalism in democratic politics. The attack on Acheson by McCarthy and his ilk appalled Mike, who told his son of his sympathy for Acheson and his wonderment that the United States could "get any decent, intelligent people to take jobs in Washington". But Mike saw "emotionalism" not only in the witch-hunt for domestic subversives but in Acheson's own policies towards East Asia, the United Nations, and the non-Western nations of the world. The gap between, on the one hand, Mike and Escott Reid and, on the other hand, Wrong and Acheson was the division between idealist and realist in one sense. In a broader sense, it derived from a different view of what American leadership must mean. The metaphors of leadership for Acheson were those of the front lines, where loyalty is cherished and doubts are banished. Those metaphors Mike rejected in favour of those of community and co-operation. The Canadian-American relationship, he said on April 10, "means marching with the United States in the pursuit of the objectives we share. It does *not* mean being pulled along, or loitering behind".[71]

After 1951, Mike's relationship with the U.S. was not the same. Later, in August, Elizabeth Bentley, in her testimony before the Senate Internal Security Subcommittee, named Mike as one who had "passed" information to Soviet agents. The charge, which broke down when Bentley was more precisely questioned, nonetheless seeped into the press and spread among right-wing circles, contaminating Mike's reputation. Acheson, a fellow victim, had much sympathy for Mike, but, in response to the torrents of abuse that had swirled about him, he had adopted a defensive posture that was less tolerant of differences, harder-edged, sometimes acid. At home, Truman succumbed to the pressure and expanded the grounds allowed to the loyalty boards for dismissing public servants. Abroad, his administration was more wary of dissent and chafed against those diplomatic constraints through which Canada, Britain, and others gently tugged to alter the path of the American behemoth. Not only Canada thought it was "trailing behind": Louis Heren, a former editor of *The Times,* wrote: "The United States became more than the first among equals. Generally speaking, it saw the European allies as so many Germanic tribes guarding the eastern glacis of the American empire [while] levies were confidently expected to be sent to fight elsewhere...."[72] Even Acheson, with his profound appreciation of the intellectual traditions of European culture, sometimes acted as if he held this belief. Others, especially on the swelling Republican right, surely did.

In July, negotiations began with a view to ending the war that had settled into a stalemate along the thirty-eighth parallel. But the war dragged on for two years as agreement proved elusive. The United States and China, the major antagonists, were profoundly suspicious of each other, and communications between them were mere fragments transported, with considerable difficulty, by intermediaries. Truman's decision not to repatriate North Korean and Chinese prisoners against their will was the major obstacle. Canada did not play a large part in these negotiations; Mike, however, did.

He was a candidate for the presidency of the U.N. General Assembly for 1952, and, despite rather lukewarm American support, he was elected with the Soviet bloc opposing and the Arab bloc abstaining, the result of his earlier work on Palestine.

Inevitably, Korea was the major issue of Mike's General Assembly presidency and, unavoidably, he clashed once more with Acheson. In his memoirs, Acheson writes about the "Menon cabal" and accuses Mike of being a major co-conspirator with India's Krishna Menon, whom Acheson despised. The plan was to end the war by repatriating prisoners through the creation of an independent commission. Mike and Paul Martin, who was representing Canada at the United Nations in the fall of 1952, did work with Menon, whom they also found difficult. Unlike Acheson, however, they believed his influence in the non-Western world was potentially valuable. Both wanted to end a conflict that had gone on too long. Acheson warned Pearson that he was "bothered" by this initiative and, in his memoirs, speaks of the "sophistries" of Menon and Pearson. In the end, the initiative failed, but Acheson's comments wounded Mike, who did not take issue in detail with Acheson in his memoirs but rather reproduced a long memorandum written at the time. The most recent analysis, however, suggests that Acheson's sense that he was not trusted and informed was, in fact, true.[73]

The age of "easy and automatic relations" had indeed ended. No longer the reluctant debutante on the international stage, the United States increasingly wanted to design the sets and direct the play. As the United States did the casting, selecting by itself the villains and the heroes, Pearson and Canada did not lose interest in the play but resented being cast as bit players. Still, it was, as Mike said in 1952, the only game in town, and he was never a player who left the game.

CHAPTER THREE

THE
PEACEMAKER

The dream has a specific content. Nothing in it suggests an age of
innocence and peace in the future, when "the wolf shall dwell with
the lamb" and "a little child shall lead them"; nor is the goal a "land
flowing with milk and honey," where men shall live without
effort.... Should he, by some stroke of fortune or through his own
exertions, enter the promised land, he will fully accept continuing
work and increasing anxiety as the price he must pay if he does not
want to be cast out of his paradise. Once there, the grandchild of
Irish peasants, propelled towards North America by the dream,
could no more freely shed his cultural inheritance of thrift and
industry, hoarding and frugality, than could the Jewish child of
ghetto parentage cast off completely his age-old fear of segregation
and persecution.

> — John R. Seeley, R. Alexander Sim, and E.W. Loosley,
> in *Crestwood Heights: A Study of the Culture
> of Suburban Life* (1956)[1]

Hᴵˢ "own exertions" and "good fortune" had brought Mike
Pearson to a pre-eminent position in Canadian life. It was not
the promised land, but for many Canadians whose ancestry, like the
Pearsons', bore memories of peat bogs, pestilence, war, and depression, the fifties seemed a favoured age. John Seeley and his colleagues recoiled from the conformity of the middle-class Canadian

suburb they studied, yet they too recognized that the post-war years had brought for many Canadians a material prosperity beyond the wildest dreams of Canadians a generation before. Those middle-class Canadians upon whom these materials blessings flowed retained, as Seeley noted, an understandable scepticism about continuity of the flow. The nation itself remained, in the words of Pearson's colleague John Holmes, "a conservative society that had ... achieved precarious equipoise".[2]

Mike and Maryon Pearson in their private and public life reflected that precarious equipoise. They remained cautious about their money, their family, and their future. Maryon handled the family finances, and Mike was the frequent butt of family jokes about always forgetting his money. While he ignored the chequebook's details, he was instinctively aware of the so-called bottom line. When he entered politics and, in his and probably Maryon's view, placed his financial security in jeopardy, he sought reassurance that he would not have to fret about overdrafts, his children's education, or his pension. A great deal of such assurance came in 1948 from Walter Gordon, a wealthy Toronto businessperson, who told Mike that, given the state of the world, Mike should "take on the job" and that he would help him do it. Gordon then made a few phone calls to "friends" and created a fund upon which Mike could draw whenever he needed. The fund, cleverly dubbed the Algoma Fishing and Conservation Society, was the product of yearly "subscriptions" from wealthy friends of Pearson and Gordon, such as stockbrokers David MacKeen and Bill Harris, and Hudson's Bay Company executive Philip Chester. Mary Macdonald passed on the requests for funds to Gordon when help was needed.* Gordon claimed in the 1960s, when he and Pearson were quarrelling, that he had raised $100,000 upon

---

* Such funds had existed for other prominent politicians, including Mackenzie King and Louis St. Laurent. The existence of King's fund seems to have been widely known but was never acknowledged. The Pearson memoirs do not mention his fund, although he was certainly aware of it and its donors. On such funds and on Pearson, see Reginald Whitaker, *The Government Party* (Toronto: University of Toronto Press, 1977), 18 and 197-8.

which Mike — or Maryon, after Mike's death — could draw.[3] The fact that Gordon later recalled his efforts when he was angry suggests that it would have been better if he had not made them. For Mike, the debt he owed Gordon was not monetary, but it was real and perhaps resented, as such debts so often are.

Like King, who was wealthy when he left office, Pearson was reluctant to appear affluent. He mocked his appearance in the early 1950s on a list of the ten best-dressed Canadians. Mary Macdonald and Maryon joined in the laughter. His tastes remained those of the parson's son. The Pearsons' car was a modest Chevrolet. They continued to rent the rather ramshackle old farmhouse on Augusta Street in Sandy Hill where small shops and Ottawa University students abounded, while many of his old friends sought out the fastness of what *Maclean's* magazine dubbed "The Haughtiest Suburb of Them All" — Rockcliffe. There, houses were a more than respectable minimum of twenty-four feet apart, and no stores, businesses, funeral homes, or churches disturbed the suburban peace. Rising early each morning, Mike cooked breakfast, usually of poached eggs, toast, and coffee, and in the evening Maryon cooked the meat-and-potatoes dinner.

They did buy a cottage on the Gatineau River north of Ottawa, but "cottage life" then meant "roughing it", denying oneself many of the conveniences that the mid-century city represented.[4] In its own fashion it was a denial of modern society, though of course a modern affluence was needed to buy a cottage. But cottages, it was thought, were wonderful for the children and grandchildren, closer to nature, and far from the madding crowds and the consumer comforts of mid-fifties America.*

---

* Pearson's friend Frank Scott mocked the "call of the wild" so many affluent Canadians responded to in a mid-1950s poem:
   Make me over, Mother Nature,
   Take the knowledge from my eyes,
   Put me back among the pine trees
   Where the simple are the wise.
   "The Call of the Wild", in F.R. Scott, *Collected Poems* (Toronto: McClelland and Stewart, 1981). Used by permission.

Geoffrey and Patsy both went to private schools. In one of his pre-war broadcasts for the BBC, Mike had praised the virtues of the North American public school system, only to be hoist with his own petard when a British friend asked why he sent his own son to private schools. He blamed Maryon, but his actions and the pride he expressed in Patsy's and Geoff's achievements belie his protests. Patsy went to Toronto's élite Bishop Strachan School and Geoffrey went to Port Hope's Trinity College School, which the redoubtable Bishop Strachan long ago had founded to educate a ruling class. Breaking with family tradition when he entered the University of Toronto just after the war, Geoffrey chose not Victoria College, of which Mike became chancellor in 1951, but the Anglican fortress of Trinity College. Patsy followed tradition by choosing Victoria, from which she graduated in 1950. She then moved to London, Ontario, where she began to study nursing. Her future husband, Walter Hannah, was also in London, where he was studying medicine at the University of Western Ontario.

In the early 1950s, Maryon and Mike knew, as parents suddenly do, that their children had grown up. To Patsy, Mike lamented her too-rapid maturity. "It's hard and a little sad," he wrote on her twenty-first birthday, "to think that tomorrow you'll be 21." Now Patsy made her choice to follow Walter to London, despite her parents' misgivings and their concern that she was "too young". It was the 1950s, when "everywhere in film, television, and advertising" one saw loving couples embracing under the "trees of new suburban homes" and when the age of marriage dropped lower and birth rates rose higher than at any other time since the First World War. Patsy's decision to follow Walter not only to London but also into medicine (nursing) upset Maryon. Perhaps she was troubled because she recalled how, in the mid-1920s, she had given up her own ambitions to be a writer and to study in order to become a faculty member's wife and to have a family. She had wanted Patsy to be an artist, but it was not to be.

Mike himself seems to have stood back from the contest between mother and daughter. He was more willing to intervene with his son when, early in his second year at Oxford, Geoffrey and Landon Mackenzie decided to marry. Landon, from London, Ontario, was a thoroughly delightful young person, charming all who came near her with her warmth and intelligence.* She had studied English and Philosophy at Trinity College, where she had met Geoffrey. She immediately charmed Mike. Nevertheless, when Geoffrey told his parents in early October 1951 that he and Landon would marry in December, Mike asked him to wait:

> I *do* understand and appreciate your feelings, your desires and your hopes. I do also — and this is I suppose important — feel very happy that Landon and you are going to "join up" (an inelegant way of putting it). We have no reservations about this and we will do our very best to help you in any way that we can. Anyway, it is not a question of helping — but of sharing. That is what a family is for. But you will, in your turn, appreciate that your news was a surprise — a rather breath-taking one — because after all December is only a few weeks away.... You know as well as I do, that people like you and Landon and us, when we take this step — we mean to take it "for the duration" (I wish I could avoid these military terms). That, therefore, a delay of a few months — or even a year — is not going to matter very much.

He asked Geoffrey to "wait for a time", but Geoffrey and Landon did not. They married on December 26, 1951.[5]

To a later generation keen to detect the role of gender differences within the harmonious family, the Pearson family offers intriguing evidence. It was hardly a typical family, but it does reveal

---

*In February 1951, Geoffrey had been invited to the Canadian high commissioner's residence to meet Princess Margaret. His father, who had met her, sent on the following advice: "You will, I think, find Margaret an engrossing partner — but remember she is much above your humble station so don't get ideas worthy of a musical comedy! I found her an agreeable girl to talk to — and suggest as subjects of conversation and in the following order of priority, dancing, travel, sex, and Beowulf." Lester Pearson to Geoffrey Pearson (Feb. 1951, PPP).

how strong the pressures of society then were — people "like them" entered marriage "for the duration". It also reveals, however, the pressures for individual choice within the family unit. Among the images of the fifties' family, the Pearson family falls quite happily between the genial patriarchy of Robert Young in "Father Knows Best" and the surly rebellion of James Dean in *Rebel without a Cause*. In the fifties, the Canadian family, like the nation, seemed in a state of "precarious equipoise", clinging to real and imagined traditions while peering, with trembling and titillation, towards the sexual and generational "liberations" of the sixties.*

Mike reflected this muddle when he tried to understand what happened to his own family in 1951. Just before he wrote Geoffrey asking him to reconsider his decision to marry so quickly, he had written to Geoff about Patsy's decision to follow Walter Hannah to London. "Patsy left us last night to work out her own destiny in her own way — or Walt's? — but not ours, and we have no complaint about that...." They had no complaint, perhaps, but there was concern, some sadness, and, frankly, some confusion and guilt as Mike groped to explain and accept why Patsy had made her own choice. It had been, he told Geoffrey, "a very unhappy and disturbing time", one that had caused Maryon much "anguish". "It is, of course, true — as you both have on occasions told us — that no generation ever understands that which succeeds it — and with the bewildering changes — and shattering events of the last 25 years, that is possibly true of my own generation to a deeper degree than any that preceded it. But it works both ways of course." Mike had

---

* Douglas Owram emphasizes the influence of depression and war on post-war attitudes: "This was a generation that had fought hard for the idea of home. It was also a generation in which the balancing act of a democratic marriage, traditional work roles, and the upheaval of the war years sat uneasily. Home was a fragile concept and always under threat." Pioneering research on the subject is found in Owram's "Home and Family at Mid-Century" (Paper presented at Canadian Historical Association Annual Meeting, May 1992), and in Veronica Strong-Boag, "Home Dreams: Women and the Suburban Experiment in Canada, 1945-1960", *Canadian Historical Review* (Dec. 1991), 471-504.

been away so much; Geoffrey's and Patsy's life had been so different from his own. "When I look back I am acutely and guiltily conscious of my own failures as a father. I wonder if my father felt the same way. I don't think — in fact I know that he was no fonder — had no greater affection for me than I have for you and Patsy — was no closer to me in the sense that he could share intimate experiences with me — and get me to pour out my feelings to him." Despite the emotional reserve so characteristic of British-Canadian families, he felt that his father had never "failed" him; rather, he had given him a secure base upon which his solid future was built.* He implied that he hoped Geoffrey shared that sense.[6]

Certainly Geoffrey appears to have done so. In a study of twentieth-century families, some American scholars have argued that it was Mike and Maryon's own generation that differed the most from their parents' in attitudes and behaviour, and that the norms of Mike and Maryon's generation were closer to their children's.[7] The Pearsons appear to confirm that argument. In the same letter in which he pondered generational differences, Mike added: "By the way, there are some External Affairs Exams towards the end of November and you might as well write them." Geoffrey did, and on May 5, 1952, before the results were officially released, Mike told Geoffrey: "You can stop worrying — you are on the list and pretty near the top. Congratulations — good show as we say at Oxford." Mike had no doubt that Geoffrey should continue following the path he himself had trod with such distinction. When Mike's old friend Larry MacKenzie, the president of the University of British Columbia, inquired in June 1952 whether Geoffrey might be interested in a faculty position, Mike, while telling Geoffrey he did not want to influence him, told him to think not of the present but "10 or 15 years ahead". Did he want to be an "assistant or associate professor" or an ambassador? The question for the Pearsons was rhetorical. Despite

---

* The letter had begun: "I have just come home from a very interesting luncheon at the PM's — Acheson, Morrison, Schumann [*sic*], the PM and I — we settled everything."

oft-expressed longings for the serene cloisters of academe, Mike privately never regretted his decision to seek the rewards and frustrations of public life.[8] But did Maryon?

Maryon, in the 1950s, began to complain about the demands of public life — and others began to complain about her. In his diary, Arnold Heeney, then ambassador to Washington and Mike's first under-secretary in 1949, writes about a dinner party where Maryon was present: "She gives me the creeps and I cannot be at ease with her — because she dislikes me I suppose. She has managed, so unnecessarily, to acquire so many critics, poor woman. I wonder what the basic reason is for her discontent."[9] Heeney failed to note her many friends. Mike is taciturn about Maryon's discontent in his memoirs, but he does give an example of it. Once after a day of campaigning in Algoma, Maryon and Mike found themselves

at a meeting of party officials from the various sections of the constituency. The survey of campaign progress was over by ten o'clock or so, and the moment for another snack had arrived, when the chairman said "Is there anything to bring up?" [Maryon] who, as was her custom, had been attentive but silent all day, spoke up, to general surprise and pleasure: "Yes, I would like to bring something up." "What is it?" asked the chairman with respectful interest. "Twelve cups of coffee and eight doughnuts."[10]

The customary silence is perhaps more telling than the tart response. In the late 1940s and early 1950s Mike's absences were longer, his preoccupations less Maryon's, especially as the children's lives passed beyond parental sway. That most gregarious of public figures, Mike Pearson, could be very solitary in private, and for Maryon such moments must have been frustrating. She told a Norwegian interviewer that she believed politics were "a man's work", but that she did express her opinions to Mike. She added, however, that "there are times when he makes me believe that my opinion does not interest him in the slightest". Mike seemed to leave his work at the office. "Even when surrounded by people," Patsy recalled, "he's able to withdraw into himself." "The usual Sunday afternoon picture," Mike wrote to Geoffrey in Oxford in 1950. "I am in the big chair with the Radio on — Mum over in the corner of the couch reading a book with ideas (in which I am naturally not interested!) and responding negatively to my periodic suggestions that she should go upstairs and dress or we will be late for a 6:30 party at the Chateau with Philip Chester."[11] In Patsy's account of her home, her mother is the "tidy person" who allowed Mike to throw "a suit on the bed and never think to pick it up". He was sentimental about birthdays and valentines, but "Mum is usually the one to buy the cards". She was also the one who would "always arrange boxes of food, a cake and other goodies, too" when the children were away at school. And invariably she was the disciplinarian. "When we got into mischief he was likely to melt away or disappear behind a newspaper," Patsy recalled.[12]

Mike seems to have believed that gender created different spheres, both infused with different "mystiques". Because Patsy "used to trail the maid all over the house with duster and mop, and played until [she] was ten," her father, in her view, "never took [her] studies seriously". The presence of women at political and sporting events that men alone had once attended struck him as something on which he should comment. It was, he often said, a sign of changing times. Nor were women much welcomed in External Affairs or the inner sanctum of government where Mike was so comfortable. When the National Council of Women met with the cabinet in 1953, he regarded them as politically naïve and even a bit comical.*

---

* "Today at 12:00 o'clock the Cabinet, or part of them (some of my male colleagues must have been frightened), received a delegation from the National Council of Women, who wished to present resolutions to the Government. They were a strange bag — I mean the resolutions, not the ladies! — notable particularly for the relatively inconsequential things that some of them dealt with, while a lot of important developments or possible developments, were ignored. There was nothing about peace, the United Nations, or international affairs, but something on race track betting, love comics, and sex offences. The P.M. was at his best with the ladies and by the end of the hour they were practically on his neck." Pearson Diary, Jan. 23, 1953, MG26 N8, v. 5 (NAC).

Neither the times nor her husband did much to make Canadian public life palatable to Maryon and, as Mike's sphere enlarged and came to draw her in, she chafed against its boundaries, resenting many of the demands it made upon her.

Mike, in fact, seems to have been uneasy with his views and the pre-eminence he gave to his public life. He missed many of the graduations, birthdays, and wonderful moments of a young child's life that become so boldly etched upon a parent's heart. As Patsy later said, these absences meant that the "family relationship had to be lived so much in our minds and hearts". There, he lived it richly. Although his own relationship with Maryon seems to have been testy in the late 1940s and early 1950s, he clearly regarded her as the glue that held the family together. When he confessed to Geoffrey his hope that he had been the father to his son that Ed Pearson had been to him, he had no such doubts about Maryon. Even his own beloved mother, he told his son, "could never have centred her deepest hopes and love on me as your mother has on you and Patsy. There is really no dross of any kind in that gold", although Mike did admit that Maryon's hard crust meant that "you have to go deep, often, to find that vein".[13] That vein linked Mike to Maryon and to the family, and its richness provided much of the confidence he exuded in his public life. When his grandson Paul was born in 1954, the letter he wrote to Patsy from Geneva reveals not only the significance he attributed to what he was doing but also the role that he believed Patsy should and would play:

A warm welcome to my little grandson, who by now no doubt has already expressed vocally his opinion of the world into which he has been ushered. We will have to work harder to make it better than it is now.... Probably he and all those who are arriving with him ... will do a better job than we have done, and bring a happier and healthier state of affairs to the world. For some time before that happens, however, he will have to depend on you for the affection and guidance which will make all the difference to him in the years ahead. As the world becomes more confused, and as life becomes more complex — as outside forces weigh on us and batter at us with greater intensity — home — and all it stands for — becomes more and more vital as the foundation of the good life.[14]

There are echoes here of buried experience, of an eighteen-year-old drenched in patriotism and Christian faith who believed, in the language of the time, that "His Mother and his God" should be his very first thoughts, and of a young man steeped in the duty to serve. Of a young diplomat who struggled to preserve the world from the barbarity of "male" passions, and, not least, of a marriage that in time cauterized the dream that Maryon once had of a life where she and Mike would "be together" and "do and think together". The dream had died, and the world that Mike had known was, by 1950, close to its dotage. Perhaps some of his beliefs are not fashionable today but, as the world that formed him has passed into history, we can at least understand the context in which they were created.[15]

In 1954, when Mike wrote to Patsy about his new grandson, most Canadians and his family believed that Paul's grandfather was doing a great deal to make the world "a happier and healthier place". He had become the best-known Canadian, a personal symbol of "the colossus — stirring between the 49th parallel and the polar sea", as a normally gloomy journalist described his booming homeland in those days. In 1952 Mike had been offered the position of NATO's first secretary general when it seemed that position mattered more than almost any other in the world. He had been president of the U.N. General Assembly in the fall of the year and had almost become U.N. secretary general. A Soviet veto and, perhaps, a poor campaign manager — his old British friend Gladwyn Jebb — ended his chances, but St. Laurent, in discussing the possible appointment with Mike, had said he would soon step aside and had hinted broadly that Mike should take his place. There seemed few limits upon his potential.[16]

Others had similar thoughts, especially when he turned down the NATO position, one that he himself had said was "the biggest job in the world at the moment". In April 1952, Michael Barkway wrote an extremely flattering article on Pearson for *Saturday Night* magazine in which he argued that, despite Mike's apparent lack of desire for the post of prime minister, it might appear to him "the only way to ensure a continuance of his policy of safeguarding Canada's position by promoting the greatest possible Atlantic unity".[17] With the fourth year of the government's term approaching and with St. Laurent turning seventy, talk of elections and the Liberal leadership swirled around Ottawa. There were constant rumours that Pearson would be shifted to a different portfolio to give him "domestic" experience, but he appears not to have wanted to move, and St. Laurent agreed with him. When he was not "shuffled", stories appeared suggesting that Mike's heart was not in domestic politics and that the office of prime minister had no allure.[18]

Those who knew him better, or — more importantly — could influence events, thought that, in the words of the eminent journalist Bruce Hutchison, "Mike can be had". Hutchison, moreover, made it clear that he and his friends wanted him. After the U.N. position fell through,* Mike apparently told Hutchison's friend Grant Dexter that he wanted the leadership and that finance minister Douglas Abbott was his principal opponent.[19] Mike learned soon after this conversation that Abbott wanted out of politics after the election. If St. Laurent left in a year, as he had told Mike he intended to do, Mike was the logical successor. Jack Pickersgill, who had left the powerful position of secretary to the cabinet and clerk of the privy council, where he had enormous influence, to become a politician and minister of citizenship and immigration, favoured his close friend, Walter Harris, who replaced Abbott as the finance minister in 1954. However, Pickersgill seems to have lost influence when he left

---

* At a luncheon with Mike on February 12, 1953, Hutchison indicated distress that Mike might become secretary general: "He says it is all fixed now that I am to be the Liberal leader, and that I am betraying my country!" Pearson Diary, Feb. 12, 1953, MG26 N8, v. 5 (NAC).

the bureaucracy for politics, and Harris himself told Dexter he would not have much chance against a politician who had been dubbed the "world's best-known Canadian".[20]

That summer in 1953, Queen Elizabeth began what nostalgic imperialists termed the second Elizabethan age. In her loyal Dominion, the great British actor-director Alec Guinness, directed by the eminent British director Tyrone Guthrie, inaugurated Canada's Shakespearean festival in the sleepy southwestern-Ontario railway town of Stratford. And her French-Canadian and Irish Catholic prime minister, Louis St. Laurent, told a rather surprised cabinet that he was "a devoted admirer of the Royal Family in general and [Elizabeth] in particular, and thinks that the monarchy is more solidly established than ever".[21] Indeed, St. Laurent's Irish Protestant foreign minister worried whether St. Laurent's affection for the Crown was not impeding his political judgement because he refused to permit the noxious atmosphere of an election to becloud the glories of the Coronation. Eventually, the election was called for August 10, with Elizabeth on the throne and most things right in the world.

Stalin died in March, the Korean War ended in July, and American dollars flowed across the Canadian border, passing through the rich resources of the Shield into the wallets of Canadian workers and voters. The Conservatives under former Ontario premier and old Pearson acquaintance George Drew blustered ineffectively in the House of Commons and on the hustings. The CCF, in the Liberals' eyes, seemed little more than an amiable annoyance. In 1952, the CCF leader, Major (his name, not his title) Coldwell, had questioned the decision by NATO to emphasize a military build-up in Europe. This roused Mike, who, in unusually strong terms, castigated Coldwell's stance. To Geoffrey, who seems to have had leftist notions and some sympathy for the CCF, and to Peter Waite, Mike privately explained that he agreed with Coldwell that there should be more attention paid to economic linkages and development but that, at the present moment, the challenge of the Soviet army must be the major concern. If only Coldwell had come to him, confidentially, before he made his rash charges he would not have spoken as he had.[22] And so, in the summer of 1953, with the Queen on the throne, peace at home, Stalin in his grave, and old age pensions in the people's pockets, St. Laurent put on his grey felt hat and charmed the country once more.

One who was not charmed, the historian and Liberal critic Donald Creighton, recalled later that "Government by party had virtually ceased to exist. Instead the Liberals had become the party of government. And it was as the neutral instrument of perfect administration that they approached the general election of 1953."[23] Bias notwithstanding, Creighton captured the spirit of that "listless, holiday" election in which more than 200,000 voters did not bother to return from the lake to vote. Mike himself commented in his diary on the curious Canadian political world where "the best political talks are ... the non-political ones".[24] A young Conservative convert, Dalton Camp, marvelled at how the wealthy Liberal campaign in "an age of growing media sophistication" made St. Laurent — a corporate lawyer, after all — into a "man of a familially common mould, everyone's handsome aging uncle, doting on the children, — whimsical, a little patronizing and a whole lot more visible". What the electorate saw of George Drew — "a harsh, malevolent puritan — and a stuffed shirt to boot" — they mostly did not like. The Liberal victory was inevitable. Three weeks before the campaign's end, Brooke Claxton told the campaign team to cut costs drastically, not because money was short but because victory was certain.[25]

Dexter and Hutchison thought that St. Laurent gave the Liberals solidity; Mike gave them "sex appeal". The combination was effective, for the Liberals were returned with 171 seats, and Mike was returned with an increased majority in Algoma East. He had briefly flirted with the idea of an urban riding rather than immense Algoma with its long distances and scattered villages, but Algoma's varied and rugged character pleased him and he remained its member until he left Parliament fifteen years later. Mike and Maryon spent much time in the constituency during campaigns, although his celebrity required his attendance at political meetings elsewhere, where Liberal votes were less certain. The 1953 election campaign is mentioned only briefly in the Pearson memoirs. Mike tells of the time when Liberal MP Leo Gauthier of Sudbury, who helped him greatly with patronage and politics in Ontario's north, asked Mike to throw out the first ball at a Sudbury baseball game. Mike hesitated, claiming that no baseball fan wants a game delayed by politicians. Gauthier scoffed: "Nonsense, it will be just fine. I know my people." So Mike threw, Gauthier hit, and a local Liberal notable caught, while the crowd remained noticeably quiet. Walking off the field, Mike said: "Leo, that wasn't very successful." Leo smiled and said: "Don't be silly, that was a triumph, not a single boo."[26]

There is little about politics in Mike's memoirs, at least in the sense that Leo Gauthier, Paul Martin, Jimmy Gardiner, or C.D. Howe know "politics". In his outstanding study of the Liberal Party under King and St. Laurent, Reginald Whitaker can find no traces of Pearson's hand in political organization. As a cabinet minister, Pearson took organizational responsibility for eastern Ontario, but in reality he was "only a front man for Senator W.A. Fraser", who was not even in the cabinet.[27] Mike was a splendid political performer on the church-basement, chicken-supper political circuit, where his remarkable charm, his skills as a raconteur, and his lode of baseball statistics made him a political diamond. But he was a political ornament, not a hard stone that cut the fabric of Liberal politics. This preciousness had two major effects. First, it protected Mike from the knocking on doors and the "bashing of heads" that politicians like Paul Martin had to do so regularly. Martin and others eventually came to resent the fact that their labour at doorsteps, constituency meetings, and Sunday-morning church services counted for little, and indeed, might be held against them as evidence of being "overly ambitious", as St. Laurent said of Martin to Pearson in 1953. In that peculiar political atmosphere of the mid-1950s, to be too political was unseemly.[28] Secondly, Mike's position meant that he received a poor education in the details of the Liberal Party and the Canadian political system. Like his predecessor, St.

Laurent, and his successor, Pierre Trudeau, Pearson kept his distance from his party's eager embrace. Mackenzie King, who had for so long savoured and succoured the party's many appendages, left a party more satisfied and fulfilled than did his three successors.

After the 1953 election, the Liberal government, like Dorian Gray, suddenly seemed to wither and scowl. St. Laurent became less sure, C.D. Howe more cranky. Brooke Claxton, who had shared King's fascination with and mastery of political details, decided, significantly, that Metropolitan Life's boardroom offered greater pleasures. Lionel Chevrier, a competent minister and fine orator, left to built the St. Lawrence Seaway, and Abbott became a Supreme Court judge. Mike quickly noticed that the domestic pillars upon which Liberal foreign policy stood were eroding, and he worried about his and his party's future. Within External Affairs, 1953-54 also marked a turning point, as Mike tried to sort out the problem of placing his senior diplomatic colleagues in appropriate posts. He found the task difficult; indeed, his indecision made the task much more difficult than it should have been. The episode was a harbinger of similar problems with personnel that Mike would have as prime minister. Still, anyone in his office with his background at the time would have had difficulties.

Three distinguished Canadian public servants who were his close friends posed the greatest problem. Norman Robertson and Hume Wrong, under whom Mike had served when he was a public servant, had been in London and Washington since 1946. A.D.P. Heeney, whom Mike had persuaded to become under-secretary, believed that Mike had promised him the Washington embassy after the under-secretaryship. Mike persuaded him in 1952 to take the new post of ambassador to NATO, but it did not satisfy him. Heeney complained in his diary and intrigued with his friend and rather unhappy replacement as under-secretary, Dana Wilgress, to improve his lot. When it seemed possible that Mike might become secretary general of the United Nations, Wilgress told Heeney to write to Mike expressing "natural regret of a prospective termination of a close and pleasant association" followed by the expression of "hope that [Heeney] would see the fulfilment of your desire to be appointed to Washington before he finally relinquishes the portfolio".[29] This intrigue would have seen Wilgress going to Paris and Hume Wrong returning to Ottawa, but Mike had other notions about Washington. He raised the topic with Walter Gordon and also spoke to St. Laurent about Graham Towers. Gordon was puzzled, since he knew that Heeney had been promised the post. He told Mike that he would not consider the appointment in such circumstances.[30]

In fact, the appointment of Gordon would have continued a Canadian tradition of leaving the major ambassadorial posts for senior political appointments, a tradition that Pearson, Wrong, and Robertson had dramatically broken. Such was External Affairs' eminence in post-war Ottawa that its own officers secured these ambassadorial plums. This brought diplomatic competence, but there was about it, in Grant Dexter's view, "the setting of musical chairs". "Normally these boys [the career diplomats] would be the advisers to the high commissioner and the ambassadors — not the Great Men in person. The Great Men would be the G. Howard Fergusons, Vincent Masseys and the like. The boys have got into blue chips, by accident, and are certainly cashing in."[31] His old friends brought the chips to Mike, who was now the banker and not the player. He was, they thought, slow in redeeming the chips and miserly in assessing their value. Not surprisingly, grumbling began. When Mike appointed Wilgress as under-secretary rather than Hume Wrong, Dexter saw that there was an "element of competition here and Hume, perhaps, does not have a proper attitude to his minister". Later, Jack Pickersgill strengthened Dexter's suspicions when he told him that Mike "felt inferior" towards Wrong and Robertson and "feared being cramped and dominated."[32]

Mike did fumble, then and later, when dealing with difficult questions of personnel and personality. Neither charm nor a diplomat's evasiveness can overcome personal ambition and pride. Pearson's transition to politics inevitably complicated his personal and professional relationship with Robertson and Wrong, and there was surely some degree of rivalry there. But too much can be made of this rivalry. The fact that Mike had served under Robertson and Wrong and his intimate knowledge of their frustrations with political superiors naturally affected the relationship among the three. He had the warmest memories of their brilliant collaboration in earlier days, but he knew Rebecca West's warning that one should never relight an old cigarette or rekindle an old flame. He and they were not who they had been before.

Cigarettes, cocktails, and incredibly hard work had made Wrong and Robertson quite unhealthy men by the early 1950s. Mike knew this and worried about both of them, as an employer and as a friend. He finally appointed Heeney to Washington and Wrong as undersecretary in the late spring of 1953; on doctor's orders, however, Wrong delayed taking the job until he had a three-month rest. When Wrong finally took up his position in November 1953, Mike's premonitions proved correct. Wrong's health failed within two weeks, and he began to die.

As Wrong was dying, Mike stayed near. In early January he asked Lew Douglas, the wealthy American who had worked with Mike and Hume when NATO was formed, if he could help to find "a great house or cottage where Joyce could do the cooking" and where Hume could rest. Mike apologized for writing, but he was "somewhat at a loss to know to whom to write". In any event, it was too late. Wrong's hypertension worsened. Mike wrote to their old friend Tommy Stone, then the ambassador to the Netherlands, on January 23, and told him that Hume "in all probability, will have passed away" by the time he received the letter. He told Stone how he had spent most of the night with Joyce Wrong at the house "helping to get him to the hospital where he at least could be freed from some of the agony that he was suffering at home". Mike carried him to the car and drove him just before midnight to the hospital as Joyce quietly wept. The next day Hume died. Mike wrote a long letter to Robertson the next day. "To me," Mike claimed, "it is a terrific blow because of our very old and close friendship. I was, of course, counting on him greatly to help me in my work, and I shall miss his wise counsel and assistance, but that is a small matter compared with the loss of such a long and good friend."[33] It had been a quarter century since Hume Wrong welcomed Mike Pearson to a Washington summer where the brightest rookie in External and its most cynically witty young diplomat "spent most of [their] spare time reforming our elementary and rather absurd diplomatic service".[34] That service was, by 1954, far from elementary and certainly not absurd, in large part because of what the two had done together. No doubt that summer in Washington, the year in London when Joyce (who gave Mike Hume's treasured fountain pen) and Mike and Hume played Chinese checkers into the night as the *Luftwaffe* and the RAF jousted above, and many other memories lingered in Mike's mind at a dinner party in March. At that party, a departmental secretary wrote to a friend, "Mr. P. talked and talked about Mr. W., and how much he missed him". Mike summarized his thoughts best when he wrote, in a private letter in March, that "it is still hard to adjust myself to Hume's absence and indeed ... that will never be possible completely. I must be getting old," he mused, "because I find new friends and experiences pale and inadequate beside the old ones."[35]

Like so many of his generation, Hume Wrong had worked himself to death. Mike, only three years younger than Wrong, saw what the horrible wars and anxious peace of his century had wrought upon those who had served its most worthy causes. Unlike many of his generation, he saw that such past service no longer could justify pre-eminence. If Mike is to be criticized for his dilatory and evasive manner when he dealt with appointments and administration in External, he deserves credit for recognizing that his generation should not cling to its old beliefs and eminent positions, but should gracefully welcome a new generation of Canadians.

When Hume died, Mike wrote immediately to his three senior diplomats, Tommy Stone, Arnold Heeney, and Norman Robertson, asking for their suggestions for an under-secretary. He pointed out that he did not think previous under-secretaries should return, thus ruling out Robertson and Heeney. Instead, he suggested much younger people, notably Gordon Robertson, Mitchell Sharp, and Jules Léger. In the end he picked Léger, even though at first Mike himself had thought him too young. Léger, who was only forty-one and was the first francophone under-secretary, remained in the position for the remainder of Mike's term as minister.[36] There was some grumbling about the appointment, but Léger was clearly the prime minister's choice, and Mike's.* Pearson and Léger did not work together closely — indeed, Mike made it clear that Léger would concentrate on administration — but they respected each other and were effective.

Léger later said of Pearson, Robertson, and Wrong that they had a blind spot where French Canada was concerned. Perhaps, but in 1953-54 Mike was casting some glances towards Quebec, and the choice of Léger reflected this new interest. He was telling Geoffrey that his greatest regret was his failure to learn French, and he not only took on a francophone under-secretary but also became a mentor to a young francophone MP, Jean Lesage, whom he asked to write to him in French.[37] Léger, an American official reported, represented a new brand of "fairly young, intelligent cosmopolitan French Canadians [in Ottawa] with close connections in Quebec". They would leave their mark on Ottawa, Quebec City, and Mike Pearson.

For three years after 1953, however, few domestic affairs left their mark upon Mike. Even more than before, he left the department alone. The department may have regarded Mike as "one of us", but for that reason his involvement in personnel matters and day-to-day administration was difficult. Moreover, there were so many more important tasks before him. Nineteen fifty-three was a decisive year

---

* One senior ambassador complained that the "Catholics" and the French Canadians were "collaring" the best posts. In fact, Léger was the first Catholic under-secretary since Sir Joseph Pope, and the major ambassadorial posts, Washington and London, were occupied by Protestants. Jack Pickersgill, however, did tell Grant Dexter that the Léger appointment was an attempt to turn Léger's eminent brother, Cardinal Léger, "from Duplessis and attach him to St. Laurent". Dexter Memorandum, May 27, 1954, Dexter Papers, TC744 (Queen's).

for him and for international relations. Stalin's death brought the hope of a Cold War thaw; the new Republication administration of Dwight Eisenhower brought a new defence policy that emphasized, in Secretary of State John Foster Dulles's words, "more basic security at less cost". This meant a greater reliance on an American-based intercontinental bomber force and on the threat of nuclear retaliation, and less upon ground troops, particularly troops stationed abroad. It was, Mike noted, a new policy that had major implications for Canada.[38] He had told the cabinet in 1950 that he could not accept, as some military authorities argued, "that the atomic bomb is just another weapon". The "psychological and political consequences of the employment of the bomb, *or the threat of its employment* [italics added] ... would be incalculably great."[39] The Eisenhower-Dulles "New Look" in defence did, in fact, treat the bomb as just another weapon and used the threat of its use as a psychological and political weapon. "Brinkmanship" and "massive retaliation" were the chilling garlands that cloaked the "New Look" in American strategic policy. And they troubled Pearson.

Since 1945, Mike had concentrated upon building institutions, the U.N. and NATO particularly. He had been president of the U.N. General Assembly and had steered the NATO council through a difficult period. After 1953, this institutional focus shifted. In the case of the U.N., its limits as an institution seemed clearer and the opportunities to shape it fewer. The experience of the U.N. presidency had taught Mike that the Cold War circumscribed what was possible. Although he said nothing, the loss of the secretary generalship a second time was understandably disillusioning. In the case of NATO, the hopes of 1948-49 for a broader Atlantic community had withered as old fears and animosities combined with tighter domestic budgets to halt NATO's growth. These institutions mattered less to Mike and to international negotiations and diplomacy after 1953. The new American Republican administration was more inclined to unilateralism, to dealing with other states directly, and to asserting American power independently and aggressively. The new Soviet administration seemed inclined to cast off Stalinist suspicions and to express greater willingness to lower the tensions between East and West. The post-1953 terrain, then, was less certain, more dangerous, but, for an experienced and clever diplomat like Mike Pearson, more exhilarating. "He is," Arnold Heeney wrote in his diary in 1955, "now at the height of his international usefulness."[40] He was indeed.

That usefulness was evident in many areas, even though Mike held no official international positions as he had earlier. His advantages were more than a quarter-decade of diplomatic experience, contacts that few others had, and, as ever, a bit of luck. The new secretary general, Dag Hammarskjöld, liked and admired him. He had played tennis in the 1930s with Anthony Eden, now the British foreign secretary, and had heard the prime minister, Winston Churchill, rant about Nazis. Another old British friend, Roger Makins, was British ambassador to Washington where Dwight Eisenhower, whom Mike knew from wartime and NATO work, was president and John Foster Dulles, a long-time acquaintance though not a friend, was secretary of state. Unlike the Americans, Mike had Nehru's respect. The Indian prime minister, who was seeking to create a buffer between the superpowers, used Pearson and Escott Reid, Canada's high commissioner in New Delhi, as intermediaries between India and the West, so much of which Nehru distrusted and so much of which distrusted him.[41]

Despite these advantages, there were problems, particularly with the United States. Mike's and, for that matter, most Canadians' doubts about the Republicans were part of the problem. Roosevelt had won Canadians' hearts in the 1930s and 1940s, and Republicans had done little to counter that romance. Certainly the "red-baiting" by some Republican senators, such as Senator Joe McCarthy, and their newspaper friends, such as the *Chicago Tribune*, annoyed most Canadians. Mike himself became a target of their wrath and suspicion in 1953, when he rejected a request by the U.S. Senate Internal Security Subcommittee that Igor Gouzenko be allowed to testify before it or be interviewed by it. Gouzenko had told a *Chicago Tribune* reporter that he might be able to help the subcommittee, which had "run out of leads". He did not, apparently, offer new information but only advice, but this important distinction was lost in the whirlwind his comments caused. The American right, irritated with Mike's actions in the final stages of the Korean War, took umbrage when he refused to allow Gouzenko, who was living anonymously under the protection of the Canadian state, to testify. Infuriating rumours had circulated about Mike himself since the 1951 testimony of Elizabeth Bentley to that same committee. No matter that Bentley herself largely retracted the charges; the rumours continued to seep into some American journals and newspapers.

The State Department, frightened of the committee and facing purges itself, renewed the request to have Gouzenko testify, and Pearson, speaking for the Canadian government, rejected it, claiming that Gouzenko had no new information and that an American congressional committee had no jurisdiction over Canada or Canadians. The RCMP had advised External Affairs that Gouzenko's motive was "an entirely selfish one". He had written a book and, in the view of RCMP superintendent George McClellan, would "go to any lengths to get his name once again splashed across the headlines of the United States newspapers". McClellan also feared that individuals whose names were not mentioned in 1946 because they were innocent would undoubtedly be identified before the committee, with disastrous results.* Mike took the Mountie's advice and, at once, faced a barrage from senators Jenner and McCarthy and their supporters.

---

* McClellan, whom Gouzenko apparently hated and suspected of being a Soviet agent, continued: "In my opinion this man has developed into a money-hungry, luxury-loving publicity seeker whose whole purpose in life is to endeavour to recover the large sums of money which he dissipated, and to live the life of ease to which he became accustomed.... I think it would be disastrous from a security point of view if Gouzenko were permitted to appear before a Congressional Committee. As you know these Committees are prepared to name names and quote unproven allegations in the most publicity seeking manner possible without regard for the rights or privacy of the persons named." J.R. Lemieux, quoting McClellan, to G.P. deT. Glazebrook, Oct. 30, 1953, Pearson Papers, MG26 N1, v. 33 (NAC); and, on McClellan and Gouzenko, see Peter Worthington's comments in John Sawatsky, *Gouzenko: The Untold Story* (Macmillan: Toronto, 1984), 135.

The Baltimore *Times-Herald* fulminated: "The best that can be said against Lester Pearson and his followers in the Canadian pinko set is that they are dangerous and untruthful." Victor Lasky, the noted right-wing journalist, rehearsed the old charges Elizabeth Bentley had made about Mike's leaks to the Soviets and added the charge that he was "covering up" for others like Herbert Norman (see Chapter 5). And Colonel Robert S. McCormick, publisher of the *Chicago Tribune*, who vacationed in Canada and bestowed crisp $50 bills for a song upon a young Brian Mulroney,* denounced Mike Pearson, as "the most dangerous man in the English speaking world".[42]

McCarthyism nauseated Mike Pearson as much as it titillated Colonel McCormick, and he instinctively turned away from it at the first strong whiff, as he did, for example, at dirty jokes. His manners bore the mark still of the Methodist parson's son. When students at Victoria College, his alma mater, "tried" Senator McCarthy and burned an effigy of him as a Hallowe'en prank, he indicated to the principal, A.B. Moore, that he did not find the incident amusing, however offensive McCarthy had been to Victoria's chancellor.[43]

Others defended him more appropriately, including the opposition leaders in the House of Commons.+ The Conservative foreign affairs critic, John Diefenbaker, railed against the affront to Canada's sovereignty and its foreign secretary, and David Lewis of the CCF wrote ("My dear Mike") to express his disgust at "the dirt

---

* "Any time he came to Baie Comeau, he asked for me, and I'd go sing. I'd perform any song that he'd want. He'd just name them and I knew them." Mulroney, quoted in Ian Macdonald, *Mulroney: The Making of the Prime Minister* (Toronto: McClelland and Stewart, 1984).

+ Mike's troubles in Washington did not help him in Moscow. *Pravda* in 1953 accused him of "devotion to American moneybags" and of working for "the enslavement of the Canadian people by the American monopolies". Mike's early years as a sausage stuffer and junior clerk were misunderstood as a "career in one of the leading American concerns for the production of weapons, Armour and Company ...". Such were the misunderstandings of the Cold War's height. Quoted in a speech by David Croll, House of Commons, *Debates*, Nov. 23, 1953.

which the irresponsible clique of demagogues in the United States has thrown at you" and to praise Mike's "restraint". The major Canadian newspapers, with the peculiar exception of the Montreal *Gazette*, voiced similar sentiments.[44] But it was left to Maryon to confront the matter directly.

As the Canadians and Americans quarrelled over Gouzenko, President Eisenhower visited Canada. At an unofficial meeting with cabinet, the Canadians avoided the topic of Gouzenko. That evening at dinner, Maryon did not. When confronted by Maryon about McCarthy and the irresponsible American press, the president "replied that the foreign press made far too much of Senator McCarthy, and seemed to think that in that regard the American press were less to blame". That, Mike told St. Laurent, was "a doubtful conclusion". Nor was the authority of the opinion strengthened by Eisenhower's statement that "he never read the newspapers because they merely confused, exalted, or irritated you".[45] In truth, Eisenhower's and Dulles's reactions disappointed the Canadians greatly. Arnold Smith, Mike's speech writer and special assistant and a strong anti-Communist, wondered privately whether the State Department had made any effort to dissuade the senatorial inquisitors. As Professor B.S. Keirstead later wrote, Canadians had "the uneasy feeling that if the State Department or President Eisenhower wished to do so, they could express their regard for and confidence in Mr. Pearson in much stronger terms than in fact they did …". The overall relationship turned slightly sour. "Canadians had an uneasy feeling that Mr. Pearson's virtues of patience, intelligence, and sensibility were not appreciated in the United States, even among the responsible makers of policy, and this meant, or so Canadians concluded, that American policy was apt to be dictated by impatience, lack of intelligent study, and insensibility to others."[46]

And yet by 1953 no relationship was more important to Canadians. Mike, while often frustrated with the character of American policy and leadership, recognized that his major task was to manage that relationship effectively. In his letter of support to Pearson,

David Lewis had wondered whether "the noisy group in the United States is not as big an obstacle to peace as is Moscow". Mike did not share this opinion: the United States, for all the problems it caused, was a nation with democratic leadership and instincts, whose leaders could not be compared with the despots who ruled the Soviet Union.[47] Even in the report to St. Laurent about Maryon's disappointing conversation with Eisenhower, Mike spoke of the president's "admirable" speeches and even defended Dulles when Eisenhower, most inappropriately, said privately to Mike that Dulles was "exceptionally equipped for his present post in every respect but one — his inability to make a good personal impression on people at first meeting or discussion". Yes, said Mike, but this "handicap ... was usually overcome when people got to know him better". For good measure he told "Ike" that his own opinion of Dulles had gone up, an opinion, he told St. Laurent, that was sincerely expressed and shared by the British. Personal differences and resentments, for this experienced diplomat, did not get in the way of managing the relationship.[48]

One difficulty in the relationship that Mike had dealt with since the steamy Washington summer of 1929 disappeared with the Canada–United States agreement to work jointly to build the St. Lawrence Seaway. In the spring of 1954, Joseph McCarthy crumbled before the television lights, during the Army-McCarthy hearings. By the end of 1954, Ambassador Heeney was reporting from Washington that the Americans were no longer expressing hopes for "improvement" in Canadian-American relations, and the "somewhat touchy situation" at the beginning of the year had been replaced by "great friendliness and frankness". Nevertheless, Heeney noted, "the tendency of the needle of Administration policy to fluctuate pretty wildly" had caused much difficulty.[49] It certainly did for Mike Pearson in 1954.

The problem, once again, was Asia, and the United States' policy towards Asian revolution. External Affairs wanted no part of the "defence of Formosa" and remained wary of American aims in Indochina where, in early 1954, the French forces faced defeat. Mike had responded to hints in 1953 that the United States might not "stand idly by" as Ho Chi Minh's forces triumphed. He warned that, while there could be no compromise with Communist aggression, "this does not mean ... that we should assume that every anticolonial, nationalist or revolutionary movement is Russian Communist in origin or direction, any more than we should assume that with patience and sympathy every Asian Communist leader can be turned into a Tito".[50] Not long after this article appeared came the Battle of Dienbienphu and a telephone call from Dulles and Eisenhower to St. Laurent and Pearson asking what Canada thought of an American intervention, including a possible nuclear strike to aid the French forces. Not much, was their answer and that of the British.[51] Eisenhower, in fact, had placed impossible conditions on American intervention, including allied agreement, and his calls were a means of strengthening the non-interventionist side. Dulles, too, was a nuclear swordsman more in talk than in deed or formal recommendation.[52] Nevertheless, the call, coming within a month of the test explosion of the American hydrogen bomb at Bikini, underlined how high the stakes were.

The end of the Korean War and the approaching victory of Ho Chi Minh in Indochina brought Asia to the forefront of the international agenda. The Korean War had ended with an armistice, not peace; Communist rule in China had hardened; and the retreat of empires had left political chaos in its wake. Dulles, the so-called China lobby, and the Conservative and Social Credit parties in Canada's Parliament * called upon the West to halt or even roll back the tide of Communism in Asia. Mike saw opportunities in danger, but he trod

---

* The rhetoric could be extreme. Social Credit member J.H. Blackmore said: "This insatiable monster is the Turko-Mongolian-red conspiracy which the free world faces today." The plot was "to bring the whole world into abject and perpetual servitude to an absolute world government, the personnel of which will be clandestinely selected by Turko-Mongolian reds or their dupes". Conservative frontbencher Howard Green declared: "If North America is ever invaded it will be from Asia, not from Europe, and it will be by the red Chinese." House of Commons, *Debates*, Mar. 29-30, 1954.

cautiously because he knew Asia so little. So must the historian. Asia was not only the battleground where most fell during the Cold War but is also the subject that has caused the most acrimonious disputes among Cold War historians. The distinguished Canadian scholars Douglas Ross and James Eayrs differ strongly in their perceptions of Canadian policy in this period. Professor Ross sees Canada and Pearson as seeking a perilous balance that was constantly threatened by the winds of war and revolution. In this quest, they acted "in the interests of peace", the title of Ross's massive study of Canada and Indochina. Professor Eayrs sees the willingness of Canada to acquiesce in much American policy in the 1950s as "the roots of complicity", the subtitle of his study of Canada's involvement in the Indochinese revolution. Both write in the aftermath of Vietnam, and their analyses reflect the advantages and disadvantages of hindsight.[53]

Looking at the mass of documents that landed on Mike Pearson's desk in 1953 and 1954, one gains a sense of how he placed Indochina and Asia within his understanding of Canadian national interests. First, he sought to limit direct Canadian involvement and to channel such involvement through the United Nations (as in Korea) or the Commonwealth. Secondly, he fretted about the exclusion of India from the peacemaking process. The United States had marshalled its block in the United Nations to defeat a resolution that India be a part of the Korean peace conference. The effect of this slight was enhanced by a United States' decision to give Pakistan $25 million in aid. Thirdly, he worried about France; its governments were unstable, its National Assembly was refusing to ratify the European Defence Community, and its case gained little sympathy from the British and the Americans either in their colonies or in Europe. From Paris, Geoffrey urged understanding of France upon his father, who respected the opinion and its source. Fourthly, and finally, Mike sought to minimize differences between the United States and Great Britain, though Britain's leadership in 1953-54 troubled him. Churchill sought desperately to meet with Stalin's successors; Eisenhower would have none of it. After "slow, waffling and indecisive cabinet meetings", Anthony Eden would explode about Churchill,

"The Old Man", to his secretary: "This simply cannot go on; he is gaga; he cannot finish his sentences."[54] But Eden himself grated upon the Americans, who found his manners patronizing* and who distrusted him after he, in American eyes, pulled back from a commitment to join them in an Asian security pact. Undersecretary of State Walter Bedell (Beedle) Smith reported to Washington after one angry encounter that Eden and Lord Reading "staged a demonstration of petulance and annoyance, the like of which I have never seen before ... their attempt to distort and deceive was so obvious that even Molotov could not swallow it...." Eden, for his part, believed the Americans wanted to "run the world". On the shoals of such personal animosities the "special relationship" floundered perilously.[55]

Repairing that relationship remained for Mike the principal aim for Canadian policy, as it had been throughout his career. Yet a relationship repaired by a joint U.S.-U.K. Asian intervention would destroy the Commonwealth and would inevitably embroil Canada in the conflict. In February 1954, the United States, Britain, France, and the U.S.S.R. agreed that the Geneva Conference on Korea planned for April should be paralleled by a simultaneous conference to deal with Indochina. The Canadians were direct participants in the former, which ended on June 15, 1954, and were indirectly involved in the latter, which continued until July 21. Mike attended the former, but found it "discouraging, complicated and frustrating". There was no Korean peace, and the conference was memorable for Dulles's refusal to shake hands with Chou En-lai and for his general bad manners. He went home early, but not before complaining bitterly that no one defended the United States against Chou En-lai's bitter attack.[56] Pearson worked with the British to maintain a balance, spoke in stern anti-Communist terms that would have pleased an American Republican, chatted amiably with Chou En-lai (which brought him a rebuke from the Americans for "fraternization" and the gift from Chou of a book on Chinese

---

* Mike never liked Eden's propensity to greet him with: "Oh hello, my dear." He much preferred Ernie Bevin's working-class twang: "Gddy, me boy."

brush-paintings on rice), and privately reassured the Indians that their interests were respected. When the conference seemed to be crumbling, he asked Reid, his high commissioner in New Delhi, to suggest to India in "a casual conversation" that it use the Commonwealth to have a conference on Asian security. Washington, whose dislike of India was "pathological", was not to learn that the suggestion came from Canada. Nothing came of this plan, but the efforts of Mike and his officers John Holmes and Chester Ronning may have influenced a bit the final outcome of the Geneva Conference on Indochina, which did reach an agreement that brought a temporary truce to that tragic land.[57]

When the agreement was reached, Canada, to its surprise, was proposed as a member of the International Commission for Supervision and Control (ICSC) in Vietnam, along with India and Poland. Mike had been extremely cautious about Canadian involvement in Asia, especially when there was no U.N. cover. But 1954 was the glorious summer of Indo-Canadian harmony (to be followed by increasingly severe winters of discontent), and Geneva, while frustrating, had at least silenced the artillery in Indochina. The Americans did not want Canada to accept the proposal and themselves refused to do more than acknowledge the peace terms. A sullen Dulles persisted in advocating a Pacific collective defence pact, and in early September 1954 the doubtful but harassed British joined the Americans and six others to form what Mike privately termed the "meaningless" Southeast Asia Treaty Organization (SEATO).[58] Canada, most happily for External Affairs, received no invitation to join.* After some

---

* The Conservative and Social Credit parties had strongly urged Canadian membership. Mike, in a May 28 speech where he attacked "the international Communist conspiracy", placed impossible conditions on Canadian membership. Professor Ross takes delight in pointing out that one who in 1954 avowed such a pact "to combat an immediate threat" from aggressive Asian Communism was none other than Professor Eayrs, who so harshly criticized Pearson's co-operation or "complicity" with the U.S. later. Such are the dangers for the scholar who seeks to change history as well as record it. See Douglas Ross, *In the Interests of Peace* (Toronto: University of Toronto Press, 1984), 70n.

debate, Canada did accept the invitation to join the ICSC. It did so because of the association with India and because Mike recognized that the ideal world of collective security could only be built upon the foundation of international co-operation, the strength of whose bricks could not be known until they faced the test of time. This brick eventually disintegrated, but, as Mike told Eden at the time, there was "no disposition here to evade this responsibility which may, however, turn out to be onerous as it was unsought". Unsought or not, the responsibility of a nation that, since 1945, had lectured others about their responsibilities was clear.[59]

Professor Eayrs and, from a different perspective, Dr. Peter Gellman have found contradictions in Pearson's apparent commitment to internationalism, but those contradictions were ones Mike himself recognized and used. He did not deny that collective security had to be selective, but believed that the habit of co-operation was essential and could come only from international participation or, as he would have said, international responsibility. Like Reinhold Niebuhr, who restored the concept of original sin to post-war American liberalism, Mike applied the same lesson to the Cold War: "Since the sources of conflict cannot be eliminated they must be controlled"; and different sources required different methods. Not for him sentimental assumptions about Asian communism as "merely agrarian reform" or arrogant assumptions like that of Dulles at Geneva that heaven's truth lay within his worldly policy. "A moral approach to problems," Mike wrote in the aftermath of Geneva, "does not require that we should see all of them in simple terms of challenges to righteousness, or of black and white. Indeed the contrary is true, and gray is the prevailing shade."[60]

At Geneva, Mike's name came up in a historic meeting among Eden, Molotov, and Chou En-lai. Molotov introduced Chou to Eden — "rather like an anxious mother bringing a farouche daughter out into polite society". Eden's secretary recorded the conversation:

Next topic, the Americans. Chou-En-Lai very bitter against them — "Helping Chiang Kai-Shek to kill Chinese." "They hate and are

95

jealous of China." A.E. — "On the contrary, they have loved China, and when their relations went wrong it was an emotional disappointment. Their vast new powers and responsibilities. Their honourable intentions. Ask Pearson. Canada close to U.S. but independent." Molotov — "Is Canada so independent of the U.S.?"[61]

Eden never answered. The next year the Soviets sought the answer themselves.

After Geneva, the international skies did clear. The new Soviet leadership loosened Austria from its grip, began to issue invitations to foreign leaders, and talked about revising "Stalinist military science" in view of the awful prospect of the hydrogen bomb. Eisenhower, too, saw more wisdom in Churchill's urgings of a meeting with the Soviets and developed in his own mind "the clear conviction that ... the world is racing toward catastrophe". He proposed an "open skies" plan of arms control and in the summer of 1955 met with Nikita Khrushchev and Nikolai Bulganin in Geneva. The world hailed the new "spirit of Geneva".[62]

In June 1955, Mike travelled to San Francisco for the tenth anniversary of the signing of the U.N. Charter. On leaving one of the meetings, he was suddenly surrounded by five Soviet representatives, including Soviet foreign minister V.M. Molotov. Molotov asked Pearson to join him in a private room, where he invited him formally, with a curious little bow, to visit the Soviet Union.

Mike discussed the invitation with St. Laurent on his return to Ottawa, and both agreed he should accept. Earlier that same year Fisheries minister James Sinclair had agreed to attend an international whaling conference in Moscow. Moreover, the visit seemed opportune in light of international events, especially the thaw in the Cold War. The Soviets knew that Mike had played a major part in the formation of NATO and that he had been a strong defender of the increase in the military strength of the alliance. He was certainly no pacifist and, as Professor Joseph Levitt has pointed out, he was surprisingly doubtful about disarmament schemes.[63] And yet he was

among the most prominent Western voices calling for more contacts and understanding between East and West. In short, it was
worth an effort on the part of the Soviets to convince him that post-
Stalinist Soviet Communism would have a more congenial face.

Several factors, in addition to Mike's eminence among Western
diplomats and Eden's comment to Molotov, may have prompted
the invitation. In 1955, the Soviets issued a series of invitations to
world leaders, the most prominent being Nehru and Adenauer.
Moreover, the Soviet press in 1955 showed increasing interest in
Canada. The hope for future trade appears to have been the principal reason for this new interest, but it is noteworthy that Soviet
commentary on Canada was growing more favourable in its analysis
of Canada's political scene. Nevertheless, the major reason for the
invitation was probably Pearson's own interest in visiting Moscow.
In November 1954, after he had spoken in Paris with John Watkins,
Canada's ambassador in Moscow, Mike wrote to Watkins: "When
will I be able to go Moscow in disguise? I have been talking so much
about co-existence these days I think I should examine it on the
spot." Watkins had established close contact with Soviet officials,
and it is highly probable that he reported Pearson's interest to them,
although Robert Ford also claims to have made the approaches that
made the visit possible.[64]

In planning the visit, Mike asked John Holmes, who had served
in Moscow, spoke some Russian, and was splendid company, and
George Ignatieff, scion of one of the most distinguished families of
Czarist times, to accompany him. Ignatieff warned Pearson that his
ancestry might prove an embarrassment to the mission,* but Mike
dismissed his worries saying, "George, if you're any trouble I'll
simply dump you."[65] In the course of planning the visit, the Soviets
expressed their interest in discussing a potential trade agreement,
but Mike was reluctant to expand the agenda to include trade.
Nevertheless, in deference to the Soviet request, Mitchell Sharp,

---

* Ignatieff's father, Count Paul Ignatieff, was a member of the pre-revolutionary
government. He fled the Bolshevik Revolution and the Soviet Union it created.

associate deputy minister of trade and commerce, was added to the Canadian delegation. Ray Crépault of External Affairs completed the official contingent. Among the journalists covering the visit were René Lévesque and Richard Needham. Maryon accompanied her husband, as did two cases of Canadian liquor, which, Crépault added, "should get them to Paris where it will be replenished".[66] Neither the Canadian people nor Mike's mother were informed of the liquid accompaniment. The supply was needed for the many toasts that followed.

In preparing for the visit, Mike also let the Soviets present the agenda, which they did after considerable delay. He resisted until the last moment the Soviet interest in exploring a trade agreement. He finally agreed to discuss trade "over, say a three year period", but told Watkins that he should not demonstrate "undue enthusiasm" for such an agreement. He was also cautious in his expectations for the visit in general. Despite this caution, the Canadian government was nonetheless intrigued with the notion that the Soviet Union wanted both trade, especially in wheat, and a stronger political linkage with Canada.[67]

On October 5, 1955, the Canadians stepped down from their plane at Moscow airport to be greeted by the Soviet dignitaries, headed by Molotov. To mark the occasion, Moscow Radio broadcast a talk entitled "Common Interests of the Soviet and Canadian Peoples" that heralded the "noticeable improvement" in Soviet-Canadian relations that had occurred "lately". The improvement in relations apparently had not resulted in improved knowledge, for the announcer expressed the hope that *Prime Minister* Pearson's visit would be an important step in the further development of Soviet-Canadian relations.[68] Events of the next few days suggested that the Soviets did indeed attach great significance to the visit: The top Soviet officials came to the Canadian Embassy party; Molotov, Malenkov, and Kaganovich gave their time freely and seemed well briefed. Pearson remained cautious in his remarks and in his reaction. He hesitated when asked to sign a joint communiqué on his visit, responded to toasts calling for "peace" by toasting "peace and security", and questioned the need to sign a trade agreement. He wrote in his diary: "You don't or you shouldn't, sign an agreement of this kind, especially with Russians, without a good deal of care and consideration."[69]

While Mike was suspicious of Soviet statements and stagecraft, his scepticism vanished when he encountered the landscape and the people of the Soviet Union. Technical people, such as the director of the Agricultural Exhibition — "a wonderful, old horny-handed farmer type" — impressed and charmed him. The miles of barren wreckage that he passed on his way to Peterhof outside Leningrad rekindled in him some of the warmth Russia's war effort had created in 1943. His discussions with "not high political communists, but administrators, artists, engineers, scientists, technicians, etc." revealed that they had a genuine fear of war and of "American designs" upon the Soviet Union. Yet he wondered whether the politicians were not using this genuine fear to gain support for their harsh policies.[70]

The visit has been described in colourful and informative detail in the memoirs of Pearson and George Ignatieff, and in both cases the accounts are based mainly on contemporary diaries. Of historic importance was the agreement to begin the sale of Canadian grain to the Soviet Union. The most memorable event was the extraordinary drinking party that occurred when Pearson and his group visited Khrushchev and Bulganin at a luxurious mansion near Yalta in the Crimea. There in Government Villa No. 4, the former palace of the noble Yousoupov family, the most extraordinary personal encounter between Canada and the Soviet Union during the Cold War took place.

Accounts vary of the meeting, but none deny that Khrushchev's deportment astonished the Canadians. Several items of controversy endure. The Canadian party comprised Pearson, Ignatieff, Ray Crépault, and John Watkins, and some journalists. The evening began with a formal discussion of Germany and NATO in which Khrushchev lectured Pearson on that organization's many iniquities, the worst of which was its plan to rearm Germany. Pearson responded by arguing that NATO was purely a defensive alliance and that its military character was a response to the presence of Soviet troops throughout Eastern Europe. Years later, René Lévesque, who thrust his microphone before Khrushchev, said that in this encounter Khrushchev clearly bested Pearson. He left Pearson "on the canvas", Lévesque claims. This reminiscence, however, may have been coloured by later political animosities between Lévesque and Pearson. Clearly, contemporary press accounts based upon the tape of the encounter do not agree (nor do Pearson and Ignatieff). Moreover, that is not what Lévesque reported in 1955. There is, however, no doubt that Khrushchev's bluster and roughness stunned Pearson and that it took him a few moments to regain his balance. Maintaining his balance became ever more difficult as the Soviets plied their guests with continuous shots of pure vodka.[71]

Another allegation, based upon a KGB defector's tale, is that Khrushchev taunted John Watkins about his homosexuality. The taunt certainly might have happened, because Khrushchev was not above such crudeness, but the evidence suggests it was unlikely. Ignatieff denies he heard any such remark, and he understood Russian. Even if it were a casual slight that Ignatieff did not hear (and, by his own admission, he did consume eighteen shots of vodka laced with hot pepper), it is certain that such a remark would have shaken Watkins. His account of the evening, however, does not suggest such a predicament.

The evening itself caused concern and did little to reassure the Canadians. Mike had a cold; a sicker Maryon stayed behind in the drafty Moscow hotel. Khrushchev met them — "the squat, tough-looking Ukrainian peasant, [with] very baggy trousers, a waddling walk, a mobile face with signs of a sense of humour, and no social graces, obviously, of any kind". Their conversation, in retrospect, is chilling. When Mike said that the West "sought only defensive strength adequate to deter aggression", Khrushchev bluntly retorted that its aim was "to impose solutions" on the U.S.S.R. Khrushchev then said that only Russians or Germans knew war. The rest of the West did not know how to fight, and this time the Germans wouldn't fight. NATO would simply fall apart when the first shot was fired. Mike replied that any world war would be far worse than the last. Khrushchev pointedly added: "This time Canada would not be geographically secure."[72]

At 12:30 a.m., with eighteen vodkas in each bloodstream, the Canadians marched out, heads up, to their car. The next morning, the car swerved around the curves of the spectacular Black Sea cliffs, stopping before a monument to Marshal Kutusov. At that very spot, their Soviet expert said, the great marshal lost an eye defeating the Turks. Build another monument five miles back, Mike said, for that is where I lost my stomach.[73]

Mike seemed to lose many hopes on that journey. Khrushchev had behaved abominably. His manners were reminiscent of the barbarians who had ruled the Third Reich and whose brutality Khrushchev had acclaimed with his taunt that only the Germans knew how to fight. George Ignatieff said that the Crimean visit was like calling on Hitler at Berchtesgaden. The West, Mike then knew, had no option but to stay the course. It would not be easy, but there was no alternative.

Canadian ambassador Watkins had worked with a friend whom he called "Aloysha" in making the arrangements for the Moscow visit. Aloysha, whom Watkins described as a historian (the disguise for many scoundrels), was, in fact, Oleg Gribanov, one of the KGB's highest-ranking and most ruthless officers. "Aloysha" was present that bizarre night in the Crimea. After the visit, it was "Aloysha" who expressed Soviet discontent with Mike's attitude upon his return. At a "supper" at Aloysha's apartment in February 1956, the host told the Canadian ambassador

> in an outraged tone that Mr. Pearson had accused the Soviet Union of having aggressive aims in its foreign policy and of imperialism. He had tried to frighten the Canadian people by telling them that the Soviet Union would attack them across the North Pole. Surely he must have seen when he was here how eager the Soviet people

were for peace after what they had come through and that the Soviet government had not the slightest intention of attacking anybody. I recalled that Mr. Pearson had remarked several times since his visit to the Soviet Union that he did not believe that his country desired war. That was true, Anatoly said. He had said many good things but why should he spoil them by accusing the Soviet Government in an important speech broadcast to millions of people from the Canadian Parliament of aggressiveness and imperialism. And the American papers, Aloysha interrupted, have come out with big headlines to say that the Canadian Foreign Minister, who has just returned from a visit to the Soviet Union, says that the Soviet government plans to attack Canada.

Surely he had not said that. Well, that was the implication; he had said that it was a threat to Canada. And it looked very much, he continued, as if these attacks had been timed to coincide with the arrival in Canada of the Soviet Trade Delegation, since they had appeared in the press on the very day of their arrival and seemed calculated, for some reason, to make their task as difficult as possible. I was sure that this was pure coincidence and that there was no desire to create difficulties for the Soviet Trade Delegation. Anatoly agreed that probably there was no such intention in the timing but thought that the effect must be the same.

But why should he accuse the Soviet Union of having aggressive aims and of imperialism? You could call it what you liked, I replied, but the fact was that the Soviet Union was a kind of large and powerful imperium which, by reason of its power and policy, dominated a large region even outside its own borders. Now I know you are going to come back to your favourite subject [the 1948 Soviet-backed Communist takeover in] Czechoslovakia, Anatoly put in. Well, there are plenty of others, I laughed, for example, Poland, Hungary, Roumania, Bulgaria, Albania etc. But these countries had independent governments, Anatoly said. And surely I would not say that the Ukraine, for instance, was a colony in the old 19th century imperialistic sense. I certainly could not agree that the Ukraine was very independent in its foreign policy, for instance, or for that matter any of the others from any evidence I had of their voting in international assemblies, for instance. It was clear that they would not dare vote against the Soviet Union.

Aloysha then took the old familiar line that the reason they voted with the Soviet Union was because they agreed with its policy. There are a great many of these old stock arguments brought forth during the evening and they are certainly not worth reporting.

Aloysha then claimed that Mike had said in the Soviet Union that "he would not say nasty things any more". Watkins said he did not recall the comment and added that he thought the frankness between Khrushchev and Pearson had been useful. "Aloysha agreed, but said that it was one thing to talk across a table in private and another to attack the Soviet Union before a large audience."[74] The despatch annoyed Mike, and it is important to examine the reason for his annoyance. Pearson had reported on his Soviet trip to the House of Commons on January 31, 1956, had made several speeches, and had circulated his diary of the trip to Canadian and British officials. In all cases, Pearson emphasized his continuing pessimism about the Soviet Union's aims. Indeed, in the House of Commons he criticized press reports that had omitted the word "professed" in discussing the Soviet leadership's declarations of peaceful intention. For him, "the Russian regime, which embodies communist imperialism is achieving a strength, a solidity, a dynamism that is impressive — indeed, it is frightening." The danger was if anything greater because, for the Soviets, "man is only material for management". This call for "peace" that he heard constantly might be genuine on the people's part, "but that is not important unless it can influence the policies of the leaders of the people and there is not so much evidence of that. Mr. Khrushchev's idea of peace, and he made no secret about it when he talked with me, is illustrated by his determination to break up NATO an aggressive organization, so he claimed, aimed at Russia and therefore a threat to peace."

The visit, Pearson admitted, brought trade advantages and possibly some advances in scientific, technical, and human exchanges, but the November 1955 foreign ministers' meeting had shown that "Soviet words differed from Soviet deeds" and that "not a single basic objective of Soviet policy" had changed. The fundamental objective, it remained clear, "is security for the Soviet Union and the triumph of communist ideology in a world of communist states controlled and dominated by Moscow ...."[75] When Watkins* presented his "friend" Aloysha's views at such length in February 1956, making clear his pessimistic evaluation of the Soviet leaders' intentions, Mike responded with unusual bluntness:

> I do not recall making any unpleasant remarks about Russia or its people since my return, but I have criticized publicly and strongly some aspects of Russian Government policy. My visit did not reassure me in regard to the peaceful aims of that policy, but certainly did convince me that the people themselves, whatever might be the

---

* Watkins was recalled soon after this exchange. Security officials later investigated him after it was learned from Soviet defectors that Watkins, a homosexual, had been compromised. He had had sexual liaisons in the Soviet Union that the KGB photographed. His successor, David Johnson, was also a homosexual, who had to leave the Canadian foreign service in 1960 because of his homosexuality. After 1955, homosexuality became grounds for dismissal, or at least security decertification. It has been alleged by a former Canadian security official that Johnson too had been compromised. Details, however, remain sketchy, and Canadian files are only partially open. The Pearson government adopted a more liberal policy towards homosexuality in 1963, but by that time about 100 homosexuals had been dismissed for "security reasons". See J.L. Granatstein and David Stafford, *Spy Wars: Espionage and Canada from Gouzenko to Glasnost* (Toronto: Key Porter, 1990), 103-14; and the *Globe and Mail*, Apr. 24, 1992.

Granatstein and Stafford conclude that Canada and, by implication, Pearson, were naïve to send two homosexuals to Moscow, since the KGB probed all "weaknesses" and, in those days, homosexuality was a public crime and thus subject to blackmail. It must be added, however, that there is no evidence that Pearson or his officials knew Watkins and Johnson were homosexual and that External tended to send bachelors to posts like Moscow, which were thought to impose great hardships on families.

views of their rulers, did sincerely desire peace. You might tell your friend Aloysha one day that if he wants to convince me of the pacific intentions of his Politburo friends, he should explain why they find it necessary to have 400 modern submarines. A submarine is hardly a defensive weapon, especially when it is an ocean-going one capable of carrying atomic weapons.

As for the complaints about the "nasty" tone of his speeches, Mike responded that Khrushchev's recent remarks "could hardly have been nastier".[76]

The British, reading reports on the visit, said there was little new except for the "colour", but it was the "colour" that permeated the fabric of Canadian policy after the visit. Nineteen fifty-six brought the chilling of the spirit of Geneva, the Twentieth Party Congress, the Soviet crushing of Imre Nagy's regime in Hungary, and the first knowledge of the existence of sophisticated new Soviet rocketry. John Watkins' diplomatic reporting, which had emphasized his contacts with the Soviet bureaucracy and the possibilities of human contacts across the ideological chasm, seemed less convincing after the visit. Pearson saw in the Soviet Union a power that would not soon crumble and a leadership that was vain and erratic. He returned more concerned, more fearful about the future, and more certain that the Soviet experiment was cruel and an anathema to all who cherished democratic and liberal principles. The Soviet Union appeared stronger than ever, as it seemed to be effectively harnessing education and science for its political purposes.[77] If the visit's aim was to allay fears and build confidence and respect, it failed to do so. Mike and his colleagues came home knowing that the Cold War would not soon lose its chill.

CHAPTER FOUR

SUEZ

My I have appreciated Canada since I left it and I think we are easily
the best as well as the most civilized.... [Alexandria] is one of the
worst places in the world [but] it was no temptation to me who has
been brought up in as good a home as I have. All it serves is to make
one hate evil and to appreciate everything that is good.

— L.B. Pearson in Egypt, November 1915

I had not heard this story of Mike Pearson succeeding Ismay [at
NATO]. I must confess that my enthusiasm would be very limited.
We know the family's views on Colonial questions.

— Anthony Eden to Selwyn Lloyd, May 3, 1956[1]

MIKE PEARSON's understanding of good and evil was no longer
that of a dutiful, eighteen-year-old, Protestant parson's son
cast by war upon Egypt's very foreign shores. After two brutal European wars, he, like most thoughtful Westerners, no longer believed
that "civilization" so uniquely coincided with Western and Christian
values. In a 1955 lecture series at Princeton University, he expressed
the view that "the most far-reaching problems arise no longer
between nations within a single civilization but between civilizations
themselves". He saw in "the yearning and the effort of the people of
the Islamic world, of India, and of South-east Asia" a movement
that was "exciting and ... full of promise for the world".[2] The

107

"vision" of the West, he acknowledged, had weakened "during the first four decades of this century", and the "arrogant Pharisaism and smug satisfaction with one's own superior righteousness" that had corrupted Western colonial attitudes was no longer acceptable.[3] He, like other Western liberals, was increasingly embarrassed about the racist and imperialist ways of the West's past and now emphasized the West's recognition of the individual as "the fundamental criterion of all things temporal". That recognition, he told an American National Council of Churches meeting in 1954, had been "one of the great liberating forces of history" whose "monuments ... are the achievements of the Renaissance, of the great humanist movements, and of liberal democracy".[4] This force must not be lost as the West adjusted to a new world where its "habit of authority", so fundamental to its imperialist expansion since Columbus, no longer prevailed, because the rulers had lost their own confidence and the ruled had regained theirs.

A "habit of consultation" had to replace the "habit of authority", but, as historian Dr. Peter Gellman cogently argues, Mike Pearson did not share the idealist's hopes that such changes would come quickly.[5] The West itself had too many bad habits, memories, and wounds to co-operate easily; but it had shared traditions, through which the "habit of consultation" and eventually co-operation could be developed. In the negotiations that led to NATO, it was Pearson and Escott Reid who expressed most strongly the belief that the treaty "should not be exclusively military in character and that there were economic and even spiritual defences against Communist attack which should not be overlooked".[6] These non-military defences were overlooked in the following years as NATO, under American leadership, rallied militarily to reinforce Western Europe in the early 1950s. Fearing that the Soviets might attack or provoke internal discord in Europe while the Americans were preoccupied in Korea, Canadian and American soldiers returned to Europe and the Europeans themselves rearmed. But the Soviets still had many more divisions and, of course, the atomic bomb. As a result, the Americans looked for more support and saw it in Germany, their recent enemy, and in Greece and Turkey, so far from the Atlantic but so near to the Soviet Union. The thought of German rearmament terrified Germany's neighbours. France felt humiliated and wondered, in the private thoughts of its president, Vincent Auriol, "whether really the only reason we are part of the Atlantic pact is to be the target of humiliations?"[7] The admission of Greece and Turkey, in Mike Pearson's private view, ended "any real hope of building up Atlantic institutions and, if you like, modifying national sovereignty in the interests of security and progress ... ".[8]

The French scurried to find safe refuge through a European solution. Three great French leaders, Jean Monnet, Robert Schuman, and René Pleven, came forward with proposals for European economic and military integration. The European coal and steel community (the Schuman-Monnet Plan) created a common market for those important commodities among France, Benelux, Italy, and West Germany. It was the embryo of the European Common Market, and the brilliant response of Europe to pleas from North America and Britain that old divisions on the continent be broken down. Following on this action, the French premier, René Pleven, proposed a plan in October 1950 whereby Germany would be rearmed within a European army under the direction of European political institutions. This plan and its aftermath, the European Defence Community, which was created in May 1952 and defeated in the French National Assembly in August 1954, delayed the rearming of West Germany and poisoned NATO council meetings in the early 1950s.

France got little sympathy in Washington and often not much more in Ottawa. Both governments had to convince their voters that once again they should pay enormous sums to defend Europe. Moreover, Germany had historically tilted between West and East, and the North Americans believed it was important that the Europeans stitch together the tightest ropes to bind Germany to the West, as German Chancellor Konrad Adenauer appeared to want to do. Mike told Canada's ambassador in Paris to warn Schuman that "there is a very real danger that if there is delay in implementing these policies [U.S.] opinion may swing in the opposition direction [towards isolationism]. Indeed the same forces in public opinion manifest themselves in Canada." T.C. Davis, the Canadian ambassador to Germany, was much blunter: "The only final alternative to a Russian-dominated Europe is a Europe to a considerable extent dominated by Germany." That opinion, External officials told Davis, was "at variance" with Canadian policy. But in Ottawa, as in Paris, old memories died hard.[9]

What had certainly died by 1951 was the heady vision of a North Atlantic community in which a revived and integrated Europe would balance the growing weight of American influence in Canadian life. Like Donald Creighton, his former colleague in the University of Toronto History Department, whose biography of John A. Macdonald he greatly admired,* Mike believed that Canada's identity depended upon the nourishment that flowed from its links to Europe and that without such links the economic and political sinews of Canadian nationhood would shrivel. NATO in 1949 seemed to offer such links, but by 1951 the alliance's purposes seemed mainly military. NATO in the early 1950s had forcefully closed the gates to the barbarians without, but it had not done enough to build a sense of community within.

Mike shared the American and British belief that rearmament must be NATO's pre-eminent concern, although he did think the Americans were tactless in their persistent demands for increased expenditures by the Europeans and Canada. When CCF leader M.J. Coldwell criticized NATO for emphasizing the military aspect while

---

* Although Creighton later had a poor opinion of Pearson's diplomacy in the 1950s and even claimed to have been personally snubbed, he responded a bit too warmly to a letter from Pearson in 1953, in which Pearson praised the Macdonald biography's first volume: "I am even more pleased by the very welcome personal letter which you have written about my book. After all, we were colleagues I believe, for at least a year, and I still venture to think of you as a professional historian. Praise from an amateur is all very well and very welcome, but a historian feels naturally much more impressed when a fellow historian commends his work." Creighton to Pearson, Feb. 11, 1953 (PPP).

ignoring economic, cultural, and social questions, Mike firmly rebuked him. He told Geoffrey privately that the first concern had to be building up the forces in Europe. That alone would give Europeans the confidence to build free institutions that could endure.[10]

And yet Mike privately acknowledged that Coldwell had a point. He too "deplored" the fact that this military "concentration endangered the 'Article 2' idea of the Pact", the development of a North Atlantic community. In July 1951, therefore, he proposed to the Americans and the British "a complete re-examination of all the machinery for European co-operation, economic, social and military; to see whether it would be possible, as a result of such a re-examination, to separate the military and non-military aspects of NATO". Thus, Turkey and Greece could participate on the military side, while Ireland and Sweden could join the Atlantic non-military side. This "Atlanticist" vision appealed to the Scandinavians, to the Dutch and Belgians, and to some American diplomats such as Theodore Achilles.[11] But even within Canada there was dissent. Just as Mike became the chairman of a committee to study the possibility of closer economic and social co-operation in the fall of 1951, his ambassador in Washington, Hume Wrong, reflecting Dean Acheson's cynical appreciation of Article 2, declared that "the idea of the creation of a 'political Commonwealth of the North Atlantic' is in present circumstances so remote from attainment that to discuss it as an aim of current policy is unrealistic".[12]

Mike did discuss it, but Wrong was right: as an aim it was unrealistic, and the Pearson committee made a very general report to the Lisbon NATO council meeting in February 1952. When in 1952 Achilles hinted to the Canadians that they should establish a precedent and make American trade restrictions on Canada an Article 2 issue, Pearson resisted the temptation, knowing that such a tactic would only annoy Acheson and other Americans who did not share Achilles' Atlanticist enthusiasms.[13] There was a small step forward, however. NATO did decide at Lisbon, with Mike as the council's chair, that there would be more consultation among NATO members and a secretary general to give leadership. Mike turned down the post of secretary general, which went to Lord Ismay, "a bluff, John Bull type of Englishman". He did not regret his decision, for "Pug" Ismay told Mike after a few months in the job that he had had more authority as "a first subaltern in the British army than as Secretary General of NATO".[14] Ed Ritchie of External Affairs' Economic Division, in an ably argued memorandum, tried to reassure his minister that "the alleged loss of momentum in the Alliance" might be more of a "shaking down" in preparation "for the longer and steadier cruise".[15] But what was the direction and who would be the pilot?

These questions troubled Mike for the remainder of his life. He was a part of "the NATO generation", that group of Western leaders who received their political education in the 1930s and 1940s and who profoundly shaped the post-war world. With memories of the nationalist excesses of the 1930s and the successful allied co-operation of the 1940s, they valued internationalism as a goal in itself and supranational institutions as schools where habits of co-operation could be learned. Monnet and Schuman in France, Spaak in Belgium, de Gasperi in Italy, Stikker in the Netherlands, Lange in Norway, Macmillan and Jenkins in Britain, Hickerson and Achilles in the United States, Adenauer and Erhard in Germany, and Pearson, Reid, and Robertson in Canada shared this common faith. As with all faiths, the tenets of post-war Atlantic internationalism were understood differently by its adherents, but there was a recognition that a common creed did exist that bound together lives and fates across the North Atlantic. Despite the eminence of many of the faithful, it had become clear by 1953 that, apart from NATO's military successes, the faith had not been justified by enough good works.

The problems were a product of both past commitments and present fears. Among the past commitments were the old European empires, especially the French and the British. Many of the French and British troops that could have served NATO in Europe were occupied in far-flung corners of their tattered empires: Indochina, Kenya, Malaya, and other colonial wars and battles. Because Canadian and American troops took their places on the European front line, it meant that indirectly Canada and the United States were supporting the attempts of the Europeans to shore up their old empires. This fact made many North Americans very uneasy, including President Eisenhower, who believed that, in his own words, "the standing of the United States as the most powerful of the anti-colonial powers is an asset of incalculable value to the Free World".[16] It was an asset that soon diminished in worth, but in the 1950s in their dealings with their NATO allies the Americans often emphasized it.

This emphasis usually infuriated the British. It also annoyed the Canadians, who had no strong anti-colonial tradition and who knew well the imperial swagger of some Americans. Nevertheless, the Canadian government was generally supportive of the American view that the Europeans should shake off the dust of their empires and focus upon their own continent and the threats within and without it. When in 1950 Britain's Labour government decided that the "Durham miners" wouldn't stand for British participation in the Schuman-Monnet Plan, Mike agreed with Dean Acheson — and most later historians — that Britain had made "her great mistake of the post-war period".[17] If Labour worried about the British worker and British socialism, the Conservatives who came to office in 1951 worried about the Commonwealth, Britain's world role, and the special relationship with the United States. In the early 1950s, Britain let Europe down. France, left alone, began to tremble.

These events weighed heavily upon Canada and upon those who charted its path in the world. The change in American strategy with the Eisenhower administration and the advent of long-range Soviet and American bombers after 1953 made North American defence a new priority. A "crash program" began to give North America an "early warning system" and an air-defence plan. Mike worried that North American defence was being separated from NATO. He urged European participation in North American defence and its integration within NATO structures, but "the Americans would have none of this concept, which, they thought, would interfere with their own control". Moreover, Canada's "own service people also, [he suspected] preferred bilateral dealings and arrangements with Washington".[18] When the Korean War ended and European worries about an immediate Soviet attack eased, former European colonies began to reject more adamantly and successfully their erstwhile overlords. These struggles threatened NATO, and Pearson devised a strategy to save NATO while avoiding entanglement in decolonization.

There were three elements in his approach: first, he continued to urge closer European integration; secondly, he, like the Americans, urged Britain to free itself as quickly but as peacefully as possible from colonial responsibilities; and thirdly, unlike the Americans but like the foreign ministers of smaller NATO powers, he argued for more formal consultation within NATO councils.

Although European integration stirred fears in Canada that future markets might be lost (and they were), Mike did not hesitate to urge such integration. In December 1953, as the French dithered about confirming their membership in the European Defence Community, Mike wrote a letter to the French ambassador graciously acknowledging the French premier's thanks for his support of French concern about German rearmament. He claimed that such understanding of the French position came naturally "because of our history, our traditions and our origins". Nevertheless,

> because we are North Americans, we also appreciate and share the anxiety of the government in Washington that European arrangements should soon be completed which will make it easier for us to co-operate to the full within the North Atlantic coalition by associating Germany in some form with our purposes and our plans, and by subjecting her to the same kind of collective obligations and responsibilities undertaken by others. . . .
>
> Canadians, because of their experiences since 1914, are in a good position to know that "continentalism" is not enough, while Frenchmen, whose history has, in this century, been so much more tragic than ours, must be even more aware that any move towards European unity, while essential, can only be safely undertaken when

there are close and continuous lifelines across the Channel and the Atlantic. One of the most heartening things of the post-war period has been the establishment of these lines.

These lines, Mike concluded, were now "strong enough to stand the strain, psychological and otherwise, of German inclusion in our agreement".[19] They were, but it was a close call.

Dulles's announcement of the "New Look" in American defence strategy, Ho Chi Minh's successes against the French in Indochina, French fears of becoming a second-rank nation, and Churchill's belief that Britain was still a major power almost undid NATO in 1954. When the French turned down the EDC on August 30, 1954, British foreign secretary Anthony Eden called a "Nine Power Conference" to pick up the pieces. Mike joined Eden in trying to persuade French Premier Pierre Mendès-France that Germany had to be incorporated within European defence. Mendès-France — "a tough, dark, unprepossessing little man who doesn't waste time on social graces — or on alcohol" — piled condition upon condition, until Eden and Pearson warned him that the failure of the conference would destroy NATO and turn the Americans away from Europe. The conference did not fail, because Eden boldly gave a pledge that the British would station four divisions and the Tactical Air Force on the continent for as long as the majority of the continental allies, united within an expanded Western European Union, wanted it. "This was," British historian Geoffrey Warner has written, "a remarkable diplomatic achievement, especially in view of the almost total and inexplicable paralysis on the part of the United States, and one that undoubtedly merited the tribute subsequently paid by the Belgian foreign minister, Paul-Henri Spaak: 'In 1954 and 1955 [Eden] saved the alliance'."[20]

In 1955, West Germany joined NATO* just as the "Geneva spirit" thawed the Cold War. European economic co-operation became

---

* Robert Schuman, when told that the West German army would goosestep but in rubber-heeled boots, responded: "This time we won't hear them coming."

concrete with proposals for a common market. NATO's place in these changes seemed unclear, and so did Canada's in this new Europe. Mike grasped the opportunity to re-emphasize the traditional Canadian interest in greater consultation and co-operation in non-military fields. He reiterated to Spaak in February 1955 his complaint that Britain and the United States had concentrated too much on the military side of NATO. In the fall of the year he went public with his views in the prestigious American journal *Foreign Affairs*,[21] and at the December 1955 meeting of NATO foreign ministers he argued for a reconsideration of NATO's functions.

"The constant harping by the Canadians," historian Joseph Sinasac writes, "may have annoyed their American and British counterparts (who thought the Canadians self-righteous and even hypocritical), but by 1956 it appeared to have finally paid off."[22] It paid off because others began to realize that the military glue that held the alliance together was no longer as strong as it had been. The face of Soviet Communism no longer seemed quite so threatening. A weary France elected a socialist government that mused about a "middle way" between the superpowers, and a cash-starved Britain began to cut back its military commitments. Dulles worried about what this meant, and in April 1956 he said that it was time for NATO to stand "for something", not simply against something.[23]

At the NATO ministerial meeting that took place on May 4 and 5, 1956, two weeks after this comment, Dulles repeated his argument and frankly declared that NATO "had reached a critical moment in its life". Anticipating Dulles's initiative, Mike had asked his department to prepare proposals that would deal with the alliance's ailments, notably the lack of consultation and discussion among its members. At the NATO meeting, however, his hopes that Dulles's words would bring action were quickly dashed. Dulles himself presented no "concrete proposals", and "all that he and the United Kingdom ... were able to offer in working towards this end was [a] proposal to establish a committee of three Ministers to advise the Council on ways and means to improve and extend NATO cooperation in non-military fields ...". Without allowing time for consultation — hardly a good omen — Dulles told the press about the committee and told them who should be its chair: L.B. Pearson of Canada.[24]

Halvard Lange of Norway and Gaetano Martino of Italy joined Mike on this committee to evaluate the possibility of non-military co-operation in NATO. They were soon dubbed "the three wise men". This disturbed Mike, who complained to a friend: "Some are born wise, some achieve wisdom, and some, I fear, have wisdom thrust upon them. We three seem to be in the last and most dangerous category." That summer the wise men found wisdom in short supply among their NATO colleagues. Martino was inexperienced and took relatively little part in the exercise. Lange, a most able foreign minister whom Pearson greatly respected, lacked the staff resources that Canada possessed. As a result, the bulk of the committee's work was done by Canadian civil servants and by Pearson.[25]

NATO's future dominated his time and thoughts during the spring and summer of 1956. It did so even though he left Paris in May pessimistic about what he could accomplish. A meeting with Dulles in mid-June did not lift his spirits, for Dulles cloaked his earlier pronouncements on the need for co-operation with many layers of caution. The United States would consult when possible but, as a great power, it reserved the right to act alone.[26] The British, whom he saw next, dragged him into a crisis that revealed how a power no longer so great found loss of status difficult. When Mike arrived in Britain on June 17, he had dinner at the Canadian High Commission with Norman Robertson and British foreign secretary Selwyn Lloyd, who told him that the British, for economic and strategic reasons, had to reduce military spending drastically and were planning to announce a unilateral decision to withdraw a couple of divisions from the continent. Mike understood the strategic arguments but "felt that if this British policy were to be implemented unilaterally, without consulting the NATO Council and without trying to secure a new, and agreed, defence directive", the result could be disastrous for NATO and Anglo-American relations.[27] Mike's arguments carried little weight with Lloyd, Eden's curious choice as foreign secretary, a man who once said: "I do not speak any foreign language. Except in war, I have never visited any foreign country. I do not like foreigners."[28] Mike was more effective with his old friends Harold Macmillan and Eden, and the decision was delayed. Nevertheless, the incident brought little promise of future consultation or effective leadership.

On the continent, new visions of a European economic union glowed more vividly than old memories of Article 2. The smaller nations were generally (though not unanimously) sympathetic to more co-operation and consultation, but they were pessimistic about the possibility that the larger powers would agree. France, like Britain, continued to believe it was a great power that retained the prerogative to act independently when its own interests required it to do so.[29] Mike had told the Australian foreign minister, Richard Casey, when he began his task that NATO would "either have to do something to strengthen itself in the non-military field, especially in the area of political consultation, or it will wither away as the menace of Soviet military aggression seems to lessen".[30] By the fall, he knew that the chances for closer consultation and transatlantic co-operation were not good. In September he, Lange, and Martino began to work on the final details of the report knowing that they could suggest no more than modest reforms. The continental Europeans were turning towards continental integration; the British remained imprisoned in their memories of past glory; and the Americans were intoxicated with the strong brew of globalism they had begun to imbibe after the war.

Like tiresome Cassandras, the Canadians harked back to the days when NATO was born, when Pearson, Reid, and others had talked, in Churchillian terms, of the new world's saving and uniting with the old and, in traditional Canadian terms, of using Europe to balance the influence of the United States. Mike knew in the summer of 1956 that these hopes were largely barren and that NATO would remain principally a military alliance so long as Soviet forces threatened it. But he was not a military man, and when others raised his name as a possible successor to Pug Ismay in 1956 he quickly

Mike and Maryon Pearson listening to the 1948 election returns in Algoma East with Duke Pearson, Mike's older brother (left), and his wife, Connie (right).
(*Sudbury Daily Star*)

As Canada's External Affairs minister, Pearson signs the Japanese Peace Treaty in San Francisco in 1951. Dean Acheson, the American secretary of state, is above and behind him.
(Canapress Photo Service/Wide World Photo)

According to Liberal political analysts, this photograph of Pearson with Winston Churchill produced the most positive responses among Canadians polled. (National Archives of Canada [NAC]/PA 117590)

Pearson listens to the controversial new American secretary of state, John Foster Dulles, in 1954; C.D. Howe, minister of Trade and Commerce, smokes in the background.
(Douglas Cameron/ NAC/C-20021)

Friends of a kind: British foreign secretary (later prime
minister) Anthony Eden (far left) and Dean Acheson (left)
would not like Mike's handling of the Suez crisis.
(United Nations)

Pearson in India with Prime Minister Nehru, "one of the most subtle and
difficult men whom I had met, an extraordinary combination of a Hindu
God, and an Eton-Oxbridge type Englishman". (NAC/PA-165518)

Geoffrey and Landon Pearson on their way to France,
where he took up his first diplomatic posting in 1953; by
the 1980s Geoffrey was Canada's ambassador to the
U.S.S.R. (Pearson family)

Mike meets Soviet premier Nikolai Bulganin (right) and Communist
Party leader Nikita Khrushchev in the Crimea in 1955. The hand
thrusting the microphone between them belongs to reporter
René Lévesque. (NAC/C-90373)

squelched the rumours. Nevertheless, he worked with characteristic dedication on the report of the Committee of Three, not realizing that, unknown to him, others were working with equal dedication to undermine the fundamental principles of consultation and co-operation on which NATO had been founded.

One of those was Anthony Eden, whom Mike had met in Geneva in the 1930s. There he had played tennis, shared gossip, and sipped Scotch with Britain's youngest foreign secretary since 1851. Eden was, Sir John Wheeler-Bennett recalled, "the Golden Boy, slim, handsome and charming", who typified the generation that had survived the war "to fight for the ideal of making the world safe for democracy".[31] It was Eden who had persuaded Mike that sanctions should be applied against Mussolini through the League, and it was Eden who embodied, in those last months before the *Luftwaffe* and the *Wehrmacht* swept through Poland, the belief that Britain represented a fundamental decency that would not abide the outrages of the European dictators. On the tennis court and in the Palais des Nations in Geneva, however, Mike saw that the "Golden Boy" was exceptionally high-strung and wondered how he would face the tests the future would place before him. Still, Eden represented for him the most congenial face of British Conservatism in wartime and afterwards. He became even more sympathetic towards Eden after 1953, when Churchill, teetering towards senility, hesitated to give up the prime ministership to the crown prince, Eden. And in 1954-55, as NATO seemed near collapse over French-American intransigence, Eden's willingness to commit Britain to the continent won his warm admiration. Eden personally asked that Pearson attend the Commonwealth Prime Ministers' Conference in 1955. Eden, Mike wrote after the conference, had been at "his best and most impressive". Churchill had beamed as his protégé and soon-to-be successor presented a "clear, comprehensive, and even dramatic analysis" of European developments. When Churchill finally stepped down in April 1955 and Eden succeeded him, Mike was delighted.[32]

Pearson looked to Eden as a sensible and experienced diplomatist who could help him tame the erratic policies of Dulles, particularly towards China. The attitude was reciprocated. On the eve of the 1955 Commonwealth Prime Ministers' Conference, Eden told Norman Robertson in London that he was "anxious" to talk with "Mike" in view of "recent developments over Formosa". Soon after Mike's arrival, he was invited to Eden's country home — "a rambling structure filled with the most unsung collection of Victorian furniture, bric-a-brac and odds and ends". Their views were "along the same line; to do what we can to hold the Americans back from rash support for Chiang Kai-Shek", while recognizing the Republicans' political difficulties.[33] They tried to place some reins upon Dulles but found that he balked at such restraints. Difficulties with the Americans, in fact, drew Canadian and British officials closer together in 1955.

But Canadian-American relations got worse in 1955, and Dulles's personality and policy were serious problems. Ambassador Heeney in Washington began to find Dulles personally unattractive. After a dinner party in March 1955, he wrote in his diary: "Our dinner for the Dulles' was quite good except for the Ds who are really without any of the social attributes." Dulles was, in Heeney's view, "a strange almost gauche creature" who had no charm. He did possess intelligence and ambition but, in Heeney's view, he was not "a great man".[34] Mike too found Dulles difficult and increasingly believed he was a clumsy diplomatist. When Dulles visited Ottawa in 1955, Mike anticipated the visit in a letter to London and Geoffrey: "[Dulles] is going to pay us an official visit on Thursday and Friday of this week. It will be interesting to see the impact that he will make on Ottawa. Certainly, Ottawa is not likely to make much of an impact on him — unless he slips on the mud and slush which is now engulfing us."[35] In a letter to Geoffrey the following year, Mike called Dulles "stupid" in his reaction to the historic Khrushchev speech denouncing Stalin at the Twentieth Party Congress.[36] Dulles reacted too quickly, too suspiciously, and almost invariably without consultation of his allies. Before a 1956 meeting at which Eisenhower and Dulles said that they would kick the U.N. out of the U.S. and take the U.S. out of the U.N. if China got in, Dulles had offered Pearson a ride on his plane to the meeting at White Sulphur Springs. It was a small plane and Mike was strapped in beside Dulles, just behind the pilot. As Mike fought off air sickness, Dulles chattered about the world. But one remark forced Mike to respond when Dulles almost "sneered" at the Canadian insistence on consultation:

> You Canadians are always complaining that we never consult you about our policies. "Ike" as you know, is a great golfer and, who knows, he may want us to play a few holes together on this visit. If we do and the score is all square on the 18th green, I'll wager that you will intervene just as I am about to make the deciding putt to demand that I consult you about it first.

Mike briefly shook off his air sickness and replied: "If I did, Foster, it would be merely to tell you that you were using a No. 9 iron."[37]

Dulles irritated Mike and Mike irritated Dulles, but, to the credit of both men, there was surprisingly little rancour on either side. (A few days after Dulles's death, Acheson pronounced at a dinner party: "Thank God Foster is underground."[38] Mike, however, mourned his colleague's death.) Neither he nor Dulles made their differences personal. The result was that when the time came to work together, they could. That time came in 1956.

Nineteen fifty-six was a presidential election year in the United States. As always, others watched anxiously as the Americans passed through their peculiar quadrennial rites. This year there was even more concern because Eisenhower had suffered a heart attack in September 1955 and in June 1956 had a sudden and serious operation on his stomach. He stayed in the presidential race, but was too weak to give leadership in the critical summer of 1956.[39] Foreign policy, therefore, was completely in Dulles's hands while Ike recuperated. Unfortunately, this absence of presidential leadership came just as a serious crisis was developing in the Middle East between Israel and its Arab neighbours.

Mike was sometimes called "Rabbi" Pearson because of his early support for partition and the State of Israel. He had gained international attention for his work at the U.N. on the Palestine question; and because of the differences between the United States and the United Kingdom on the Middle East, he continued to emphasize, in his diplomacy, the centrality of the U.N. when Middle East troubles appeared. The rise of Arab nationalism, the numerous border incidents, the failure of the Arabs and Israel to reach a peace agreement, and the influence of the Cold War on Middle Eastern politics made effective diplomacy difficult. The British and French had traditional interests in the area; their imperial successors, the Soviet Union and the United States, had new ones. In 1954, Dulles, eager to line up Arabs in his world-wide anti-Communist legions, offered substantial quantities of arms to Egypt and approved military aid to Iraq, which had joined with Turkey and Britain in a defence pact. No arms were to be given to Israel, with the result that it turned to Canada, whose foreign minister, it believed, might be sympathetic to its pleas and whose F-86 Sabre jets were the best fighters of the time.[40]

Pearson was willing and C.D. Howe, the trade and commerce minister, was enthusiastic because of the cash Israel offered. Dulles told the Israelis that he supported this sale, but privately he forced the Canadians to reject the request. The tactics infuriated Pearson, especially as the Americans, the British, the French, and, in mid-summer 1955, the Czechs, as surrogates for the Soviets, flooded the Middle East with arms. The Czech sale of arms to the increasingly nationalist prime minister of Egypt, Gamal Abdel Nasser, raised the stakes — and the fears — in the Middle East. Dulles reacted with a secret peace plan and tried to control the requests to buy arms that now intensified. To use Mike's metaphor, Dulles had chosen a driver where he should have used a putter; not surprisingly, he lost control of his shot.[41]

Mike was becoming increasingly wary about Middle East politics. He feared the rhetoric and the blend of religion and state. In his memoirs, Pearson claimed that "nothing" at the U.N. equalled "the venom and the fury of the Arabs".[42] It repelled him, recalling for him the nationalist excesses of the 1930s. When his cabinet colleague

Robert Winters asked Mike to see a Lebanese-Canadian, John Seaman, on the subject of Israeli-Arab relations, Mike agreed to meet with him but not with a Mr. Massoud, "because of his violent prejudices and his previously distorted and inaccurate statements on Canadian policy". Massoud nevertheless accompanied Seaman, but remained in the outer office. Mike agreed to shake hands with Massoud after Seaman assured him that Massoud had been "too violent and prejudiced" in the past, but that he was now seeking a better relationship with the government. Massoud, "obviously more emotional and Arab in his approach" than Seaman, joined the conversation and said to Pearson that "no country could do more to assist in easing tension between Arabs and Jews than Canada". Pearson expressed agreement that Palestinian refugees should be resettled and that Canada should play a part.[43] More important than Massoud in persuading Mike that there were legitimate Arab grievances and fears beneath the rhetorical excesses was Egyptian foreign minister Mahmoud Fawzi. Mike knew Fawzi from the U.N. and liked him. In July 1955, Fawzi visited Ottawa to reassure Pearson that Nasser's acceptance of Soviet arms and Pan-Arab nationalism was not so threatening as some North American commentators suggested. Egypt, Fawzi claimed, recognized "the communist imperialist threat and is strongly anti-communist". He deplored the recently created Baghdad pact among Turkey, Iraq, and Britain because it had brought the Cold War into the Middle East. He warned, however, that it was the issue of Palestine that was mostly likely to bring war. He told Mike that the Palestinian refugees should receive compensation for the lands and homes they had lost and that a territorial readjustment should be made. Mike asked "what would be the chances of public opinion in Egypt and the other states accepting this solution, which fell short of their public demands". Fawzi thought they would and added that, despite Canadians' strong public support for Israel, their influence "always commanded respect because of their sincerity and objectivity!" Pearson, much flattered, described Fawzi in his report on the visit as a "moderate, wise and honest person".[44]

Fawzi persuaded Pearson to visit Nasser, who did not seem so moderate and wise. On his return from his Soviet trip on November 10, 1955, Mike met Nasser, who was "quite as impressive and attractive a personality" as Fawzi had claimed. There was no bluster; rather he gave "an impression of sincerity and strength without any trace of arrogance or self-assertion". Nevertheless, he spoke constantly of Israeli aggressiveness and claimed that he had no choice but to turn to the Soviet Union for arms. Mike warned Nasser about the arms race that was developing: "Egypt felt herself threatened and weak — therefore she strengthened her armaments for security. No one could object to that in principle, but the result was that Israel would then feel insecure ... and in her turn would get more arms." Nasser agreed it was all "very unfortunate and even dangerous". He did say that the Arab states would recognize Israel, provided that the refugee and territorial questions could be settled. The path to these negotiations, however, would be tortuous, and Nasser, in Pearson's view, did not see the dangers of "supping" with the Soviet devil. He left Nasser without "optimism as to the possibility" of a political solution soon.[45]

Pearson was one of several international personalities who was used as a "channel" for Egyptian-Israeli dialogue.[46] After his return from Cairo, he met with the Israeli ambassador, Michael Comay, and Moshe Sharett, the prime minister of Israel until November 1955, when he became foreign minister. The Sharett visit in early December was made necessary by criticism from Canadian Jews that Pearson had visited Cairo but not Tel Aviv. The visit was not reassuring. Mike wrote that Sharett, who was regarded as a moderate compared to his successor as prime minister, David Ben-Gurion, was "quite inflexible in his determination not to yield a pint of sand to the Arabs". British cabinet minister Reginald Maudling, who had visited Ottawa a few days later, reported to British foreign secretary Selwyn Lloyd that Pearson said the Israelis "were likely to be extremely stubborn about making any concessions at all".[47] When Pearson met with Comay after Sharett's departure, there was a more critical tone in his remarks. He chided the Israelis for the harshness of their response to guerrilla incursions and rebuked Comay personally for remarks at a rally in Ottawa's Capital Theatre, where he had allegedly spoken of "a state of emergency" for Canadian Jews. Comay claimed that he had been misquoted, but the incident revealed two important facts. First, Pearson, like most of the political leaders of those pre-multicultural days, deprecated the linkage between Canadian domestic groups and foreign governments and their quarrels. Secondly, he may still have been "Rabbi" Pearson to some, but he had begun to question some tenets of the faith.[48]

Nineteen fifty-six began with Pearson well informed about and familiar with the principal figures in Middle Eastern politics and their views. While he was very worried about the growing tensions, he told Maudling that he didn't think an Israeli pre-emptive attack on Egypt was likely.[49] Moreover, he believed that the Israelis must be armed as a deterrent to the Egyptian arms purchase. He had told the Israeli ambassador that Canada would look sympathetically on Israeli requests for arms. The requests came, and so did complications, as Dulles blocked the sales and the opposition in the House of Commons criticized Canada's role as a "merchant of death" in the Middle East.[50]

Despite his interest and fears, events in the Middle East after March 1956 were not followed closely by Pearson because of his responsibility for the NATO report and because domestic politics, in the form of angry debates about the proposed TransCanada Pipeline and quiet whisperings about the prime minister's and the Liberal Party's health, placed additional demands on his time. What little time he devoted to thinking about the Middle East led him to conclude that the United Nations was the instrument through which the dispute should be mediated. Beyond that, there was, in historian Michael Fry's concise summary, "a deep seated concern over refugee and relief matters, involvement [through the U.N.] in the maintenance of armament agreements, and a willingness to play a modest, stabilizing role in arms transfers [which] complemented a mistaken belief that incremental, confidence-building measures, both political and economic, could help bring about a comprehensive settlement of the Israeli-Arab dispute."[51] The problems, Mike told Geoffrey in February, were so much worse because Britain, France, and the United States could not "get together". They were, in fact, moving farther apart than he realized.[52]

Professor Fry perhaps exaggerates Pearson's belief in the effectiveness of confidence-building measures. In March 1956, after Eden and Lloyd briefed him on the Middle Eastern situation, he told Terry MacDermot, the Canadian ambassador to Greece, that the more he heard about the Middle East, "the more depressed you get over the chances of an agreed and permanent settlement". So far as he could see, there "doesn't seem to be much hope … for the parties getting together. The best we can do is to hope that they don't get together in the wrong way by shooting at each other."[53]

His fears were not alleviated by Dulles's tendency to approach Middle Eastern problems with characteristic suspicion of Soviet influence on the one hand and European imperialist interests on the other. These bifocal lenses distorted Dulles's view of the Middle East and led him to proceed erratically. His increasingly confused policy towards the Middle East was apparent when he met Mike in May 1956. The United States, Dulles said, would not sell F-86s to Israel but would like to have Canada sell some so that Israeli pilots would be ready to fly them in an emergency, when the United States itself would be willing to supply the Israelis with F-86s. Quite apart from Dulles's hypocrisy, Mike was disturbed by his lack of faith in the U.N. as an instrument through which settlement might be achieved.[54]

If Dulles was confused, Eden was angry. When Mike met him in early May, he was "nervously and physically exhausted and, therefore, somewhat overwrought". Jordan had refused to join the so-called Baghdad Pact, which Eden saw as a symbol of continuing British influence in the Middle East. When young King Hussein dismissed "Glubb Pasha", the legendary British commander of the Arab Legion, and Nasser's anti-British rhetoric intensified, Eden was infuriated — and disoriented. His secretary, who himself wanted strong action against Nasser, despaired. Eden, he wrote in his diary, "seems to be completely disintegrated — petulant, irrelevant, provocative at the same time as being weak. Poor England, we are in total disarray." If not then, it certainly was to be later.[55]

For Eden, in that summer of 1956, Nasser became the symbol of the many challenges British influence and power faced. Nasser, in his mind, became Hitler and Mussolini, the two ranting madmen whom he had stood up to in the 1930s. The difference between Nasser, the embittered nationalist product of Western imperialism, and the European dictators of the 1930s eluded the understanding of Eden and many of his senior ministers and advisers. It did not elude Dag Hammarskjöld, the U.N. secretary general, who in 1956 tried to mediate the Middle East disputes. But the U.N. chief's efforts were, in the words of his biographer, "impressive but unavailing".[56]

Hammarskjöld's work there and elsewhere had greatly impressed Pearson, who had come to know the man well after he, rather than Mike, had become secretary general in 1953. When Hammarskjöld returned from his Middle East mission in the spring of 1956, Mike suggested that, when Hammarskjöld came to Montreal to accept an honorary degree at McGill, they "might spend some quiet hours together ... preferably at our cottage up the river", talking about the Middle East. They did not do so then, but the letter's tone ("My dear Dag") reflects the easiness that existed between them, an easiness that was lacking with Dulles and, increasingly, with Eden.[57] This personal link mattered in the months ahead.

As spring became summer, the Middle Eastern situation deteriorated quickly. Nasser's willingness to accept more Soviet arms, his calls for a united Arab front, and his anti-Western rhetoric made Britain and the United States much less willing to consider the large-scale loans he sought for the Aswan Dam project on the Nile. Despite strong warnings from their ambassadors in Cairo, the United States and Britain decided to withdraw the offer to finance the dam. Dulles bore the bad news to the Egyptian ambassador on July 19. The British, who, to their annoyance, were informed of the move after it was made, followed the Americans and withdrew their own offer.[58] Less than a week later, Nasser stunned the world by nationalizing the Suez Canal. The British reacted angrily. Macmillan called Nasser "an Asiatic Mussolini". Eden became more determined to destroy him — and he wanted support.[59]

He immediately told St. Laurent and other Commonwealth premiers: "We cannot allow [Nasser] to get away with this act of expropriation and we must take a firm stand." The tone and the substance of Eden's message prompted Mike to send Norman Robertson a warning:

> I am deeply concerned at the implications of some parts of Eden's message; especially as I doubt very much whether he will receive strong support from Washington in the firm line which he proposes to follow. A talk which I have just had with the United States Ambassador here strengthens these doubts. Surely the UK government will not do anything which would commit them to strong action against Egypt until they know that the U.S. will back them.
>
> I am also worried as to the meaning to be given Eden's words, "We believe that we should seize this opportunity of putting the canal under proper international control and permanent arrangement." Surely with the Russians dissenting and supporting Egypt, the UK do not think that this can be done, as they profess to hope, "by political pressure" alone. There remains force — which they visualize as a last resort. But is it not clear that to be effective enough force would have to be used to destroy the Nasser government and take over Egypt. Any effort to use force, in fact, would in all likelihood result in an appeal by Egypt to the UN. That would be bringing the UN into the matter with a vengeance, and by the wrong party.

Pearson told Robertson that he should continue to stress that the U.N. must be brought into the dispute. "This may not be practicable," Pearson advised, "but it certainly shouldn't be dismissed without the most careful consideration. It might well be argued *that if an international dispute is of such a character that force is envisaged, it is also one that should be brought before the UN in order to try to avoid the use of such force.*"[60] (The emphasis is Pearson's.)

Mike's views deeply offended Eden, a fact that Eden and other British officials concealed at the time and even in their memoirs. The evidence, however, is conclusive. On learning that the Canadian government thought the U.N. should be brought in, Eden told the Commonwealth Relations Office to tell the Canadian government that "there was no intention of taking action in the United Nations about the Suez Canal situation".[61] When the British high commissioner in Canada reported on July 30, 1956, that the Canadian Broadcasting Corporation had a commentary by a "Professor of Political Economy from the University of Alberta" that argued that the U.S. and the U.K. had provoked Nasser, Eden wrote on the telegram: "Lord Home. Please speak. This is Canadian govt again. We must react." On the same day, Eden read the telegram reporting Mike's statement to the house on the Suez nationalization in which he condemned the seizure but refused to give any additional comments. He wrote on the despatch: "miserable".[62]

Eden grasped at morsels. The high commissioner had reported that the eastern Canadian press had generally supported Britain's strong statements. Eden told the high commissioner that he was struck by the fact that the press was ahead of the government and that the High Commission should keep the government "up to the mark".[63] Acting on this advice, the high commissioner called on Pearson, who expressed willingness to help the British in their predicament and who supported the idea of a conference of concerned parties. Otherwise, he was unyielding. He said that while the Canadian government "did not feel justified in offering their views when not invited, Mr. St. Laurent felt very strongly that the use of force could only be effective if the whole of Egypt and not merely the Canal were occupied and that these measures offered no hope of a solution". While Canadians generally supported Britain's hard line, the British high commissioner had little hope for the government, which, he snidely commented, "will act with typical Canadian caution".[64]

Eden, it is now clear, thought Pearson and Canada hopelessly cautious — "wet", as Margaret Thatcher so memorably dubbed those she believed had too-flexible spines. Pearson, it is equally clear, was suspicious of Eden's intentions and judgement long before the battle began in the Middle East. He was more aware than he suggests in his memoirs that the British were considering the use of force. Similarly, Eden was more ill-disposed towards Canada than Canadians knew at the time or than his own memoirs indicated. Suez is too often interpreted as the product of serious misunderstandings. In fact, Pearson's analyses of late July and early August were, in the words of Professor Granatstein, "extraordinarily prophetic". He saw that the British and the French were serious about the use of force, that they would have little support, and that they would ignore the U.N. and the U.S., and, or course, Canada. Such actions, Pearson feared, would split the Commonwealth, damage NATO, and make Moscow the winner.[65] The British, too, knew very early where Canada was likely to stand.*

> She is [a British official wrote] unlikely to move significantly in advance of the U.S. If the U.S. fights, Canada may be prepared to do so too....
>
> The probability is that if the U.S. neither contribute nor wholeheartedly endorse military action Canada will not do so either. Indeed, depending upon the U.S. reaction, it is possible that Canada would endeavour to restrain us from resorting to force, and refrain from public support for our action if we nevertheless went ahead.[66]

When Britain went to war, Canada had always answered, "Ready, Aye, Ready". Eden should have known that this time it would not.

His imperial breeding stirred up in him a sense of betrayal and, more seriously, disbelief. In mid-August, Robertson told Commonwealth secretary Lord Home directly that if Britain attacked Nasser

---

* Canadian Conservatives had their suspicions about Canada's future stand. When asked by John Diefenbaker whether Canada stood with Britain and France or with the United States, Pearson evaded the question by disingenuously denying that there were differences between the two sides. House of Commons, *Debates*, Aug. 6, 1956.

it "would be brought before the UN as an aggressor" and he doubted that either the Commonwealth or the U.N. would survive. Moreover, Canada would not support the U.K. if it did so. Eden angrily responded to Home's report of the meeting. "I think that this should be taken up with the Canadian govt.... It is far worse than anything U.S. govt has ever said." In reality, it was not. Eisenhower had made clear his opposition to the use of force, but Eden chose to cherish distant hopes. Moreover, Lord Home told Eden it was not worthwhile to pursue the question with Canada. The Canadians were left out of a conference of major canal users that took place in August, and they ceased to be consulted seriously.[67] The conference failed to find a solution and probably served to strengthen Nasser's resistance.

Indeed, the major Canadian contribution at this time came not from Ottawa but from Duck Island in Lake Ontario, where Dulles, on vacation, dreamed up the notion of a Suez Canal Users' Association* which he hoped would delay confrontation and provide time to find a scheme to have the canal run by the "Users", with Egypt deriving compensation only for its expenses. Mike, who arrived in Europe for a NATO council meeting on September 5, thought the plan foolish. He told the NATO meeting that the best approach was to go to the U.N. The Soviets might use a veto, but the majority support for the proposals of the London Conference would offer "important and valuable support for subsequent negotiations". He argued that force had to be ruled out, "except as a last resort and [used] only in accordance with the principles we have accepted in the NATO Pact and the U.N. Charter". In his memoirs, Eden claims that Pearson "was averse to military sanctions, [but] he did not exclude them in the last resort". That interpretation is obviously

---

* The difficulty of the scheme was apparent early when the original acronym, CASU, was rejected. The Dutch foreign minister warned it was too close to *casus belli*, the Portuguese foreign minister said it meant "balls" in Portuguese, and the French said it sounded something like "breakarse" in French. See Alistair Horne, *Macmillan 1894 - 1956* (London: Macmillan, 1984), 414.

incorrect, and Eden's private comments to British officials revealed above indicate that he knew it.[68]

In Paris in mid-September, Mike became increasingly frustrated with Dulles's "Users" scheme and with British and French intransigence. He did not think Canada would be invited to join the "Users" group and was pleased he could avoid it. He resolved that he would not leave Paris but "stick to his NATO job" there. The "Users" proposal, on closer examination, seemed both impractical and unwise. What, he asked on September 27, "is the next move? Force, without USA support, or an appeal to the Security Council for some backing for this latest proposal" — backing that was unlikely to be forthcoming.[69] The appeal to the Security Council finally came, but it seemed much too late.

Upon his return to Canada, Mike gave a long report to the cabinet on Suez on September 27. His discussions in London and Paris had convinced him that the British and the French were united in their desire to make Nasser back down. When they saw that he would not do so, there would be "very real danger". They should have submitted the dispute to the U.N. at once but had done so much too late. He added, prophetically, that the final result would be the exposure of French and British weakness, and "it was clearly not in Canada's interest that these two allies should be weakened".[70]

On September 21, the Canadian cabinet, on Pearson's advice, had agreed to sell twenty-four F-86 jets to Israel at a rate of four per month. The Israelis launched raids against Jordan a few days later, and the sale was delayed. Foreign Minister Golda Meir reassured Pearson that the fighters were for self-defence and their importance lay not in their military prowess but in "the moral effect of your decision on those who still have not reconciled themselves to our existence and independence".[71] The sale, which Dulles had covertly encouraged, is best explained by reference to Pearson's emotional links with Israel, his sense of impending conflict, and his fear that Israel might be left alone to face increasingly well-armed Arab opponents. In a classic Canadian balancing act that deeply irritated the British, Canada simultaneously agreed to sell wheat to Egypt.[72] In mid-October, Mike told the House of Commons that Canada had maintained its impartiality and that it was "important that [Canada's] position should not be prejudiced by premature commitments which appear to be neither desirable nor necessary". In that way, Canada might "get to play a part in negotiations" leading to a settlement of the Suez crisis.[73]

In fact, neither the Canadians nor the Americans knew what was happening at the time. Feeling cut off from British information, Dulles asked Ambassador Livingston Merchant to "see Mike and see if they are in touch with [the British] and if Mike can get the feel of it".[74] But Mike, too, had lost his feel, as Eden and his senior colleagues drew back from the Canadians' antennae. On October 22, with Eden and his leading colleagues' agreement, Selwyn Lloyd crossed his Rubicon, the English Channel, and met French and Israeli officials in Sèvres to plot a war. It was agreed that if Israel attacked Egypt, both countries would be offered an ultimatum to withdraw from the canal area or face British-French attack. The Israelis, of course, would; the Egyptians naturally would not. British and French bombs and paratroopers would then rain upon Egypt. It was a preposterous conspiracy. Even Robert Rhodes James, Eden's most sympathetic biographer, admits that the ultimatum was "a pretext for achieving the destruction of Nasser. But it was so obvious a pretext that one still wonders why [Eden] believed it would not be seen as such."[75]

On the evening of October 29, 385 Israeli paratroopers floated down thirty miles from Suez, and other Israeli troops began attacking Egyptian border positions defending the Sinai and Gaza. The next day, as planned, the British and French issued an ultimatum demanding that Egypt and Israel stop fighting and withdraw ten miles from the canal, which would then be "temporarily" occupied.[76] Eisenhower, campaigning for the November 6 presidential election and anxious about the Hungarian revolt against Soviet rule that had broken out four days earlier, learned of the ultimatum from the press. So did St. Laurent. Both were enraged; their foreign ministers felt personally betrayed. Robertson, who prided himself on his personal friendships with British officials, had been misled by these friends. Mike grasped for details. He asked Ambassador Jean Désy in France what was going on. "I have an uneasy feeling that there is something going on between the French and the Israeli government which the French have not bothered to tell us." Moments later, Eden rose in the House of Commons and revealed that the British were involved in the scam as well. Robertson called from London saying that "not only had he been given no inkling of what was under consideration" but that, even when directly questioned, British officials had not said that "anything extraordinary was contemplated".[77] In short, they lied.

St. Laurent called Mike to his office. Red-faced with Irish anger, he threw Eden's telegram towards Pearson and asked, "What do you think of that?" The telegram, which had been sent to the U.K. high commissioner only one hour before he spoke, was didactic in tone and dishonest in its details. He claimed to be worried about an Israeli attack on Jordan and to have "warned" the Israelis "off Jordan absolutely". Nasser, however, had made it clear that Britain had no obligation to defend Egypt. The Suez Canal was another matter, and if the Israelis and Egyptians continued to fight, Britain must take military action to defend it. In the despatch sent to ever-loyal New Zealand, Eden concluded:

> Your constant and friendly understanding have given us the greatest encouragement through a period of great tension and I am sure we can look for your continued support until we can see this through. We will keep you informed daily through the High Commissioner. But I want you to have at once this personal message from myself to give you the background for your own information.

With Canada, it was different:

> Clearly there are risks in intervention. But the risks of hesitation and delay are in our judgment greater, and unless hostilities can be brought to a close at once, they risk developing into a wider conflict

involving others. I know that we can look for your understanding and much hope for your support in our endeavours to limit its scope and to bring about a truce so that a permanent settlement can be worked out which will pacify this turbulent area.

For Eden, Canada was no longer a close part of the family. For St. Laurent and even Pearson, the feeling was the same.[78]

Eden's letter infuriated them. To Robertson, Pearson expressed open distrust of Eden and deep disappointment in Britain. Nevertheless, he beseeched St. Laurent not to react too bitterly. He therefore drafted the reply himself. His major and immediate purpose was "to let Eden know he could not count on [Canada's] support automatically". This time Canada would not answer, "Ready, Aye, Ready".[79] The St. Laurent–Pearson reply refused to accept that either the Israeli attack or the ultimatum was justified. Three items concerned Canada most. The first was the impact on the United Nations, whose position was undermined by the British-French-Israeli joint action. The second was the Commonwealth, whose unity was threatened. India had already denounced the British action. The third was "the deplorable divergence of viewpoint and policy between the United Kingdom and the United States". The profound differences brought "distress to all those who believe that Anglo-American co-operation and friendship is the very foundation of our hopes for progress toward a peaceful and secure world".[80] That foundation was now trembling. Mike knew that he could do nothing to affect matters in London, where Robertson anxiously waited for his calls to be returned.* On the afternoon of Thursday,

---

* Arnold Smith met a friend who was a senior official in the Foreign Office but critical of the Anglo-French moves. Nevertheless, he had little love for Canada. "My informant [Smith reported] also said that the bitterness about the Canadian attitude on Suez was as great as that against the Americans. He said that the decision to sell Egypt wheat been regarded as a stab in the back in a moment of Britain's crisis and need. In all this, he said, Canada had been even softer than the Americans." Smith to Robertson, enclosure in Robertson to Pearson, Nov. 1, 1956. MG26 N5, v. 85 (NAC).

November 1, Pearson flew to New York, taking with him "jottings on bits of paper" that had on them his plan for action. The headings apparently were: immediate cease-fire; a U.N. force to patrol Arab-Israeli boundaries and, if necessary, the canal zone; and the creation of machinery for a permanent political settlement in the Middle East.[81]

"Lester Pearson is a big man from a country that is a small power," the *New York Times* had declared in May 1956. He was, the *Times* claimed, probably better known abroad than in Canada. So it seemed to John Holmes, who flew with Mike to New York. When they arrived at the electric and chaotic U.N. Assembly, diplomats and U.N. officials "kept rushing up" to Holmes saying, "What's he got? We hear Mike's got a proposal. It's high time. Can he do it?"[82] Both the *Times*, where Mike's friend "Scotty" Reston extolled his virtues, and John Holmes, who marvelled at his master's ways, might exaggerate Mike's prominence, but it does seem true that no one quite had the advantages he had, in those days, in the U.N. corridors. He had kept Canada uncommitted since the crisis began and had consistently urged that the U.N. was the proper forum. Now, finally, its moment had come, and Mike was there. He found chaos.

Hammarskjöld was rumoured to be resigning. The U.S. delegate, Henry Cabot Lodge, brushed off his British and French counterparts. The Soviets voted with the Americans, their great antagonists. Resolutions calling for Israel to withdraw and for peace came forward with near-unanimous approval. The British and French vetoed them. Pearson saw that the key was to find a plan acceptable to the British and French that could be sold to others as one that was not inspired by them. The clue came from Robertson, who sent a telegram to External on the morning of Mike's departure. Mike probably did not see it until he arrived in New York, but his actions suggest that when he did he immediately grasped its significance. Robertson had spoken with Sir Ivone Kirkpatrick, the senior Foreign Office official, and had told him that Pearson was "turning over in [his] mind the possibility of proposing a cease fire, to be followed by a major diplomatic conference to deal with the whole context of Middle Eastern and North African questions, and that as part of this approach it would be essential to set up an adequate UN military force to separate the Egyptians from the Israelis." Kirkpatrick, most significantly, replied that, in the debate on the censure motion his government faced that afternoon, Eden would say, "but police action there must be to separate the belligerents and to prevent the resumption of hostilities between them. If the UN were then willing to take over the physical task of maintaining peace no one would be better pleased than we." Kirkpatrick, who had with him his French counterpart, Jean Chauvel, said that such a force should not be simply "notional ... thought up as a diplomatic gimmick to meet this evening's diplomatic requirements". For the first time, Robertson saw an opening. "This is not much," he told Mike, "but it is something." It was up to his long-time colleague to widen the opening in the dense thickets of General Assembly politics in New York.[83]

That day in New York was, perhaps, the most dramatic in U.N. history. Hungary announced its withdrawal from the Warsaw Pact, declared its neutrality, and asked for U.N. protection. The bombing of Egypt began, and tempers flared between old friends. While John Holmes, Geoffrey Murray, a young but very able External Affairs officer, and Bert MacKay, Canada's permanent representative, worked the corridors crammed with nervous and puzzled diplomats, Mike went immediately to Hammarskjöld and presented the idea of the U.N. force minutes before the Special Assembly convened at 5:00 p.m.[84] Hammarskjöld was pessimistic.

The assembly met to consider an American motion calling for an end to the fighting and an immediate withdrawal. As the debate went on long into the night, Mike took no part but sat at the Canadian desk, right below the speaker's lectern, scribbling notes and chatting amidst the din with dozens of delegates who approached him. MacKay, Holmes, and Murray moved through the corridors, among the other desks, and about the North Lounge, where Walter the bartender mixed "superb whiskey sours until the gavel finally banged the Assembly silent" at 4:30 a.m.[85] Hammarskjöld wondered why Mike had said nothing in the debate on Dulles's resolution. He speculated that it was because Mike was uncertain about his peace proposal. In truth, Mike wanted to avoid commitment and to maintain a position where he would offend no one. Canada thus abstained on the U.S. resolution. Australia, New Zealand, France, Israel, and, of course, Great Britain, opposed it. Sixty-four voted for it. In the early Manhattan morning after the vote, Mike rose and said that the resolution merely called for a return to an unacceptable status quo. What was needed was a provision for a "United Nations force large enough to keep these borders at peace while a political settlement is being worked out". It was, John Holmes later wrote, "one of the most potent conditional sentences in UN history", and reflected Pearson's "ruthlessly pragmatic" approach to the crisis. Dulles grumbled: "Canada is unhappy and wants to be a mediator."[86] For once, he knew his neighbour well.

Dulles, nevertheless, encouraged Mike to pursue his idea of a U.N. force, as did other delegates. He met Hammarskjöld just before 5:00 a.m. and, finding him still sceptical, arranged to have lunch the next day. They all skipped breakfast.

He found Hammarskjöld still sceptical at noon. Where would the force come from? Apart from the British and French forces, which were all too near, the other potential forces were too far away; meanwhile guns now blazed, bombs rained down, and threats and counter threats abounded. Hammarskjöld seemed paralysed by his pessimism, even though the British and French had not yet landed their ground forces. After their lunch on Friday, Mike flew back to Ottawa for a Saturday morning cabinet meeting. By now, it was clear that the Soviet tanks had turned around and were rolling back to Budapest to crush the Hungarians and their revolt. The Soviets, Mike told the cabinet, were "showing the true character of their regime". It made Suez all the more regrettable.[87]

The sombre cabinet approved the U.N. "police action". Heeney then tried out the idea on the Americans in Washington. Dulles had just gone to the hospital with what he thought was appendicitis, but was really cancer. His assistants, who met with Heeney, worried that the U.N. force might be seen by Afro-Asian opinion as "legitimizing the present operation". Mike went back to the cabinet and suggested that a "Committee of Five" be set up to report upon the establishment of an "intervention force". Canada would not necessarily be a member of this committee if it was thought that all members should be those who supported the withdrawal resolution. Britain and France would be asked to delay the troop landings. India would be asked to co-sponsor the resolution in order that non-aligned support might be won. Robertson in London and Heeney in Washington would seek the approval of governments there. The cabinet accepted the initiative. Mike left the cabinet meeting and went to Uplands airport. Never a good flier since he had crashed in the First World War as a trainee for the same Royal Air Force that was now dropping bombs on Egypt, Mike shunned the reporters flying with him: "All I wanted to do was look out the window and think about what I ought to do, how I ought to do it, and what the consequences would be." His preoccupations made him forget to get airsick.[88]

He reached New York at 6:45 p.m. on Saturday night, November 3, just as another late-night session was beginning. He brought good tidings and soon received them. The British had accepted his proposal, believing that their own forces and the French would be the central part of the U.N. force. The Americans, with an election three days away and Soviet tanks rolling towards Budapest, desperately wanted to erase Suez from the centre stage of world opinion. They saw Mike's plan, under Hammarskjöld's rather than the proposed Committee of Five's control, as the best option among many bad ones. The Indians had their own resolution that demanded immediate withdrawal within twelve hours. The Indians had rallied Afro-Asian opinion behind it, but, fortunately for Mike, Arthur Lall, India's U.N. representative, was a decent, moderate man who did not insist that the Afro-Asian resolution must have priority. He and Mike made a deal. Each would support the other's resolution. And so Mike moved a resolution, drafted by Lodge of the United States, for a U.N. peace force. Lall, unaware of its provenance, supported it. Canada in turn supported the Afro-Asian resolution. The die was thus cleverly cast for a Middle East peace force before the British and French forces had even landed.[89]

At 2:00 a.m. on Sunday morning, November 4, fifty-seven nations voted for the Canadian resolution and no one opposed it. A crowd swarmed around Mike to congratulate him. Eight hours later, Hammarskjöld, who had gloomily forecast doom for Mike's plan, convened the informal planning committee that created the force. Convinced now that the force offered not only prospects of peace but also a greater part for the U.N. in international security, Hammarskjöld moved with determination, demonstrating what his biographer rightly claims was "firm and unquestioned leadership".[90] Within the next forty-eight hours, the Israelis trounced the Egyptians, the British and French landed in Egypt, the United Nations Emergency Force (UNEF) took form, Egypt accepted its presence, Eisenhower was re-elected, and the British and French agreed to a cease-fire. Soviet tanks slaughtered Hungarians, as "volunteers" gathered in the U.S.S.R. and China to serve against the "imperialist" invasion of Egypt.

The force took form with a Canadian, General E.L.M. "Tommy" Burns, as its commander, and the U.N., quite unexpectedly, seemed to have worked. Those anxious days that began with the Israeli thrust into Egypt ended with Eden's ashen-faced declaration that Britain would accept the U.N. resolution calling for a cease-fire and intervention by UNEF. Eden first thought and strongly hoped that UNEF would include British and French troops and thus cloak their operation with U.N. respectability. There was to be no such face-saving; as Mike said, that would be like having the burglars guarding the safe.[91] Even the Canadians, to their great annoyance, faced exclusion at one point because the Egyptians objected to the presence of Canadian ground troops, with their British traditions and badges, and to the obvious and large presence of a country so identified with the history of the British Empire.*

This objection, which annoyed the Canadians greatly and which took up most of Mike's time in the two weeks following the November 6 cease-fire and many pages in his memoirs, was resolved through the intervention of Hammarskjöld, Eisenhower, and India. The resolution was unsatisfactory: Canada sent no ground troops, only specialist units. Nevertheless, this compromise prevented acute political embarrassment. Mike himself was personally offended and blew up at the Egyptian U.N. delegate. Nor was he happy about the agreement reached with the Egyptians by Hammarskjöld; in his view, it gave the Egyptians the right to decide whether UNEF could remain. Mike warned Hammarskjöld that the legal arrangements for UNEF were badly flawed. Eleven years later, another war proved, in Sir Brian Urquhart's words, that "Mike was right".[92]

Some consolation came the next fall when the telephone rang on October 14 and a Canadian Press reporter told Mike he had won the Nobel Peace Prize. He responded, "You mean nominated." No, "*won*". Mike's immediate comment was a memorable "Gosh". He called Maryon at a beauty parlour where the waving of her hair was interrupted. Hammarskjöld, rumoured to be a nominee himself, immediately and publicly declared that the award was "a warmly deserved recognition of the consistently intelligent support and leadership that through the years you have given to the cause of international peace". That evening the Pearsons dined with Queen Elizabeth and her new prime minister, John Diefenbaker, at Rideau Hall. Pearson was very much the centre of attention — to his delight and Diefenbaker's understandable dismay.[93]

The new prime minister had not supported Mike's efforts a year earlier. In the House of Commons, Diefenbaker, then the Conservatives' foreign affairs critic, continued to demand, as he and his colleagues had since the Suez crisis began, that Canada back Britain.

---

* After 1956, Pearson began speaking more openly about the need for a distinctly Canadian flag. The incident with Nasser seems to have strengthened his view that Canada needed its own flag.

The early moderation of the complaints gave way to bitter condemnation when war began. Led by the *Globe and Mail*, the Conservatives questioned the St. Laurent government's judgement in opposing Britain at war. Former Conservative leader Arthur Meighen, who had wanted Canada to say "Ready, Aye, Ready" in 1922 when Britain contemplated another war in the Mediterranean, came forward in the *Globe* to express his high regard for Eden and "his opinion that Canada might well have taken an example from Australia in its early and outspoken support of the British position".[94] After the cease-fire, the contretemps over Canadian participation in UNEF, and the humiliation of Britain and France, the tone turned bitter. The House of Commons met in emergency session in late November, and the Conservatives moved an amendment deploring the "gratuitous condemnation of the action of the United Kingdom and France which was designed to prevent a major war in the Suez area". St. Laurent lost his temper and bluntly said that "the supermen of Europe" could no longer have their way in the world. Mike, equally rashly, declared that Canada would not be a "colonial chore-boy" who simply ran around and shouted, "Ready, Aye, Ready". It was a foolish comment. The Conservative amendment lost, but that debate won the Conservatives many votes in the next election.[95]

Mike defended himself and his government publicly and privately, then and later, by arguing that the real aim of Canadian policy was to help the British escape from the disaster they had created for themselves. "No matter what Howard Green [the most vociferous Conservative critic] may say ... we know that the government in London are grateful for the line we followed."[96] In fact, whatever Mike's hopes and declarations, they were not so grateful.

Eden had thought Mike's attitude "miserable" from the earliest days of the crisis. Even critics of Eden told Canadian friends at the outbreak of the war that the Canadians had let Britain down, had sided with the Americans, and were the focus of as much resentment as the Americans. Charles Ritchie dropped into London on November 13 and found hostility. It seemed "like a desertion on my part and no doubt many of my friends here think that it is a desertion of them on the part of Canada". His closest friend, the great Anglo-Irish writer Elizabeth Bowen, put it plainly to him: "What if we *are* wrong? If one of my friends made a mistake or committed a crime I would back them up. It is as simple as that." As Nasser gloated, Britain retreated, and a broken Eden took refuge in, of all places, Ian Fleming's Jamaican villa. Even Ritchie seemed to believe that Canada's voice was too loud in the anti-British chorus. "I hope," he wrote on November 24, "that in Ottawa they realize that the time has come to help to save the face of the British over Suez." The British "will remain the best bet in a bad world", and Canada "should not be too much influenced by unreal majorities of the United Nations".[97]

Later British writers tend either to ignore Canada's role or to echo faintly some of the bitterness of the time. Macmillan's official biographer, Alistair Horne, more knowledgeable about Canada than all but a few Britons, had only one reference to Pearson. He refers to Pearson's introduction of "the notion of the United Nations peace-keeping force — with the concomitance of repeated Arab-Israeli warfare that would accompany its failure".[98] A nasty review, indeed. Even David Carlton, a hostile biographer of Eden, does not believe that the Canadian efforts were calculated to save Britain from itself or that Eden was well disposed towards Mike's efforts. On November 3, Carlton writes, Lester Pearson "most unhelpfully set about mobilizing support for the rapid creation" of UNEF.[99] Nor have all reviews been enthusiastic on the other side of the Atlantic. While Dulles and the *New York Times* commended Pearson, Acheson did not. He believed that "Mike was being a little woolly and not paying enough attention to the power aspect, and to the need to deal with a situation in firmness".[100] Nor did Howard Green change his mind about his criticisms at the time. Britain and France were "our two mother countries", not simply the "supermen of Europe". Canada had no business attacking them when they had been provoked by a thug like Nasser.[101]

Peace did not come to the Middle East; more wars followed.

Nasser exposed UNEF's weakness when he expelled it in 1967 and war began. As the British and French retreated from the Middle East, the Americans took their place, and one can certainly argue that they showed less sensitivity to and understanding of that area's delicate balance than the Europeans had done. France, embittered by Britain's abandonment of their war, cast its lot with Europe and for an independent nuclear deterrent. Britain, ironically, became more dependent than ever on the United States, because Suez exposed how weak Britain was economically and militarily and how potent American opposition to its world-wide aims could be. The United States, which had so righteously condemned its allies for lack of consultation, saw little reason to consult others in its own adventures. Vietnam was kept off the NATO and U.N. agendas, as Suez never was.

For Canada, as for others, Suez was a watershed. The four who guided Canadian diplomacy at New York through the crisis were Pearson, Holmes, MacKay, and Murray, scions of that British Protestant stock that had rallied to Britain's side throughout Canadian history. What they saw in 1956 was British leadership that, contrary to Acheson's view, lacked an understanding of power in contemporary international politics. Like Eden, Mike too had read Henty and Kipling. But for him the romance of empire had given away to a vision of a system of international rules and organizations that would restrain the bandits and bullies of the world more effectively than British gunboats ever had. And it was Mike, not Eden or most of his colleagues, who heeded Kipling's advice to keep one's head while all around were losing theirs. When word reached London that Israel had refused to accept the cease-fire demand, a refusal that meant Britain could go to war, all but two cabinet members laughed and banged the table. David Carlton acidly remarks: "Those present were for the most part men of considerable private wealth from the best families in the land; most were declared Christians; many had fought gallantly in world wars against front rank adversaries; and most had attended prominent public schools where they would inevitably have been raised on the ethical values of

Tom Brown's Schooldays."[102] Most of the Canadian cabinet had been raised on the same values, had fought in the same wars, and had shared the same faith; but when they met on the eve of the British bombardment of Egypt they did not laugh and bang the table, but rather accepted the judgement of Mike Pearson, who loved London most among cities and Britain second-best among countries. For them, what was happening was tragic. History suggests that their judgement was right, their behaviour better. Tom Brown had taught them well.

The Canadians were not fully candid with the British about the likelihood that British forces would be allowed to participate in the U.N. force. Moreover, the Canadian eagerness to contribute a larger force to UNEF seems somewhat zealous. If the Canadians forgot Henty, they remembered Baden-Powell too well and were overly enthusiastic in their desire to become Queen's Scouts. And yet, in retrospect, Pearson's work does represent a remarkable accomplishment in diplomacy. The UNEF initiative strengthened the United Nations, moderated the tensions between Washington and London, and helped to maintain both the Commonwealth and NATO. On November 1, catastrophes seemed imminent to the most objective observer, but most did not occur. That they did not owed something to the presence of Pearson in New York that fall. Gunnar Jahn, the chairman of the Nobel Committee, said that Pearson won the prize because of "his never-tiring determination and his exceptional ability to put forward constructive ideas for the solution of a problem". Pearson believed, Jahn claimed, "that the basis of any negotiation on international problems must be an attempt to understand the other party and meet him halfway…".[103] At the United Nations in 1956, no one tried harder than Mike Pearson to understand the other party. In the end, he said in his Oslo lecture, "the whole problem returns to people; yes, to one person and his own individual response to the challenges that confront him".[104] He had responded brilliantly to the challenges that confronted him. His triumph became the emblem that he carried forth into new challenges on less familiar terrain.

CHAPTER FIVE

GRITTERDÄMMERUNG

The Canadian whose father accepted Canada as a spiritual dependency of some external power is thinking of it now solely as a nation in its own right. Though the nation is diverse, confused, self-centered, a little dizzy and smug from success at the moment, it has become cognate and organic. The Canadian knows better than his father knew, that he belongs to it and no other.

— Bruce Hutchison, *Canada: Tomorrow's Giant*, in June 1957[1]

BRUCE HUTCHISON, Canada's finest journalist, took "a casual, disordered tour" across Canada, in 1956-57, "not by the main highways but mostly on the side roads". He discovered "a curious and little-understood people with a surprising past and a future rather important to mankind." He thought he saw, in that high noon of post-war prosperity and middle-class nationalism, a new nation on the path to becoming "tomorrow's giant".[2] Hutchison was one of a group of Canadian print journalists who helped to define and communicate the smooth blend of Canadian political nationalism and internationalism of which Mike Pearson had increasingly become the national and international symbol. Hutchison and his close friends Grant Dexter and Max Freedman of the *Winnipeg Free Press*, George Ferguson of the *Montreal Star*, Kenneth Wilson of the *Financial Post*, and Blair Fraser of *Maclean's* celebrated, for their many English Canadian readers, the post-war successes of the Liberal governments. It seemed to them the best of times. Looking back three decades later in an "old man's" lament, Hutchison saw no reason to change his mind: "Canadian peace-keeping forces were ... spread around the world, and the nation's repute reached an all-time peak." Canada was, he wrote, "every-body's friend, the international darling or fortune's fool".[3]

Hutchison was a St. Laurent Liberal to the bone, but even those who had shed or never worn Liberal colours have regarded the Liberal governments of the 1950s as remarkable in their talent and managerial efficiency. Dalton Camp, who worked on George Drew's federal campaigns in the 1950s, admitted that for all the Tory criticism of St. Laurent's government, "the Liberals were in fact competent". The Tories, Camp wrote, were "hopelessly out-manned, outmanoeuvred, and outclassed" by the experienced Liberal ministers. Political scientist Reginald Whitaker is highly crit-ical of the Liberal Party's policies under King and St. Laurent, but he too emphasizes their great skill in ensuring that the party never rejected "the support of the vested capitalist interests, while at the same time never losing its credibility with the voters as a part of democratic reform...". This equipoise "left it precisely the flexibility and freedom of action to 'wheel and deal' in the centre of the politi-cal spectrum and to make the kind of practical accommodations necessary to maintain its hold on power".[4]

The centre in the mid-1950s was capacious and Liberal. The great divisive conflicts of Canadian political history when the centre did not hold seemed to have vanished. When Hutchison toured Quebec in mid-winter 1956, he was reassured. He recalled the 1930s, when Lionel Groulx publicly predicted that there would inevitably be a separate Laurentian state and R.B. Bennett privately told Hutchison that he agreed. But both had been wrong: "They had been watch-ing the side eddies, not the main current of Quebec life." The great-est figures of French Canada had been "moderates working with the moderates of other provinces", leaders like Laurier, Lapointe, and, of course, St. Laurent. Never had the French-Canadian nationalists controlled federal politics and, Hutchison implied, never would they do so. In a Montreal nightclub, he shared snails and wine with Roger Lemelin, whose "Plouffe family" interpreted "French Canada" to "English Canada" through the new medium of television. "Engorging a snail," the massive writer with burning eyes denounced "the politicians who only divide us. The people unite — always. Nothing can stop that union in the end." There could be no doubt: "the great movement is toward the center, not the other way." As Hutchison walked back to his hotel, the cross on Mount Royal grew dim as Montreal's skyline engulfed the dawn. The new Montreal was obscuring its separate past. Hutchison had seen Quebec's future, and he had no doubt it would work.[5]

When Mike Pearson first thought of politics in the mid-1940s, shortly after the conscription crisis of 1944, he worried about his lack of knowledge of Quebec. The healing of Quebec's wounds was foremost on the national agenda, but he knew little either of the patient or of possible remedies. The wounds healed more quickly than many thought possible, and in the 1950s most English-Canadian politicians shared Bruce Hutchison's belief that the forces of modernization, represented by Montreal's new bank towers and Louis St. Laurent's business approach in Ottawa, would triumph over those traditional forces represented by the cross on Mount Royal and Maurice Duplessis's conservative nationalism in Quebec City. With such beliefs and a French-Canadian prime minister, Ottawa placed Quebec's complaints at the side. Mike retained some of his earlier worries about his ignorance of French Canada. After he asked that his parliamentary assistant, Jean Lesage, write to him in French, Lesage did, most elegantly. But Jules Léger and Pearson did not develop a close relationship after Léger's 1954 appointment as under-secretary. The department's business was done in English. Indeed, Allan Gotlieb, who joined the department in 1957, later recalled that officers "could be paid to learn Russian or Spanish or Chinese but not to learn French". Marcel Cadieux, who was concerned about the unilingual character of the department in the 1950s, questioned the lack of support for instruction in French only to be told that the department could never support French-language training because that would mean that French was being treated as a foreign language! In the East Block in the 1950s, the winds of change that were gathering in Quebec went unnoticed, until the cyclone of the 1960s blew away that calm forever.[6]

Louis St. Laurent was an effective windbreak after 1948, but by the mid-1950s his strength was waning. He was seventy-one when he was re-elected in 1953 and, after the election, speculation began about his successor. Douglas Abbott, the genial and able finance minister, whom many thought a likely heir, unexpectedly left politics at fifty-four to take an appointment on the Supreme Court. Defence minister Brooke Claxton, who had wanted to be prime minister but who lacked Abbott's "light touch" and charm, also resigned, to join Metropolitan Life. Lionel Chevrier left Parliament and the Transport ministry to head the St. Lawrence Seaway Authority, where he would supervise the construction of the massive project that symbolized the self-confident mood of the nation. All were younger than Pearson, and their resignations and St. Laurent's age and obvious physical deterioration made Pearson and others think about his future.[7]

By 1956, Pearson knew some decisions had to be made. Intimations of mortality were increasingly numerous. He was fifty-nine; his father had died at sixty-three. Hume Wrong, his closest companion in the service, died at fifty-seven. Many of Mike's generation who had fought in the First World War and worked through the nights of the Second sustained by stimulants and cigarettes were showing the effects of their efforts. Mike and others, for example, worried about Norman Robertson: he was younger than Pearson, but his health was "starting to give way under the strain of chainsmoking and his relentless sedentary life".[8] The excitement of the war years and post-war reconstruction had disappeared as mid-1950s government seemed more and more the administration of things. In 1954, Graham Towers retired from the Bank of Canada at fifty-seven because he was bored and because, like Claxton, he wanted to taste the more lucrative rewards of the private sector before he finally retired.[9]

Mike, too, was often bored. He and Maryon had bought a house in 1955. In fact, they owned two houses in 1956 — the one on

Augusta Street, the other a duplex on Cobourg. Maryon had been dickering for both properties and managed, to her embarrassment, to purchase both.[10] After a peripatetic life, the Pearsons finally had a home — and its responsibilities. On a February Saturday in 1956, Mike told Geoffrey that he had enjoyed a game of curling in the morning, but the afternoon found him "as usual" in the office. He wished he could curl more "but the pressure of Parliamentary, Political and Departmental work has been, as usual, heavy and unremitting". He was being forced to be less the "statesman" and more the politician and was clearly uncomfortable with the change. There were real mistakes the government was making, and St. Laurent was "tired and discouraged and not giving as much confidence or leadership". The ministers were acting too much as individuals and not enough as cabinet colleagues; Howe was, in Pearson's eyes, the worst offender. There was, naturally, "much gossip about the political future and much pressure" on Mike to indicate "that [he] would accept the leadership if it were offered". So far, he told Geoff, he had been "firmly negative — but I am becoming worried about the future. If I continue on this course — or even more, if I get out altogether when the PM does —which is what I want to do — there will be a lot of people who will accuse me of running away from a responsibility and a duty."[11]

This indecision marked Mike's attitude that year. Three items required decisions, and they were difficult. There was a touch of Mackenzie King in the effectiveness of his ditherings; a comparison he would deplore but one that has some merit in the view of others at the time.* First, he had to decide whether to accept the secretary

---

* In March 1956, *The Readers Digest* asked Pearson to tell it "the best advice" he ever had. He recalled one late-night conversation with King that ended with, "If you ever become a person of political position and influence, young man, never forget that in the course of history, far more has been done for mankind by preventing bad actions than by doing good ones." That, however, was not the best advice. His uncle in Chicago was given credit for the advice: "Happiness in work is an essential ingredient for happiness in life." "The Best Advice I Ever Had", Mar. 19, 1956 (MG26 N1, v. 19).

generalship of NATO. He cared deeply about NATO, regarded it as one of his major achievements, and was a confident participant in NATO councils. His name surfaced immediately in the early winter of 1956 as a possible successor to "Pug" Ismay, who it was rumoured would not seek a second term. Mike's membership on the "three wise men" committee kept his name at the forefront of NATO discussions. He remained coy, even in private. Paul-Henri Spaak of Belgium was, characteristically, more direct. When he heard that the position might become open he was immediately "tempted" and asked the Belgian NATO representative to lead his campaign. In September 1956, Mike told Charles Hébert, Canada's ambassador to Belgium, that he did not want the job, or at least it *seemed* that was what he had meant. A month later, when Pearson's candidacy was being promoted by some Britons and Americans, an annoyed Hébert recalled the earlier conversation:

On that particular occasion you had remarked how weary you were of being constantly on the move and that…
a) you had little taste for a job which involved uprooting yourself and Maryon from Canada and starting afresh in Paris,
b) you could not see how you could free yourself from your present governmental and practical responsibilities,
c) you thought that Ismay's successor should have a fluent knowledge of French.

Pearson then instructed Hébert to ask Spaak directly if he was interested. He did, and Spaak replied immediately: "I had no thought of seeking the appointment because I understood that Mike was interested in it." Spaak added that he was certainly interested if Mike was not. If Mike had not wanted to convey that message, what did he want?

He was, one suspects, unsure. Moreover, the need for decision had come at the wrong time. The Suez crisis thoroughly entangled him, as events and Spaak moved forward. At the request of the Americans, Pearson himself proposed Spaak's nomination in

December 1956, and the Belgian was elected unanimously. Spaak, in his memoirs, generously noted that his triumph "was partly due to the fact that Lester Pearson, who would no doubt have been greatly preferred to me had his services been available, did not figure as a candidate".[12]

A second decision was demanded by the Liberals of Algoma East, who were urging their distinguished member to agree to a nomination meeting in his far-flung constituency. The election was sure to come in 1957, and the bitter Algoma winters made an early meeting essential. As Mike mediated between Israelis and Arabs and Americans and Britons at the U.N., Mary Macdonald used her own combination of skill, charm, and knowledge to maintain peace with strength in Algoma East: "I just saw in the Sudbury Star that Mr. Murray suffered a $25,000 fire at the Shequandah farm. That is really too bad and I have sent a note." At another time she had to turn off a Pearson broadcast because Norman Beauvais and Art Jackman called saying a complaint had been filed against their mail delivery service: "they wanted to know if it meant they couldn't carry the mail. I had to tell them of course [they could], and lecture them (nicely) ... because they have not yet sent in their application." They said they wanted to check with a lawyer before they submitted it, but Mary told them "to just fill it in and get it down here. After all their action is not now *legal* and your hands would be tied if they don't help you to help them."[13] Mike and Mary felt comfortable with these people — trappers, pilots, storekeepers, and small-town Canadians — and his stays in their spare bedrooms, roadside cottages, and downtown hotels gave him a sense of the Canadian quotidian, a sense that so many of his foreign-minister counterparts never had or felt need of. Mike, like his clergyman father, realized that the Liberal faith, like the Christian faith, gained strength if the believers saw evidence of many good works. And in Algoma East, in Mike Pearson's day, there were many. He never promised to build a dock "right around Manitoulin Island" or to accumulate "a government-financed stockpile of uranium at Elliot Lake which would top the highest hill", as an opposition member once charged; but, with Mary Macdonald's help, he did cause many docks to be built and much uranium to be bought. By the fall of 1956 the riding was in politically good shape, and "Auss" Hunt of the local Liberal executive made plans for a nomination meeting on October 15. "They are most pleased," Mary Macdonald reported, "because it signifies your intention to remain."[14]

Remain he did, and in doing so he went a considerable distance towards making a third decision, the most significant one. By 1955 it was becoming clear that the government had lost much vigour and that the prime minister was a shadow of what he had been when his government was young. Even a great admirer, the journalist Bruce Hutchison, confided to Grant Dexter, another Liberal sympathizer, that "the Old Man is really through" and that a new Liberal leader should be found soon.[15] C.D. Howe, cabinet minister for a generation, reflected on the government's malaise in March 1955: "He spoke nostalgically [to A.D.P. Heeney] about the days of King — he and the P.M. were of another generation — there were too many new faces around the table —[Finance minister] Walter Harris was not like Abbott. He thought Mike the right man for the leadership but he'd have to raise a finger."[16] Many others thought Mike the "right man" and watched his finger movements anxiously as St. Laurent's health faded.

Walter Gordon had been urging him to consider the leadership since he first entered politics. And, as Patrick Brennan has clearly demonstrated, many of English Canada's leading journalists, notably Bruce Hutchison, Grant Dexter, Blair Fraser, and George Ferguson, had agreed that "Mike was the man". Having pored over their private and public writing, Brennan concludes: "The degree of respect and affection for him displayed by the press, and especially the top-ranked men, had no equal anywhere else in the government and not infrequently bordered on hero worship."[17] Pearson valued and cultivated this "responsible, civilized relationship" between politician and journalist, one that seems impossible, if not unsavoury, to observers of a later day embittered by Vietnam, Watergate, and the assorted other ills of the middle and late Cold

War. In the post-war years, however, the consensus on foreign policy was remarkable, embracing not only press and public but also moderate left, centre, and right. For journalists like Ferguson and Hutchison and for the majority of English Canadians, again in Professor Brennan's words, "Pearson articulated and symbolized the hopes of a nation — their hopes — and through his diplomatic achievements made Canada mean something in the world." In those times, that meant a great deal.[18]

Despairing over the future of the government and hoping to make "Mike lift a finger", George Ferguson, editor of the influential *Montreal Star*, wrote to Pearson in February 1956 suggesting that St. Laurent might resign.[19]

The question of the succession assumes therefore an immediate importance, and I hope, as you study it, you will set aside whatever personal preferences you may have in the matter, and do your thinking in terms of national duty and responsibility — high-sounding phrases which I usually reserve for un-read editorials. Your object when you entered public life was to pursue the advocacy of certain vital policies beyond the point to which you were held by the restrictions of the civil service. What has happened since then makes this logic and argument a good deal stronger than it then was. After all, at that time, there was a successor to King and you and he saw fairly well eye to eye on the policies in question.

Since then, the Cabinet has been very gravely weakened and if you look at the Gallup Poll on the Colombo Plan in The Star of Wednesday, February 22nd, you will see what public opinion is drifting to. We are going to have a fairly long period of critical years, and the plain fact is that, without you, the Cabinet's policies will drift from bad to worse. There is lethargy, selfishness and cynicism in the Cabinet, in Parliament and among the public, and in my judgment, they are on the increase.

I do not want to indulge in personal judgments about your colleagues, but there is not a single one of them who is really fitted for the real task. There is administrative competence and manipulative skill. There is precious little principle and, outside yourself, and the Prime Minister, no leadership at all.

Ferguson's judgement was harsh but was widely shared. Blair Fraser, the *Maclean's* columnist whom many came to consider the fifties' conscience, visited Charles Ritchie in Bonn in April 1956 and told the Canadian ambassador that "the Liberals are in trouble in Canada and that they will lose the election". In Fraser's view, "they have depended for much of their influence on the support of a small group of publicists, professors, civil servants, and men of influence, and it is this group whose support they have lately lost". Fraser, of course, was a significant voice within that group, and he knew well the mood he described. It would soon get worse.[20]

In the spring of 1956, C.D. Howe, whose autocratic ways were annoying his younger cabinet colleagues, was eager to finish his last great megaproject, the TransCanada Pipeline. He brought forward the pipeline bill, which provided for American control for a brief time to allow the company to pay for and absorb the large quantity of steel pipe that was necessary to get the line to Winnipeg that summer. Included in the bill, which was already controversial because of the American ownership, was a proposed loan of $80 million to support the construction from Alberta to Manitoba, an amount that private investors were unwilling to put up. Cabinet approved the loan proposal on May 7; the only way to meet the construction deadline was through the use of closure. On May 14, Howe introduced his bill with a strong attack on opposition leader George Drew and ended his speech with the announcement of closure. The House of Commons exploded. Walter Harris and Jack Pickersgill had worked out a timetable that provided for closure at the various stages of debate.

Closure had not been used since 1932, when Mackenzie King, then opposition leader, denounced it as "autocratic power to the nth degree". Howe had given the opposition a bloated target — Texas oil millionaires controlling Canadian resources plus an arrogant ministry that listened to the Texans rather than Canadians.

From early May to "Black Friday", June 1, the House was in tragi-comic chaos, with sessions ending at dawn and animal noises echoing throughout the chamber. Amid the din and chaos, old men shook fists at each other, MPs broke into satirical song, and the prime minister was mocked as "Silent St. Louis", the puppet of Howe and his Texas friends. On Black Friday, the speaker declared it was Thursday, the centre aisle swelled with angry members, and the Chamber echoed with "Onward Christian Soldiers" from Tories and the CCF, while the Liberals tried to drown them out with "We've Been Working on the Pipeline". It was, perhaps, one of Parliament's blackest moments. Pearson was appalled. So were most of his friends; and so were many Canadians. All the ministers had to speak to defend the government. Pearson did so — poorly, partisanly, and late at night. Stanley Knowles of the CCF, who played a central role in the attack on the government, recalled it as "a silly speech ... but it was obvious that he was just doing his duty to fill time". Pearson seems to have thought better of it, suggesting that "some of our members may have thought when I sat down amid jeers and hoots and cheers that perhaps this fellow might make a good leader of the party after all". The Hansard record, however, suggests that Knowles was closer to the mark.[21]

After the debate ended, Howe told a friend that he would not want to face an election immediately but thought that "the long term reaction will be definitely against the Conservatives".[22] To be sure, the polls showed only a slight reaction, the Conservatives seemed an unappealing bunch, and their leader, George Drew, was ailing. Nevertheless, shrewd political observers sensed that the polling results concealed a profound disgust with what had happened, and a loss of confidence in the government. The effect of the pipeline debate on Pearson was to increase his own uncertainties.

His indecision is reflected in his sporadic conversations with A.D.P. Heeney, who was contemplating his own future, though Mike was more reticent with those who urged him on. In December 1954, Pearson told Heeney with much enthusiasm that Walter

Gordon was to enter the government in the spring. Heeney "formed the impression, on no evidence, that LBP will stay the course and be a candidate for the leadership". A year later, he was hearing rumours that Mike might appoint himself Heeney's successor. In early 1956, he told Heeney that he wanted "to get out". Evidently Heeney had earlier mentioned a position at McGill University as a possibility, and he suggested it again. Mike said he would be happy there. Heeney told him that he believed Pearson should stick to government "as a matter of conscience". The next day Mike "referred again to his own future".[23] It was clearly bothering him. He thought he might want to be chairman of the International Joint Commission, or high commissioner in London, but he would prefer a university. When Heeney said he should take the leadership, Mike deflected the implied question by saying that "he had hoped to be able to come out publicly for [Walter] Harris." He could no longer support Harris, who was being promoted for leadership by Jack Pickersgill and some others. If he were offered the leadership "unopposed he supposed he could not refuse".

These conversations occurred the week of George Ferguson's letter urging Mike to seek the leadership. Heeney was in Ottawa during the last bad stages of the pipeline debate and found Pearson "having a wretched time torn between distaste for the unpleasant features of his public life and ... his very active sense of responsibility". Heeney again urged him to remain because no one else in the government could "maintain the momentum of our national life" or had "the moral quality for leadership of the govt".[24] A few days later, in Washington, Pearson spoke of his "revulsion at the petty politics and preoccupation with partisan advantage...". He mentioned the possibility of the NATO secretary general's position. Then, with characteristic ambivalence, he said: "If ever he'd had a desire for political life (and the leadership) the experience of the past months had cured him — except when he saw the way Geo. Drew behaved and the tactics of the opposition, well — And there he left it." Still, Heeney left the conversation believing that "they" could persuade him to take the leadership if it was offered soon and "virtually unanimous". Heeney hoped the offer would come soon.[25]

It did not, to the surprise of many. Just as Mike decided to stand again for nomination in the fall of 1956, St. Laurent decided to remain as Liberal leader for the 1957 campaign. Howe later said that, at the time of the 1953 election, he and St. Laurent had agreed to retire "after a year or two", but St. Laurent "changed his mind about retiring, which was a mistake, both for him and for the party".[26] And so, in the wonderful but probably apocryphal quip, "they'd run St. Laurent even if they had to run him stuffed".[27]

By the end of 1956, the chill that fell upon the world in the aftermath of Hungary and Suez had enhanced Pearson's position, within his party and among most of the press. He seemed the obvious successor to the septuagenarian prime minister. Bruce Hutchison's year-end *Financial Post* column detected a "tide in the affairs of men" that seemed "to be sweeping [Pearson] inevitably into the Prime Minister's Office".[28] Walter Harris had been tarnished by his role as Liberal tactician in the pipeline debate, and before the 1957 election the decision to increase the old-age pension by only six dollars bestowed upon him the deadly sobriquet "six-buck Harris". Some of Pearson's and Harris's colleagues later spoke of Harris as the heir apparent, but there is stronger evidence that the pipeline fiasco had mortally wounded his chances.[29] Prime Minister St. Laurent did not help matters for Harris in a verbal jousting with John Diefenbaker in January 1957. The new Conservative leader took notice of Pearson's refusal of the NATO secretary generalship. Then, looking at Harris, he suggested that "some" of Pearson's colleagues had hoped he would take it. St. Laurent responded by saying that he had known Pearson for "some time" and had come to feel that "he was dedicating his life to the service of his country". And, Arthur Blakely of the Montreal *Gazette* continued, "he went on to lavish such praise on Mr. Pearson as rarely comes from a Prime Minister speaking of a Cabinet colleague". The corridor "buzzed" after the speech.[30]

The passing of years has not stopped the "buzzing". Many of Pearson's colleagues, including Walter Harris, later said that Pearson had long harboured ambitions for the leadership and that his public stance of reluctance was pretence or fear of losing. Douglas Abbott, for example, believed that once Pearson realized he could not be U.N. secretary general, he was determined to be leader. Historians have frequently agreed, pointing to advances in Pearson's career that were clearly the product of deliberate action and choices.[31] Indeed, earlier chapters have pointed to several instances, such as Pearson's entry into External Affairs, where what appeared to be chance was, in fact, calculation. In his own memoirs, he speaks briefly of his decision to contest the leadership and suggests that the leader's position was one for which he "had no particular desire". He felt, however, that he had a "public obligation", whatever his personal feelings and his doubts about his qualifications.[32]

Was Pearson "ambitious" as so many who worked with him privately then and publicly later claimed? The question is important, not only because Pearson's colleagues suggest he was disingenuous but also because an examination of the evidence illuminates many recesses in our knowledge of the man and his times. To Pearson, ambition was not a virtue. He knew, of course, that Brutus had said Caesar was ambitious and that even Marc Antony had admitted it was "a grievous fault". Vaulting ambition was not a quality much honoured in Methodist homes, especially that of Ed Pearson, who knew his Shakespeare as well as his Bible. Like sex, it lurked in those pre-Freudian corners, fascinating in its mystery, tantalizing in its promise, and terrifying in its implications. It emerged only in the most private moments, to be handled daintily like precious china at Sunday teas. Sex moved out of the shadows in the twentieth century, but ambition remained concealed behind curtains. Mike could not seem to be ambitious; talent would reveal itself.

His attitude tells us much about himself, his background, and, most of all, the milieu of Ottawa during the Liberal ascendancy of the 1950s. Pearson's "crowd" bears many similarities to its British counterpart, described so well by Lord Annan: a group of males from the best schools, with liberal social values, who saw in "self-less" government service the highest calling. Wrong, Heeney, Robertson, Pearson, Reid, Ritchie and even the editor George Ferguson were all Oxford men and bore that institution's mark. Too much ambition was terribly "non U", as it had been at Oxford, where effortless excellence received the highest acclaim. It was not always so in Canada, for Mackenzie King was very ambitious and did not bother to hide it. But his leading public servants were embarrassed by his ambition and his willingness to get his hands very dirty indeed in the morass of party politics. By the 1950s, ambition had become suspect among Ottawa's mandarins. Their reaction to Paul Martin's leadership ambitions was telling. Christina McCall, who interviewed many of the "crowd", concluded: "It was Martin's unhappy lot throughout the St. Laurent and Pearson decades to bear the disdain that had been reserved previously for Mackenzie King...." Martin "wanted power, curious creature, and he let people see this base desire". For the Protestant, English, male, very "U" mandarins in the Liberal Party and its bureaucratic and journalistic associates, "Pearson-the-Pure-in-Heart had been designated for the succession by St. Laurent-the-Saintly and had accepted the imprimatur after a graceful show of reluctance".[33] It all seemed "beyond politics" and, in their view, that was where it belonged.

It is easy to mock this anti-political, pure-in-heart stance. In 1956, as Mike moved with such seeming reluctance towards his political destiny, a young Irish Catholic senator from Massachusetts was exploring his very great ambitions by openly pursuing the Democratic vice-presidential nomination and, in doing so, was revealing that the new generation of politicians would not be ashamed of ambition. And in Canada, the Conservatives broke with the spurious gentility of Bay Street and chose John Diefenbaker, a prairie populist whose dark eyes burned with ambition. It is not surprising that the "Liberal élite" found it hard to take Diefenbaker seriously.

They were far more liberal than democratic, and not at all populist. When Diefenbaker engaged in "wild showmanship" during the pipeline debate, it provoked, among Pearson's colleagues, "ribald comment over our coffee cups". His election to the Conservative Party leadership in December 1956 provoked a "relieved reaction" among Pearson's crowd.[34] Despite their worldly sophistication and their brilliance, there were forces that they could neither understand nor counter.

Their world — or, rather, the way they saw it — echoes faintly to later generations because in them were so many echoes of what went before them. Talk of duty, honour, and conscience came very easily. When Mike spoke to Heeney about his decision, such terms came freely from him — they came, more tellingly, in Heeney's reflections in his diary: Mike must accept the leadership as "a matter of conscience"; he shows a "sense of responsibility"; and he has the "moral quality" for leadership. Both Heeney and Pearson were parsons' children, and such language was bred in their bones. It atrophied as post-war disillusionment and secularism set in. The Second World War and the Cold War that followed, however, refilled the empty vessels of the western Christian legacy for Pearson's "crowd" and created a strong brew that fortified the Liberal élite in the post-war era. Simultaneously, their innate suspicion of the demagogue and of appeals to popular emotions deepened as Hitler's and Mussolini's ranting remained in their memories.

Ambition, then, was unseemly; but there was more to Pearson's indecision than a reluctance to seek the Liberal leadership and, nearly everyone assumed, the prime ministership. Politics themselves were regarded with disdain by the Liberal élite. Reg Whitaker has brilliantly analysed the Liberal Party's evolution in the 1950s into "in a curious sense a non-partisan party":

> ... however one approaches the question, it seems reasonable to conclude that the Liberal party, as a political party, was growing less distinct, that the party was more a vehicle for élite accommodation, involving not only the élites of the two linguistic and cultural

groups in Canada but the bureaucratic and corporate élites as well, than a partisan organization. When partisanship got in the way of élite accommodation it was partisanship that was usually discarded.[35]

Mike Pearson liked this flavour of 1950s Liberalism. The Cold War brought a remarkable consensus on Canada's foreign policy, and he extolled this non-partisan approach at home and abroad. When the pipeline debate and the Suez crisis shattered the non-partisan consensus, Mike became angry and uncomfortable. He spoke of the "revulsion" he held towards partisanship and told Geoffrey how he loathed stepping down from his non-partisan pedestal.[36]

This anti-political attitude is deeply rooted in Canadian intellectual history. Stephen Leacock and other English-Canadian imperialists ridiculed "the little turkey-cocks of Ottawa, fighting as they feather their mean nests of stick and mud, high on the river bluff".[37] Ed Pearson in his wartime Chatham pulpit also spoke of the need for Ottawa's politicians to put aside politics to serve a higher purpose. As young diplomats, Hume Wrong and Mike passed many evenings mocking their political masters, lamenting the politicians' fickle, second-rate ways. When Mike moved from the under-secretary's office to the minister's office he and Mackenzie King cloaked it in non-partisan rhetoric, presenting it as a simple promotion. King's description of Pearson's appointment was an extraordinary statement, one that caused Eugene Forsey to erupt in anger.[38] Perhaps Mike did not notice Forsey's eruption, for in his memoirs he says his entry into politics felt like "being promoted from general manager to president in the same company". However, he was never so close again to his old colleagues, and "politics" as much as seniority was a source of this progressive alienation.[39]

Vic Mackie, a veteran journalist who accompanied Mike on campaign swings through Algoma East, recalled that Mike "didn't like campaigning for an election.... didn't like pushing himself forward". Despite "his wonderful personality and easy-to-get-along-with nature", Mike found it difficult "to stick out his hand and ask for a vote". Fortunately, the enthusiastic Mary Macdonald "egged him on and pushed him forward and would take him around and introduce him to people and say, 'This is a man who wants to be your next Member of Parliament.'"[40] In his memoirs, he pays tribute to "politics and politicians", claiming they "deserve far more respect in our democratic society than they receive". But he then betrays his fears:

> I had none of the gifts of the actor who can play on people's emotions and produce the mass frenzy that leads not only to irrational support for good causes, but also for causes evil and dangerous. I have always suspected and distrusted those who could arouse the masses by working on their emotions, turning favour into frenzy, support into hysteria, and normally rational human beings into howling mobs.... But the exaggerated appeal to fanaticism, to a false and deceptive hope, or to a vision which cannot possibly be realized can result only in disillusionment — this kind of thing, so common in today's politics, I have always disliked and distrusted, almost as much as I have abhorred the marketing of politicians and policies as though they were detergents or deodorants.

These aspects of modern politics threatened democracy through the undermining of the individual voter's "sense of responsibility".[41]

Foremost among the threats to that "sense of responsibility" in the fifties was Senator Joseph McCarthy's campaign to purge American government of Communists, a campaign that, in Pearson's view, played on emotions to produce "a mass frenzy". In 1957, that frenzy overflowed into Canada and, in the comment of Arnold Heeney to his diary, "cast real shadows on relations with the USA and on the standing of [Pearson] at home in this his finest year".[42]

The shadows were cast by the suicide of Herbert Norman, Canada's ambassador in Cairo and a target of American congressional anti-Communists. Norman, in the judgement of the United States Senate Subcommittee on Internal Security, and of some others who have examined his career, notably Professor James Barros, was at best a Soviet sympathizer, at worst a conscious and secret agent of the Soviet Union's imperialist aims. Others, such as Pearson and Professor Roger Bowen, treat Norman as a victim of McCarthyism, one whose early flirtation with Communism became a scarlet letter that no amount of service to Canada's and the West's purposes could remove. An official report that examined all relevant Canadian documents and declared Norman guiltless of subversion has not stilled suspicions.[43] As with so much of the literature on the Cold War, particularly on espionage, the sources are exclusively Western. The absence of evidence from the "other side" seems to produce a surprising certainty of conclusions. The final answer to the Norman riddle probably lies within the dusty files of the KGB, which may eventually yield the answer. Whether Norman is "guilty" or "innocent", the effect of the Norman affair on Pearson's career and life was significant. As Heeney suggests, the "Norman affair" did cast shadows upon Pearson, not only in 1957 but in the decades that followed.

"Murder by Slander", read the *Toronto Daily Star* headline of April 4, 1957. On that morning, Norman left his ambassadorial residence in Cairo, walked to a building, took an elevator to the eighth floor, walked up one floor to the roof, removed his glasses, watch, and cufflinks, looked at the sidewalk below, waited for it to clear, then jumped. Just weeks before he died, the U.S. Senate Subcommittee on Internal Security had raised his name again, and, just as before, the news leaked to the press. Norman, like Pearson, had his finest diplomatic hour during the Suez Crisis, but the revival of the old rumours about his links to Soviet espionage quickly changed his mood. The thought of returning to Canada for interrogation, as he had in 1950, and of once again being asked to "name names" depressed him. In the House of Commons in March, Pearson had defended Norman against the allegations that had been leaked to the newspapers and condemned those who sought to smear him "by slander and insinuation". Norman thanked his minister and the others who supported him but, in a cable, told Pearson he found the charges "vexing and discouraging".[44] They remain so.*

In the 1940s both the State Department and External Affairs had turned to the universities to find experts on Asia. Both departments had shown surprisingly little interest in the area until Japan began to loom as a potential threat allied with Fascism in Europe. During the 1930s many academics and some journalists had paid attention to East Asia, fascinated by the impact of modernization on traditional societies and the turmoil that accompanied it. They clustered around the Institute of Pacific Relations (IPR), attending its conferences and publishing in its journals. The young scholars included Herbert Norman, Owen Lattimore, and such Asians as the economic historian Chi Ch'ao-ting.[45] The locations for IPR conferences were (for academics) glamorous: Shanghai (1931), Banff (1933), Yosemite (1936), and Virginia Beach (1938). Many of the institute's members had lived in East Asia when they were young, as Norman had. They were often, like Norman, children of missionaries, and their parents' experience as teachers and doctors among the Asian poor made them sympathetic to reform movements. In the 1930s the increasing militarization of Japan and its imperialist ambitions in Asia horrified them. Simultaneously many of them, again like Norman, became proponents of Asian revolution, especially as Mao Tse-tung gathered his peasant forces to fight off the Japanese and to expunge corruption in Chinese society. The IPR had a distinct leftist tinge. But in the context of the 1930s, with Japan linked with Fascism, China enduring its brutal onslaught, and Western institutions dealing so fecklessly with disorder, the dream of socialist revo-

---

* Even the end of the Cold War and the passing of so much time have not ended the fascination of some. "St. Lester of Pearson: a day of reckoning" was the headline in the Canadian gossip monthly *Frank* in April 1992. The story continued: "Disciples of much beloved former prime minister St. Lester of Pearson are in high anxiety over the latest nail in the coffin of Pearson's old friend Herbert Norman." It was reporting on a *National Review* article (Mar. 30, 1992) which said that the latest "nail" in Norman's coffin meant that "Canadians [can] get on to the even more important matter of former Prime Minister Lester Pearson and his activities as Counselor of [the] Embassy in Washington during World War II." Canadians already have (see vol. 1, ch. 12).

lution and internationalism was seductive to these scholars. In 1940, the IPR published Norman's book *Japan's Emergence as a Modern State: Political and Economic Problems of the Meiji Period*,[46] which very clearly bore traces of the Marxist debates of the 1930s.

Norman had encountered the cutting edge of Marxist thought at Trinity College, Cambridge, between 1933 and 1935, a time when the Depression's sting and Fascism's success jolted young Cambridge men loose from tradition. Anthony Blunt, then a young research fellow at Trinity College and himself a clergyman's son, much later recalled how "quite suddenly, in the autumn term of 1933, Marxism hit Cambridge". Blunt had been on sabbatical that term, but when he returned he "found that almost all my younger friends had become Marxist and joined the Party; and Cambridge was literally transformed overnight".[47] The wealthy young American Michael Straight, who arrived at Trinity College in the fall of 1934, moved from the Socialist Society to the Communists that fall: "The Socialist Society had two hundred members when [Straight] went to Cambridge and six hundred when [he] left. About one in four of them belonged to Communist cells." It did not seem a giant step to move from socialism to Communism, as it did later. The Soviet Union, terrified by the Fascist threat, called for a common front: "On all of the issues that we cared about," Straight recalled, "militant Socialists and Communists held the same opinions."[48]

For Norman the step from socialism to Communism was easy, for he arrived already convinced that the future would and should belong to socialist revolution. At Trinity, the most brilliant students shared these beliefs. Guy Burgess was, perhaps, the most outstanding as well as "very good looking in a boyish, athletic, very English way". Norman, an insecure, physically frail, but thoroughly intellectual Canadian, was drawn like a moth to the bright flames of this group. It was the charismatic John Cornford, Darwin's great-grandson, soon to die in the Spanish Civil War, who "influenced ... him more than any of" his other friends, "and under his tutelage [Norman] entered the Party".[49]

Whether he bore a Party card is irrelevant; he was at one with them. Norman left Cambridge in 1935 to return to Canada, where he taught at Upper Canada College. He sent money to the Loyalists in Spain, moved in left-wing circles, and was eventually dismissed from his job. A Rockefeller fellowship took him to Harvard. In the United States, he again found friends who were drawn to Marxist approaches, including Shigeto Tsuru from Japan, in whose apartment the FBI came across him in 1942 as he tried to collect some of Tsuru's papers. The result was an FBI file.[50]

By the time this strange encounter occurred, Norman was a member of the Department of External Affairs. The department had been seeking a Japanese-language expert for the Tokyo legation for many years. With his new Ph.D. in hand, Norman had seemed the ideal person, and he served in Tokyo until December 1941. He was interned after Pearl Harbor, but a prisoner exchange freed him. Upon his return he was assigned to the so-called Examination Unit, an intelligence operation, where he was responsible for the Japanese intelligence division.

It was in this sometimes comical operation that Norman came within Pearson's ambit. Pearson was the chair of the Associate Committee of the National Research Council, which supervised the Examination Unit, and he continued to exercise informal supervision of its American liaison when he left Ottawa for Washington.[51] The unit's records suggest that the work was tedious. Even before Norman was repatriated, the Americans had suggested that he would be very useful to them. They could compare their analyses with his own and with those of their counterparts in British intelligence. On November 4, 1942, Pearson wrote a letter of introduction for Norman to Colonel William Donovan of the U.S. Office of Strategic Services, and the arrangement was completed.[52]

Norman remained in Ottawa and Pearson in Washington until the war's end. They had infrequent contact. There is nothing in the records to indicate closeness, although there was obvious acceptance by Pearson of the importance of Norman's work and the excellence of his skills. James Barros suggests a closer relationship, intimating that Norman's tendency to shun old leftist acquaintances, which two sources mention, was the result of Pearson's warning to him. There is, however, no evidence to confirm that there was such a warning and, considering that the shunning occurred so soon after Norman's return, it seems unlikely. Moreover, Pearson had worked to end internment of Canadian Communists after the German attack on the Soviet Union. Why would he tell Norman to shun the left, when the left was now so ferocious in its opposition to Nazism, which was, of course, the enemy?

At a lively and probably bibulous dinner at the British first secretary's residence in 1943, Pearson himself agreed that the Soviets "were winning the war for us"; and he went out of his way to try to coax reticent Soviet diplomats out of their shells at international gatherings that year.[53] It is not surprising (though Barros suggests it is) that in October 1944, when Pearson encountered a Soviet diplomat who lacked a shell — Anatoly Gromov, first secretary of the Soviet Embassy in Washington — he asked Norman Robertson to check out who Gromov might be. He received no answer, but it is scarcely surprising that a Canadian diplomat, aware of the significance of Soviet aims for the post-war settlement, should be interested in whatever crumbs of information such a Soviet might let fall at lunchtime. Gromov was, in fact, a notorious KGB operative.[54] Pearson also may have had dinner with Herbert Norman and "some others" at some Soviet Embassy event in Ottawa in the late spring of 1945, and Emma Woikin, the External cipher clerk later convicted of spying, may have been helping the Soviets' cook with the dinner preparations, but the evidence is flimsy and it seems most unlikely that the Soviets would in any way involve Woikin in such an event, since she was already their agent. In any case, the Canadians' presence at such a dinner would not have been improper.[55]

Gouzenko's revelations came later that year, and they were a lightning bolt that exposed not only Soviet infiltration of Western agencies but also the weakness of the Western security apparatus. The Western-Soviet alliance may have been a bad marriage, but it was sustained by those threads of trust that bind together the principals in a common life. Gouzenko and the brutal sweep of the Soviets through Eastern Europe weakened the threads and, finally, severed them. The divorce was bitter, and old relationships were quickly ended.

In 1946 and 1947 Pearson became convinced, in his own words, "that there was such a thing as Kremlin-directed communist subversion ... and that the safety of the state was involved". Escott Reid, a socialist in the thirties who often expressed admiration for the Soviet worker state, became its most bitter critic in the Department of External Affairs. An old friend of Pearson, King Gordon, who had visited the Soviet Union in 1932 and had thought, like others, that he had seen the future working, disavowed such views. In 1947, Norman visited a former Cambridge classmate who had made the same journey to Communism in the 1930s. Norman told Victor Kiernan, who was then teaching at Cambridge, that his heart was still in the "right place" but that his life and work required him to be discreet. One of his External colleagues and Cambridge acquaintances, Harry Ferns, had talked too much about his Marxist faith and had been dismissed from External. Israel Halperin, a friend from undergraduate and Toronto and Ottawa days, had been implicated by Gouzenko, and Norman's name was in Halperin's address book. Leo Malania, an External Affairs officer with a more sympathetic view of the Soviets than most, left External in 1946 because Emma Woikin, the cipher clerk identified by Gouzenko, had lived with the Malanias.[56] Small wonder that Norman thought he must be discreet. And to the south a whirlwind was mounting, as Congress cast a suspicious eye upon Americans whom they suspected of what had suddenly become treason.

One such target was the senior State Department official Alger Hiss, whom John Foster Dulles whisked away from suspicion to install, as president of the prestigious Carnegie Endowment. In Canada, Hume Wrong, less an evangelical than a cynic in his strong anti-Communism, managed to secure a United Nations job for a grateful Malania in 1946. (Malania eventually became an Episcopalian priest.)[57]

When Donald Maclean attended an interview for a post in the British Foreign Office in 1935, fresh from Cambridge and commitment to the "Party", he was asked about whether he had "communist views". He did "an instant double-take":

> Shall I deny the truth, or shall I brazen it out? I decided to brazen it out. "Yes," I said, "I did have such views — and I haven't entirely shaken them off." I think they must have liked my honesty because they nodded, looked at each other and smiled. Then the chairman said: "Thank you, that will be all, Mr. Maclean."

He passed with flying colours.[58] No one had bothered to ask Norman such a question in 1939. But he too would probably have passed even if he had "brazened it out" as Maclean had. Nineteen forty-six was the year of a sea change in the West and in its concept of security. Reaction against the earlier lack of concern about Maclean in Britain, Hiss in the United States, and Norman in Canada heightened the fears of those suspected and the suspicions of those who had fear. The foreign offices in the Anglo-American democracies — the élite service linked with the best schools and the oldest traditions — became the focus of most suspicions. It was a heady brew for the demagogue.

When, therefore, on February 9, 1950, Senator Joseph McCarthy charged, without evidence but with great bluster, that there were 205 Communists in the State Department, the battle lines were drawn. Thus began, Pearson wrote, "the dreadful trail of McCarthy and the 'witch hunts'". As Pearson recalled with unusual bitterness, McCarthy was "one of the most horrible creatures of the twentieth century. I loathed and detested him."[59] Indeed he did. In May 1950, Pearson publicly denounced "the spectacle of innocent and respectable people being persecuted and almost destroyed by innuendo and unjustified suspicion". Such tactics would only help Communists whose aim was "to create fear, insecurity and suspicions" that "public officials" including even "the great Secretary of State himself" might be disloyal. He expressed the hope that the West would "refuse to throw overboard our liberty, remembering that communism is declining in free countries...". Its defeat would come from the preservation of liberty under law and "the eradication of social injustices". These words were scarcely likely to temper the anger of the more extreme American or Canadian anti-Communists. He did add, however, that Canada had given to the FBI the names of 163 Americans who had been mentioned in the investigation of the Soviet spy Klaus Fuchs. The FBI in turn gave the RCMP Canadian names. Among the names passed in 1950 was that of Herbert Norman.[60]

By this time China was "lost"; Alger Hiss had been convicted of perjury; and the Soviets had "the bomb", which the Klaus Fuchs spy case suggested traitors in the West had given them. The change was as sudden as it was fundamental. The prominent American sinologist John Fairbank realized that "people could no longer be taken at face value". When he told a board meeting of the American Institute of Pacific Relations that his fellow board member Alger Hiss should not be interrogated because everyone had the right to his own opinion, he was rebuked and had to offer a different formula: "Every man must be accountable for his own actions."[61] No group was held more accountable than intellectuals, particularly those who studied East Asia and who cheered Mao's march towards the Forbidden City.

Owen Lattimore, Norman's friend, an intellectual and a former American official in China, was called by McCarthy the "top Soviet spy" in 1950, and to many Americans the charge made sense. A biographer of Lattimore has sought to prove that he was a mere scapegoat. Yet, one reviewer noted, while there is no solid evidence that Lattimore was what McCarthy suggested he was, the close scrutiny of Lattimore's biography conveys "a feeling that Lattimore was fated to end up McCarthy's victim. There is [as one reads the book] a growing sense of horror that the destiny of this thoughtful but guileless man is going to be the inquisition."[62] The same seemed true of Herbert Norman. His life history had too many associations, friendships, commitments, and coincidences that seemed to lead him towards the inquisition. Mike Pearson was determined that such an inquisition would not try Herbert Norman. For him, the new standard Fairbank described would not obtain: what mattered were actions, not opinions.

In 1950, the FBI and the RCMP sifted through the pieces of the Norman puzzle and found some that did not exactly fit. When the RCMP prepared a report, Pearson asked to see it before it was sent to Washington. The RCMP had already sent it, and the FBI had more details on Norman to add to its bulging file. By 1950, Norman was a major figure in Canadian diplomacy. His Japanese expertise was highly prized at the war's end, and he went to Washington, where he served under Pearson briefly and then replaced him on the Far Eastern Advisory Commission. In Tokyo he evaluated Japanese leaders as part of an investigation of war crimes. Most important, he joined the staff of General Douglas MacArthur as MacArthur presided over the construction of the post-war Japanese government. In a position to influence policy, Norman supported liberal, democratic, and, it is certainly true, socialist and Communist forces in the reconstruction of Japan. He raised the suspicions of Major-General Charles Willoughby, MacArthur's intelligence officer, who was most unfavourably disposed to the Communists Norman had freed in 1945 and sympathetic to the military officers whom Norman wanted to try as war criminals.[63] It was Willoughby's complaints about Norman that brought him to the attention of the Senate committee investigating McCarthy's charges against the State Department. Norman was "named" by Iowa Republican Senator Bourke Hickenlooper, and his world was never the same.

He was ordered home in October. External was worried, not so much about Norman's background as about what "the Americans, particularly [FBI director] Hoover" might make of it.[64] Norman was examined by Arnold Heeney and Norman Robertson and by the RCMP. On the one hand, Pearson is criticized by Norman's favourable biographer, Roger Bowen, citing the feelings of Norman's wife, for not standing strongly behind his officer. On the other hand, Norman's strong critic, James Barros, rebukes Pearson for attempting to moderate the scrutiny of Norman and to restrict the information about Norman that was sent to the FBI.[65] In fact, Pearson was in New York at the time, thoroughly absorbed by the Korean War, concerned about American policy in East Asia, but more fearful than ever before about the threat of international Communism. He tried to hold back the RCMP report, but he did allow the department and the RCMP to examine Norman. It is difficult to imagine that he had any choice. He knew the force of McCarthyism and Hoover and realized that to defy them at that moment could end the influence he hoped to have on American policy. It was the RCMP that brought forth the evidence against Norman, but it was External that conducted the inquiry and maintained control of the final decision. Pearson insisted that the final decision on Norman's fate must remain with External. Like any police force that sees a court exonerate one whom it believes guilty, the RCMP was resentful. So was the FBI.

By the time Norman met his questioners in 1950, he knew that an answer like Donald Maclean's to his Foreign Office examiners in the 1930s about his Communist beliefs would be unacceptable. That year his friend Owen Lattimore, whose background was so similar to his own, showed how few the defences were against such charges. During the questioning, Norman took refuge in ambiguities, half-truths, and — in some cases, it seems — lies. He did emphasize that he had done nothing that in any way was disloyal to Canada and offered to resign if his past embarrassed the department. Professor Barros claims that the investigation was a "whitewash" and the Robertson-Heeney-Norman interview was "a discussion among gentlemen of breeding". The interview was indeed polite, but the questions were direct and, as Bowen points out, the experience must have been all the more difficult for Norman because of the atmosphere.[66] Robertson himself had been a socialist at Oxford in the 1920s, and on the strikers' side of the barricades in the historic 1926 British general strike. He knew what youthful passions were, and his own life was a lesson in how thoroughly they could be lost. The "Common Room" background of the three explains the tone, which was fundamentally different from that of the Senate committees that confronted Americans. Norman was very clearly considered innocent until proven guilty; and in 1950 there was certainly no evidence available that proved Norman guilty of disloyalty. The evidence against him was circumstantial and based principally on associations rather than actions.

Norman's interrogation was the direct result of the FBI's discovery of his name in Israel Halperin's notebook seized for the Gouzenko trials. Pearson had seen the notebook and, apparently, the references to Norman, Halperin's former classmate. George Glazebrook's "impression from [Pearson's] remarks at that time was that this was one of several innocent people mentioned in reference to addresses and social engagements".[67] The External and RCMP questioning of Norman had produced nothing more substantial. Coming as it did in the difficult winter of 1950-51, when even "the great Dean Acheson" was deemed a suspect by some Americans, it is scarcely surprising that Pearson accepted the finding that Norman was not a "security risk". In a meaningful and surely provocative gesture, he appointed Norman head of the American and Far Eastern Division, a position Norman assumed in January 1951.

That year relations with the Americans were bad, especially over American policy in East Asia. On April 10, Pearson gave his Toronto speech, in which he said, all too memorably for his American critics, that the days of "easy and automatic relations" between the United States and Canada were over and that Canada would not be "merely the echo of somebody else's voice".[68] Pearson had caught the attention of Americans who expected Cold War allies to be echoes, and they sharpened their focus on him and on Canada. On August 7, 1951, Karl Wittfogel, testifying before the Senate Subcommittee on Internal Security investigating McCarthy's charges, identified Herbert Norman as a member of a "communist study group". Immediately, the committee counsel, Robert Morris, read into the record the FBI information on Norman's ties with the Institute of Pacific Relations that had been leaked to him. Pearson reacted quickly, condemning Wittfogel's comments as false but even more the method in which the information became public. He said that "reports" about Norman's alleged sympathies had surfaced earlier but had been "carefully and fully investigated" and that Norman had been given "a clean bill of health".[69] The Canadian press reacted angrily to the subcommittee's attempt to snare a Canadian, and the Canadian government sent a protest note to the State Department deploring Congress's method. On the day the protest was sent, the subcommittee defiantly called Elizabeth Bentley to testify. She "named" Pearson, and Morris linked him tightly with Norman.[70]

The information leaked, as it always did. Pearson's knowledge of the absurdity of the charges against him and his anger about them hardened his attitude. The pressure on Norman intensified, however, particularly when, in May 1951, his Cambridge contemporaries Maclean and Burgess defected. These defections, the appearance of new information on Norman, and the very apparent American unwillingness to deal with Norman in his official capacity led to another investigation of his background in January 1952. This time Norman told more, admitting to being close to the Communists if not actually to possessing a Party card.[71] The 1950 investigation, which Pearson used to clear him, had obviously been incomplete. In the second investigation, George Glazebrook represented External, but the RCMP had two officers, Superintendent George McClellan and Inspector Terrence Guernsey. The questions were harder; the result less satisfactory. Norman tried to recapture the mood of the earlier investigation but failed. He gave Glazebrook an autographed copy of his book. Glazebrook thanked him warmly, but then said to Norman, "You know this will never go away." Norman agreed. On leaving, Guernsey, convinced then as later of Norman's guilt, said to Norman, "You certainly have loyal friends in External." After the investigation, Pearson read the record and concluded that, contrary to his own statement of August 1951, Norman had been a Communist at Cambridge, but that he remained a loyal Canadian public servant. He shifted Norman from the sensitive

American and Far Eastern Division to the relatively innocuous Information Division. He then appointed him high commissioner to New Zealand, telling him that the posting was "a renewed expression of the confidence of the Prime Minister and myself in you and your service to the country".[72]

Pearson, however, did not clarify his earlier statement exonerating Norman of Communist association in light of the new information that indicated the statement was untrue. His anger towards McCarthyism deepened. In 1953, Pearson's refusal to allow Gouzenko to go to Washington to testify irritated the Senate Internal Security Subcommittee. Simultaneously, Pearson denied that a Canadian official had provided the FBI with information that bore upon the guilt of Harry Dexter White, a senior American public servant. This angered both the subcommittee and the FBI. J. Edgar Hoover asked his deputies to "Let me have memo on what our files show on Pearson", and Bentley's charges against Pearson suddenly appeared in the press. Hoover was angry: he scrawled on one memorandum: "Then Pearson had better stop mouthing his half truths as pertain to the FBI." The FBI's strong ally, Colonel Robert S. McCormick of the *Chicago Tribune*, joined the chorus; it was on this occasion that he called Lester Pearson "the most dangerous man in the Western World".[73]

During the next year, 1954, the new medium of television let North Americans see the face of McCarthyism. In the Senate hearings, McCarthy attacked a young witness, then boorishly read a newspaper as the witness's lawyer, Joseph Welch, spoke. McCarthy interrupted rudely and regularly until suddenly Welch turned on McCarthy: "Let us not assassinate this lad further, Senator. You have done enough. Have you no sense of decency, sir? At long last, have you no sense of decency?" He walked out to thunderous applause. McCarthy ranted on, demonstrating, in James Reston's words, "with appalling clarity what kind of man he is".[74] The applause for Welch was loud in Canada, too. Like the evil wizard in childhood nightmares, McCarthy melted into the floor, and those who had been close to him when he performed his demagogic magic — the Kennedy brothers among them — quickly scampered away. The FBI stopped worrying about Pearson, and entries in his file ended — for a while.

Reflecting this quiescence, Pearson told Norman in April 1955 that he would not want to see him leave the foreign service for a university post, adding that "more responsible jobs" were awaiting him in Ottawa. At year's end he offered him Cairo, where Norman arrived just in time for the Suez Crisis.[75] Then in March 1957, after much praise for his work in that crisis, Norman learned that his name had come up once more in testimony to the Senate Subcommittee on Internal Security. John Emmerson, an old friend of Norman's, was asked by Robert Morris whether he had known Norman, "a Communist". Emmerson denied he knew that he was a Communist, but then unhelpfully added that Norman was currently Canada's ambassador to Egypt. Senator Jenner's ears pricked up: "You say he is now Canada's Ambassador to Egypt?" and Jenner wondered whether he was there when Donald Maclean was. Then Morris read into the record a list of charges against Norman. They quickly became public, and more followed.[76]

Pearson reacted angrily. The *Globe and Mail* reported that Pearson's denial of the charges "was as scathing a denunciation of the activities of a friendly foreign government as has ever been heard in the House of Commons". Pearson, the report continued, "is ordinarily the embodiment of calm caution", but not that day. He also pointed to the earlier security check and the press releases of 1951 and said that the government stood by them and "treated with contempt" this latest farrago of lies from Washington.[77]

Pearson's anger arose partly because the issue had been dormant so long, but partly because he was determined to smother the charges, which came at an exceedingly bad moment. He was working with the Americans, the British, the Israelis, the Egyptians, and the U.N. to bring a more lasting settlement to the Middle East. The day after he spoke in the House he was at the U.N. in New York emphasizing the importance of Egyptian co-operation with the United Nations Emergency Force. Here Norman could play a role.[78] From New York Pearson left with St. Laurent to meet Eisenhower and Macmillan in Bermuda to discuss a wide range of problems, the Middle East in particular. Norman was not among the topics covered, at least in the formal record. Mike returned to Ottawa just before Norman plunged to his death.

In the House of Commons, all parties deplored Norman's suicide. Diefenbaker asked whether Canada would cease to share information with the United States if congressional committees breached security so blatantly. Eisenhower expressed the hope that the incident could be forgotten and praised the fine Canadians who served under him — a classic Eisenhower *non sequitur*.[79] Privately, Eisenhower expressed sympathy but said he could not criticize Senator Jenner, who was "nuts", because such criticism was exactly what Jenner wanted. His comments, Heeney wrote, were not "satisfactory, I fear".[80] The *Washington Post* was blunter. Its April 5 editorial cartoon by Herblock showed death as a grinning skeleton pulling a folder labelled "Herbert Norman" from a file drawer labelled "Hearsay Reports".

The suicide put the committee on the defensive, but only briefly; then a counterattack began. The FBI file on Pearson was reopened; Morris dragged out the Bentley charges again and the fuller information about Norman found its way to opposition leader Diefenbaker and Social Credit leader Solon Low. A New York FBI agent reported that in the New York NBC studio Pearson had been "so violently uncomplimentary about the U.S. that one of the engineers threw the switch and started recording his comments prior to the broadcast". The tapes were to be located "because if they were it might well be possible to put Pearson in his proper light". Hoover asked for "complete summaries of all we have on Norman and Pearson".[81] The pot was beginning to boil; it threatened to overflow on Friday, April 12, in the House of Commons as Diefenbaker and Low probed to discover what the government really knew. Pearson returned to the House to answer the attacks. In doing so he admitted that Norman had associated with Communists and intimated that an RCMP report passed to the United

States had been a subcommittee source. The minister's statement, the journalist Harvey Hickey wrote, "was widely regarded as disappointing, raising more questions than it answered".[82] The questions remained unanswered; three days later, St. Laurent called a general election. Pearson thought the Norman affair would be an issue, but it was not.

Mike told Heeney that he had "been more upset by this sad affair than anything else in his experience". It had produced the worst "wave of anti-Americanism" that he had ever "experienced". The 1951 clearance bothered Pearson. "At that time," Heeney wrote, "Mike, with considerable courage, took the responsibility of underwriting Herb's loyalty without qualification though we could not in the nature of things *prove* him clean."[83] Obviously bothered, Pearson wrote to St. Laurent on April 15:

> We have been accused of not clearing this matter up in 1951. At that time, we affirmed and re-affirmed our loyalty in Mr. Norman as an official of the Government and as a patriotic Canadian, and for years afterward [there was] no reference to the matter in the United States. I do not agree that we should have made all the evidence available at that time. This is absolutely contrary to our way of dealing with security cases, a way which has been effective in protecting national interests and is just to individuals. In this case, disclosure would have focussed a great deal more attention on the incident than was actually given, and in the atmosphere of 1951, this would have been unjust and unfair to Mr. Norman, and might well have driven him out of the service.

He could not have answered simply "yes" or "no" to Diefenbaker's questions without giving out the evidence. More important, "If we made all the evidence now available, we would merely be raking up a lot of old insinuations and charges dealing with situations and activities which took place before Mr. Norman ever joined the Department and which did not affect his loyal service to the Department subsequently."[84]

He told Dick Casey, his good friend and Australia's foreign minister, that Norman was a "fine and sensitive person, but not tough enough to stand the innuendoes and insinuations" from Washington. He had tried to help matters by disclosing that Norman had "consorted" with Communists as a student, but it had not stopped his opponents from exploiting the information. He told Casey: "You have to be tough to live in the world today."[85]

Indeed, the world was becoming "tougher" for Lester Pearson, his government, and his friends. The Norman controversy illuminates a great deal about Pearson, the Liberal government, and their times.

If Norman had been an American diplomat, he would not have survived the first interrogation. His interrogator, the FBI, would have told its allies in Congress of his faults and, like Norman's friends Lattimore and John Service, he would have been hounded from the public service. In Canada, the police force was firmly controlled by the executive. So was the information about Norman: Pearson and his colleagues kept matters to themselves. Pearson told St. Laurent on the eve of the election that his purpose in keeping silent was to protect "our officials from slanderous implications". He spoke of the lack of "elementary decency" in the subcommittee's approach. He deplored the fact that the Norman affair might become subject to "party politics".[86]

These sentiments, even this language, were those of Pearson's age and of the St. Laurent government. They are, where individuals are concerned, most liberal, but they are not democratic. In Canada, the Cold War consensus on foreign policy, the rapid post-war economic growth, and an extraordinary similarity of background and viewpoint among Canadian élites suppressed the democratic forces that were behind the popular uprising of fear and democracy that McCarthyism represented in the United States. At the end of his memorable *See It Now* program on McCarthy, Edward R. Murrow told the audience that the fault of McCarthyism lay not in the stars but in "us". Decades later, James Barros points to "the gentlemen of breeding" who kept Norman's secrets to themselves. McCarthyism's failure in Canada may be the victory of élitist tendencies in Canadian political life in the post-war period.[87] It was also, however, the victory of civility and decency.

Pearson's subordinates in External spoke of their minister as "one of us".[88] There was the aura of the Common Room, where ideas are alive but the personal is absent. Like their British counterparts whom Lord Annan describes so brilliantly in *Our Age*, they were the secular heirs of spiritual parents and their lives bore that mark. The religion their fathers had served they had left behind. Most did not talk about this fundamental break with their parents' world, and Mike never did with Ed or Annie Pearson. There were also divisions between men and women, wives and husbands, that marked that age. The fishing trip was "off", Pearson told Harry Crerar in 1956: "As so often happens these days, the insistence of a wife on also being present threw a wrench in the works."[89]

But for Pearson's crowd, as for Annan's in Britain, their age was passing quickly. In 1955, Cold War pressures led to the creation of a unit to investigate the presence of homosexuals in positions requiring security. Maclean and Burgess had been homosexuals; homosexuality seemed a security risk. Pearson, Robertson, and Robert Bryce, who himself had known Norman and was subject to suspicion because of youthful socialist activities, accepted the need for such a unit. Robertson and Bryce supervised it, and its activities led to the "resignations" of several officers from External. In the minds of Oxbridge men, a man's private sexual preferences were his own business, even if the law at the time made certain preferences illegal. This "gentlemanly" stance was no longer possible, and all that could be done was to keep the "names" a secret. Suez, with its lies in Britain and the sense of betrayal in Canada, was also profoundly corrosive. Elites had failed, and their secrets seemed evasions or lies. In Canada, John Diefenbaker, a westerner and an outsider, tapped a democratic strain that the memory of wartime unity, the demands of Cold War consensus, and the magnificent achievements of the élite Canadian diplomatic corps and the post-war Canadian economy could not close off. For Pearson's crowd, as for Annan's, government had been by discussion. "Out of discussion came policy, a policy which was further modified by more discussion. Bargains and trade-offs were not considered signs of weakness, they were considered sensible compromises."[90] By 1957, this style was worn less comfortably by Canadians. The American alliance seemed less beneficent; Liberal paternalism less benevolent; and the charm of compromise less attractive. Canadians looked for a government more willing to heed other voices, a government with the air of the corner store, not the Senior Common Room. In June 1957, Canada elected John Diefenbaker. Lester Pearson endured to lead in the next age, but that age would never be his own, as the post-war age had been.

CHAPTER SIX

THE DUEL

I went to the polling booth in 1957 still very angered by the pipeline debate and by what the government had done, fully intending to vote CCF.... I even looked up the name of the CCF candidate in Ottawa West because there was very little campaigning. And I saw Mike's face just as I was about to put my "x" down. It was Mike's face, nobody's else, that came before me and said to me, "tch." And I said to myself, "I cannot vote against the party that has Mike Pearson."[1]

— Pauline Jewett, future Liberal and New Democratic MP

PAULINE JEWETT may have seen Mike's face when she marked her ballot in 1957, but for many other Canadians the memorable face of the 1957 election campaign was John Diefenbaker's. His intense eyes, powerful voice rich in staccatos and crescendos, and razor-edged wit starkly contrasted with Louis St. Laurent's lacklustre performance. When the campaign began, Liberal victory seemed certain. The March 1957 Gallup Poll, taken shortly before the election call, showed support for the Liberals at 46.8 per cent and for the Conservatives at only 32.9 per cent, a result very similar to the outcome of the 1953 general election (48.9 to 31.0) when the Liberals won 171 seats and the Tories only 51.[2] St. Laurent was so certain of victory that he did not bother to fill Senate vacancies and sent a letter to Kwame Nkrumah, Ghana's founding prime minister, telling him he looked forward to meeting him after the election.[3]

Pauline Jewett voted Liberal because she thought of Mike Pearson and wanted him to be St. Laurent's successor. The 1957 campaign made it clear that Pearson himself was willing to step into St. Laurent's shoes. A week before the June 10 election, the *Globe and Mail* reported that Pearson had been the busiest Liberal campaigner. He had travelled more than 15,000 miles and spoken in sixty constituencies. When he spoke in Manitowaning in Algoma East on June 2, it was the first time he had spoken in his own constituency in a month.[4] His return was overdue, for it was clear to an outside reporter that this time Pearson faced a challenge in Algoma East. His opponent was the mayor of Thessalon, former Liberal "Meet the Man" Mulligan. By the time Pearson returned a week before the vote, "Meet" had the riding "in a tizzy ... and observers talking about the possibility of an upset". A *Globe and Mail* reporter who accompanied Mike on the campaign trail said that ordinarily "his memory for names, his charm, his sobriquet (everyone regardless of politics follows the doings of our Mike), his ease with the little man", would assure him victory. It helped that Algoma East "has had more public works in the last eight years than any other riding in Canada". This time, however, uranium had created the new city of Elliot Lake with 13,000 residents, 1,800 of them in trailers. When the residents complained about the shortage of housing, the former civil servant blamed "remote bureaucrats [who] did not understand the particular needs of a distant area". After a stormy session, Pearson managed to have 135 applications for government-subsidized loans approved. The reporter noted that "whether this will save his bacon remains to be seen on June 10th".[5] Perhaps it did, for on June 10, Canadians saw Pearson elected while several of his colleagues fell — notably C.D. Howe, who was defeated by CCF candidate Douglas Fisher, and Walter Harris, for many the preferred successor to St. Laurent.

One of those who preferred Harris was Jack Pickersgill, who later suggested that St. Laurent was "almost" the Liberal Party's only asset in the 1957 campaign.[6] Opinion at the time does not support this view. The powerful *Winnipeg Free Press* criticized the old ministers of the government — a criticism that clearly included St. Laurent — but nonetheless urged a Liberal vote because it was a vote for a government that included a "young" man, sixty-year-old Lester Pearson, whose "ability far outshines anyone else in the party …". In analysing the campaign, John Meisel noted how the Liberals used Pearson's "undoubted success … as an excellent example of how difficult it would be to replace the Liberal cabinet…". *Le Devoir*, less than a week before the election, pointed out that most Liberal ministers had to stay close to their constituencies because of unhappy voters. Pearson, however, was said to have had "les succès oratoires" comparable to the considerable oratorical successes of John Diefenbaker. Alone among the government ministers, Pearson had reason to rejoice in the campaign, which for him had been "un véritable triomphe", even in Victoria, where the voters were very accurately described as "les plus impérialistes du pays…". St. Laurent had shown it would be his last election, and in the campaign "M. Pearson se signale comme le plus fort candidat à sa succession."[7]

The campaign did put many in Pearson's political debt — and these debts would bear interest at a later date. As one reporter who accompanied him said, "he … played the party wheelhouse — with a workload that would kill a horse". He had "taken it all with a grin", but the exigencies of constituency politics and the disorganization of the Liberal campaign did try his patience: "Arriving from London at Malton at 9:23 a.m., no one met him and he was left to pace the waiting room for half an hour like an immigrant, just off the ship. When W.A. Robinson, candidate in Simcoe East, finally showed up, he greeted the minister airily: 'You big shots are always late, so I figured it for a quarter to ten.'"[8] By the time Robinson met the "big shot" minister, the Liberal campaign was limping badly. In fact, Pearson's "success" in Victoria was an attempt to "repair the damage" done by an uninspiring St. Laurent speech in the same city.[9] The worst moment came on June 7 at Toronto's Maple Leaf Gardens, where party organizers brought together the Ontario candidates with the leader to celebrate the "Peace, Prosperity and Security" that St. Laurent and his party had bestowed on the suddenly unappreciative nation. The day started badly for the Pearsons. Mike campaigned that morning in Chapleau in Algoma East. The party chartered a small plane to bear the Pearsons to Toronto. Fog made the take-off difficult, and once the plane was in the air the fog thickened. The pilot assured the two passengers that they need not worry, he was following a valley he knew well. At the moment of reassurance, Mike recalled, "a hill appeared right ahead of us. We must have chosen the wrong valley. Up and away — barely." The rest of the flight was bumpy and frightening until they came to stormy Toronto. "Airsick, battered, and a shade bewildered," Pearson was whisked from Toronto Island Airport to the platform at the front of the Gardens. The hecklers outshouted the faithful; St. Laurent looked and sounded very much the "old man" the hecklers declared he was. A young boy of fifteen came forward to the platform and, before a dumbfounded prime minister, tore up a Liberal poster bearing St. Laurent's photograph. Liberal organizers rushed forward to hustle the protester away but succeeded in knocking him down the steps and making his head crash into the cement floor. The hushed crowd focused on the unconscious boy, and St. Laurent stared in speechless consternation. Three days later the Liberals lost,[10] and the Tories took 23 of 24 seats in the Toronto-Hamilton area.*

---

* Only in northern Ontario did the Liberals maintain a lead (9 to 3). In the Toronto-Hamilton urban concentration the Conservatives took 51.4 per cent of the popular vote (39.8 in 1953) to 19.8 for the Liberals (39.9 in 1953). National results were:

Liberals	105	(40.9% of popular vote)
Conservatives	112	(38.9%)
CCF	25	(10.7%)
Social Credit	19	(6.6%)
Others	4	(2.8%)

The Liberals' higher popular vote is explained by its high totals in Quebec (57.6 per cent compared with only 31.1 per cent for the Conservatives). See Peter Regenstreif, *The Diefenbaker Interlude: Parties and Voting in Canada* (Don Mills: Longmans, 1965), 32.

The defeat was a shock. So accustomed were Canadians to Liberal governments that *Maclean's* went to press with an editorial that began: "For better or for worse, we Canadians have once more elected one of the most powerful governments ever created by the free will of a free electorate...."[11] The Liberal government once was powerful, but by June 1957 what voters saw was a prime minister who, in Peter Newman's memorable image, "Like a faulty radio ... would have his good and bad days, sometimes fully aware of the events around him, at other times fading out completely, and viewing the world with the unknowing, glassy stare of the very old".[12] To this tired presentation, Diefenbaker responded with fiery speeches, replete with dramatic gestures, crescendos, pauses, and diminuendos, which, in the words of John Meisel's excellent academic study of the election, conveyed effectively a vision of a country "on the verge of greatness if it could only get rid of its old and inadequate government". A vote for Diefenbaker would ally a voter "to those who were creating a dazzlingly bright and promising future".[13] Howe and Jimmy Gardiner, both in their seventies and both members of the King cabinet in 1935, were easy targets. St. Laurent's and the government's reluctance to support the south Saskatchewan dam hurt Gardiner and western Liberals badly. It became clear that "the prairies' most aggressive defender no longer counted for as much in national attention or decision-making as he once had...".[14] Pearson himself seemed to feel Howe was the cause of many of the government's problems, and some of Howe's campaign gaffes were egregious.* But it was somewhat unfair to blame Howe, for he proved invaluable in raising campaign funds, including those for Algoma East. Moreover, Pearson

---

* The most famous occurred when he was confronted by a western farmer whom he gruffly rebuffed with a finger in the farmer's midriff and the comment: "It looks like you've been eating pretty well under a Liberal government." The satire *My Fur Lady* brought down the house with such lines as "Uncle Louis, Uncle Louis, tell us what to do and Howe". See Robert Bothwell and William Kilbourn, *C.D. Howe* (Toronto: McClelland and Stewart, 1979), 325, 325n.

himself bore some responsibility for the defeat.

Like Jack Pickersgill, with whom he shared deep respect and affection for their leader, Pearson could not publicly blame St. Laurent for the Liberal loss.[15] He was also aware that some of St. Laurent's problems derived from foreign policy and that St. Laurent had been Pearson's most vigorous defender. Indeed, St. Laurent's most famous outburst — the angry statement that "the era when the supermen of Europe could govern the whole world is coming pretty close to an end" — occurred in a debate in which Pearson's work at Suez was being bitterly criticized by the Tories.[16] In the campaign, hecklers in English Canada taunted St. Laurent with "supermen, supermen". Polling data from 1957 do not show unequivocally that Pearson's work during the Suez Crisis hurt the Liberal Party. Nevertheless, John Meisel's thorough and objective assessment of the campaign does suggest that the Liberal cause was hurt by the charge that the Liberals had "knifed" Britain and France in the back.[17] The Tories regularly pointed to Pearson's tarnished halo. The most bitter comment came from the redoubtable mayor of Ottawa, Charlotte Whitton, who pointed to the housing problem in Elliot Lake in Algoma East and commented: "It's too bad Nasser couldn't help Mike Pearson to cross Elliot Lake when Mr. Pearson did so much to help him along the Suez Canal."[18]

Underlying this criticism and implicit in Diefenbaker's campaign was the belief that the Liberals and, in particular, Pearson had embraced the United States too warmly and had distanced Canada from Britain and the Commonwealth. Walter Gordon's Royal Commission on Canada's Economic Prospects had presented its preliminary report in December 1956, and its mildly expressed concern about the post-war growth of American investment in Canada permitted John Diefenbaker to claim that the Liberal government was allowing Canada to "inexorably drift into economic continentalism".[19] Gordon reflected a broadening stream of anti-Americanism that swelled slightly at Suez and briefly became a torrent when Herbert Norman leapt to his death. The U.S. Embassy in Ottawa was disturbed by the Canadian mood. It even

reported on a lecture on John A. Macdonald given by historian
Donald Creighton, who had been troubled since the late 1940s by
the "Americanization" of Canada but, like so many others, had
avoided expressing his profound doubts about the post-war American alliance. The embassy reported to the State Department on
March 13, 1957, that Professor Creighton's lecture was "purportedly
historical" but was, in fact, "obviously political" and anti-American.
Creighton had referred to U.S. bases in Canada as a "primitive
form of military imperialism", a view that no Canadian political
party, "excluding the Communists", had espoused. The report continued: "While it can be expected that in an election year it may be
considered expedient for Conservative politicians to raise the bogey
of 'American domination', the Embassy is surprised to find this tack
adopted by a man of unquestioned intelligence who is held in the
highest regard in Canadian academic circles. Whether this is a
portent of things to come during the election campaign is too early
to tell". As a portent, it was accurate.[20]

In fact, Pearson himself was angry with the Americans and
shared some of Gordon's concerns.[21] And yet the American alliance
was the cornerstone of his post-war foreign policy. He was deeply
committed to the defence of the West against the threat that he
believed Soviet Communism represented, and he knew that the
defence depended upon an American commitment to Europe.
Raised on a fear of American isolationism, profoundly thankful for
the triumph of American internationalism in the post-war years,
aware that, historically, waves of anti-Americanism had defeated
Liberal governments, Pearson tended to keep his concerns and fears
to himself. Occasionally, his frustrations burst through this reserve,
as in April 1951 when he angered the Americans by criticizing their
East Asian policy; or, again, when Americans harassed Herbert
Norman. Normally, he kept his concerns private or expressed them
only to friends like Heeney or Gordon. George Glazebrook, who
had known Pearson well and who had shared Pearson's British-
imperial enthusiasms in the early 1920s, perceptively said that
Pearson's dilemma was finding a way to oppose the Americans

without being anti-American. By June 1957, maintaining that balance was difficult, and the Liberals felt the consequences as English-Canadian Protestants, led by the university-educated, responded to the nationalist sirens sounded by John Diefenbaker.[22]

After the election, C.D. Howe, who went to bed on election night after he was defeated but before the final returns were in,* grumbled to the American ambassador that it was a good time for the Liberals to be defeated.[23] For Pearson, the defeat seemed at first a tragedy, but upon mature consideration he too realized that his position had been growing more difficult. Nationalist questions about Canada's post-war alignments paralleled American frustrations with Canadians. At one level these became evident in the Norman affair when American congressmen spread innuendoes about the Canadians' and, in particular, Pearson's lack of concern about the Communist threat. Sputnik's launch in 1957 and the pathetic failure of the Americans to toss a grapefruit-sized radio into space to match the Soviet triumph reinvigorated Cold War fears, as did, more legitimately, the brutal Soviet suppression of the Hungarian rebellion. The government also faced hard decisions about air defence in the wake of Soviet advances in long-range bombers and their tests of intercontinental missiles. Wisely, the Liberals put off the decision until after the election, but it could not be long delayed.[24] And it must be added that Pearson himself no longer had the cachet that had allowed him a rare freedom and influence in London and Washington. Suez had severed many ties with London and left distrust between Britons and Canadians at the highest level. In Washington, the doubts about Pearson arose during Korea and grew in its turbulent international aftermath. Livingston Merchant, the American ambassador in Ottawa between 1956 and 1958, though

---

*His loss was all the more bitter because he was defeated "by 'a young Socialist librarian' whose histrionics on TV proved remarkably effective". That "socialist librarian" was Douglas Fisher, who later became a prominent television personality. Ambassador Livingston Merchant to Julian Nugent, June 18, 1957. State Dept. Records 742.00/6-1157 (National Archives).

outwardly very friendly to Pearson, told Acheson, who was also friendly in personal contacts, that he, like Acheson, no longer had great faith in Pearson: "I recall one experience with him at Geneva in the spring of 1954 as well as several since which forced a radical revision of the estimate I had earlier formed on the Embassy-State playing grounds…" when the State Department baseball team confronted the Canadians led by their athletic and able ambassador, Mike Pearson.[25] By 1957, those days were gone, never to return in Mike Pearson's lifetime.

Acheson may have thought that Pearson conciliated too often, listened to those he should not, and, worst of all, chased idealistic will-o'-the-wisps when hard reality faced the West. But Pearson with his faults was preferable to John Diefenbaker. One of the first post-election letters Pearson received came from Acheson, who urged Pearson "to plunge into the task of leadership which I know you don't want but which is now plainly your destiny". In his reply, Pearson made it clear that he had already decided to follow Acheson's advice. Maryon, he added, "has been converted by the national defeat into a party combatant and is becoming quite reconciled to a life of opposition poverty and political conflict".[26]

If the loss saved Pearson from difficult times and decisions, it also cleared his path to the Liberal leadership. Walter Harris lost his own constituency. Robert Winters, a promising young minister who appealed to the Liberals' business constituency, also went down to defeat. Paul Martin won his Windsor seat, but his potentially powerful base in southwestern Ontario was fatally weakened by the loss of most members in the area. The parliamentary Liberal party after June 10 was overwhelmingly a French-Canadian party. Of its 105 members, 62 were from Quebec; 13 others were in constituencies outside Quebec where francophones made up a large percentage of the electorate.[27] Mike actually thought the number was higher (80), and he saw it as a reason for the Liberal government not to prolong its tenure, citing the minority situation. When the distinguished Queen's University economist (and passionate Liberal) Clifford Curtis recommended "hanging on", Pearson politely but firmly disagreed, pointing to the overwhelmingly francophone character of the Liberal caucus and the need in any Liberal cabinet to appoint francophones as the ministers from Manitoba and Alberta because the only Liberal representatives from those two provinces were francophone.[28] St. Laurent agreed that the government must resign. It did, and on June 21, 1957, John Diefenbaker took office.[29]

St. Laurent remained as leader through the summer and through increasing demands that he step down. In the meantime, Pearson's friends, especially those in the press — Grant Dexter, Bruce Hutchison, George Ferguson, and Blair Fraser — urged him to grasp the challenge and worked to ensure that he succeeded. Their work now, Grant Dexter privately said, was to "help Mike shine".[30] In August 1957 Hutchison wrote to Mike from his Vancouver Island "camp", as Canadians and Americans used to call rustic retreats, where he had "no decent paper, no typist and no ideas ... only rain and a diminishing woodpile". He did have something to say, however: "the sooner you are on the bridge the better for the party and the nation." His "only clear purpose ... in politics [was] to see you in the Liberal leadership and then in the East Block". He didn't even want a senatorship to remain not only "an axeman" but also a "Mikeman".[31]

On Labour Day, September 2, St. Laurent's son, Renault, called Mike and asked that he and Lionel Chevrier come to visit their leader at his summer home in St. Patrick on the lower St. Lawrence. Chevrier and Pearson journeyed to St. Patrick on September 4. They were met by Renault and his brother-in-law, Mathieu Samson, at the Quebec station. On the trip to St. Patrick, Samson and Renault told them how depressed St. Laurent was and how much he wanted to resign. Nevertheless, he worried that a resignation would be interpreted as "running away from duty". Upon their arrival, Pearson and Chevrier (whose presence would negate charges that the anglophone Pearson had forced St. Laurent to resign) were shocked at the sight of a weary, dejected, and unresponsive St. Laurent. A few days before, St. Laurent had told the press he would not resign and that he would travel to Ottawa to meet the caucus for the fall season. It was clear to his family and to the visitors that such a course was impossible. Renault asked Pearson to draft a statement indicating that St. Laurent wished to resign as leader but would stay on, if health permitted, until the new leader was chosen. Pearson worked on the text past midnight and showed it to Chevrier the next morning. They then gave it to St. Laurent, who "stared uneasily at the draft, at times reading, at other times merely brooding".[32] Then, finally, he approved it. They decided to release it on Friday, lest "nasty people" suggest that Pearson and Chevrier had forced their leader to resign. Chevrier recalled that St. Laurent hesitated to resign until Pearson promised he would seek the leadership. For whatever reason, modesty or forgetfulness, the request is not mentioned in Pearson's memoirs, but there can be little doubt the promise was made.[33]

"'Mike' Pearson Heavy Favourite As Next Leader", the *Toronto Daily Star*'s headline declared the day after St. Laurent's retirement. Mike was already at a Young Liberal meeting at Presqu'île Point, where he encountered his two most likely opponents, Walter Harris and Paul Martin. The *Star* barely noted the presence of Martin and Harris but gave full coverage of Pearson's call for "a charter of the new liberalism of 1957 — not 1857". The Young Liberals greeted him with "wild enthusiasm", a standing ovation, and a prolonged chant of "We want Mike, we want Mike". Pearson, it was reported, had the support not only of Liberal youth but also of "nearly two-thirds" of the Liberal MPs who had sat in the last House of Commons and who could be expected to exercise their influence in support of Mike in the constituencies.[34]

Howe let it be known that he wanted Mike; and Jimmy Sinclair, the most outspoken and unpredictable of St. Laurent's ministers, declared that Pearson would succeed St. Laurent. The influential Jack Pickersgill called on Walter Harris, his closest friend in the government, and told him that "Pearson was our only hope" and that he intended to support him.[35] Harris decided not to run. Paul Martin did, but the journalists quickly claimed that his chances were bad, not because he lacked political skills and support but because the party had to choose an English Canadian and, preferably, a Protestant to recover the dozens of seats they had lost in the English Protestant bastions in Ontario and the Maritimes. There Pearson would be the favourite. John Bird, a journalist usually thought of as Conservative, saw only Pearson's age (sixty) and his lack of training as weaknesses. Otherwise, Bird was clearly captivated by Pearson's record and style. His comments, which came before the award of the Nobel Peace Prize, are a good reflection of the coverage he received and of the emotions that carried Pearson to victory in the January 1958 election: "Mike Pearson's best claim to the leadership is not his undoubted popularity, his common touch. It is that indefinable thing called 'size.' He is a big-time man, big enough to be a leader. As world statesman, Pearson has already shown that the home town boy can bat with the best of them in the biggest league of all. And Canadians like their prime minister to be a man they can be proud of in any company."[36] Indeed they did, and do, and the Nobel Peace Prize, announced in October 1957, assured Pearson of the victory. As momentum thrust him forward others clung to him, not for the ride so much as for the chance to influence his direction.

Canadians and Liberals knew very little about what direction Pearson wanted to move. He told the young Liberals at Presqu'île that Liberalism must take the middle road. The *Toronto Daily Star* mildly rebuked him, saying that the middle of the road "is not the best position from which to win the race. The shorter course is in the inside of the track — the left side, left of the Conservative runners." In fact, few knew where Pearson stood, and that was an advantage. Liberals and others rightly regarded Paul Martin as being on the left. The crusty and conservative C.D. Howe used to taunt him by calling him "my Communist friend", and Howe quickly made it clear to Martin that he would not consider supporting him for the leadership. Pearson, in fact, was one of the few in the cabinet upon whom Martin could count for strong support when he presented programs as Health and Welfare minister, but because Pearson rarely spoke on domestic issues and was often absent, he did not acquire the reputation of being among the few left-Liberals of the cabinet.[37] Certainly one could not discern his views on domestic questions from the speeches that he gave in the House of Commons or elsewhere in the months before the January 1958 leadership convention. He said almost nothing in the House on the social legislation of the Diefenbaker government, but concentrated on such questions as the "careless and quick" North American Air Defence Agreement and the Conservatives' notion of diverting Canadian trade to Great Britain. In the case of the latter, he showed his hand slightly by describing Britain's offer of free trade to Canada as a proposal that "has not been exceeded in economic matters for many years in this country". Diefenbaker's proposal of "shifting" trade from the United States to Britain he regarded as "protectionist". He emphasized, however, that he "did not favour the old 19th century idea of free trade, but the freest possible trade with a minimum of restrictions and on the widest possible multilateralist basis".[38] Free trade if possible, but possibly not free trade.

This elusiveness on issues other than international ones was noticed. One journalist commented ten days before the leadership convention of January 14-16, 1958, that if Pearson was chosen leader he would be "something new for Canadian public life: a major party leader with virtually no previous record — good or bad — in domestic politics". The award of the Nobel Prize on October 14, 1957, seemed to assure a victory that already was very likely.[39] The front pages of newspapers were filled with tributes to Pearson. In Toronto, which had gone strongly Conservative, Walter Gordon used the non-partisan Canadian Institute of International Affairs to organize a dinner for 2,000 people to honour Pearson, and Toronto Mayor Nathan Phillips declared December 19 "Lester Pearson Day". Pearson's speech to the gathering was broadcast on local CBC television, as were the tributes by politicians, diplomats, and, as Gordon put it, "assorted Cardinals, Rabbis, Bishops, Moderators and various lesser fry".[40]

The *Toronto Daily Star*, which was very much influenced by Gordon and had already backed Pearson, described how "the former Toronto newsboy and son of a Methodist minister" accepted "humbly" the description of Pearson by U.N. General Assembly president Leslie Munro as "the great Canadian who is one of the foremost citizens of the world".[41] It was wonderful politics, all the more so because it was cloaked in non-partisan garb. Paul Martin, who had officially declared his candidacy a few days before,* must have known that he had no chance. At least Pearson's backers believed he should have known: Martin, they complained, was actually trying to influence delegates and organize support for himself by telephoning. It was not the kind of "gentlemanly play" that had been anticipated, and Mike was told to "ask people to speak to the delegates in their parts of the country".[42] Others, including former Windsor mayor Senator David Croll and Jack Pickersgill, criticized Martin's overly aggressive campaign.[43] Martin's memoirs reveal more than a touch of bitterness when he comments that "some of Mike's cronies in the press sought to put forward the view that he was just sitting back and leaving the politicking to me, [but] this was far from true". Contemporary accounts and records (but not Gordon's or Pearson's memoirs) confirm Martin's view. While Pearson's campaign was deliberately low key, it had buttons, hoopla, and subtle but effective pressure. Moreover, it rested upon a clever media strategy that generated enormous free publicity.[44] True, the formal structures were weak, and Keith Davey is correct in his claim that there was an appalling "lack of organisation" and an "ezey-ozey way of doing things" at the convention itself. Yet it is equally true, as Maurice Lamontagne recalled, that "there was no need to have a formal organisation".[45] The die was cast and, besides, in those days "gentility", as Martin dubbed it, brought its own political rewards.

The Liberals gathered late on a cold January fourteenth at Ottawa's exhibition grounds, where the Coliseum, popularly known as the "cow palace" because of its bovine function during the exhibition, was decorated with Liberal red and white bunting and

---

*Pearson officially declared his candidacy in Algoma East on December 4 in the same hall where he was nominated as a candidate in 1948. He left six days later for Oslo.

photographs of Laurier, King, and St. Laurent. So effective was the refitting that "the ripe odor of the farm yard has been displaced with sweet smelling odor of a disinfectant — or almost".[46] There were four candidates, but one of them, Mayor Don Mackay of Calgary, withdrew and supported Pearson. Reverend H.L. Henderson of Portage la Prairie barely received enough support to be nominated. Martin's campaign was feisty, but ultimately futile. The Quebec delegation, guided by Pearson's former parliamentary assistant, Jean Lesage, opted for the English Protestant, Pearson, and not the French Catholic, Martin. When the vote was taken on January 16, Pearson had 1,074 votes and Martin only 305. The "smiling, boyish looking" Pearson promised he would travel across Canada to meet as many Canadians as possible, and Martin pledged complete loyalty to the new leader.[47] The party's platform shifted to the left, mainly because John Diefenbaker's Conservatives were passing some important social legislation and were crowding the political centre.

The convention's mood influenced its immediate aftermath. Pearson's acceptance speech, Grant Dexter of the *Winnipeg Free Press* wrote, was hard-hitting and promised "vigorous opposition" that could lead to an election soon. He reported that the convention generated enthusiasm for a full-fledged assault on the Diefenbaker government.[48] Others, including Martin and Jimmy Gardiner, counselled caution, as did the editorial page of the *Free Press*. Pearson listened neither to his veteran colleagues nor to Dexter and Bruce Hutchison, who also believed that forcing a quick election would be unwise. On January 14, before the convention opened, Mike had met with his most enthusiastic journalistic supporters, Dexter and Bruce Hutchison. When they suggested that a less aggressive strategy should be followed, Pearson curtly said: "It's no use, Grant. I've made up my mind. We're going to force an election. That's final." The convention, of course, reinforced his aggressiveness, and his acceptance speech promised that the government would fall "and soon".[49]

Pearson's bold stance faced a test on January 20 when the minister of finance was to make a motion to resolve the House into a

Committee of Supply. On that occasion it was usual for the opposition leader to move an amendment to the supply motion; his doing
so is deemed to be a want of confidence. The party's decisions on
the question of tactics, the weariness of Pearson after the four nights
of convention, and the absence of many veteran politicians on the
weekend following the convention left Mike to his own devices.
Aware that he had to maintain the "fighting stance" in the
Commons that he had promised at the convention, he spoke to Jack
Pickersgill, who was far more knowledgeable than he about the
workings of Parliament and politics. Pickersgill, who worried about
forcing an election so early, came up with what he thought was an
ingenious device. Pearson would harshly condemn the government,
especially for its economic policy, which was bringing a recession to
Canada, but would then demand that the government resign rather
than call an election. The governor general could then call upon the
Liberals to form a government. "Then the Socialists would vote
against the motion, an election would be avoided, and the Liberals
could not be accused of cowardice."[50]

The Liberals and Pearson were not accused of cowardice, but of
arrogance and stupidity.* When he moved, seconded by St.
Laurent, that the failure of the Canadian economy required the
restoration of "a government pledged to implement Liberal policies", the jeers of the government bench accompanied guffaws from
the Press Gallery. Mike sat down and knew at once that his "first
attack on the government had been a failure, indeed a fiasco". In his
own words, Diefenbaker "tore me to shreds".[51]

Diefenbaker spoke for two hours and three minutes, taunting
Pearson: "On Thursday there was shrieking defiance. On Monday
there was shrinking indecision." He waved a document entitled
"The Canadian Economic Outlook for 1957" that showed, Diefenbaker claimed, that the government had known then that there
would be an economic downturn. It was a confidential report that a

---

*Mary Macdonald and Maryon advised against the Pickersgill strategy, but most of
those Pearson consulted thought it "very clever". He did not consult widely.

200

prime minister had no business revealing, but this breach of etiquette mattered little that day to Diefenbaker. It did later, when its author, Mitchell Sharp, resigned from the public service and joined with the Liberals to topple Diefenbaker.[52]

The disaster became a débâcle after Diefenbaker called an election on February 1, 1958, for March 31. "Dief's" first campaign address was a triumph, the Liberal *Winnipeg Free Press* reported. His audience of Young Progressive Conservatives were "on the edge of their chairs as he played upon their emotions like a master".[53] So was Canada by the end of the campaign, as the electricity of that first meeting passed through political halls in every province. The Liberal campaign faltered badly. Pearson asked Senator John Connally to be the campaign manager in English Canada. His later recollection was that he was "horrified" because he "had no touch or feel for this kind of thing". He told the Quebec manager, Charles G. (Chubby) Power: "Chubby, this is a terrible thing to have happen to the party, because I don't really know this party. I know a lot of people in it; but most of the people I know outside of Ottawa are the Members." And there were not as many members as before, and they soon found that they could not leave their constituencies to help others.[54] Pearson pledged tax reductions, social programs, efficient government, but to no avail. The Gallup Poll in March showed that the Diefenbaker appeal cut across party lines, geographic divisions, and ethnic rivalries.[55] Pearson tried to make an issue of the fact that Diefenbaker had called a winter election, but that only served to remind voters that the Liberals at their convention had demanded an election. Pearson's crowds were smaller, often silent, and quick to leave the hall. The high moment of the campaign for Pearson was a rally at the University of Toronto where he said he could not compete with the "agitated eloquence" of his opponent and tried a "quiet reasoned approach". He admitted Liberal sins of the past and "the more hardened and cynical of his followers" were heard to "groan aloud". He left pleased with his performance, but the crowd was small, and most students and most university-educated people wanted John Diefenbaker (53.1 to 26.6

per cent).[56] At the University of Manitoba, the boos for Mike Pearson were louder than the cheers. The meeting was unhappy. After the meeting, at Herbert Moody's home, Maryon was grumpy and, to her brother's horror, turned her sharp tongue upon Tom Kent, the editor of the *Winnipeg Free Press*, and left the articulate young Englishman speechless.[57]

The campaign was not what Maryon and Mike had imagined it would be when, a year before, they decided he should seek the Liberal leadership. Jack Pickersgill knew that his Newfoundland seat was safe and scurried back to his Rockcliffe home to cast a vote. He met Pearson on election day and said: "Mike, you haven't any illusion that you're going to win this election?" Mike answered: "None whatever. I hope we might get about a hundred seats."[58] They didn't. On March 31, election night, Mike's friends "Charlie" Lynch and Blair Fraser, who hosted election coverage on television, watched in amazement as the Tories swept the country, leaving only 49 Liberals, 8 CCF, and no Social Credit. The Tory slogan was "follow John", and most of Canada did.

That night Mike, a slightly wilted carnation in his lapel, watched the result at Ottawa's Château Laurier after a supper of oyster stew. He kept his sense of humour as he quipped to a friend that "the oysters were wonderful" but "the television show was about the worst I ever saw". The night's best line belonged to Maryon, who mournfully watched Liberals fall everywhere but in Mike's Algoma East: "We've lost everything. We even won our own seat."[59]

The taste of defeat was bitter, even when laced with wit. Diefenbaker's Conservatives had gained the greatest electoral victory in Canadian history. In Quebec, the Liberals' bastion that had withstood Toryism in June 1957, Diefenbaker's appeal proved irresistible as the Conservatives took 50 of the province's 75 seats. It was a rout, and its extent was Mike's fault. As he realized what was happening to him and the Liberal Party, he attacked what he called "the cult of personality, whether expressed in terms of dictatorship or demagoguery". Diefenbaker's style was demagogic, but his promises in 1958 were, in fact, more cautious than Pearson's, who promised a state medicare scheme, a national pension plan, and a tax cut. These promises seemed desperate bribes to an electorate tired and distrustful of Liberalism, while Diefenbaker's "forensic eloquence shone brightest in his word pictures of the future which awaited Canada with a Conservative government providing the physical means, mainly roads and railways, of developing the far north". Audiences shared his vision and his scorn for Pearson's "igloo to igloo" description of the sinews that would bind the North together. Mike simply seemed to lack imagination — and political education. Pearson, the veteran columnist Richard Jackson noted, "hasn't discovered yet that people want to be entertained as well as informed", and that politics were "also fun and games for the campaign and the crowds". The last week in Kingston, the Pearson cavalcade slowed at a traffic light, and a friendly bystander remarked: "Mr. Pearson, you are a very nice man, but go home, you're wasting your time."[60]

After the election, Mike and Maryon had to decide whether Mike, who would turn sixty-one on April 23, was wasting his own and his party's time by remaining as leader. There was really no choice: he saw no alternative leader and was not willing to enter history as the Liberal Party's greatest failure. He would stay and face the considerable challenge of rebuilding his party. The task seemed awesome. He had performed poorly wherever he tried to throw political punches, as in his first parliamentary speech, his weak contribution to the pipeline debate, or his fighting acceptance speech at the Liberal convention. His avoidance of "domestic issues" and clear preference for the non-partisan platform throughout his years in the House of Commons had hurt him badly in his first campaign as leader. But his problems were not merely oratorical and stylistic. His speeches, actions, and private papers reflect a confusion about what he thought his party should be and who should help him shape it.

There were competing visions of what the party should be, and each reflected a different influence upon Pearson. Each has left its mark upon the interpretation of the rebuilding of the Liberal Party after the deluge that swept away so much of the old structures.

Three distinct interpretations can be identified. The first appears in the work of Bruce Hutchison, Canada's most eminent journalist of the 1950s, who told his friend Dean Acheson in 1963 that he was "doing his best to make Mike Pearson prime minister...".[61] He and his close friends Grant Dexter, George Ferguson, and Max Freedman, and other anglophone journalists like Blair Fraser and Kenneth Wilson, were charmed by Pearson's personality, animated by his internationalist vision, and committed to the optimism of post-war Canadian nationalism. Hutchison and his colleagues were probably the major force in explaining and promoting Pearson in his years as foreign minister. They shared his vision but, in the end, he did not advance theirs. Still, they admired the man. In 1990, when asked simply what he thought of Lester Pearson, Bruce Hutchison quickly declared, "I loved the guy".[62]

Hutchison and his friends did not cease to love the guy with "the beefy figure, the round pink face and boy's grin", and the "high-pitched voice, faint lisp and corny jokes", but they were much worried about their protégé as he stepped down from the lofty heights of diplomacy to the bargaining and battering of everyday politics.[63] In October 1957, Grant Dexter told *Winnipeg Free Press* editor Tom Kent, whom owner Victor Sifton had brought over from England's *The Economist*, that the economist John Deutsch had had a talk with Mike about domestic politics. Deutsch had told him that a Liberal leader must be with the "little guy" and against the "interests". He warned Mike against protection, combines, and "grants", by which he meant social assistance programs. The right policy was freer trade and non-discrimination, the classic liberal choices. When Mike inquired about agriculture, "Johnny bulked floor prices, parity prices, quota controls etc. all together. These, he said, must be avoided because they were bad politically and economically. They were stupid on all counts." John Deutsch, a close friend of Hutchison and Dexter and a fellow western Canadian, had set out the tenets of the Liberalism they cherished, a faith that began in Manchester in the nineteenth century and flourished in the twentieth century on the grain-rich prairies of North America.[64] The core beneath its hardy husk was a scepticism of distant, big governments and the "interests" that swarmed around them.

Hutchison, so genuinely fond of Pearson, did not blame him for the 1958 disaster. He told Dexter that "Mike would have been overwhelmed no matter what he did in the campaign. If he walked across the waters of the Ottawa River, if he had turned water into wine or fed the multitudes on loaves and fishes, indeed if he had performed Resurrection, he still would have been defeated...". Nevertheless, he did have "deep misgivings" about the Liberal Party in the future. He suspected that the Liberals, in response to Tory protectionism, "will swing sharply to the Left, in the direction of more welfare, more Danegeld, more Keynes and more of everything I don't like".[65] This swing would "devalue" both the Canadian currency and Canadian politics. Dexter and Hutchison had already identified Walter Gordon and his Toronto associates as the force pushing Mike towards the Liberalism they did not like. And they were right.

Walter Gordon had not always been on the left. In the 1940s, as a wartime special assistant to C.D. Howe, he had mocked Liberal politicians of the day who advocated social welfare measures. His friendship with Pearson was established in the 1930s but was strengthened enormously in 1948-49 when he took the lead in organizing support for Pearson's entry into politics. Through him, Pearson spoke to the Toronto Board of Trade in January 1949, where Gordon told him he was "a great hit". "Everyone," Gordon assured him, "just takes it for granted that you will be the next prime minister." Pearson neither then nor later contradicted Gordon's flattering prophecy, but he did say he was "very conscious of the debt of gratitude which I owe you...".[66]

He owed him more than the introduction to the Toronto business community. Gordon arranged the fund that financially assisted Pearson's entry into politics and helped with his expenses thereafter. The character of the fund, the "Algoma Fishing and Conservation Club", is illuminated in a 1957 series of letters. One "club member", John McCarthy (the son of Pearson's former superior in Washington, Leighton McCarthy), wrote to Gordon, enclosing a cheque "for the regular quinquennial assessment" for the club. He added:

> The last time we discussed the affairs of the Club I was surprised to
> learn that its finances had become somewhat impaired. It was disap-
> pointing to hear that inside reserves were now having to be used for
> purposes which should be properly considered as current mainte-
> nance work (i.e. fence mending etc.)
>
> I believe that my family were one of the charter members of this
> Club. The aims and objectives of the Club, as stated in the original
> prospectus were highly commendable and worthy of our continued
> whole-hearted support.
>
> The recognition which the chief executive officer of the Club
> has received for his work — not only on a national but also on an
> international scale, more than amply justifies the confidence of the
> Club's founders.

Pearson took time to interrupt his election campaign to write to
McCarthy:[67]

> Walter Gordon has transgressed the anonymity rules of member-
> ship in the Algoma Fishing and Conservation Club to the extent of
> sending me a copy of your letter ... but I certainly don't feel like
> taking punitive action against him. As for you all I can say is that the
> janitor and steward for the Club is deeply touched by the generous
> thought of such an esteemed charter member and is inspired to pay
> even more attention to the property in the future than he has been
> able to do in the past.

The Gordons and Pearsons became friends, and their friends
became each other's friends. Bill Harris, a Toronto stockbroker and
old friend of the Pearsons who gave the club $1,000 in April 1957,
and his wife, Ethel, offered their Hobe Sound, Florida, home as a
retreat from the political wars. Each winter, and in some springs, the
Harrises entertained the Pearsons in Florida. In the summer,
Hudson's Bay Company president Philip Chester and his wife,

"Issy", whom Mike liked enormously, gave hospitality to the Pearsons at their Magnetowan cottage, where they played "sailors' bridge, drank gin and tonic", and Mike caught bushels of pickerel.[68] When Mike needed help in his office after the leadership race, Philip Chester seconded John Payne from the Bay to Pearson's office. The Pearsons had become increasingly comfortable in the fifties — and in their fifties — with these business people, and those moments Mike grasped free from his crowded schedule he gave to them.*

Liz and Walter Gordon were as charming as they were rich. Over dinner at their elegant Toronto Rosedale home, the witty and civilized Gordons would mock the pretentious and the philistine as "maids tottered around bearing heavy platters of roast lamb and crystal decanters of claret".[69] Walter was also an unusual businessperson in that he genuinely enjoyed politics, bureaucrats, and even intellectuals and was willing to use the capital he accumulated in his business enterprises to acquire a stake in their worlds. In the later 1940s, after the death of Joseph Atkinson of the *Toronto Daily Star*, Gordon used his accounting skills and political influence to

---

* The Pearsons lacked the financial resources of their social friends, but their own circumstances improved in the 1950s. As a cabinet minister he earned $25,000 per year. His salary, however, fell to $10,000 in 1957 after the defeat of the Liberal government. To supplement his income he began writing a newspaper column. The Gordon "Fund" earned about $4,800 per year. The greatest boost to his financial well-being was the Nobel Prize, which brought approximately $43,000 along with the honour. Maryon handled not only the household finances but also investments. The Nobel money was set aside for "a rainy day" that never came. When Mike died, Maryon's brother, Herbert Moody, told Philip Chester that Maryon was surprisingly well off, the result, he suggested, of free homes, food, and vacations. The Pearsons did live rent-free in the opposition leader's residence, Stornoway, between 1958 and 1963 and then in the prime ministerial residence at 24 Sussex Drive until he left office in 1968. Herbert was actually unfair to his sister. She invested very shrewdly, thanks to the excellent investment counsel of her close friend Graham Towers, the founding governor of the Bank of Canada. Mike himself took little interest in investments or money. He never carried a wallet, stuffed bills in a "clump" into his pocket, and frequently had to borrow money from aides. In this peculiar approach to everyday finances, Pearson fits securely within a Liberal tradition from King to Trudeau.

assist the Atkinson family in maintaining control of the *Star*. They were understandably grateful, and Gordon's influence on the *Star* in the succeeding decades was remarkable. The paper, for example, assigned a reporter in 1957 to assist Pearson in his leadership campaign, and Gordon regularly consulted with the *Star* about its political coverage.[70]

Not everyone admired Gordon's ways, however. C.D. Howe was furious with the recommendations and, indeed, the existence of Gordon's Royal Commission on Canada's Economic Prospects. Pearson had recommended External Affairs officer and distinguished poet Douglas LePan as the commission secretary, and from him Pearson heard criticism of Gordon's demanding and authoritarian ways. Gordon was determined that the commission would reflect his increasingly Canadian-nationalist views. When the economist John Young wrote a study of Canadian commercial policy that did not reflect such an approach, Gordon took pains to disavow it.[71] Mary Macdonald also had doubts about Gordon. While never criticizing him directly in her letters to her "boss", she subtly hinted that Gordon's wealth and pretensions bothered her. "Oh," she wrote in April 1953 about some customs problem, "Mr. Gordon telephoned yesterday. I guess he survived his trip to New York, and it reminded me of his wife's visit to Paris in June, although I guess you fixed that up now." She hinted later that Gordon was too eager to appear on television about his royal commission.[72] What probably irritated Macdonald most, however, was Gordon's attitude towards Pearson. Christina McCall summarizes well the tone of the Pearson-Gordon correspondence of the 1950s. Gordon, she writes, "regarded Pearson as a wholly admirable man who might know his way around international negotiating tables but who was too much the innocent intellectual to be able to look after his own political or economic welfare".[73] The attitude must have annoyed Pearson, but in the aftermath of the disastrous election of 1958, his political and economic welfare needed much improvement and Walter Gordon could best produce it.

Hutchison and Dexter grumbled as Gordon's influence grew.

"Johnny" Deutsch had warned Mike of the nonsense emanating from Liberals "like Walter Gordon and Bob Fowler", but Mike argued with him "not on his own but as a reflection of Fowler and Gordon". He asked if Canada should not "accept this age as the age of grants" and recognize that the market cannot always produce justice for "the little fellow".[74] They hoped that *Free Press* editor Tom Kent, who had strongly criticized the Gordon Report, would bring some balance to Gordon's influence. Kent did go to Ottawa to help Pearson in January and February 1958, but to their horror he soon was sporting the "leftist nonsense" they heard from central Canadians like Gordon. Kent, Hutchison told Dexter, "simply doesn't understand human beings and tries to construe politics in an economist's chart, a magic formula which is guaranteed to produce prosperity if you only add the figures up right". "What is the new Liberalism anyway?" Hutchison asked after the election, "Keynes and Kent? Debt and deficit? More government and less taxes? A slight revision of the Regina Manifesto?"[75] Hutchison, in fact, got most of it right.

Liberalism veered to the left after 1958, leaving Liberals like Hutchison and Dexter clinging to the threads that linked them personally to Pearson but unable to pull the threads in a way that moved policy. Kent quickly influenced Pearson, not only because he had an enormous capacity to produce policy memoranda, but also because those memoranda argued most effectively that Liberalism must "mean" something if it was to survive. Mike's old colleague, social democrat and historian Frank Underhill, wrote to him as a friend on the fateful day he moved his unfortunate motion and pointed out that Tom Kent was "the only Liberal editor at present writing as if he had readers above high school entrance intelligence levels". He recommended that Pearson try to present himself as "an intelligent, thoughtful leader, and not a cheap evangelist like Diefenbaker". In doing so, he should realize that "Liberalism belongs to the left, or else it becomes meaningless". Mackenzie King's fierce critic in the 1930s admitted to Pearson that "Mr. King had the right attitude, and he prevented both the Progressives and the C.C.F. from getting anywhere in the country…. Your enemies should be always on the right, as his were."[76]

The advice reflected Mike Pearson's own thoughts, and the Liberalism that he advocated after March 1958 was as "impatient" as Underhill, Kent, and Gordon, increasingly his major advisers, had urged it should be. Underhill had said that such a Liberal course was the only one that youth would follow, and again Mike agreed.[77] Here Gordon helped, too.

When he was hiring management consultants for his business, Gordon would reportedly say, "Get them young, quick-witted, and flexible and you won't have any trouble teaching them techniques."[78] In the summer of 1957, with a tired St. Laurent hanging on as leader, a group of young Torontonians organized a group, "Cell 13", to breathe fresh air into the party. They quickly took over the Toronto riding associations and pledged their support to Mike Pearson. Just after the Nobel Prize was announced, Cell 13's organizer, Gordon Dryden, wrote to a member of Landon Pearson's family and encouraged him to join others in rebuilding the Liberal Party.

Dryden had seen Pearson that summer and offered to help reform the party. He told Mackenzie that he had brought together a group of reform Liberals who were dedicated to helping get Pearson elected. Among them were Barney Danson, Keith Davey, Royce Frith, Phil Givens, Robert Stanbury, Richard Stanbury, Jim Trotter, David Greenspan, and Vernon Singer. They would "clean out" the old executive and move from there.* They soon learned that "Walter Gordon … had the ear of Pearson", and he began to attend their meetings. He came wearing the Clarkson, Gordon uniform — "sober suit with waistcoat, rep tie, striped shirt, polished Oxfords, dark hose secured by garters" — only to encounter a sports-jacket, bow-tie crowd. There, in Keith Davey's words, Walter learned that

---

* Move on they certainly did. Danson and Robert Stanbury were future Liberal cabinet ministers; Frith, Davey, and Richard Stanbury became senators; Phil Givens mayor of Toronto; Singer an MPP; and the others prominent party officials.

politics were fun, while Davey began to wear three-piece suits. Each impressed the other, and soon Gordon made the young Toronto broadcasting executive national director of the shattered Liberal Party. When Davey asked Mike Pearson what his salary would be, Pearson said: "Ask Walter Gordon." That was the way it was for some time.[79]

Toronto had been Tory for generations. At the last minute before the 1957 election, St. Laurent finally appointed a Toronto cabinet minister, Paul Hellyer. The Diefenbaker government had great cabinet strength from Toronto, and Queen's Park was thoroughly blue for another generation. The decisions Pearson made or, perhaps, allowed to be made in 1957-58 cast the mould of the Liberal Party for the future. The influence of the west and of St. Laurent Liberalism, already weak, waned as Hutchison, Dexter, and their group moved to the side. The Pearson Liberal Party and its heirs bore the stamp of urban, increasingly ethnic, rich, and media-centred southern Ontario. It was a flavour profoundly distasteful to John Diefenbaker and many other Canadians, but for Liberals at the time it became a wonderful elixir.

Gordon provided most of the money and recruited much of the staff for Mike Pearson after 1958. There were other influences upon Pearson. The economist Maurice Lamontagne counselled him on Quebec, and a young Cape Bretoner, Allan MacEachen, who had been defeated in 1958, also offered advice. MacEachen was a particular favourite of Maryon, not least because the proud Scot sent her a bottle of Scotch each Christmas. Maryon liked Tom Kent much less, but Mike became increasingly attracted to his fertile mind and skilled pen. Then there was the caucus.

MacEachen seems the exception to the general rule that held among Pearson's advisers: none had knocked on doors or kissed babies in election campaigns. By 1960, the Liberal caucus was casting a wary eye towards the group clustered around Mike's office. Their interpretation of what happened on "the road back" is ably presented in Jack Pickersgill's account of the opposition years. Pickersgill's focus is clearly on the House of Commons, where he, Paul

Martin, and Lionel Chevrier, along with other caucus members, used their brilliant debating skills to taunt, irritate, and expose in contradiction Diefenbaker and his government. It is a convincing account, but is completely at odds with those of Tom Kent and Walter Gordon who (especially Kent) focus on the creation of an extra-parliamentary party structure and policy.[80] Pearson's memoirs, as one might expect, give credit to both his colleagues and the platform. The caucus, in retrospect, was much more effective than anyone could have predicted in April 1958. It is true, however, that Pearson seems to have relied less on his parliamentary colleagues than one would expect. There is evidence, for example, that his first bad parliamentary experience left a residue of suspicion. "Mike is reaching the point, and very rapidly," Grant Dexter wrote in May 1958, "where he will not listen seriously to Jack."[81] Certainly he did not listen to Pickersgill as often as he heeded Gordon and Kent in those times.

Pearson, fortunately, had the ability to make those around him believe that he listened, understood, and even sympathized with what they said. In opposition, he was able to use this ability to bind together through his own person different approaches, persons, and organizations. But the record suggests that the decision to move the Liberal Party far away from St. Laurent Liberalism, to shift towards welfare capitalism, and to emphasize a definite policy stance on a broad range of issues — the latter rightly considered to be dangerous for an opposition party — was Mike Pearson's own decision. It was through him that Davey and Dryden met Gordon. It was he who plucked Tom Kent from the bosom of the *Winnipeg Free Press* and who encouraged Kent to promote the "leftist" policies the old *Free Press* crowd so deplored. And it was Pearson who asked Mitchell Sharp to organize a Kingston Policy Conference in September 1960. There Kent and Gordon forged their alliance and presented policies that would become the legislation in a Pearson government that transformed modern Canada.

CHAPTER SEVEN

THE LIBERAL HOUR

On the sun-washed morning of April 22, 1963, Lester Bowles Pearson, riding in a borrowed blue Buick and dressed in a well-worn morning coat, drove up to the front door of Government House to be sworn into office. When he drove away again ... he turned for a moment to his press secretary, Richard O'Hagan, and said ... "You know, Dick, somehow I feel like myself again."
— Peter Newman, *The Distemper of Our Times*[1]

JOHN DIEFENBAKER'S government began to crumble in 1960. Two years after it had received the largest mandate in Canadian electoral history, the Conservative government, which had seemed so fresh and vigorous, suddenly appeared unable to make decisions or to keep in step with the times. Just as its triumphs were so much the product of John Diefenbaker's political skills, so its disintegration was, to a large extent, the result of his own weaknesses. Prominent among these was a personal enmity that he directed towards those he believed were denying him the fruits of his victory. By 1960, he had come to resent Lester Pearson.

It was not always so. Diefenbaker had been the Conservatives' external affairs critic in the 1950s, and he contributed to the bipartisan foreign policy identified with Pearson. Their personal and professional relationship was good. Pearson, for example, responded to Diefenbaker's best wishes on his 1955 Soviet trip with a short note that expressed regret that Diefenbaker could not join the party in Moscow. A more telling indication of Pearson's attitude towards Diefenbaker is found in Mary Macdonald's letters in the mid-1950s, in which she reports on Diefenbaker's activities and comments without a trace of the suspicion or condemnation that she reveals when she mentions Tory leader George Drew.[2] Suez and Herbert Norman changed her tone, but Diefenbaker was not so harshly critical of Pearson as his colleague and future foreign minister Howard Green had been on those occasions. Indeed, Norman asked Pearson to pass on his thanks to Diefenbaker for his support immediately after the American Senate Internal Security Subcommittee raised his name.[3]

In the 1957 and 1958 campaigns, Diefenbaker's sarcasm and invective were reserved for Jack Pickersgill, C.D. Howe, and his long-time Saskatchewan rival, Jimmy Gardiner. So decisive was his victory in 1958 that he could afford to be generous to Pearson, and his private letters to his wife and confidante, Olive, reflected such generosity and, perhaps, sympathy.[4] But the mood quickly changed, as the Liberals in the House of Commons opposed his policies with increasing effectiveness. Their effectiveness derived partly from the remarkable parliamentary skills of Pickersgill, Paul Martin, Lionel Chevrier, and, after 1958, Paul Hellyer, and partly from the difficulties that beset the Tories in 1959 and 1960. The government document that predicted an economic downturn, and that Diefenbaker used so effectively to ridicule Pearson's non-confidence motion in 1958, had proved to be accurate. The long post-war boom that had provided the foundation for stability reached its end in 1959-60, and so did the relative harmony between John Diefenbaker and Lester Pearson.

Between 1960 and 1967, the personal enmity that marked the relationship between these two Canadians poisoned the political atmosphere. Although Diefenbaker and Pearson "made up" in their memoirs and claimed that the public animosity was merely a partisan covering that concealed respect, their protests are unconvincing. In private, Diefenbaker mocked Pearson and reserved his

Dr. Gunnar Jahn presents Mike with the Nobel Peace Prize in Oslo in
1957, for his creative diplomacy at the United Nations.
(Douglas Cameron/NAC/PA-114544)

Retiring Liberal leader Louis St. Laurent (right) with
Pearson and rival Paul Martin as the Liberal leadership
battle begins after Pearson's return from Oslo.
(Douglas Cameron/NAC/PA-114542)

Reporter and author Bruce Hutchison at the Liberal
convention in 1958. Hutchison was a long-time Pearson
promoter who helped Mike with his speech-writing at
this time. (Douglas Cameron/NAC/PA-117113)

Mike Pearson with his mother Annie; his faithful letters to her tell us a great
deal about him. (Gilbert A. Milne)

Mike and Maryon surrounded by staffers and colleagues at the Château Laurier on election night 1962; defeat was near. (John Young/*Maclean's*)

Mike meets Quebec premier
Jean Lesage at the
province's Liberal convention in 1963, when Lesage
finally endorsed the
federal Liberals.
(Douglas Cameron/NAC/
PA-113500)

Mike and John F. Kennedy on the terrace of the President's summer home
in Hyannis Port, during a two-day "informal work session" in 1963.
The two leaders quickly became friends.
(Canapress Photo Service/Wide World Photo)

Maryon, Patricia Pearson Hannah, and her son Paul with Mike at a
1963 Liberal campaign rally in Maple Leaf Gardens. (Capital Press)

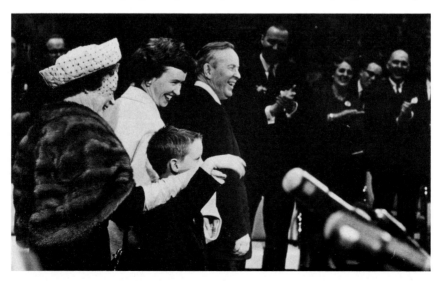

harshest barbs for him. Pearson, his confidante Mary Macdonald recalls, had difficulty believing anyone was fundamentally evil, "with the possible exception of John Diefenbaker". Others close to Pearson largely share her view. As always, Maryon was bluntest. She referred to Diefenbaker as simply "that horrid man from Prince Albert".[5]

Their enmity was probably inevitable. Although Diefenbaker, like Pearson, was born in Ontario of British-German Protestant stock in the 1890s, his experience led him to different conclusions about Canada and different approaches to politics. In his memoirs, Pearson analysed their differences:

> My background of official and diplomatic duty, along with my own nature, tended to make me more interested in issues, in finding solutions to problems, and in trying, rather to convince doubters that my answers were right than to make sure they were politically feasible as well as right in themselves.... I might have been more effective had I been a politician from the beginning, working my way up from the backbenches, learning on the way to curb my weakness to find something worth supporting in nearly every pro- posal of an adversary, and remembering that in party politics all is black and white....[6]

He might have been more effective as a politician, but he would not have been Mike Pearson and he would not have been prime minis- ter.

What drew so many different people to Pearson were those qual- ities that seemed to make him not a politician, but someone who lis- tened directly to them. He had "something", his political opponent Grattan O'Leary wrote:

> I never knew what it was — a kind of instant receptiveness increas- ingly professional over the years backed up by real and decent concern. He always gave the impression of being genuinely inter- ested. His fault as a politician, if it was a fault, was his ability to place

himself in the other person's position: he had all the tricks of a negotiator. Finding out how one side felt, then playing it back to the other side.[7]

In fact, this receptiveness was "professional", acquired by years of diplomatic experience where sensitivity to "the other" was fundamental to his achievement. It was effective, but in time it could create misunderstandings, as receptiveness was mistaken for agreement.

Diefenbaker's schooling came not in London's clubs over aged claret or in U.N. corridors where different tongues and ways compelled a cosmopolitan manner, but in the country stores, fishing parties, and bitter politics of Saskatchewan, a province whose promised future never came and where, as its socialist premier Tommy Douglas, said, "the only protection the Tories had in the [1920s and 1930s] were the game laws...".[8] Tories rarely won anything in Saskatchewan — government contracts, judicial appointments, or elections. Diefenbaker lost federal elections in 1925 and 1926, provincial elections in 1929 and 1938, the Prince Albert mayoralty in 1933, and Conservative leadership contests in 1942 and 1948. He was sensitive to his German name, carrying a letter from professors during the First World War certifying that he was of "Canadian birth", and later he never hesitated to proclaim his loyalty to the British crown. To reach his goal he worked ceaselessly, shunned social life, and vacationed rarely. He seemed different and an outsider, not only in Ottawa in the forties when western Tories were rare, but even in the 1920s in Prince Albert when, as an austere young lawyer, "tall, stiff [and] formally dressed", he strode to his Prince Albert law office along an unpaved street, passing trappers, bush pilots, farmers, Cree Indians, and gold miners.[9] An introvert like so many politicians, Diefenbaker was incapable of being "genuinely interested", which Pearson appeared to be. He needed crowds and the life he gave them he fully shared. But, as Basil Robinson, Diefenbaker's assistant and most perceptive analyst, has observed, he had "little feel for team play".[10]

The styles, then, were different. Diefenbaker was a populist; Pearson distrusted the irrationality of populism. Reading through their papers, one is struck immediately by how different their worlds were and how much the experience of an "Ottawa man" like Pearson differed from that of a prairie lawyer whose world was that of the small town, with its service clubs, its fears about next year's crop, and its sometimes stifling pressures to conform. Even in Ottawa, Diefenbaker had few friends, and in opposition, as he was from 1940 to 1957, his tendencies to stand alone were not constrained. He knew few insiders, could not travel to London, New York, or even Toronto or Montreal and find welcome in their private clubs, and was distant not only from the so-called Liberal establishment but also from what he derisively and rightly called the "Bay Street Boys" who were so influential in the Conservative party under George Drew. The most representative of these was the Toronto businessperson J.M. Macdonnell, who was active in the Canadian Institute of International Affairs and who sat at the head table when the institute honoured Pearson's Nobel Prize.

In his memoirs, Diefenbaker claims that he put Macdonnell in the cabinet because Olive felt sorry for him and said his heart would be broken if he were left out. At his swearing in, Macdonnell allegedly told Olive that "because [Diefenbaker] had forgiven his subterranean plots" against him, "he would never again be disloyal. It was not very long," Diefenbaker wrote, "before he returned to his former ways." Another Torontonian and a former student of Pearson's at the university, Donald Fleming, received a more senior ministry than Macdonnell, a minister without portfolio, but as minister of finance he never had Diefenbaker's trust. Neither did the able Davie Fulton, who, like Macdonnell, had gone to Oxford as a Rhodes scholar.[11] Diefenbaker distrusted them; but he did not ignore them, as he did his colleagues from Quebec. He had won the leadership without Quebec, and in 1958 he had won Quebec without a Quebec leader. One minister Diefenbaker did trust, Alvin Hamilton, reflected Diefenbaker's own views when he wrote in 1959 that the key to Tory success was holding the west: "With the Maritimes and Ontario reasonably steady and the West with us a good number of Quebec seats will always come to us."[12]

In 1960, for the first time since the election, the Liberals pulled ahead of the Tories in the Gallup poll, and in September they held a "Study Conference on National Problems" at Kingston. The model was the Liberal summer school organized by Vincent Massey in 1933 against the wishes of Mackenzie King, who, with some justification, thought that Massey was trying to impose upon him a more definite and more liberal platform than he wanted.* It is a measure of how different Mike Pearson was from Mackenzie King that he was the main proponent of the Kingston conference and that his hope was for a conference that would bring together independents and Liberals and define, for the party, a more progressive and activist platform. As with Massey's conference, the Kingston conference deliberately invited few members of Parliament, its agenda implicitly rejected the policies of the last Liberal government, and its organizers hoped it would attract new supporters to the party, some of whom might become candidates.

In retrospect, the conference seems to have been a remarkable success. Peter Newman, who attended the conference, later described it as "the most important single source of Lester Pearson's lieutenants and advisers" and pointed out that "of the 196 men and women who attended, 48 were later named to senior appointments in the Liberal administration". J.W. Pickersgill, the only MP to speak at the conference, describes it as "the most important event of 1960" for the Liberals and emphasizes its importance in recruiting candidates and supporters. Others, noting the remarkable similarity

---

* As King travelled to Alice and Vincent Massey's home in Port Hope, he had a dream in which "curiously enough [I] saw first one snake in the grass come out of a marshy ground — a little one — and a little later a larger one .... concluded it was a warning to be careful — I wondered if it could mean that by any chance my hosts were not to be trusted." Mackenzie King Diary, Sept. 3, 1933 (NAC).

between the record of the Pearson government and the policies pre-
scribed by some of the speakers at Kingston, have described the conference as "a forecast of the future". For Pearson himself, it was "the
beginning of our comeback".[13] For Jean Chrétien, three decades
later, it was a model for a study conference to define Liberalism for
the 1990s.

Assessments at the time were much less flattering. Political journalist Harold Greer, who was usually friendly towards Pearson,
dubbed it "an unmitigated political disaster" which revealed a party
disorganized and divided. Kingston, Greer wrote, "was an egghead
conference and Mr. Pearson ... is something of an egghead
himself". The politician, Greer averred, "must think with his liver".
There is, accordingly, "a constant quarrel because the intellectual
begins by saying he doesn't know, an admission which is fatal for
the politician". Greer correctly detected a chasm between the
politicians and those who "thought" or who at least wanted the
Liberal party to develop a coherent program for the next election.
A perceptive assessment of the conference by a young Toronto
banker, R.M. MacIntosh, that was widely circulated after the conference, echoed some of Greer's views. The few MPs who were
there, apart from Pearson, "seemed not very sympathetic to the
purposes of the Conference...". Paul Martin "could almost be
heard to mutter, 'Enough of these bloody ideas — let's get back to
politics'". Jack Pickersgill was clearly unhappy in his final luncheon
address, not only with the interventionist schemes that were proposed and the criticisms of the United States, but also with the
charge, which he most vigorously refuted, that the St. Laurent years
had accomplished little.[14] But these objections were mild compared
to the bitter attack by Pearson's early and fervent supporters Bruce
Hutchison and Grant Dexter.

The most striking contribution to the Kingston conference
was a speech by Tom Kent that challenged Canadian Liberals and
was, in MacIntosh's words, "a very well-written case for the broad
extension of economic assistance to the underprivileged in the
fields of health, education, old age assistance and other fields". So

bold was his prescription that Frank Underhill,* a founder of the Co-operative Commonwealth Federation who told all who cared to listen that he had voted CCF in 1958 despite Pearson's pleas that he not do so, accused Kent "of importing Manchester Guardian–Fabian socialism to a cold climate and to a fast-changing society where security could not receive so much emphasis". If Kent's recommendations were regarded as too sweeping by a socialist, they appalled Hutchison, Dexter, and Victor Sifton, owner of the *Free Press*, who had Dexter write a critical report on the conference for the paper.

By September 1960, Kent had left the *Free Press* to work in Montreal for Chemcell Limited, and there were bad feelings after his departure. Sifton, Hutchison, and Dexter had first encouraged Kent to work with Pearson and had urged Pearson to employ Kent's skills, but by 1960 their differences were great and fundamentally ideological. The economist John Deutsch, a close friend of Hutchison and Dexter, had warned them earlier that "Tom" had a "blind spot". He was "thoroughly Liberal" on trade and on "freedom of the individual", but had problems on the question of "expansionism". Deutsch explained this aberration in personal terms: Kent's father had been unemployed for a long period, and "Tom" stopped "thinking with his head, the moment an argument on unemployment, underdevelopment — of expansion versus non-expansion [begins]". Deutsch, Graham Towers, and others had been "working on him" and would get "tougher". But the lesson

---

* Underhill had published a collection of his essays in 1960 entitled *In Search of Canadian Liberalism*, which he dedicated to his former colleague at the University of Toronto, Mike Pearson. Pearson, who was fond of Underhill, corresponded with him after becoming Liberal leader. Underhill recommended in January 1958 that Mike should start some summer conferences "as Vincent Massey did years ago at Port Hope". He urged Pearson to listen to "intellectual and educated people". In his reply Pearson said that the letter "persuaded me to bring Tom Kent" to Ottawa to advise him and that he agreed with the direction the party must go. Underhill to Pearson, Jan. 20, 1958; and Pearson to Underhill, Feb. 11, 1958, Underhill Papers, v. 13 (NAC).

did not take, and at Kingston Kent demonstrated how committed he was to a wide-ranging program of social reform and "expansionism".[15] The problem, it now seemed, was that Kent had convinced Pearson.

Pearson was aware of this problem. He wrote to the highly influential Hutchison after the conference ended and deprecated the "gross" misrepresentations by the press of what had happened at Kingston. Of course there was controversy, but what was the point of a conference "of this kind, especially one designed for 'liberals' if we cannot receive, discuss, support or destroy proposals and ideas?" He shared Hutchison's concerns "about the trend of things in this country which reflects itself in the extension of government action, with all that that implies ...". Any increase of government authority "is only and always the extension of the area of individual freedom and of a realization of its true meaning". There must be change, for "sound reform is preservative rather than revolutionary ...". The letter did not convince Hutchison, whose liberalism was different from Pearson's and Kent's. He told Dexter that Mike's thinking had a "woolly quality" to it and wondered what would "come from it" at the National Liberal Rally from January 11 to 14, 1961.[16]

C.D. Howe, the symbol of 1950s *laissez-faire* Liberalism, died on January 4, 1961. He had been "distressed" over what had happened at Kingston, where he thought "left-wing intellectuals" were too prevalent, notably Tom Kent, whom he "heartily disliked".[17] Walter Gordon, whom Howe had snubbed for some time after 1957, was the rally's policy chairman. The resolutions called for, among other things, health insurance, regional development funds, urban renewal, a national scholarship plan, greater unemployment assistance, pension reform, increased social investment, limits on foreign control of the Canadian economy, complete processing of raw materials in Canada, and a Canadian flag. Tom Kent, who had written the most trenchant critiques of Gordon's royal commission, and Gordon had "made up" at Kingston and worked together closely for the Ottawa rally. Kent had wanted his remarks at Kingston to be "off the record" and was annoyed when Pearson allowed the press to hear them. It was Gordon who overcame Kent's reluctance and convinced him he should participate in shaping policy resolutions for Ottawa, which, of course, would make Kent's commitment public and his influence obvious. Gordon wrote to Kent after the rally (which he termed a "great success") and told him, with much validity, that "it would have been a ghastly failure without all the preliminary work that went into the policy issues, in which you played the biggest part".[18]

That part deeply disturbed Hutchison and his friends, who saw that their kind of western-Canadian Liberalism had lost the sympathy of Pearson. The convention's support of deficit financing was appalling but expected:

> What I didn't expect was that Mike should so casually destroy that whole image of Responsibility which he has tried so painfully to construct, and which he has encouraged us to build up for him. Nor did I expect that he would assure you (as I understand from Victor) that there would be no plan for a general tax cut and, within a week, would endorse such a plan with enthusiasm. That shakes me. Mike has had three great tests (1) the famous vote-of-confidence resolution in which he fell on his face; (2) the tax holiday of the 1958 election ... and (3) the present party platform. He has failed every one of them.

Hutchison said he was "blowing off steam" to Dexter and no one else:

> I keep a stiff upper lip. But I am disgusted, not with social reform, or even public spending but with the sheer cynicism and wild idiocy of imitating the Tories and deceiving the public about taxes. This just shocks my moral sense, or what's left of it. What happened to Mike's head and morals? Well, they may be right about these things politically. The Canadian public may be crazy and debauched enough to believe them. We may be fighting history and not a mere Rally of the Grass Roots statesmen. If so, God help us.

Business people would never support the party, "unless Mike finds a way to repudiate or reinterpret this poisonous heresy. And even if he does, who is running the party anyway? Gordon, Lamontagne and Tom Kent, I would guess. Cry havoc."[19]

Havoc or not, Hutchison's guess was not wrong, so far as party policy and organization was concerned. In 1960 Gordon and Pearson reached an agreement whereby Gordon would head the reorganization of the Liberal Party and chair the policy committee for the National Rally. Gordon's demands were clear and bluntly expressed. They included agreement with Gordon's views on economic policy, particularly those on "modest steps to counteract" the U.S. "takeover" of Canada's economy. He also made it clear that he expected the Finance portfolio after a Liberal victory and a commitment from Pearson that, if Gordon entered politics, Pearson would not leave for some "international position". In July 1960, Gordon had sent Pearson some of his policy proposals, and, according to Gordon's record, "he agreed *completely* [italics in original] with my ideas". Gordon then committed himself to assist financially, organizationally, and electorally.[20] At the Kingston conference, Pearson's speech had a major section on foreign investment that drew directly from Gordon's memoranda. The deal, it seemed, was done.

But why was it done? After Kingston and the policy rally, Pearson faced criticism not only from Hutchison and his group, but also from business people who distrusted Gordon's and Kent's plans, and from some of his parliamentary caucus, who worried about the influence Mike had granted to Gordon and Kent. Indeed, in his history of "the road back to government", Jack Pickersgill has only two references to Tom Kent, one trivial, the other critical.* In Pick-

---

* Pickersgill describes a parliamentary debate when Diefenbaker ridiculed the Kingston and Ottawa conferences and Tom Kent, "the leader of the leader". When Pearson referred to John Fisher on Diefenbaker's staff and said, "Body by Fisher", Diefenbaker quickly retorted: "Body by Fisher is a great deal better than Brains by Kent." Pickersgill makes no further comment. J.W. Pickersgill, *The Road Back by a Liberal in Opposition* (Toronto: University of Toronto Press, 1986), 150.

ersgill's account of how the Liberal Party travelled the road back to power, no credit is given to Kent and his work. Mary Macdonald also told Mike, especially after Kingston, that he should not rely so much on Gordon and Kent. Between the Kingston conference and the National Rally, the Pearsons spent a winter vacation with the Towerses, and Graham undoubtedly let Mike know how little he thought of Gordon's economic notions — as he continued to do until Gordon finally failed. And we know how C.D. Howe and his friends grumbled in their ample armchairs in the Mount Royal Club that winter before Howe died.[21]

One can suggest several motives to explain Pearson's actions. First, the parliamentary session of 1958-59 convinced Pearson that the Liberals, though few, could be effective in exposing Diefenbaker's weaknesses. On the first anniversary of the 1958 "day of national madness", Mike wrote to Landon and Geoffrey that the "present session of Parliament has shown that the liquidation [of the Liberal Party] has not been effective...". He was "more comfortable" than before because he knew that they could not be humiliated in the House so long as the Liberals had Martin, Pickersgill, and others. He need not worry about their competence or their loyalty. It was an advantage that John Turner, Robert Stanfield, Joe Clark, and even John Diefenbaker did not have, and it permitted Pearson to give Gordon and Kent the latitude he did.[22] Secondly, he had no alternative to Gordon. In his letter to Landon and Geoffrey, he mentioned that the Liberals were gaining in the country, but not because of any organizational work the Liberals themselves had done. He told Hutchison that he had wanted Dave Sim, a former deputy minister, to be his national organizer but it did not work out. He asked Toronto businessperson Bruce Matthews to be party president and treasurer, but Matthews failed to raise sufficient funds and his political outlook was, in Mike's words, "conservative".[23] Intellectually, Mike believed the party should move left, and Matthews would not be enthusiastic about this movement, however strong his "Liberalism by tradition". In 1958, Mike "was idealistic enough to hope that our expenses, including a substantial part of our campaign costs could be met from membership dues and annual donations from the party faithful". Such hopes, as always, were futile. Gordon's demands were great, his tone a trifle patronizing;* but his fund-raising abilities were proven. He was, moreover, a *rara avis*, a businessman who wanted a "leftist" and "progressive" party and, perhaps most important, enjoyed people with ideas, like Tom Kent. After Gordon committed himself, $200,000 came in quickly, as did new faces, an "action plan", a "Leader's Advisory Committee", and an attempt to discover who and where Liberals were. Gordon, Keith Davey later recalled, came to their daily meetings with a long, detailed agenda and made decisions quickly. Pearson, whom Davey met twice a week, had no agenda. He would start a meeting by opening the desk drawer and twirling a Dad's cookie at Davey, and seldom answered a question with a yes or no. Instead he left Davey to interpret such comments as, "Well, Keith, if that is really something you feel you must do ..." as the "no" it was.[24] Gordon filled many gaps created in the Liberal Party by the cyclone of 1958 and the choice of a leader who found "politics" difficult.

Finally, Pearson came to rely on Tom Kent after 1960 because he sensed that this recent arrival in Canada could see more clearly than others what the future would bring and how the Liberal Party and Mike Pearson might become part of that future rather than being overwhelmed by it. Not only the Liberal Party but also the Co-operative Commonwealth Federation had been shattered. The CCF began to rebuild through a formal alliance with Canadian labour and its transformation into the New Democratic Party (NDP). More important, the New Democrats brought Tommy Douglas to Ottawa to be their leader. He had governed Saskatchewan since 1944 and had just given it the medicare the federal Liberals had promised since 1919 but had never delivered.

---

* "Further to my letter of yesterday, I have now arranged for John Gellner and Jim Eayrs to meet you at my house at 6:30 p.m. on Sunday, March 1. Gellner, Eayrs and you are to talk about defence." Gordon to Pearson, Feb. 20, 1959, Pearson Papers (NAC).

While Hutchison and others were startled by the "leftist" character of the Kingston conference and the National Rally, some on the left declared that they had heard it all before in the Liberal platform of 1919 and in the King government's Green Book proposals of 1945. Why were the 2,000 delegates brought to Ottawa, and what was all the cheering for? asked Ramsay Cook, a young historian attracted to the NDP then taking form and to John Kennedy's challenges to young Americans: "The Liberals now have a guide for the future which is no more radical than Mr. Diefenbaker's promises, and less in tune with twentieth century Liberalism than the program which John Kennedy offered.... Clearly the new Pearson is but the old King — with a dash of Walter Gordon." Cook had mockingly entitled his article "Not Right, Not Left, But Forward", a remark Mike made when a hostile reporter suggested that the new party program was "leftist". He had given Cook and others an easy target.[25]

Kent made the target more difficult to hit. Why Pearson came to rely upon this young Englishman whom Mike's old friends disliked so much, who insisted on so much of his time, who challenged him constantly, and who aroused so much suspicion among the caucus becomes clearer when one looks at what Kent gave him. In June 1960, Kent sent on to Pearson a letter about Canada he had sent to "his old friend Jo Grimond...", a "delightful privateer in British politics" who had become Liberal Party leader. It was just after Kennedy had won the historic West Virginia primary, the Soviets had shot down Francis Gary Powers' U-2, Eisenhower had lied, Khrushchev had exploded, and the fresh winds of careful embrace between East and West had turned acrid. Kent's letter is a remarkably prescient document that captures the political emotions that animated North Americans in the sixties:

> There are now, I think, many signs that the submerged nine-tenths of the conservative iceberg in North America is melting rapidly. We will soon be in a new reformist phase — which will, one may hope, be reflected in the display of less doctrine and more understanding in U.S. relations with the rest of the world.

In U.S. domestic affairs, the basic fact is that the conservative phase produced no move back towards laissez-faire; despite all the talk, what its opponents call "creeping socialism" was not arrested. The next reformist phase is therefore likely to take even the United States a considerable way further in the creation of what I like to call a welfare economy — which means (as opposed to socialism) an enlargement of the public sphere not in production as such but in consumption — larger public expenditures on education, health, housing and other services.

Our task in Canada is to implement these desirable trends while meeting the considerable structural economic difficulties that are replacing our boom times of the '40s and '50s. Because of those difficulties, there are ways in which our Canadian problems in the '60s may have much more in common with Britain's than they had in the past. In any event, they provide, I think, a most significant challenge to a twentieth-century liberalism; our response could be of considerable significance far outside Canada.

If we can get a Liberal government with Mike Pearson as Prime Minister, I would have few fears about the adequacy of the response. The danger is that this, like so many political issues, will be pre-determined: we will never have the chance to do the big thing adequately unless we plan imaginatively for it now, as a small opposition and a disorganized party. Any real chance of success depends, I think, on Mike taking the crucial, ideological initiative before the end of this year.

It's urgent to get a new image of the party before the public, and to re-invigorate its organization — which depends partly on personalities but also on clarifying a political attitude to fight for. With a good many conservative forces still operating inside the party, that's far from easy. But it badly needs to be done, preferably in the form of a personal political testament by Mike — a statement of his philosophy and general policy which would provide a rallying-point for all the people who want to be liberal reformers but have little guidance as to what that means in the 1960s.

In Canada it is necessary to explain why the Liberal today,

without being any less concerned about freedom, would much extend public expenditures on education, health (including medical insurance and sickness benefits), housing and urban renewal. This has to be combined with a national policy for securing more equality among our still very diverse regions. There have to be sound policies for broadening the economy and raising employment levels; for increasing our trade and improving our payments balance; and for giving Canadian defence and foreign policy a satisfactory role in the world.

Primarily, I would say that Liberals need to shift the emphasis of their thinking a good many notches (in our case) towards egalitarianism. That's essential if we really want to regain the radical role that, in Britain, Socialism has muffed and that here is at the moment hopelessly spread among individuals rather than parties. We have to show that we really do want to create a much more equal society. And I would emphasize, too, a more skilful society (more "educated" having rather an odour to it) — which is not only of obvious importance but can have, I think, considerable political appeal. Indeed, the emphasis on the need for greater human skills, for the maximum use of our brainpower, perhaps helps as much as anything to clear away our nineteenth-century hangover about economic liberalism and gladly accept the more collectivist framework of contemporary economics and administration; the Liberal policy is not to wring our hands over the way that science and universal education are taking the world, but to insist that this necessary collectivist framework can and should be fashioned in such a way as to broaden, not narrow, the individual initiative and responsibility that will be more rewarding to individuals who are more skilful, who have more security and who live in a more equal society.

Kent had forecast a future that he enthusiastically looked forward to shaping. [26] The enthusiasm was infectious, and Mike caught it.

The die for a Pearson government was cast in 1960 and 1961, and Pearson's principal task thereafter was to keep those who found other shapes more comely from wandering too far from their old political mate. Pearson called on Hutchison just after the rally whose resolutions had caused Hutchison to have "nervous indigestion", to use Jack Pickersgill's description of the effect of the event on some Liberals.[27] Hutchison was prepared to confront him and had him to dinner with the crusty Jack Clyne, "our largest tycoon". The confrontation misfired: "[Pearson] is so charming ... and so honest that I find it hard to quarrel with him." Hutchison, who had his own self-deprecating charm, told Dexter that really it was not an argument with Mike "but with a tide of history, the wave of the future. A new generation has taken over in Washington and, at the Liberal convention, in Canada and it won't listen to the mutterings of an old man like me. We now belong to the ages." But, Hutchison wrote in his cottage outside Victoria with the vines in bloom, "it's spring here, flowers everywhere, April temperatures and now I shall repair to the garden where there is peace and no deficit finance. Nature is always in surplus, thank God."[28]

Mike himself, as Gordon feared, was tempted to retreat to the more fragrant orchards of international diplomacy where he had so long flourished. With the assistance of John Holmes, who left External in 1960, he tried to write a major work on "the world in 1960", but too many current events on the international scene and political exigencies in Canada prevented its publication.* His letters to Geoffrey reveal how much he yearned for what lay behind him. He wrote to Geoffrey just after the 1960 summit between Khrushchev and Eisenhower had collapsed in the wake of the U-2 incident and told him that he had written an article for *Foreign Affairs* and would be writing another for the *New York Times* "on assignment": "All of this takes up time, of course, that should be devoted to attacking the government in the Commons on the price

---

* John Holmes gave me his copy of the manuscript. He drafted the chapters after a discussion with Pearson, and Pearson revised. It was the same pattern that Arnold Smith used in drafting *Democracy and World Politics*. Pearson had drafted many speeches for others and found it easy to have others draft them for him. Mr. Smith's copy of another Pearson work is inscribed with a note indicating that in that book, it was "my own words".

of eggs." But there was not a word about the price of eggs or other domestic matters. Instead, he talked about "an interesting week" he had spent in Chicago at a conference on world tensions, "another flight from domestic politics". At the conference, a decision was made to create an "International Council on World Tensions", which would be funded by prominent individuals and foundations to undertake a five-year program, and which would concentrate on Asia and Africa in an effort to find means to reduce "tensions". The organizers "pressed him hard" to become the council's first president and offered him a large salary. He admitted to Geoffrey that he was "very tempted". His first concern was whether "this kind of job" could make a contribution. His second concern was justifying to his friends his abandonment of Canadian politics.[29] He did not accept the offer of the position, although he remained wistful about the world he had lost and weary about the "politics" that were now his lot. He told Geoffrey in early 1961 that he wanted an election soon: "Then I would know. Either new and inescapable responsibility as head of a government or freedom from politics. Either prospect would be satisfactory — especially the latter." Certainly his private letters reflect neither interest nor joy in the doings of Ottawa or his political tasks. This indifference contrasts strongly with the obvious excitement that he derived from another "World Tensions" conference, this time at Geoffrey's former college, New College, Oxford. It was all "vastly instructive and interesting" for Mike, as he learned about Asia and Africa from their politicians and intellectuals. The "new, young black leaders", like Kenneth Kaunda, impressed him as "speakers and persons". The experience and, of course, Oxford made him "nostalgic and sentimental".[30] "In the kind of life I lead now," he told Geoffrey and Landon, "with domestic politics and party preoccupations pressing one hard — and I'm not enamoured of these pressures as you know though I do my best to disguise this. With this kind of life, I don't seem to find time for the more important things in life — such as telling Landon and you how very proud I am of what you have both done in your work and your lives." Landon and Geoffrey were then in Mexico City, where Geoffrey was first secretary at the Canadian Embassy. "I wish," Mike concluded, "my own present career gave me as much contentment, shall I call it 'inner cleanliness' as yours does."[31]

The carapace he donned to conceal his discomfort in the political world was sometimes transparent, and his pain as he carried out his political tasks was too obvious. One senses in these remarks Pearson's fear of entrapment, of losing his freedom, of making commitments that he would rather not make. After the Ottawa rally, he did not contact Gordon for more than two months, to Gordon's annoyance and puzzlement. Did he worry about becoming ensnared in policies he did not favour and in commitments he would rather not have made?

The evidence is circumstantial, but we do know that Pearson found opposition extremely uncomfortable and that Gordon asked for commitments that were exceedingly broad in scope. The section of Pearson's Kingston conference speech on economics and trade does not reflect what he said publicly and privately about such subjects before and after the conference. It is true that he was concerned that a too-large percentage of foreign investment in Canada and Canadian export trade was American, but his response — and, for that matter, Liberal policy — was to diversify and seek a broad "Atlantic" trading area. He criticized the Diefenbaker government's trade-diversion policy and its opposition to British entry into the Common Market. He urged the Canadian government to embrace a British "free trade" proposal first made in 1957 and repeated in 1960 as a "first step" in the creation of an "Atlantic Economic Community". Any "narrow" or "protectionist policy" would be "out of step with history".[32]

In fact, Mike was not marching in step with history, for the evidence now suggests that his vision of an "Atlantic Economic Community" was almost certainly chimerical, especially after the French rejection of Britain's membership in the Common Market in early 1963 because French president General Charles de Gaulle believed that Britain would be an American "Trojan Horse" within the community.[33] Nevertheless, Mike's statements reveal the difference in emphasis on trade and economic matters between Gordon and himself. His knowledge of and interest in such affairs were, by his own admission, not great. He was therefore less committed to economic policies than he was to policies in areas where his expertise was greater. Still, he must have been uncomfortable, and it must have shown.

After Mike finally contacted Gordon in April 1961 after the National Rally, events moved quickly, partly because of Gordon's determination and partly because an election was likely within a year.[34] Gordon secured Keith Davey as national director in May 1961, and organized a policy committee to draft an election platform. He began, with the assistance of Davey and Toronto lawyer Dan Lang, to seek candidates, and formed a Leader's Advisory Committee, which Pearson chaired and Gordon vice-chaired. Later, Gordon became not only chair of the National Campaign Committee but also a candidate for Davenport riding in Toronto. Davey proved indefatigable in his efforts to restructure, reinvigorate, and centralize party operations. Davey and Gordon paid close attention to provincial wings and broke with precedent by having the provincial campaign chairs appointed by the national leader. Provincial feudal structures, particularly in Joey Smallwood's Newfoundland, successfully resisted these attempts to limit their suzerainty, but there were successes — as in Quebec, where the central campaign assisted the young Montreal lawyer John Turner in gaining a party nomination. More important, Quebec Liberals embraced the practice of nominating conventions and thus abandoned the old "bosses" who normally chose candidates themselves. Turner was helped, but he had to win a democratic nominating meeting.[35] Quebec, in this respect at least, became a province more like the others.

For a biographer of Pearson, these details of party transformation present a problem. As political scientist Joseph Wearing notes: "Davey's letters and memoranda to Pearson are fascinating, cogent documents; but party organization was not a subject that greatly interested Pearson and it is difficult to judge how much importance he attached to them." Nevertheless, Pearson liked Davey, a sports fan whose affection for the hated Yankees* Pearson forgave, and gave him a remarkably free hand.[36] What affected and interested Pearson more than details of party reorganization was the presentation of the party leader in the election campaign. What Davey and Gordon wanted to present was not what Canadians saw when they looked at Pearson in 1961.

Canadians, public-opinion polls seemed to suggest, did not like Lester Pearson as a politician as much as Pearson's advisers had hoped. It was discouraging, for he had performed well in the House in 1961, especially in the so-called Coyne affair. James Coyne, the governor of the Bank of Canada, had followed a restrictive monetary policy and had made controversial public speeches that conflicted with government policy. Finance minister Donald Fleming and Diefenbaker finally decided to fire Coyne. The pretext was a change in the pension to be awarded a retired governor that raised the amount of the pension to $25,000. Fleming informed Coyne that his contract would not be renewed when it expired in December 1961, and the government began to try to undo the pension, which it alleged had been improperly increased. Professor Granatstein, who has most ably chronicled this affair, points out that though the pension was large there was no impropriety. The charge of impropriety naturally outraged Coyne and forced him to defend his integrity. In June the government presented its bill to remove Coyne from office, but made the error of preventing the bill from going to a House committee.[37]

The Liberals were careful to distance themselves from Coyne's policies, which, at a time of high unemployment, seemed restrictive in the view of most academic economists. Indeed, on January 20, 1961, Pearson had endorsed an economic program that was expansionary, featuring tax cuts, lower interest rates, and accelerated depreciation.[38] Pearson denounced the bill because it denied Coyne a hearing and because it made Coyne a scapegoat for the Tories'

---

* When Gordon, Pearson, and Davey met, the discussion began with Pearson and Davey dissecting last night's box scores, to the great annoyance of Gordon.

economic mismanagement. Through the bill, Pearson claimed, "the executive is seeking to make the elected representatives of the people rubber stamps, because they are being asked to take action without information...". Diefenbaker, who directed Conservative strategy, hated Coyne, considering him "an unregenerate Grit" who was being manipulated by his old Winnipeg friend Jack Pickersgill.* Coyne, Diefenbaker sarcastically declared, "sat, knew, listened and took" when $25,000 was dangled before him. He was going to "line up" the Grits with Mr. Coyne's thinking and annihilate them. This time, however, his threats rang hollow, for Pearson deftly persuaded the Senate banking and commerce committee to hear Coyne's case.[39]

They heard his case — and much more. Coyne released a flood of documents that revealed a government uncertain of its economic path, clumsy in its operations, and vindictive in its relations with the governor. It was a sorry tale, but its telling helped the Liberals. Sixty per cent of the 76 per cent of Canadians who had heard of the controversy sided with Coyne; only 9 per cent supported the government's case.[40] The Liberals had battled Diefenbaker and, for the first time since 1958, had decisively won.

It did not help much in the polls. Since the Liberals first pulled ahead of the Conservatives in the Gallup poll in November 1960 (44 per cent to 39 per cent), their advance had stalled and to some extent retreated. In 1961, Gordon and Davey, inspired by Theodore White's *The Making of the President: 1960*, which described how effectively John Kennedy had used polling to shape his campaign, hired Kennedy's pollster, Lou Harris, to conduct surveys for them. It was the first time such sophisticated techniques had been applied to

---

* They were close friends, and Pickersgill did speak with him and assist him during this period; but Coyne's anger was his own and needed no direction. After the death of Pickersgill's first wife, Coyne had been an "emotional rock" for Pickersgill, who never forgot the many kindnesses at that time. This emotional link undoubtedly intensified the anger in Pickersgill's attack on the government's action. Interview with J.W. Pickersgill.

Canadian politics, and it was taken very seriously. Gordon recalls that he and Davey were surprised to see that Canadians were not as critical of Diefenbaker as they had expected. Indeed, many Canadians retained an image of him as an "honest, sincere, straightforward man" — exactly what the leading Liberals believed he was not. Pearson, the surveys revealed, lacked a clear image and was seen as "a diplomat" who was unfitted for domestic politics. What had once seemed his greatest strength seemed to have become a political liability.* Even his fabled bow tie was found wanting. Harris's expert research revealed that voters liked Mike more when he wore a straight tie.[41]

Davey stuffed his own blue-and-white bow tie in the drawer. (He also ceased to wear sports jackets that may tactfully be described as colourful and turned to the three-piece blue suits that later became his trademark.) The sartorially altered Davey, along with Gordon and the Liberal Party's new and very talented communications chief, Dick O'Hagan, began to work on Pearson. Armed with Harris's surveys, the campaign planners urged Pearson to wear a straight tie, and he did. They also worked with him on his television manner after Harris's surveys showed that many Canadians thought him a "smart-aleck". They tried to deal with such mannerisms as the sheepish Pearson smile, which curiously and disturbingly followed such statements such as: "The unemployment statistics are really bad this month." He was told to keep his thumbs inside his fists

---

* The pollsters showed photographs to test reactions. The highest ratings were for the photograph of Pearson with Churchill and the photograph on the cover of this book, with scores of +41 and +28, respectively. A photograph of Pearson and a clenched fist rated the lowest, -19. Two were tied at -18, one in which he was curling, the other showing him signing an autograph. The strategists recommended that "to avoid strengthening Mr. Pearson's negative image and to increase his appeal to voters ... certain situations should be avoided. These include frivolous scenes and ones where he is shown in the pose of the traditional politician." This advice was followed and has made the search for informal photographs for this book much more difficult. "Pearson's Pictorial Appeal", Box 7, Kent Papers (Queen's University Archives).

when he was angry and to avoid long sentences and words, particularly ones where his lisp was obvious. His lisp proved a particularly difficult problem. Davey recalls Pearson's anger when a speech writer included a phrase "seven successive deficits". Pearson told his advisers: "I never want to uth [use] theven thuccethiv deficiths again." His advisers, Davey recalls, could not decide whether to laugh or cry.[42] Pearson gave the cue, and they all laughed.

The polls persuaded Gordon and his colleagues that the Liberals should emphasize the Pearson "team" and remove the spotlight from the leader. It was a wise decision. One result was an energetic candidate search that produced a talented group, including Mitchell Sharp, Edgar Benson, Larry Pennell, Herb Gray, Donald Macdonald, Pauline Jewett, and Gordon himself, in Ontario; Maurice Lamontagne, Charles "Bud" Drury, Maurice Sauvé, and John Turner in Quebec; Jack Nicholson, Jack Davis, and David Groos in British Columbia; John Stewart, Richard Cashin, Jean Eudes Dubé, and Allan MacEachen in Atlantic Canada; and the former CCF leader Hazen Argue from Saskatchewan. Pearson himself played a part in recruiting Toronto Maple Leaf hockey star Red Kelly, who probably attracted more attention than any new candidate. In general, however, candidate recruitment was not the leader's responsibility, and Gordon's efforts, excellent as they were, built up some loyalties to him that would create problems later.

As the election neared, Harris would fly to Ottawa and meet Davey at the airport. Gordon would join them and drive to Stornoway, where Mike met them at the door and always greeted them with, "Okay, how bad am I this month?"[43] It could not have been pleasant for Pearson, and his offhand comment in his letter to Geoffrey that politics were "unclean" betrays his discontent with what he endured in 1961 and early 1962. The discomfort caused by Harris's reports and the responses taken would have been justified if there had been obvious results. In his biography of Gordon, however, Denis Smith suggests that "it is a moot point whether this advice was any less occult, or any more reliable, than the impressionistic judgments of political professionals might have been".[44] Strong evidence supports Smith's perceptive suggestion that the sophisticated techniques did not produce exceptional results. The Gallup poll, for example, shows almost no movement in the standing of the two major parties, as Diefenbaker's government stumbled through 1961 and faced a serious economic crisis in 1962.* In September-October 1961, moreover, an extensive survey on leadership revealed that 53 per cent of Canadians approved of the way Pearson was doing his job (48 per cent for Diefenbaker) and only 18 per cent disapproved. More Canadians (32 per cent to 24 per cent) thought that, in a recession, Pearson would be a better leader than Diefenbaker.[45] These figures became worse the following year, and so did the standing of the Liberal Party.

When Peter Regenstreif later wrote *The Diefenbaker Interlude*, an electoral history of the period 1957 to 1963, a major theme was the deterioration of Pearson's personal support in the opposition years. Regenstreif found that Diefenbaker's "personality and qualities" attracted people to him. "In contrast, Pearson's support was strongly party identified." People chose Pearson because they preferred the party, not because they favoured its leader. When asked why they voted Conservative, 32 per cent in 1962 and 30 per cent in 1963 answered "Diefenbaker". When asked why they voted Liberal, an astonishingly low 3 per cent answered "Pearson" in 1962 and only 6 per cent in 1963.[46] Pearson, bow tie or not, had remarkably little appeal to those who had no regular party affiliation. Even Liberal supporters felt uncomfortable. Regenstreif, who was rumoured to be a Liberal sympathizer, used anecdotal evidence drawn from interviews to support his point. He quoted a Kitchener, Ontario, sales-

---

*	PC	Liberal
Nov. 1960	39	44
Jan. 1961	38	44
June 1961	40	42
Sept. 1961	38	42
Nov. 1961	37	43
Apr. 1962	34	40

man who intended to vote Liberal as saying "Pearson leaves me out in middle field somewhere. It's like a wonderful singer with a good voice singing trashy songs".[47] Mike probably felt the same way himself.

Successful or not, the remaking of Mike Pearson was one of many Canadian reactions to the election of John Kennedy in 1960. Coming at a moment in Canadian national life when anti-Americanism wafted through the air, the creation of Camelot on the Potomac quickly captured Canada's eye. It immediately disturbed John Diefenbaker, who had liked "Ike", the Kansas farm boy who became a war hero and who shared with Diefenbaker a taste for simple foods, fishing, and complicated syntax. The "new frontier", with its resident intellectuals, youthful glamour, cosmopolitan sophistication, and too-quick assumptions about what America meant and must do, had boundaries that Diefenbaker could never cross. Suddenly, his evangelical fervour, so electric in 1958, seemed as outdated as a crystal radio in the stereophonic age, especially to the young, the intellectuals, the fashionable, and the urban. Apart from the style, itself exceedingly important, the substance of Kennedy's appeal signalled a reinvigoration of the liberal tradition. Just as William Lyon Mackenzie had responded to the remarkable effervescence of Jacksonian democracy in the 1830s, and his grandson had clasped to his bosom the aura, if not the substance, of Roosevelt's New Deal a century later, Canada's liberals looked southward again for the breath of new life. Ramsay Cook had said that the intellectual content of the Kingston conference and the policy rally could be found in the book *The Affluent Society*, by Kennedy confidant and erstwhile Canadian John Kenneth Galbraith. Cook, a New Democrat, could have said the same of his own party's founding convention. In one of those fundamental shifts in American history between reform and retreat that Arthur Schlesinger, Jr., Kennedy's friend and biographer, has argued are the salient feature of American history, the liberal hour had once again struck, and the sound reverberated in Ottawa as loudly as in Washington.[48]

When Diefenbaker called the election on April 18, 1962, for June

18, his advisers correctly predicted that the Liberals would take the "Kennedy" approach, stressing the need to "get the country moving again". The Liberals led in the polls; Donald Fleming had brought forward a budget with a large deficit; and on May 2 the government pegged the dollar at 92.5 cents.[49] The mood in the House had been foul before the election, with Diefenbaker claiming that Pearson had not stood up to Communist imperialism. The reference was to Pearson's remark in an interview with Pierre Berton that if the choice were death or Communism, he would choose Communism because he could live to fight it. It quickly became "better red than dead" and brought a stream of protest. A Quebec Liberal member, Lucien Cardin, exploded in the House, charging that "From the first day [Pearson] was chosen head of the Liberal party, the Prime Minister by his cynical attitude, words and disparaging remarks about [Pearson] has revealed that in the deep recesses of his soul there burn the envious fires of the little green-eyed monster".[50] The campaign was not much better, particularly when the Tories got off to a bad start. By late April, the Liberals had moved into a significant lead (45 per cent to 38 per cent) in the Gallup poll. Mike, whose restrained language of 1958 had vanished, felt confident enough to challenge Diefenbaker to a debate, which Diefenbaker refused.[51]

The Liberal campaign, based on Harris's surveys, concentrated on Ontario, which Davey and Gordon knew so well, and on Quebec, where Jean Lesage's provincial Liberal government was very popular. The west and the Maritimes were not so well known, but there were hopes for British Columbia. There was also grumbling. Liberal Federation president John Connally expressed his strong suspicions of the influence of Tom Kent and Gordon on Pearson, but Diefenbaker's policies and personalities and Mike's ability to conciliate those who were discontented kept his diverse party together.[52] It was his greatest achievement in the 1962 campaign.

For a while it appeared that the Liberals would win at least a minority government, as Diefenbaker ran his worst campaign and the Liberals ran an innovative and often ingenious one. The

"Diefenbuck", a "dollar" with "92½¢" and Diefenbaker's wrinkled jowls upon it, was especially effective. Gordon sent out regular warnings to candidates, however, that they should avoid attacking Diefenbaker, whose personal popularity remained great in many quarters.[53] Perhaps too many attacks had already occurred, for in the final weeks of the campaign, the Liberals began to slip, as the Tories and Social Credit began to rise. In Quebec, Social Credit's Réal Caouette, an unknown car dealer and a firebrand orator, set aflame those rural areas that were suspicious of the changes so quickly occurring around them; and in doing so, he destroyed Lester Pearson's hope of forming a government.

The election-night photograph shows Mike and Maryon slouched and sad watching the results at the Château Laurier Hotel. There would be no northern Camelot. He won his own Algoma East seat, doubling his margin of victory. The Liberals won 100 seats, but the Tories had 116, even though the parties had an almost identical popular vote. Social Credit won 30 seats, 26 of them in Quebec, and the New Democrats won 19. It was a Conservative minority government, but for Diefenbaker, who had won 208 seats only four years earlier, it was a tremendous defeat. Mike felt much better when he fully realized what had happened, and his resolve to defeat Diefenbaker stiffened.

Geoffrey had written to him before the election to tell him that he had finally paid his debt to the party and could be his "own man". Mike agreed: he had now "paid [his] debt and now I am on my own".

> But "my own" keeps me here — where I am — for the present — as the work is only half-completed. If the next round is within 12 months — I'll go through it all again — hard though it is. If, however — and this is unlikely —[Diefenbaker] works out a coalition arrangement with [Social Credit] and hangs in for 3 or 4 years — then — after one session — I withdraw — if not with much honour at least without scars.
>
> If it were not for SC in Quebec — our complacent party man-

agers muffed that one* —we would now be forming a minority government. And *that* would be a real headache — in present circumstances. Imagine — with a combination of Dief and Caouette in opposition against you — with a combined majority!…

The campaign was very ragged and exhausting — but I am in good condition. Your mother was magnificent — especially as it doesn't come easy for her. But she was a real trouper and I was proud.[54]

Both Pearsons were prepared to fight another day.

One who did not see the next day was Mike's mother, Annie, who died in 1962. On election night, she had talked with Mike after it was clear that the Liberals had lost. As she had since Mike's childhood, she gently chided and challenged him while consoling:[55]

Well, I've been watching the campaign and there seems to have been an awful lot of talk about the dollar and financial matters and all that kind of thing, and I notice you've been taking part in these discussions and I was thinking, you know, that perhaps you haven't been asked to take on the Prime Minister's job at this time because you were never very good at arithmetic.

Mike's own sense of humour obviously came from Annie — and so much else. She had been, most likely, the greatest influence on his life.

Arithmetic also was the government's problem. Shortly after the election it became clear that devaluation of the dollar had not halted the financial crisis. It was an indicator of the bad relationship between Diefenbaker and Pearson that, on June 21, Diefenbaker sent Bank of Canada governor Louis Rasminsky, rather than calling upon Pearson himself, to explain the emergency measures

* The party manager in the Quebec region, the political veteran C.G. "Chubby" Power, was baffled by the Social Credit phenomenon and did not take it seriously until it was too late. Power to Bruce Hutchison, May 29, 1962, Power Papers, v. 6 (Queen's University Archives).

that the Canadian government had to take to prevent further deterioration of Canada's Exchange Reserve Fund. Rasminsky
expressed to Mike the hope that "the Liberal Party would forget
Politics" and give its support for these emergency measures, which
the government had to take. Pearson said that he would give that
support at a moment of crisis provided that he was made aware of
what specific actions the government proposed to announce on
June 24. Pearson called Gordon, who immediately reacted
strongly, because he believed that Diefenbaker and Donald
Fleming were using Rasminsky. Gordon feared that Pearson would
accept proposals from "a senior civil servant" that he would reject
from politicians. He also charged, most inaccurately according to
Louis Rasminsky, that the measures had been proposed to Canada
by the International Monetary Fund (IMF) and that their acceptance meant a significant loss of Canadian sovereignty. In any
event, no copy of a speech arrived before Diefenbaker gave it, and
Pearson did not hesitate to suggest that the measures were the
product of government mismanagement, although he did express
support on "national grounds". His "political" comment annoyed
Rasminsky, but his support for the measures upset Gordon, who
cast a cold eye on what he believed — erroneously, it seems — was
the IMF's baneful influence.[56]

In fact, the finance minister and the Bank of Canada had adopted
policies that would soon lead to a stronger Canadian economy.
Their success, however, was clouded by the abundant confusion and
contradiction that accompanied decision in Diefenbaker's minority
government. By June Mike had come to believe that the Diefenbaker government could not survive long, even if the economy
recovered. As he studied the details of the 1962 election results, Mike
was pleased that the "Kennedy" approach had attracted to the Liberals in Canada the type of people who were drawn to Kennedy in
the United States. Analysing the results, one finds Liberal strength
among the young, the urban, the university-educated, professionals,
the well-to-do, labour, Catholics, and ethnic groups. These were
the sectors that the Liberals had hoped to woo because they

believed they influenced others more than the rural and the older Canadians who still followed John Diefenbaker. In metropolitan Toronto, which the Liberals had lost in St. Laurent's heyday, the Liberals had taken fifteen seats, the Tories only six.[57] The Canada of the future seemed to be moving to the Liberal side. It seemed mere months before an issue arose that would precipitate a crisis that would cause an election.

If Kennedy's image perhaps illuminated a path for the Canadian Liberals, his policies soon helped them too. Although Diefenbaker had liked Eisenhower, there were serious differences in policy that arose between Canada and the United States in the Eisenhower years. Some were economic, especially in the area of disposal of surplus agricultural products, but most concerned the Canadian-American defence relationship. In February 1959, the Diefenbaker government announced the cancellation of the Avro Arrow and the acquisition of American Bomarc missiles for Canadian defence. The Americans had refused to buy the Arrow, which, without such purchases, was much too expensive to produce. Bomarcs were cheaper, but, as Diefenbaker said on February 20, 1959, the Bomarc's "full potential" was achieved only if it was armed with nuclear weapons. He pointed out that Canadian forces in Europe were already being equipped with "short range nuclear weapons", the ironically named Honest John missiles. Such weapons were also to be available for the F-104 aircraft, which the Canadians purchased as a strike weapon for their European forces in 1959. The "bombs" would be held by the Americans for Canadian usage under a shared-control system, but the agreement had not been negotiated at the time the Arrow announcement was made; and it never was.

Sidney Smith, the External Affairs minister who took part in these decisions, died on March 17, 1959, and was replaced three weeks later by Howard Green, a veteran British Columbia MP who had been Pearson's most virulent critic at the time of the Suez Crisis. Diefenbaker, who had long suspected that the "Pearsonali-ties" in External Affairs were feeding information to their friends in the opposition, chose a loyalist who had no background in External

Affairs but who had firm views — especially on nuclear weapons, which Green abhorred.

He was not alone. In the later 1950s the doctrine of "massive retaliation", fashioned in the early Eisenhower years, seemed recklessly dangerous as the Soviets and Americans tested hydrogen bombs thousands of times more powerful than those that had incinerated the cities of Hiroshima and Nagasaki. Moreover, the launching of Sputnik in 1957 and the clear evidence that Soviet intercontinental ballistic missiles could rain their warheads upon North America while Soviet tanks rolled through Europe, as they had through Hungary in 1956, "unhinged" the pillars upon which NATO doctrine stood. Tactical nuclear weapons such as the Honest John could halt the Soviet advance, but the costs would be unacceptably high. By the end of the 1950s, Theodore Draper comments, "the dilemma was excruciatingly acute — the next war could not be a conventional war and it could not be a nuclear war".[58]

Mike Pearson's lack of interest in economic questions contrasts strongly with his intense interest in the shifting sands of international politics and nuclear diplomacy in the late 1950s and early 1960s. No topic occupied more of his time, and his knowledge was great, his thinking sophisticated, his fears profound. In 1959, Harvard University Press published a series of lectures that he had given at the élite Fletcher School of Law and Diplomacy. John Kennedy, then a Massachusetts senator, reviewed the book, *Diplomacy in the Nuclear Age*, in the *Saturday Review* and pointed to Pearson's concern about "the dangerous ambiguities of a military policy grounded merely in nuclear deterrence". Nevertheless, Kennedy (or his amanuensis, perhaps) stressed that Pearson's major emphasis was on the need to strengthen instruments of negotiation and mediation and to assure that diplomacy furthered the reduction of international tensions. Kennedy noted Pearson's belief that NATO must have more effective "machinery for policy-making", but did not indicate whether he agreed with that belief.[59]

Deeply influenced by the arguments of Henry Kissinger in *Nuclear Weapons and Foreign Policy* and Herbert Kahn in *On Ther-*

monuclear War — arguments that Stanley Kubrick brilliantly satirized in *Dr. Strangelove, or How I Learned to Stop Worrying and Love the Bomb* — political scientist James Eayrs told the Kingston conference that Liberals should face the terror of nuclear weapons directly. For Canadians there could be no choice: geography dictated that it was "in Canada's interest to do everything in its power to make the Great Deterrent under United States control increasingly effective". To that end Canada should, in Eayr's "realistic" view, open Canada's territory, including its waters, to "United States retaliatory missiles"; acquire American anti-missile and anti-aircraft defences; and allow the atomic warheads that alone would make defence credible.[60]

Others recoiled from such analyses, including the National Liberal Rally, which left Liberal policy ambiguous and in Eayrs's view, silly.* Maryon Pearson was one who recoiled (so was Eayrs later), and she let others know how absurd she found the nuclear world of 1960. She and Patsy joined the Voice of Women in 1960. Denounced by some as a "communistic" organization, the Voice of Women, Maryon declared, was not subversive simply because it talked of peace. Women had a special role, because "men are so used to war.... This is why it's so important for women to bind together and take a stand." "The present world situation," she told another reporter, "is dreadful. It's got to be stopped. I don't understand how men have allowed such conditions to arise." In direct rebuke to those who urged Canadians to look realistically at nuclear weapons and to consider fallout shelters, Maryon said: "Men get casual and used to talking about piles of bombs here and piles of bombs there." Women were more inclined to peace because "they produce life and want to see their children live".[61]

Although Mrs. Howard Green would not endorse the Voice of

---

* The rally called for Canadian interceptors to confine their activities to "identification" of Soviet intruders, with the actual shooting left to Americans. "The proposed policy," Eayrs wrote, "has wittily been dubbed a 'policy for bird watchers', but bird watchers have more strength and stamina." James Eayrs, *Northern Approaches: Canada and the Search for Peace* (Toronto: Macmillan, 1961), 43.

Women's views, her husband's views were, perhaps, closer to Maryon's than Mike's and Geoffrey's were. Geoffrey, who was with NATO at this time, shared James Eayrs's views on the need for Canada to accept the implications of its geography and its membership in NATO and NORAD. After the Ottawa rally, which as we have seen did little to clarify Liberal defence policy, Geoffrey suggested that his father emphasize "NATO control" of nuclear weapons as a "way out", a course that Mike subsequently followed. The trouble was, of course, that NATO control was an elusive concept that never became a reality. Neither did the build-up of NATO conventional forces, which, logically, was the best method of reducing reliance on the bomb. In this situation, the Liberals and the government took refuge in ambiguity. There was, however, a fundamental difference. In 1959, Diefenbaker indicated that nuclear weapons would be obtained, and the Americans took him at his word. Subsequently, his government retreated from this statement. Although Mike had agreed that nuclear weapons could be accepted "under NATO collective control", he had not publicly — or privately in answer to Geoffrey's arguments — agreed that Canadian forces should accept nuclear weapons in Canada or Europe if those weapons were U.S. controlled, and he had not made public commitments as a head of government. He told a peace activist who wrote to him in April 1962:[62] "There has been no full scale debate on defence policy in this present Parliament which would give the Opposition Parties any real idea of all the factors involved in formulating a nuclear defence policy for the space age. So it is hard for the Opposition to be too dogmatic. In the light of the facts at our disposal, we believe that as a nation Canada should stay out of the nuclear club." Later that year the "facts" at his disposal changed.

On the morning of October 16, "Mac" Bundy came to John Kennedy's bedchamber in the White House to tell the president, still in his nightshirt, that the Central Intelligence Agency had proof that Soviet missiles were in Cuba. Kennedy, whom Khrushchev had tested before, reacted angrily: Khrushchev "can't do this to me".[63] The thirteen days that followed brought the world within an eye's blink of a nuclear catastrophe. For John Diefenbaker, it was a political catastrophe.

By October 1962, Diefenbaker's distrust of John Kennedy was profound — with good reason. Several times Kennedy had made it clear that he much preferred Mike Pearson to Diefenbaker. On his first visit to Ottawa in May 1961, at a dinner party at American ambassador Livingston Merchant's residence, Kennedy talked and joked with Pearson and ignored Diefenbaker.[64] A senior American aide later recalled that the president was "absolutely discourteous" towards Diefenbaker.* In April 1962, during the 1962 election campaign, Kennedy, whose loathing of Diefenbaker was now widely known, invited Pearson to a White House dinner. The invitation had been sent before the election was called, but this subtlety was lost upon Diefenbaker, especially when Kennedy paid conspicuous attention to Pearson. Livingston Merchant called on Diefenbaker shortly after the dinner and endured a tirade about the Pearson invitation and a threat by Diefenbaker that he would reveal the memorandum Kennedy had left behind. When Kennedy heard what had happened from Merchant, he called it "blackmail". It was, and it was badly done. Kennedy said he would never speak to or see Diefenbaker again.[65]

When Kennedy decided to blockade Cuba, he called Macmillan of Britain personally and well in advance, but sent Livingston Merchant to inform Diefenbaker only two hours before his historic television speech. The judicious Diefenbaker aide Basil Robinson, who admits the many faults of Diefenbaker, points out that in this case "Diefenbaker's upset was understandable". The blockade was, "after all, a very important development for the defence of North America, and it was [Diefenbaker] who had entered into the

---

* It was on that visit that Kennedy dropped a memorandum entitled "What We Want from Ottawa Trip". Diefenbaker had it in a vault, took great umbrage at its contents, and claimed that Kennedy had scrawled SOB in the margin. Kennedy, upon learning this, told his friend Ben Bradlee that he "didn't think Diefenbaker was a son of a bitch.... I thought he was a prick". Bradlee, *Conversations with Kennedy* (New York: Norton, 1975), 183.

NORAD agreement five years before", an agreement that provided for the "fullest possible coordination" in North American defence.[66] Diefenbaker's anger, coupled with his confusion over an External Affairs recommendation (made before Kennedy spoke) that the matter be referred to the U.N., made him appear to question Kennedy's decision and words. He briefed Pearson, but then borrowed Pearson's words for his own speech in the House, confirming for Pearson that Diefenbaker could not be trusted.[67] What followed would have been comical had the stakes not been so high. Diefenbaker refused to place Canadian forces under a NORAD alert known as "Defcom 3", and Defence minister Harkness defied him by ordering them on alert despite Diefenbaker's stand. Diefenbaker refused again the following day, by which time his reluctance was noted by a Canadian public overwhelmingly behind Kennedy's stand. Mike told Geoffrey that the House was in a foul temper, but Diefenbaker's end was near.[68]

The Cuban Missile Crisis was a chilling moment in the Cold War that stiffened Canadian spines, including some in Diefenbaker's cabinet. For Kennedy, Diefenbaker was now a marked man. For Diefenbaker, Kennedy was a sworn enemy. Other allies had also been appalled by Kennedy's failure to consult. The Dutch foreign minister, Joseph Luns, for example, opposed Kennedy's action and hesitated to act. The hesitations and objections of The Netherlands and others were forgotten.[69] Diefenbaker's behaviour, however, was neither forgotten nor forgiven, because in American eyes it fitted a pattern that could be identified as anti-American. It also troubled many Canadians and many Conservatives.

Mike was in the midst of reviewing Canadian defence policy when the crisis occurred. He had, as indicated earlier, met with James Eayrs and John Gellner in 1959 to discuss the problems of nuclear weapons. Both men were identified with the view that Canadian defence policy was wrong and that Canada had an obligation to fulfil its alliance commitment to accept nuclear weapons. Eayrs expressed the view at the Kingston conference; Gellner established a close relationship with Liberal Defence critic Paul Hellyer

and tried to influence him. Hellyer had toured military bases in the
United States and Europe in August 1961 and November 1962. He
returned from both tours convinced that defence requirements,
quite apart from the question of commitments, demanded that
Canada accept nuclear weapons. "The military people at SHAPE,"
Hellyer reported in November, "are very concerned about the indecision of the Canadian government." They had not brought "the
matter into the international political arena" but, if there were no
decision, might not be able to avoid doing so.[70]

Hellyer's prediction proved accurate when retiring NATO commander General Lauris Norstad passed through Ottawa on January
3, 1963. Confronted by reporter Charles Lynch, Norstad said that
Canada had made a commitment to provide its F-104s in Europe
with nuclear weapons. Air Marshal Frank Miller, who was standing
nearby, publicly agreed with Norstad, who had had a private chat
with Hellyer in November. The effect was devastating and disastrous for the government. Mike, like Defence minister Harkness,
had already concluded that Norstad's view was correct, and 54 per
cent of the Canadian public agreed with them.[71]

During 1962, an obviously troubled Pearson had surveyed old
friends, colleagues, and others on the subject. At the 1961 policy
rally, the party had taken a stand against nuclear weapons for
Canada's NORAD forces. They would contemplate such weapons
for the European forces only if they were subject to NATO control
and requested by the NATO council. Early in 1962, Pearson had
tried to write a defence pamphlet to counter Diefenbaker's "ludicrous" stand, but told his former External Affairs colleague Douglas
LePan that he found the task difficult. It was, he told another old
friend, "in some ways the most agonizing problem" he had faced,
because of Canada's "obligations for collective defence" and its
other obligations "to prevent the spread of nuclear weapons". No
defence pamphlet was forthcoming, but even before the Cuban
Missile Crisis, Mike had called for the establishment of a select committee to determine the issue.[72]

After Cuba, he told another old friend, University of Toronto history professor George Brown, that he still believed that Canada could play a "full part" in the Atlantic alliance without nuclear weapons, but he did see a problem in the "commitments" Diefenbaker had made. If elected, Pearson claimed, he would work to negotiate an effective non-nuclear role for Canada in the alliance.[73] Gellner and Hellyer, however, had decided that was not good enough. Hellyer, with Mike's approval, asked Gellner to prepare a draft of a Liberal defence policy, which he did by December 21, 1962. Gellner recommended that Canada "should make good on our commitments to NORAD and NATO until we can change them through renegotiation".[74] Pearson sent this paper to several people, asking for their comments. Walter Gordon took the paper with him on a trip to the west coast while he met with Liberal candidate David Groos, a defence expert.* Endorsements of the proposed policy came from Gordon's brother-in-law, "Bud" Drury, who had already urged such a policy on Pearson, Hellyer, Mitchell Sharp, Pickersgill, Groos, and others.[75] After Norstad's remarks, Mike himself went to New York for the Council on World Tensions and, at the Sheraton-East Hotel, between Broadway plays and council meetings, drafted and redrafted a statement on nuclear weapons for Canada. On landing at Toronto on his return he immediately and without consultation announced: "As a Canadian I am ashamed if we accept commitments and then refuse to discharge them."

Canada, he declared, "should end at once its evasion of responsibility, and put itself in a position to discharge the commitments it has already accepted for Canada". The Liberals, he argued, had opposed the acquisition of most weapons that required nuclear warheads and would seek, therefore, to renegotiate with the United States and NATO "a more effective and realistic role for Canada" in collective and continental defence. It was hypocritical to invoke

---

* Gordon's later statement that he was caught by surprise and did not support the change seems odd, in light of the fact that he had the Gellner document and even served as its interpreter. See Denis Smith, *Gentle Patriot: A Political Biography of Walter Gordon* (Edmonton: Hurtig, 1973), 119-20.

"moral grounds", for Canada accepted the protection of the nuclear deterrent in U.S. hands and exported uranium for military purposes. (He did not add that much of that uranium came from Elliot Lake, in his constituency.) Fulfilling the commitments was "the only honourable course for any government representing the Canadian people".[76]

Comments came quickly. A young Winnipeg Liberal, Lloyd Axworthy, wrote to say "how very disappointed and saddened" he was "to see a man renege on past principles, and deny the very policies upon which so much admiration and respect have been built". Axworthy declared that he could no longer be active in the Liberal Party. Two other future Liberal cabinet ministers who had been considering standing as Liberal candidates denounced Pearson. Pierre Trudeau labelled him the "unfrocked priest of peace" and claimed that "les hipsters" of Camelot had intrigued with Pearson to destroy Diefenbaker. Jean Marchand said he would not run because of Pearson's stand.[77] Conservative Defence minister Douglas Harkness, however, welcomed the speech and saw in Pearson's stand an escape for the beleaguered Diefenbaker government. He did not recognize how stubborn Diefenbaker would be, and how strongly Howard Green and his deputy, Norman Robertson, felt about the issue.

Diefenbaker did give a speech in the House of Commons to defend his position. He claimed that, at the recent Nassau conference between Macmillan and Kennedy to which he had invited himself (to their dismay), Macmillan and Kennedy had agreed that increasing conventional forces was more important than deploying nuclear weapons more widely. He also revealed some details of confidential talks with the Americans. The Americans were livid; Harkness issued, without consultation, his own "clarification"; and Diefenbaker faced a crumbling government.

On January 30, 1963, the U.S. State Department issued an astonishing press release calling John Diefenbaker a liar. Even Mike thought that the Americans had gone too far.[78] They had; but so had John Diefenbaker. Harkness resigned on February 4, 1963, and that afternoon Mike moved a no-confidence motion. The New Democrats had condemned Pearson's nuclear stand, but they and Social Credit were willing to support a motion condemning the "indecision" and "lack of leadership" of the government. On the cold Ottawa evening of February 5, 1963, John Diefenbaker's government was finally put out of its misery.[79]

CHAPTER EIGHT

MR. PRIME
MINISTER

We have been bouncing around the heavens, at least we did so on our way back from Ottawa. [U.S. ambassador] Walt [Butterworth] and Virginia asked us to come up for a dinner party they were giving for Mike and Marion [*sic*]....

Mike was recovering from losing a gland in his neck and from a Finance Minister's boner on the Budget, which nearly upset his government — about as stupid a performance as the Bay of Pigs. But he was laughing it off; and Marion was disliking power and position as much as she disliked its opposite. As for the rest, they were, as Walt said, a tribal society, naive, terribly serious about the wrong things, and not at all aware of their real problems, which were worth being serious about. Their best move would be to ask us to take them over; and our best move would be to say, no.

— Dean Acheson shortly after the 1963 election[1]

THE PHILOSOPHER George Grant called the 1963 election "the last gasp of Canadian nationalism". His *Lament for a Nation* was a funeral dirge for what he called "the older traditions of Canada". Diefenbaker, for all his flaws, challenged those forces of liberalism, modernity, and technology that had corroded those traditions, weakening them until they collapsed under Kennedy's determined assault upon their last wounded defenders. Diefenbaker had defied the new empire and its fortresses on Bay Street, at editors' desks, and in the universities.[2]

This interpretation was congenial to many commentators, then and later, as they tried to understand why the 1963 election seemed so significant. Certainly there was much evidence of Kennedy's interference in Canadian politics, and circumstantial evidence that it was effective. It was not Grant but Ambassador Walt Butterworth who told the dean of American journalists, Walter Lippman, that the election's "outcome holds salutary lessons which will not be overlooked by future aspirants to political office in Canada".[3] On the day that his government fell, Diefenbaker had identified the culprits who had brought him down as mere playthings of the gods who played their games in Washington. During the campaign, he invoked Macdonald and Borden, whose campaigns in 1891 and 1911 had triumphed over the forces of "continentalism", and had given, to politicians after them, a salutary lesson of what would happen if they openly flirted with the Yankee siren. But by 1963 these lessons had been forgotten. In Diefenbaker's bitter memory, it was he and the "little guys" who were left to battle against "them": the forces of Bay Street capitalism, continentalism, and Americanism.[4]

Through this lens, Grant and Diefenbaker saw Diefenbaker's celebration of what had made Canadians different from Americans* as a vain attempt to nourish those starved roots that had provided the "juice" – the nourishment – for the defining "particularisms" of an earlier Canada. In Grant's view, the Liberal Party had been pursuing policies that had led inexorably to the disappearance of Canada, and Mike Pearson had been its guide. For Pearson, "the existence of the Canadian nation was not a priority". Bitter words indeed, especially from one who knew Mike very well, who had

---

* Diefenbaker could be blunt. On March 23, he declared that "when some nations start to point out to us what we should do, let me tell you this. Canada was in both wars a long time before some other nations were.... We don't need any lessons what Canada should do after that record of service in two world wars." *Globe and Mail*, Mar. 24, 1963.

spent many long nights with him in London as the *Luftwaffe* flew overhead, and who, one night upon his return from a dreadful night of carnage in London's East End, had had the grime washed from his weary young body by his sister Alison's close friend, Mike Pearson. But Grant's friendship with Pearson ended. A major factor may have been Mike's relationship with Mary Greey, Alison's young Canadian roommate, whom Grant adored. Grant believed that in London, during the Blitz, Mary Greey had fallen in love with Mike and he with her. When Mike returned to Canada, she decided that she too would come home. Grant wrote to his mother in September 1941 and asked her "to understand & try & help". If she had ever seen Mary Greey and Mike together, he said, "you would know how absolutely suited they are for each other & how each adores the other". They were, he added, "both far too fine to ever let it interfere with his children & wife but please try to understand it & make it a natural easy thing". But the return to Canada chilled the ardour. In 1945, she went back to London where she fell in love with (and subsequently married) the Canadian historian Gerald Graham. Grant wrote to his mother that she was now in love "in a way she never loved Pearson". Grant cared a great deal for Mary Greey and after she and Mike were no longer together he cared much less for Mike.* Grant's resentments bloomed brilliantly, if eccentrically, in the hothouse that enclosed the small English-Canadian élite of the 1940s and 1950s. In the haze of that hothouse, the lens through which Grant looked at Pearson and the 1963 election became

---

* Through the assistance of John Holmes I interviewed several individuals who were in a position to comment on the relationship. The most important interview was with Alison and George Ignatieff. They were in London then and knew both Mike and Mary Greey well. Alison said that Mike and Mary were drawn together by the extraordinary circumstances of the Blitz, which transformed acquaintanceship into friendship. She did not elaborate upon the nature of the friendship. She and George Ignatieff agreed that Mike became a much more private person after he returned to Canada, and thenceforth his life was played out primarily in the public forum. The letters quoted are from George Grant to Maud Grant [September 1941], W.L. Grant Papers, MG30 D59, v. 40 (NAC); and George Grant to Maud Grant, June 16 [1945], *ibid.*

blurred. As a result, he missed much detail and distorted the image he framed.[5].

When the election was called, it was Diefenbaker's Conservative colleagues who demanded that he not lead an anti-American campaign. When it was thought Diefenbaker would resign, his replacement was to be George Nowlan, a small-town, Baptist, Nova Scotian lawyer who was suspicious of Bay Street's influence and whose Annapolis Valley roots were among the strongest of those European "particularisms" that Grant celebrated. Nowlan, like Grant, believed that his beloved valley had been made "embarrassingly superfluous" by twentieth-century technology and "the cosy Canadian-American relationship". And yet it was Nowlan who announced on the front page of the Halifax *Chronicle-Herald* on February 11, 1963, just after the government fell, that he would "quit the cabinet immediately if an anti-American election program were presented by his party".[6]

The Liberal campaign chair was Walter Gordon, who was publicly identified with anti-continentalist forces. Gordon's 1961 book, *Troubled Canada*, went far beyond anything the Diefenbaker government had ever conceived in setting forth a program to deal with Canada's loss of "a large measure of economic independence".[7] Moreover, until January 12, 1963, it was the Liberal Party that had opposed nuclear weapons, to the annoyance of American officials, while the Diefenbaker government had, on several occasions, indicated that it would accept them. This point was not lost upon State Department officials, who, in briefing the presidents, pointed out that Diefenbaker's anti-Communism was sterner than Pearson's and that Pearson did not hesitate to criticize American policies if he disagreed with them. The day after the election, James "Scotty" Reston of the *New York Times* told his readers that American officials liked Pearson "because he is one of the few diplomats here who have told them the blunt truth in the past and made them like it, even when they didn't agree...". That probably goes too far; we saw earlier that the same Livingston Merchant who briefed Diefenbaker on Cuba expressed to Acheson his reservations about

Pearson. Still, Reston is correct that the Americans did not like Diefenbaker, "not primarily because he differed with them — Pearson has differed with them much more effectively" — but because Diefenbaker personalized his battles and made wild charges, such as the suggestion that Washington could use Canada as a "decoy" to avoid nuclear attack on the United States. That, Reston declared, was a "low blow".[8]

Looking back at the 1963 election, we can observe that these "particularisms" whose passing Grant lamented had much stronger roots than he imagined. Grant's contemporary, Marshall McLuhan, who seemed to celebrate modern information technology and the "global village" it would create, was more perceptive in his forecast that the very processes of "homogenization" that Grant so feared would result, dialectically, in a reinvigoration of "particularisms", whether they be ethnic identity or regional assertiveness. Grant should have noticed that those who, in 1963, resisted Diefenbaker's "nationalist" *cri de coeur* most adamantly were Newfoundlanders and francophones. They were among the Canadians least touched by American communications technology and its "empire", and their "particularism" was most pronounced. Those who heeded Diefenbaker's call most willingly lived in Saskatchewan and Alberta, which in 1911 had overwhelmingly supported free trade (and would do so again) and whose political culture had been traditionally most willing to accommodate American innovations.[9] Moreover, many of those urban Canadians who did respond to Kennedy and his vision of America in 1963 soon afterwards retreated quickly as that vision became lurid and dissonant after his death. On the eve of the 1963 election, for example, Pierre Berton looked out his window on a "gloriously crisp winter afternoon" upon a countryside that possessed "a traditional Canadian textbook look", with A.Y. Jackson's "swirling hills, in pastel yellows and shadowed blues ... sparkled glitter on the crusted snow [with] rutted roads snaking across the skyline". Berton refused to be romantic about the "Canadian identity" that scene represented, for it had become clear to him that, "If we want a Distinctive Canadian Identity that we can wear with pride, then we must earn it". There were those "who cling to the beautiful Canadian Dream that we can go our own sweet way in the world of the States without reference to our neighbours and that we can 'be ourselves' in the nineteenth century sense". Such people wanted to preserve Canadian particularisms:

> But the vision of a Fortress Canada surrounded by an undefended and invisible cultural barrier is as dead today as the pterodactyl National sovereignty. If this election proves anything it proves that anti-Americanism is finished as a political issue. We have cast our lot with this continent for better or for worse and the people know it. The world is reassembling itself into larger units and I doubt we could escape the tide even if we wished to.[10]

The election did not prove what he thought, and a few years later Berton, of whom the Pearsons were very fond, began to ask Canadians to earn their distinctive identity by studying their past, whose "particularisms" he most lovingly and ably chronicled. National sovereignty was no pterodactyl.

And yet Grant and Berton were correct in sensing, from their very different perspectives in 1963, that things had come unstuck in Canada. In the post-war period, Canadians had, in historian Douglas Owram's words, reacted to the "instability and chaos of the 1930s and 1940s" by seeking "the conventionality and security of home and family". Post-war prosperity had eased the difficult "balancing act of a democratic marriage, traditional work roles" and the fears of depression.[11] Canadians after 1945 recalled the disruptions of political life in the 1930s and sought stability. They battened down the hatches on their family lives. The first studies of voting in the 1950s indicated that most Canadians voted as their parents or their co-religionists did. Diefenbaker's victory, however, broke this pattern. The fading memory of the Depression, the mobility that came from a rapidly expanding education system, and the unloosing of restraints of many kinds as the fear of social instability receded also contributed to a willingness to leave behind anchors that had held Canadians to traditional social and political institutions. Because he had shattered so many Canadian political traditions, there was a paradox in Diefenbaker's appeal to tradition, and many who voted for Pearson were also nostalgic for their own vision of the past. Another Maritime Conservative, Canada's ambassador in Washington, Charles Ritchie,* noted this circumstance in his diary on April 8, election day: "For some of my fellow civil servants the Liberals seem a sort of normalcy which is called stable government and seems to mean a return to old middle-class, middle of the way, reasonable, responsible, familiar Canada."[12] That Canada could never be put together again.

Mike Pearson knew that he could not put together the "familiar Canada" that Ritchie had described. He also thought that the Diefenbaker-Kennedy jousting was a sham affair, an abrasive scraping together of two gritty personalities that obscured the more fundamental issues facing the electorate. Those issues included the place of Quebec in Confederation, an issue he tried to address on December 17, 1962, in the House of Commons. With the intellectual assistance of Maurice Lamontagne (who had initially opposed André Laurendeau's January 1962 idea, but in discussion with Pearson had warmed to it), Pearson proposed the creation of a royal commission on bilingualism and biculturalism and a true "partnership" between French and English Canadians that required "equal and full opportunity to participate in all federal government services". Like the speech on nuclear weapons, this initiative was mainly Pearson's. There was reluctance on the part of Gordon and Kent, who thought other issues were bigger, and from Maurice Sauvé, who generally disagreed with Lamontagne's ideas. The

---

* Ritchie cast a cool eye upon the New Frontier and upon the so-called Liberal version of Canada, but Diefenbaker's nationalist campaign had no resonance for him. After the election, he wrote to thank Howard Green for his support but would not write to Diefenbaker: "I consider his disappearance a deliverance; there should be prayers of thanksgiving in the churches." Charles Ritchie, *Storm Signals: More Undiplomatic Diaries, 1962-1971* (Toronto: Macmillan, 1983), 46.

speech attracted favourable comment in the Quebec press and from francophone intellectuals. It appealed very much to Jean Marchand, who was considering a Liberal candidacy, but the next major speech Pearson made, the one on nuclear weapons, ended Marchand's Liberal flirtation abruptly. And, as Jack Pickersgill later said, neither speech had much impact on those grass-roots francophones who were intending to vote Social Credit.[13]

Mike began the campaign in high spirits but with full knowledge that Diefenbaker would not make his lot easy. He told Geoffrey on February 22, 1963, that "the campaign ... will be the toughest, most challenging and, I think, most important 10 weeks of my life". He agreed that he "*must* [italics in original] not be provoked or cajoled into any but a high level appeal for support".[14] That appeared to be possible and, indeed, the correct political strategy when the government fell. The Liberals had a fifteen-point lead in the Gallup poll. They had money and sophisticated polling. Tom Kent and Maurice Lamontagne, with help from some others, had improved upon "the Liberal Programme" of 1962, which had been, perhaps, the most intellectually coherent and detailed policy statement ever produced in Canada. (It bore the mark of campaigns in Kent's native Britain, where campaigns begin with the publication of policy statements, which then focus debate.) The Conservatives were in disarray. Harkness's resignation had been followed by resignations from George Hees and Pierre Sévigny and decisions by Davie Fulton and Donald Fleming that they would not run. The Liberals, in contrast, had assembled a strong team of candidates and a leader who promised responsibility. For the first time in their history, the Toronto *Telegram* and the Montreal *Gazette*, historically the strongest Tory papers, endorsed the Liberals, as did the Toronto *Globe and Mail*, whose politics were eclectic but whose editorial certainty and clarity were memorable. The Liberals seemed to have public opinion solidly with them on the nuclear issue, which, in the view of most observers, would be the main issue of the campaign.[15] Diefenbaker seemed destined to tilt at windmills, but this time it appeared likely that the drama of the spectacle would excite only a few.

Things went badly wrong. Dalton Camp, who was in charge of the Conservatives' national headquarters, began the campaign with a party "reeling from blows", with low morale and no money. At Conservative headquarters, Camp wrote his letters by hand. The Liberals, using the "Kennedy approach", had enthusiastic young volunteers, sophisticated polling analysts, and highly competent political veterans, such as Mary Macdonald and Tom Kent's assistant and devoted Liberal "the highly talented Pauline Bothwell".[16] And yet for all the talent and support, as Camp correctly observed, the Liberals "ran an unbelievably bad campaign".

The troubles appeared as soon as the election was called. In 1962, Tom Kent had travelled with Pearson and prepared most of his speeches, but the relationship was uncomfortable for both. After a meeting, Pearson wanted to watch a ball game; Kent went over the day's events relentlessly. After the election, they continued to disagree often, particularly over the Liberal pledge of medicare and on the nuclear-arms question. In 1963, it was clear to Kent that, more than before, Diefenbaker would dominate the Tory campaign. And, Kent later wrote, "given the kind of campaign that he would wage, it was inescapable in Mike's nature that he would keep trying to reply; that he would tangle with the man he now so much despised".[17] Kent had long worked closely with Pearson; but he now became a candidate in British Columbia, far away from the central campaign. There were others who were missing. Lamontagne ran again in Quebec. Lou Harris, who had been polling since 1961, had other duties and was rarely available. He was replaced by his American associate Oliver Quayle. Gordon remained campaign chair, but he too was occupied in his own Davenport riding. When the first polls came in, Gordon and Davey were shocked. The self-confidence Mike had started out with ebbed away.[18]

Mike felt comfortable with the nuclear-weapons issue, and he believed it would be the winning issue. Kent, Gordon, and Davey disagreed. Although Kent suggests that Pearson made the nuclear-weapons decision because of his sense of obligation to collective responsibility within the alliance, there is strong evidence that

Pearson looked at the polls and was influenced by them. Indeed, he was rather proud of his "political" shrewdness when he spoke about his decision later. In 1972, he told Professor Denis Smith, with some satisfaction, that the nuclear-weapons speech "was when I really became a politician".[19] He had also been "his own man", not simply a voice for party policies. When, therefore, Gordon and Davey told him that he should not emphasize the nuclear issue but should focus on the domestic "bread and butter" issues, which polling indicated were the major concerns, he was irritated.

So much went wrong. The Liberals had more money, but they faced a flamboyant opponent who was a magnet for cameras and microphones. They turned to gimmicks. The "Diefenbuck" had worked so well in 1962; in 1963, however, the gimmicks failed dismally. There were "homing pigeons", intended to signal Pearson's arrival, that never arrived. There was a children's colouring book that was unfit for children and offended many adults.* Worst of all was the "truth squad". Annoyed at Diefenbaker's wild charges, Davey decided that a Liberal should follow Diefenbaker, take notes, and then afterwards point out the lies. For this task Davey selected Judy LaMarsh, the MP for Niagara Falls and a tough campaigner. Diefenbaker quickly turned the trick to his own advantage by introducing LaMarsh at each meeting, giving her a table to make notes, and then making her the target of his rapier wit. Davey's idea backfired disastrously, with even the Liberal press aghast at the spectacle. Davey offered to resign; Mike refused the offer.[20]

The March Gallup poll revealed that the Liberals had fallen to 41 per cent, while the Tories had remained the same, and Social Credit

---

* The NDP page, for example, had a bespectacled professor wearing a mortarboard and a square, menacing demonstrator with a placard that said, "Ban the Bomb". The caption read:

This is an NDP party,
They are discussing their platform.
They are against just about everything.
Sometimes they are even against themselves.
Colour them black and blue.

had surged in Quebec. Simultaneously, it became apparent that Quebec had changed its mind about nuclear weapons. In November 1962, 59 per cent of francophones thought Canadian armed forces should have nuclear weapons. In March 1963, it was only 37 per cent, after the Quebec journalists thundered against Pearson's policy change. Suddenly, the parliamentary majority that had seemed all but certain had become a minority. Davey decided the campaign needed a new direction, and he and Gordon persuaded Pearson to promise "sixty days of decision", with a clear program of action for a new Liberal government.* Certainly, something was needed. Mike was depressed; Maryon was furious. Mike mused to reporters about the idea that Diefenbaker and he should quit and turn over their parties to younger men. His press secretary, Dick O'Hagan, was astounded and angry at these remarks, but managed to deflect attention.[21]

The Liberals' problems, however, attracted relatively little interest, because John Diefenbaker was working his political wonders on the prairies again. Peter Newman, collecting notes for his critical biography of Diefenbaker, which would transform Canadian political journalism, was on the train as Diefenbaker performed his whistle-stop magic. Newman knew Diefenbaker's flaws well, but on that train he saw his strengths, and it was "an unforgettable experience" as "the people of the flat, sad little towns turned out to hear him by the hundreds in the prairie chill" and "scrambles of children followed him adoringly".[22] "Sixty days of decision" diverted some attention from Diefenbaker's progress across the prairies, but the Liberals found the Kennedy administration, which so fervently wanted Diefenbaker's defeat, the opposite of helpful.

Newsweek, which was widely and correctly regarded as a maga-

---

* Davey had suggested 100 days, but Maryon said it would remind everyone of Napoleon's 100 days and the defeat at Waterloo. Pearson, as a former historian, agreed, although it compressed the decision and eliminated the possibility that people would think of Franklin Roosevelt's "one hundred days". It seems typical of decisions made in desperate campaigns.

zine closely linked with Kennedy, featured Diefenbaker's scowling face layered with drooping jowls on its February 18 cover. The story was nastier than the cover. Diefenbaker turned it quickly to his advantage, blaming members of the Liberal Who's Who and the lesser Who's Who for the article. On March 28, Max Freedman, the *Winnipeg Free Press*'s Washington correspondent, called Pearson at an Edmonton Canadian Legion branch and told him that he had just come from a White House dinner where Kennedy had offered any help Mike might need. Not surprisingly, Mike quickly replied: "For God's sake, tell the president to keep his mouth shut."[23] He checked quickly with the janitor to make certain no one else had heard that the White House had called. He knew what Diefenbaker might do with that delicious morsel. The very next day, the U. S. Congress released testimony given by secretary of defence Robert McNamara in which he said that the Bomarcs in Canada would draw enemy fire. Diefenbaker quickly interpreted this to mean that "the Pearson policy is to make Canada a decoy for intercontinental missiles". It was an outrageous comment, but it captured attention.[24]

On March 30, Pearson, who had an undiagnosed infection and had been told to stay in bed in the Empress Hotel before the meeting in Victoria that evening, unburdened himself to Bruce Hutchison. He mentioned Kennedy's offer and his reaction, then added that he did not know whether his campaign could go on.[25] It did, but on April Fool's Day in Vancouver he wished it had not. The hall was swarming with demonstrators shouting "Yankee stooge" and worse. They set fire to the Stars and Stripes in front of the platform. They aimed pea-shooters at Pearson and bounced peas off his swollen, infected head as he spoke. Maryon was in tears on the platform. Afterwards, thoroughly depressed, they returned to their hotel, where they agreed never to go through a campaign again. As Mike and Maryon drank a toast to their agreement, some excited aides burst in and declared that the Liberals had won at least three more seats because Pearson had not backed down. There, Mike declared, "was a loyal politician, one who puts seats ahead of everything — even ahead of soul".[26]

Neither body nor soul was in good shape in the last week of the election. The "high level" he had resolved to maintain had proven impossible. He obviously resented the attempts to reshape him, package his message, and cast the Liberal appeal at the level of what he told Geoffrey was "an 18th century illiterate simplicity".[27] When Mike was young, his political idol had been Lloyd George, whose demagogic brilliance was unexcelled. But he lost his taste for such performances, though there remained a curious fascination with them, even in the case of Diefenbaker. That fascination mingled with fear and created many of his parliamentary problems. He had been schooled in the gentility of post-war politics and was not prepared for the sudden change that came after 1957. With some doubts, he accepted his advisers' pleas that he try the new political technology of polls, focus groups, and media consultants to defeat Diefenbaker's approach, which harked back to an earlier time. He had Kent and Lamontagne deal with "issues" as Kennedy had Sorenson and Schlesinger. It did not quite work.

On April 8, Maryon and Mike went to the Château Laurier to watch the results. The evening began with a sweep of Newfoundland, and visions of a majority danced in the heads of the Laurier crowd. They dimmed somewhat as the Tories did better than expected in the Maritimes, and Social Credit won 20 seats in Quebec. Still, by the time the polls closed in Manitoba, the Liberals were leading or were declared winners in 119 seats and needed only 13 of the remaining 57 seats in the Canadian west. They fell short, winning only 10. Still, they had 129 seats, enough to break open the champagne. That night, politics was soothing for the soul as well as the taste buds.[28]

Prime Minister Pearson took office two weeks later, on April 22, one day before his sixty-sixth birthday. There were five colleagues who got special consideration and who deserved it: Paul Martin, who had been remarkable in his loyalty after his convention loss in 1958 and relentless and skilful in his performance in the Commons; Lionel Chevrier, who had been Pearson's Quebec lieutenant and also a fine performer in the House; Jack Pickersgill, the Liberal who

annoyed Diefenbaker most and who had long since convinced
Pearson that, despite the 1958 amendment error, his political skills
were remarkable;* Maurice Lamontagne, who had served Pearson
effectively as a speech writer and as a counsel on Quebec; and, of
course, Walter Gordon, without whose financial assistance, personal
contacts, and great determination Prime Minister Pearson would
not have been possible.

As expected, Martin chose External Affairs, and Gordon,
Finance; but not before Mike asked him whether he thought he
might be better suited for Trade and Commerce. Gordon reminded
Pearson, in Pearson's words, "that it had been understood between
us that he should have Finance, that he wanted it, and so it was".
The request left a doubt in Gordon's mind about Pearson's commitment to him and his policies.[29] Chevrier asked for and got
Justice. Pickersgill, to Pearson's surprise, asked for the relatively
minor post of secretary of state and the more demanding one of
government leader in the House. Paul Hellyer, who had been so
influential in the defence debate, got Defence. Mitchell Sharp
became minister of trade and commerce, and veteran Ottawa
member George McIlraith minister of transport. In classic Canadian
fashion, some ministers represented regions or interests, such as
Harry Hays, who represented Alberta and agriculture. Judy
LaMarsh was given the difficult Health and Welfare ministry and
was the sole woman in the cabinet. When Pauline Jewett asked

---

* Pickersgill, Diefenbaker wrote in his memoirs, "was the only member I've known
who could strut sitting down". J.G. Diefenbaker, *Memoirs of the Right Honourable
John G. Diefenbaker. The Years of Achievement: 1957-1962* (Toronto: Macmillan,
1976), 81. There was some talk after the election that Diefenbaker would not resign
immediately but would wait and meet Parliament. Then six Social Credit members
announced they would support the Liberals, and this action compelled Diefenbaker's resignation. There were later allegations of bribery. Keith Davey and his old
college friend Doug Fisher talked about a more formal arrangement with the NDP.
But nothing came of it after someone — the Liberals were certain it was David
Lewis — leaked the information to the *Toronto Daily Star*. See Peter Stursberg,
Lester Pearson and the Dream of Unity (Toronto: Doubleday, 1978), ch. 4.

Pearson if she might be a minister, he told her there was already one woman.[30] And that was all there would be in those years.*

The cabinet met at three that afternoon. Pearson's face was swollen from the infection, which had not disappeared, but though he was tired, his spirits were high, the best they had been since 1957. His cabinet got remarkably good reviews. Two political scientists, Jack McLeod and John Meisel, led the cheering. McLeod declared the cabinet "the most impressive array of brains ever assembled in a Canadian cabinet", and Meisel also noted the cabinet's outstanding talent, which he said promised "efficient and incisive administration". McLeod's comments are quoted in almost every book about the period and then mocked (for reasons that will be understood later), but he was correct in that Pearson's cabinet had more university degrees, technical expertise, and governmental experience in the bureaucracy and in ministries than any previous cabinet. It also had seven francophones from Quebec and three francophones from other provinces, more than any other cabinet in Canadian history. If any new government could deliver sixty days of decision, this one surely could.[31]

Mike himself had no doubts. His mood had never been so bright, his political confidence so apparent as when he wrote to Geoffrey and Landon on May 26, 1963. Maryon and Mike had spent their first weekend at the prime-ministerial retreat at Harrington Lake, and they were enjoying it. The letter is a rare expression of the Pearson thoughts that lay behind the public face, and therefore merits particular attention:[32]

I have abandoned the idyllic charms of Harrington Lake for the less idyllic burners of government — but not, I hope, for long because that cottage, the peace, the water and the co-operative fish, is going to be a life saver. Things are going well with us in parlt. govt — but, of course, it is still a honeymoon and the drab conflicts of house-

---

+ For Pearson ministers, 1963-68, see Appendix A.

keeping are only beginning. But one thing I know, that I am going to be happier, more comfortable and more effective in government — than ever I was in opposition. The problems are agonisingly difficult and complicated but we have a chance to do something about them — instead of criticising others for not doing anything or doing the wrong things. Psychologically, this makes all the difference to me. It means that though I started in right after the election and have had no let up, I feel fine, full of energy and without any need of a holiday; yet if I have had any success so far — it is in the field of intangibles, creating a better climate for Canada both at home and abroad. Morale really is higher now — especially in the civil service. We have a very efficient management govt — and we will not lose touch — as in 1956 and 57 — with public and parliamentary opinion. There will be no arrogance in this administration if I can prevent it. But there is certainly going to be lots of unpleasantness in the House of C. D. is very nasty and cannot conceal his frustrations. He misses the pomp and prestige of office greatly and obviously.

Pearson's first concern was to repair relations — which he believed had been badly damaged — with Canada's major allies, Britain, the United States, and France. He therefore flew to Britain a week after his swearing-in to meet with Queen Elizabeth and Prime Minister Harold Macmillan. Macmillan had been dragged into Canadian politics by Diefenbaker's allegation that he had counselled caution in acting on Cuba and, along with Kennedy, had said at their Nassau meeting that conventional rather than nuclear weapons should be emphasized. Neither statement appears to be accurate. Macmillan's biographer, Alistair Horne, has recently revealed how profound the dislike between the two prime ministers was, a fact of which Diefenbaker's assistant Basil Robinson was made aware. In Macmillan's opinion, Diefenbaker was "something of a mountebank ... a very crooked man.... so self-centred as to be a sort of caricature of Mr. Gladstone". The only test of a question was "the political advantage of his party".[33] Macmillan, Mike had told Geoffrey, was his kind of Conservative. It was equally clear that Mike was Macmillan's kind of Liberal. They had the kind of conversation that both loved, circling the globe, expertly settling on those parts where problems had erupted or would erupt, and then soaring again.[34]

Britain, of course, came first for visits in those days, but the more significant visit was to John Kennedy. Knowlton Nash, the closest student of the Kennedy-Diefenbaker relationship, who was in Washington when these disputes occurred, asserts, in his fine study of the conflict, that animosity overflowed from the personal dealings to block the normal channels of business and communications between the two countries. Certainly the president thought it did. It was at Kennedy's request that his assistant, McGeorge Bundy (who had approved the State Department press release that called Diefenbaker a liar), sent out a notice to numerous American government departments indicating that "progress" could now be made with the Canadians and that "negotiations should be most carefully co-ordinated under his personal direction through the Department of State".[35]

Kennedy invited Pearson not to Washington, where the black ties and toasts of official dinners would get in their way, but to the Kennedy compound at Hyannis Port, where they could relax. Mike Pearson was John Kennedy's kind of person. Kennedy, a friend once said, "still felt something of an upstart, an Irish Catholic who looked to the Brahmins for a model of how to act". According to a recent study, Kennedy's friends tended to be "upper class Protestants", and "his rhetoric and other aspects of his public style were self-consciously reserved and patrician". Much has been made of how Pearson impressed Kennedy with his baseball statistics that spring day on Cape Cod, but, as we have seen, Kennedy's interest preceded his awareness that Mike knew what Walter Johnson's earned-run average was. Mike, *inter alia,* had the Nobel Prize that Kennedy coveted, was a close friend of *New York Times* columnist Scotty Reston, whose approval the administration craved, and expressed in a North American accent that British global sense he so admired.

Moreover, when Mike arrived, Kennedy was trying to thaw the Cold War, as Mike had tried to do earlier. Kennedy's American University address in June created the warmth that resulted in the nuclear test-ban treaty, approved just before his death. Many believed it was his finest monument.[36]

May in Cape Cod brings cool winds and rain off the Atlantic, but the atmosphere was warm as soon as the two men met. Kennedy staffer Dave Powers tested Pearson on baseball, but Mike passed with high marks when he identified a relief pitcher who had blown a no-hitter in 1962. He did not tell Powers that the relief pitcher happened to be Ken Mackenzie, not only one of the few Canadians in the major leagues but also a voter from Algoma East. Canada's ambassador to the United States, Charles Ritchie, thought the meeting was "tinged with euphoria. The atmosphere was that of clearing skies after a storm — the clouds of suspicion covering Canada-U.S. relations had parted, the sunshine of friendship shone." There was also, Ritchie noted, "an atmosphere of complicity between them, as though they had both escaped — like schoolboys on a holiday — from under the shadow of an insupportably tiresome and irrational Third Party and were now free, within the limits, to crack jokes" about Diefenbaker. There were jokes; but there was also much business, and the "log-jam of pending issues was broken". Officials began to talk again, confident of their superiors' support, and several agreements began to take form dealing with the Columbia River, automobile trade and production, offshore rights, and, of course, nuclear weapons, which were accepted for NORAD forces in Canada and Canada's forces in Europe. The promised negotiations to end the commitments that brought nuclear weapons for Canadian forces, however, were not completed until the end of the Trudeau government in 1984. Kennedy and Pearson resolved that the bitter quarrel between the two neighbours must not be repeated, and they promised fuller consultation and exchanges of views.[37]

In Pearson's absence, his government quickly took form, and the dominant personalities were Walter Gordon, who, because of the "sixty days of decision", had to prepare a budget quickly, and Tom Kent, who lost his electoral battle to Tommy Douglas in British Columbia but who returned to a position that was probably much more influential than any cabinet post he might have received. He became policy adviser to the prime minister, officially "Co-ordinator of Programming". Gordon gave him that title and assisted in the structuring of the office, but there were tensions. He and Kent wanted to decrease the influence of Mary Macdonald, but she was, as Pearson said, indispensable, and she became Mike's executive assistant. Dick O'Hagan served as press officer and got on with everyone. Annette Perron was Pearson's secretary, and an irrepressible and brash young Alberta Liberal, Jim Coutts, was appointments secretary.

Gordon, concerned that the presence of so many older and senior ministers in the cabinet would give the impression of caution, told the press after the swearing-in ceremony that sixty days of decision would follow, and promised to have a budget soon. Kent had briefed a group of civil servants about the Pearson program at his home at the same time and had emphasized that the government intended to do exactly what it had promised it would do. What followed was an unpleasant exchange with some public servants, notably George Davidson, David Golden, Simon Reisman, and Claude Isbister, who took strong issue with the lack of realism in the program. According to Peter Newman, Kent told the civil servants that he was not stating what might be done but what *had* to be done. Kent believed the objections were to policy as well as process; the civil servants believed they were objecting to Kent's tone and attitude as well as his disregard for the traditions of cabinet government. Did he speak for Pearson? they wondered. Both sides were angry — and remain so to this day.[38]

Gordon had long believed that the deputy minister of finance, Kenneth Taylor, was inadequate. He told him immediately that he would be replaced by Robert Bryce. Although he had cleared Bryce's name with Mike (deputy ministers are prime-ministerial appointments), Mike believed that it was essential that Bryce remain in his current Privy Council post until July when the transfer of office would be complete. Both Gordon and Pearson regretted this later. Left with a deputy in whom he had no confidence and assistant deputy ministers who soon expressed reservations about his economic aims, Gordon brought in three outside "advisers" to help in the budget preparation. Faced with reluctance, Gordon, in his biographer's words, "put his program ahead of appeasement of the Department" and "thus inevitably challenged the Department's self-esteem and goodwill".[39] A departmental draft of the budget disappointed Gordon, and he turned to his advisers. The tension quickly grew as the Gordon budget developed, especially over the measures to restrain foreign investment, proposed by Geoffrey Conway, a Ph.D. student at Harvard and a former Clarkson, Gordon employee.

The political dangers were obvious, and Pearson soon learned how intense the departmental upset was. His major source was Graham Towers, the former governor of the Bank of Canada, who told his confidante, Maryon Pearson, that he thought Gordon was not only wrong but a fool. Maryon let Mike know her thoughts and that she agreed.* On May 31, 1963, Mike met with Gordon and Louis Rasminsky, the governor of the Bank of Canada. Rasminsky had strongly objected to the proposed change in the withholding tax on dividends paid to non-residents — a change that would favour Canadian-owned companies — and the proposed take-over tax on sales of Canadian shares to non-residents. Rasminsky warned that the Americans would react strongly. He was also troubled by the proposed surtax on higher incomes, because, in those times of the "brain drain", it might lure the best Canadians southwards.

---

* In a later memorandum, Gordon says that when Mike, with Maryon present, asked Gordon to consider the Industry department rather than Finance in 1963, he said no, at which point "Maryon suggested I should take whatever portfolio the 'P.M.' wanted me to take!" Maryon became "increasingly cool and distant with the result we saw less and less of the Pearsons". Walter Gordon, Memorandum, Dec. 5, 1965, Gordon Papers, v. 32 (NAC).

Mike did not press the matter after the meeting and, as he pointed out, no one in Finance resigned or threatened to do so. The Gordon budget went forward on June 13.[40]

It was a catastrophe, even though a few parts of the budget stand up well in retrospect. Gordon reduced the deficit by introducing several minor tax changes and closing loopholes. He dealt with the continuing problem of unemployment (according to the 1963 election polls, Canada's major political concern) by tax concessions, retraining schemes, and regional grants. He promised to move towards a balanced budget in the future. There were, however, many contradictions, because new taxes promised to be deflationary. After detailing these changes, he introduced the withholding and take-over taxes, the latter at a severe 30 per cent level.[41] The next morning the initial reviews in the Canadian press were cautiously good. A victory party followed and all seemed fine, although a drunk Finance official told "Ben" Benson, Gordon's parliamentary secretary, that it was "an ignorant budget prepared by ignorant people".[42]

The trouble began with a question from NDP MP Doug Fisher about whether Gordon and "his government officials alone" had prepared the budget speech without "outside consultation or ghost writers". Gordon was evasive in his reply. Gradually, the House learned that two of the outside consultants had been on their company payrolls. Gordon, a novice in the House, performed poorly as each answer led to another question. Economists began to criticize the budget, with Melville Watkins of the University of Toronto, later a close nationalist ally of Gordon, suggesting that the budget was not merely pre-Keynesian, it was positively pre-Cambrian.[43] Jack Pickersgill, who could not believe what was happening, tried to help in the House. But on June 18 another crisis arose outside the House, when Eric Kierans, president of the Montreal and Canadian stock exchanges and, ironically, another later nationalist ally of Gordon's, launched a vitriolic attack on the budget, declaring that "the financial capitals of the world have just about had enough from Canada". "Today, our friends in the western world," Kierans declared, "would fully realize that we don't want them or their money and that Canadians who deal with them in even modest amounts will suffer a thirty percent expropriation of the assets involved." Kierans announced that he would tell his associates to sell Canadian stocks short. Gordon panicked; markets began to fall. He met with Pearson, who urged him to withdraw the tax. He did so on June 19, *before* the markets closed, and speculators made a killing. The *Globe and Mail* and the *Winnipeg Free Press*, which had given the budget cautious support initially, demanded Gordon's resignation.[44]

He offered his resignation to Pearson on the day the *Globe* called for it, June 20. The discussion, as reported by both parties, was neither pleasant nor conclusive. When Gordon offered his resignation, Pearson said, according to the recollection of both, "Have you lost confidence in yourself?" Gordon said he had not. Mike said: "Well just carry on. We'll get over this by making the changes that have to be made." Mike had, before meeting Gordon, "seriously considered" accepting the resignation.[45] He had already asked Mitchell Sharp, a former public servant, if he would accept the position if Gordon resigned. He called Maurice Lamontagne and Allan MacEachen, his two former assistants, to Sussex Drive and asked Lamontagne if he would become minister of trade and commerce. Lamontagne realized that this meant Gordon would be leaving Finance, and he objected. Mike spoke to others about it, including Geoffrey and his old friend Fraser Bruce, now a prominent businessperson. The most explicit evidence of what he believed is found in the diary of his close friend Arnold Heeney. Heeney, who believed Gordon had been "incredibly inept" and "a serious political liability", met with Pearson in the summer of 1963. Pearson told him how troubling the Gordon situation was. Heeney wrote in his diary: "For LBP to have to strike his friend will be cruelly hard, but surely it must be done." Pearson told Heeney "that he [hoped] within a couple of months, to have induced Walter to take another portfolio; he was afraid however that he wd. insist on resigning his seat".[46]

On June 24, Sharp gave the strongest speech in defence of Gordon. Ironically, it was from notes prepared for Pearson, who thought better of speaking when Diefenbaker did not speak. Gordon felt that he was not supported, and the tone of injured pride pervades his account and that of Tom Kent, who lunched with him regularly as he endured the ordeal. The budget was much revised, to the satisfaction of many of Gordon's cabinet colleagues. Kent claims that Walter's spirits rebounded quickly and that he took the reversal stoically, but his own record of the incident suggests that he became bitter:

> I felt a bit let down.... That Mike never said a word in my defence despite the fact it was almost as much his budget as mine — my ideas but he had bought them. Second [Dick] O'Hagan with or without Mike's knowledge polled the Press Gallery as to whether I should be asked to resign. This undermined my position very considerably at a most difficult time. Third, while Mike backed me in caucus I did not feel he did so in Cabinet....
>
> On the other hand my personal position had been built up to a point where people thought I was some kind of superman. Mistakes on my part were taken as a great let-down.[47]

Heeney ruminated on the incident that involved his friends (Gordon and he were close in the 1950s), and concluded that it "will be a test not only of the political acumen necessary to a P.M. but the quality of ruthlessness, political and personal courage ... which the national interest probably requires in [the] present crisis". In short, Gordon had to go. Mike certainly wanted him to leave: there can no longer be any doubt on that question. But he could not bring himself to cut the hangman's rope. It was, in part, a sense of obligation that made him determined to have Walter make the decision. There was, however, another reason. Before Doug Fisher rose in the House to pull out one of the fragile pillars holding up Gordon's budget, he had taunted the government about the many varieties of Liberals: the Sharp Liberals, who were the moderate and efficient administrators; the Pickersgill Liberals, who believed that only Liberals should govern and were, therefore, cautious; and the Gordon Liberals, who were innovative and to the left.[48]

Pearson had little interest in, or understanding of, the economic aspects of Gordon's budget. There can be no doubt, however, that he supported the budget when Gordon explained it to him before its presentation, although he surely did have some concerns about the speed at which Gordon wanted to move, and he was disturbed about the controversy with Finance officials. But, as Professor Smith and Tom Kent have ably argued, the Gordon budget had a nationalist, *dirigiste* thrust that was, within the context of 1963, a definite statement of the direction the new government would take. Pearson clearly wanted Gordon to leave, and both men probably erred: Gordon in staying; Pearson in letting him. Nevertheless, Gordon's direction he believed to be correct, even though most of his cabinet colleagues probably disagreed. To lose him in the minority government's first months — and Gordon was too proud to go quietly — would have been dangerous. Just after the election, Frank Underhill wrote to his old colleague and congratulated him on having most of the "better educated" with him. This meant, however, that the "big business groups" were with him too, and the former CCF activist — he had voted Liberal in 1962 and 1963 — warned Pearson that he should not heed their call. What the country needed was "a modest but meaningful confrontation" between left and right, and this meant that the Liberals must be on the left, not in the centre. In his reply, Mike expressed his concern about the support of the *Globe and Mail* and the "tycoons", but promised he would keep the party "where it should be — left of centre". And that is where Walter Gordon was. There wasn't enough company in the cabinet to have him depart. Mike was left with a dilemma and an unhappy colleague.[49]

Ironically, the strongest support for such a *dirigiste* position came from Quebec, where the government of Jean Lesage had embarked upon an ambitious program to breathe life into an inactive state structure. By 1963, the Quebec state had been pumped with adrenalin and was challenging the fundamental characteristics of Canadian federalism. Lesage had been Pearson's parliamentary secretary but had left Ottawa in 1958 to lead the Quebec Liberal Party. Their relations had been warm. When Lesage was appointed to the federal cabinet in 1953 as minister of resources and development, he wrote to Pearson: "You assisted me greatly in my accession to the Cabinet. After all, you gave me the opportunity to learn the Government business and to acquire experience in the world of high policy. I shall never forget how indebted I am towards you."[50] In 1963 Lesage repaid the debt by endorsing the federal Liberals, although some grumbled that the endorsement came a bit late in the campaign. Pearson had watched, along with other Canadians, the remarkable transformation of Quebec in the early 1960s, at first with warm approval but later with considerable disquiet. As early as 1961, one year after Lesage's election, polls in Quebec revealed that "separatism" had the support of a surprisingly high percentage of the population (26 per cent in a *Le Magazine Maclean* poll; 45 per cent in a rather unscientific *La Presse* survey). Lesage responded to the nationalist gusts by demanding a fundamental revision of Canadian federalism and by promising a redefinition of Quebec nationality, by which the "state" of Quebec would become the realization of the expression of nationality: "Or le seul moyen puissant que nous possédions c'est L'Etat du Québec, c'est notre Etat. Nous ne pouvons pas nous payer le luxe de ne pas l'utiliser."[51]

The implications of such statements were not lost on Mike Pearson, even if, as he told his young granddaughter, Hilary, who was learning French at the time, he could not conjugate the verb "avoir". One of his first actions after the election was the appointment of the Royal Commission on Bilingualism and Biculturalism, to be co-chaired by André Laurendeau and Davidson Dunton. Laurendeau had proposed such a commission in January 1962 but had denounced Pearson in *Le Devoir* for his nuclear-weapons stand in 1963; Dunton was the president of Carleton University and a former journalist.[52]

Royal commissions, of course, move notoriously slowly, and

Pearson had to respond with immediate political action. On April 21, the day before Pearson's swearing-in, William O'Neill was the first casualty of terrorism in Quebec when a bomb exploded in a Canadian army recruiting office where he worked as a janitor. The next month, seventeen bombs exploded in one night in Westmount mail-boxes, and the notion that St. Laurent's son might head the royal commission ended abruptly. The monuments to Wolfe and Queen Victoria were tumbling down, and it was not a time to look to the past for anchors.[53]

If Pearson was disinclined to deal directly with economic affairs, he was fascinated with Quebec and, in Laurendeau's view, "lucid" and "well informed" on the subject. Laurendeau perceptively realized that Pearson's lack of ties with the province and his sense that mediation was needed gave him opportunities he did not have in English Canada.[54] He had indicated before his election in April 1963 that he considered "national unity" the most important problem his government faced. Pearson's commitment to dealing with the problem was unquestioned. Looking back one can see that the sincerity of his efforts and his open-mindedness were in themselves significant factors in maintaining "that continued — if frequently fragile — conviction that the Canadian experiment should not be allowed to fail".[55] But his sincerity and open-mindedness were hardly enough. Quebec needed others who could lead from within the province.

Pearson owed many debts to Lionel Chevrier, who had become the Quebec leader during the late St. Laurent years and who had given superb parliamentary service during the black years of opposition. Pearson had profound reservations about Chevrier as his Quebec lieutenant, however. Although he sat for a Montreal constituency, Chevrier was a franco-Ontarian by background, and it soon became clear that he was inappropriate as Quebec leader.[56] Moreover, Pearson was aware that Chevrier, who was first elected in 1935, was perceived as "old" at a time when the new was very much in vogue. The first Quebec reactions to the cabinet Pearson announced in late April could only have intensified his worries. As

Laurendeau saw it in *Le Devoir*, the "old guard" took the pre-eminent positions; the "new guard" remained a row behind.[57]

A memorandum written by a prominent young Quebec Liberal arrived on Pearson's desk in early May 1963, and he circulated it widely and commended it. The perspective was interesting, for this young Quebec anglophone, later a Trudeau government aide, argued that "in granting increased recognition to Quebec problems ... far from alleviating the present restlessness, it will probably increase". What was needed were strong francophone leaders who could "demonstrate the progress obtained, and, thus ... keep within bounds the inevitable pressures from Quebec". Above all others there must be a *chef,* and this position had special qualifications. The individual chosen must, among other qualifications, be accepted as a French Canadian in Quebec, be "of the spirit and generation of New Quebec", and be "a forceful orator and a dominant personality, which does not mean he has to be a Caouette". Lionel Chevrier did not fit; by the end of 1963 he had gone to London as high commissioner, a post Pearson first offered to Walter Gordon.[58]

Maurice Sauvé thought himself eminently qualified for the position, as did numerous journalists who promoted him. The Quebec caucus disagreed, as did the prime minister and the cabinet, with the exception of Walter Gordon and a few others sympathetic to him. Lamontagne had many qualifications, including personal friendship with Pearson, but he recognized his limits and refused the position. The choice, therefore, fell upon Guy Favreau, who had entered the House of Commons in 1963 and who replaced Chevrier at Justice and Pickersgill as Liberal House leader.[59]

Guy Favreau had much to recommend him. He possessed great personal warmth and had an outstanding reputation as a counsel. He had served as associate deputy minister of justice under the Conservative Davie Fulton, yet had managed to maintain strong links with the reform wing of the Quebec Liberal Party. As with Louis St. Laurent, who had brought Favreau to Ottawa in 1951, the respect for Favreau transcended politics. Also like St. Laurent, Favreau had virtually no political experience; however, he seemed to be a quick learner. Moreover, affection and respect were valued currencies in the political trade. Pearson seemed to have good reason to hope that Favreau would be to him "what Ernest Lapointe had been to King".[60]

Favreau quickly moved to the forefront. His work on constitutional reform in the summer and early fall of 1964 (the "Fulton-Favreau formula") won him considerable public and private acclaim. Pearson wrote privately to Senator John Connally about the "wonderful job" Favreau had done in dealing with the provinces in the thorny constitutional negotiations. Connally urged that Favreau's work should be publicized, especially in Quebec. "This will put him a cut above the turmoil there."[61] But the turmoil had already engulfed him, and his work was getting bad as well as good reviews.

Hal Banks was his first hurdle, and he stumbled in explaining how the notorious labour leader had managed to escape Canadian justice. In early October, on the new CBC program "This Hour Has Seven Days", Patrick Watson interrogated Favreau. In reviewing Favreau's performance for Pearson, press secretary Richard O'Hagan reported in October 1964 that Favreau "did not do himself any notable good". O'Hagan was especially concerned about Favreau's "command" of English, which had affected the clarity and precision of his replies.[62] Favreau's appointment as Quebec leader at a time when Quebec's position in Confederation was the foremost national issue placed a harsh national spotlight on him. He began to wince.

Seeing the weakness of their prey, Erik Nielsen, a fierce interrogator, and John Diefenbaker moved in for the kill on November 23, 1964. Favreau made a spirited defence, but only exposed himself more fully. Decoys failed completely. "When a big hunter is after big game," Diefenbaker taunted the Liberals, "he does not allow himself to be diverted by rabbit tracks."[63] The charges were indeed serious: that Favreau had not consulted his departmental officers before deciding not to prosecute Raymond Denis, who, it was alleged, had tried to assist drug dealer Lucien Rivard by attempting to bribe a Montreal lawyer; that he had not informed the prime minister about either his decision or the involvement of Guy Rouleau, Pearson's own parliamentary secretary, in the bribery scandal; and that he had protected his friends. Favreau reacted bitterly as, day after day, opposition MPs pursued their wounded quarry. The mood of Parliament turned foul.

In desperation, Favreau asked for an inquiry in order to halt the merciless parliamentary onslaught upon him. Pearson quickly agreed, but then left on a western tour, giving the impression that he did not stand behind his minister. More devastatingly, he did not inform the House of Commons that Favreau had, in fact, told him about Rivard on September 2, not in late November as Pearson had suggested before. Pearson's failure to speak up at once disappointed even his closest aides. Jack Pickersgill and Tom Kent, in Kent's recollection, "almost wore out our welcome with Mr. Pearson, urging him day after day that the only thing to do was to make a statement". But no statement was made to the House. Instead, Pearson wrote to Mr. Justice Dorion, informing him of the earlier decision of Favreau. The information came too late. In Kent's later view, "it was the lowest point in Pearson's political career".[64] Gordon received a note from Favreau indicating how isolated the Quebec lieutenant felt. Favreau thanked Gordon warmly for his encouragement and added: "I shall never forget … how you dared rise in the House in my defence, at the very moment when so many were speechless and I myself was performing badly."[65]

In February 1965, the Royal Commission on Bilingualism and Biculturalism issued its preliminary report, which declared that Canada was "passing through its greatest crisis in its history". Pearson, too, was facing a crisis — the catastrophic collapse of the francophone representation in his cabinet. Guy Rouleau had resigned two months earlier as Pearson's parliamentary secretary when it became clear that he had tried to intervene to assist Rivard. In January, Yvon Dupuis, who had led the Liberals' attempt to employ rough-house tactics on Réal Caouette's Social Credit, was fired from the cabinet after being charged with accepting a $10,000 bribe to arrange a race-track charter. The worst blow, however, had come on November 30, 1964, when a Conservative MP charged that Lamontagne, the secretary of state, and René Tremblay, the minister of immigration, had received furniture without payment from a bankrupt Montreal furniture company.* A cloud swirled around their ministerial and political activities, and Pearson let them know that he believed their political "usefulness had been practically destroyed". They remained, with Lamontagne embittered, until after the 1965 election, when Pearson replaced them.[66]

Lamontagne had worked with Pearson since the early, lonely days of opposition. Pearson deeply regretted what he thought he must do. In 1965, he seems to have concluded that his government's troubles came from his early laxity with his ministers. Moreover, his mail bulged with demands that he "clean up" his party. Old friends, such as the prominent United Church minister the Rev. George Goth, harangued him on the need to expunge evil from his midst. The historian A.R.M. Lower's observation that there was much rot in modern Canada provoked a most interesting response from Pearson: "As I have recently been accused of being personally responsible for the debasement of public morality in this country, your observations are very pertinent. Seriously, however, I do not agree that there are 'large areas of rot' in our country. I do not agree that the conduct of Mr. Favreau, Mr. Lamontagne, and Mr. Tremblay, however inept and ill-advised, represents any form of corruption or lack of integrity on their part." The historian had not mentioned the three Quebec

---

* Lamontagne had accepted furniture in 1962 and 1963 from a store owned by the Sefkind brothers, who had told him he could pay for it when he could. When the Sefkinds went bankrupt, he did nothing until the Bank of Montreal came after him. There were no allegations that he had given any favours. Tremblay had also bought furniture, but some was not delivered and he did not pay. He paid later, after delivery. Both, however, were tarred with the same brush, and their ministerial careers were ended. Even Erik Nielsen thought it unfair to Tremblay. See his *The House Is Not a Home: A Political Autobiography* (Toronto: Macmillan, 1989), 149–50.

ministers.[67] Pearson, nevertheless, thought of them at once and even granted their ineptitude. It was a telling reaction and a reflection of the fury he sensed had arisen in English Canada.

When the Dorion report of July 1965 found that Favreau had shown bad judgement, Pearson readily accepted Favreau's resignation, but he kept him as Quebec lieutenant and, more controversially, made him the president of the Privy Council.[68] The compromise satisfied no one. Only the husk of Favreau's former prestige and power remained.

In the view of some, Pearson's failure to defend Favreau energetically marked him as insensitive to the true nature of the situation. In this vein, Auguste Choquette, the Liberal member for Lotbinière, told Queen's University students that, since no one doubted Favreau's integrity, the commotion was simply another Diefenbaker attack on French Canada. He clearly implied that a Liberal prime minister should have fought off the attack with all the power at his command.[69] Tommy Douglas's explanation of why Pearson acted in the fashion he did is perhaps the most persuasive. In the British and Canadian tradition, Douglas claims, a prime minister does not rush in to defend the government: "You let the Minister defend it, and if he can't defend it then you throw him to the wolves." This time, however, the minister dragged others along with him. It left bitter memories and thoughts, especially among young Québécois like Marc Lalonde and André Ouellet, who were in Ottawa then as aides and stayed to govern later. They remembered and vowed it would never happen again.[70]

In the 1963 memorandum that had urged Pearson to find a solid Quebec lieutenant, the author had warned that a poor leader "would probably do more harm than good to the Federal Liberal cause", because he would become "the butt of attack". It was an accurate prophecy. Favreau could not lead; followers scattered. In Peter Newman's view, "the whole sordid business", which took place between November 23, 1964, with the first charges of Erik Nielsen, and June 29, 1965, when Dorion released his report, "seemed absurdly like an old-fashioned, low-budget gangster movie scripted by some third-rate dramatist with no regard for the authenticity of his plots". But the players were not actors, and the farce contained much that was truly tragic.[71]

While Pearson was trying to build a strong Quebec presence in Ottawa, others were dealing with the fundamental changes in Confederation that both he and Lesage believed must happen. Lesage had endorsed the Pearson Liberals in 1963, but he had made it clear that this did not mean that he endorsed the political and constitutional status quo. He had given Ottawa an ultimatum three days before the 1963 election that either Quebec would receive the right to opt out of shared-cost programs with full compensation within a year or it would take "steps on our own side to make the required decisions in fiscal policy".[72] In that same campaign, however, the Liberals had made numerous promises, including the creation of new regional-assistance schemes, an economic advisory board (which took form as the Economic Council of Canada), a new federal labour code, and national medicare and pension plans. These would require more funds in Ottawa and rearrangements of responsibilities with the provinces. Moreover, the other provinces and the parliamentary opposition warily watched the federal government's dalliance with Quebec.

Mike delegated responsibilities in the area of social and economic policy to his ministers and acted as a senior partner in a law firm does when important cases arise in areas in which he has no expertise. He gave general direction but no detailed advice. When trouble occurred at the level of the relevant minister, he despatched Tom Kent to help. Kent's memoirs are, therefore, a detailed and invaluable account of the remarkable record of social and economic legislation between 1963 and 1966. In Pearson's memoirs, these items are scarcely mentioned, and his own papers reveal how little he was involved in these areas. For example, the Canada Pension Plan, a historic addition to Canadian social security, rates barely a mention in Pearson's memoirs.[73]

His own involvement in the Canada Pension Plan negotiations was peripheral but, at a critical moment, decisive. In the Department of Health and Welfare, the new government had developed a national contributory pension plan that was based on the Liberal campaign promises. Because of its constitutional implications, this scheme naturally required negotiations with the provinces. Tom Kent worked closely with Judy LaMarsh and her ministry and produced a plan that would be a "pay as you go" scheme, with outflow roughly equalling inflow, as with American social security. Simultaneously, the Quebec government, "galvanized" by the federal action, worked out a scheme of its own whose provisions included greater benefits, a twenty-year vesting period, and higher contributions. Most important, the plan would be funded, and those funds could be used by the province to invest in the Quebec economy. The federal plan looked anaemic beside the muscular Quebec plan, which the highly capable bureaucrats of the "Quiet Revolution", notably Michel Bélanger, Claude Morin, Jacques Parizeau, and Claude Castonguay, had developed. Quebec rejected Judy LaMarsh's plan and infuriated her by presenting its own plan, a tactic that, in Tom Kent's words, "destroyed the federal government position". The other provinces "licked their lips" as they contemplated the funds into which they could dip in a Quebec-style funded plan.[74]

There were more police than governmental delegates at the Château Frontenac for the Easter 1964 federal-provincial conference when Premier Lesage presented his plans. Bomb threats came regularly; students chanted insults at the federal politicians as they emerged from the meetings. Judy LaMarsh "would never forget the sense of being an alien in my own country, my life potentially at stake whenever I moved out of my hotel room or the conference chamber".[75] Pearson reacted warmly to the Quebec pension plan, joking that "we" could join their plan, but Lesage wanted much more than simply the alignment of the pension plan through portability between the Quebec and Canada plans. He wanted more tax points from the federal government or, he threatened, he would bring in a budget that would mean double taxation in Quebec and a fundamental challenge to the Canadian federal and fiscal system. He also attacked the federal government's proposed student loans and family-allowance extensions. The meetings ended in acrimony, and Pearson and Lesage issued separate communiqués. "Profond désaccord", read *La Presse*'s headline the next day.[76]

That weekend, Maurice Sauvé, who was believed by other ministers to be the cabinet's "leak" to journalists and to Quebec City,[*] and who had been conspicuously absent from the federal government's delegation to the Quebec conference, called on Pearson in an excited state on a Saturday morning and told him that Claude Morin had said the situation was disastrous. On Monday morning, Sauvé met with Tom Kent, who, along with Gordon Robertson, had been trying to pick up the pieces. To that end, Kent had written a memorandum detailing a series of possible agreements with Quebec, the most important being opting out of shared-cost programs with compensation, a larger share of "points" of taxes for Quebec, and, of course, alignment of the pension plans. The pension plans would be aligned if Quebec would accept a ten-year maturity period for pensions rather than twenty. (That is, a person would receive a full pension after paying into the plan for ten years.) The other provinces, it was hoped, would accept this plan on the basis that they would gain funds that they could invest. Sauvé and Kent went to Pearson and urged him to send them on a confidential mission to meet Morin in Quebec City. He agreed but was pessimistic.

Kent's memorandum began with the argument that "the most single object of policy of the government is, presumably, to maintain the unity of Canada".[77] He argued that not enough had been given to Lesage to answer the demands of the nationalists in his cabinet and the province. Judy LaMarsh disagreed and, in doing so, reflected the views of many of her colleagues. She believed the new

---

* Judy LaMarsh said Sauvé leaked "tid-bits" to Claude Morin. Tom Kent said that Sauvé's "disposition to advance his position by talking to the press was notorious". Both made these comments in their memoirs. In his papers, Walter Gordon claims that Sauvé was the major source for Peter Newman, whose journalism was remarkable in its accuracy about the internal affairs of the Pearson government. A close reading however, suggests that Newman had many other sources.

plan was a "sell out" to Quebec. She was not informed of the Kent-Sauvé negotiations for the pension plan, even though the federal plan had originated in her ministry. When Sauvé and Kent went to Pearson's residence on their return, they met with Gordon, Favreau, Lamontagne, Martin, MacEachen, and Sharp, but not LaMarsh. These ministers reached a consensus, despite Gordon's understandable concern about the fiscal implications and others' fears that the opposition would criticize the "balkanization" of Canada, which Tommy Douglas most effectively did in the House.[78] Pearson, Kent later wrote, was "at his persuasive best", and Gordon, who knew he would be attacked for the tax concession to the provinces, was "too objective and too courageous to let that affect his judgment". The final details were sorted out by Kent and Gordon Robertson, working quickly with their colleagues in Quebec after Lesage approved the deal.[79]

Judy LaMarsh then realized what was happening. When she found out from leaks to the press — for which she blamed Sauvé — she was understandably outraged. She called Kent, a friend, to her office. As he walked in, LaMarsh "picked up the autographed picture of Pearson" on her desk and "slammed it face down", shattering the glass. Her resignation letter was ready, but Kent convinced her not to submit it and to support the plan. She forgave Kent but never Pearson. Her memoirs give, perhaps, the harshest appreciation of Pearson:

> ... I felt that I had been shamefully treated by my Leader. Pearson did not then, nor has he ever, even acknowledged what a dirty trick he played. I admit that circumstances may have forced his hand, but I will always maintain that he did not need to do it that way.... But if he let Walter Gordon down in the time of trouble, why should I expect more? I know leaders have enough on their plates without spending time to "baby" temperamental ministers but I have always thought that one of the signs of natural leaders of men (and women) was their readiness to take the necessary pains to keep their followers with them. Pearson just let his ministers lie where the axes

had felled them and he harmed not only himself but his administration by doing so. He lost their affection but, more importantly, their respect and loyalty.

LaMarsh became closer to Gordon, of whom she speaks well in her memoirs, but both became more isolated in the cabinet.[80]

Mike had written to Geoffrey early in 1964 after he returned from one of his increasingly regular Florida vacations at the Hobe Sound retreat with Bill Harris and his wife, Ethel. He was "tired", he said. In May 1963, he had had a minor operation, and the exhausting session that followed was punctuated with colds, which was "unusual" for him. To Geoffrey, he expressed his belief and, obviously, hope that the 1964 parliamentary session "should be less wearing than the last one. Our legislative program will be well prepared, our budget less spectacular, our cabinet more experienced and stronger. Only Dief will remain the same."[81] Dief remained the same, but, as we have seen, Mike was a poor prophet otherwise.

Nineteen sixty-four was one of the worst political years in Canadian history. In his outstanding book on the "scandals" that so plagued the Pearson government in 1964 and early 1965, Richard Gwyn noted that one effect of the scandals was the "erosion" of "the repute of the Government as a whole and in particular the reputation of Pearson himself".[82] In that noisome atmosphere, Pearson seemed to cherish international activities, where his reputation remained high and the settings were familiar. At NATO in January 1964, for example, Secretary General Dirk Stikker hailed him as a "Founding Father" and paid tribute to "his outstanding services" to the alliance, which, together with his "dedicated pursuit" of international understanding, had brought him a Nobel Peace Prize. Pearson then proceeded to give a brilliant exposition on international affairs, challenging his head-of-state colleagues while educating them.[83] He could not do the same in Ottawa.

He desperately wanted to pull the Canadian parliament out of the morass into which it seemed to have fallen in 1964. A new flag for Canada seemed to Mike Pearson an elixir that might transform his followers, wearied of the parliamentary battles and sad at heart as their heroes fell. Moreover, in the race against national division, a new flag might be a rallying symbol. Therefore, on May 1, 1964, exactly a month after Pearson flew home from the apparently disastrous federal-provincial meetings in Quebec, he spoke to the Canadian Legion branch in Espanola in his riding of Algoma East and, in the words of one reporter, showed "the courage of a Roman Gladiator ... because he has taken his argument for a new Canadian flag into the den of those who have been most outspoken in favour of retaining the Red Ensign".[84] Mike had talked about a new flag for many years, and later remarked how the refusal of Nasser to accept Canadian troops for the United Nations Emergency Force because of their British insignia had convinced him something must be done. Moreover, a new flag had been part of the Liberal platform in 1962 and 1963 and, on St. Patrick's Day 1963, he had told the House, to numerous shouts and objections, that Canada would have a new flag within two years.[85] The new flag was not mentioned in the 1964 throne speech, but the growing crisis of Canadian unity seemed to have spurred Mike into action.

Having tested the issue in Espanola, Pearson let it be known that he intended to tell the national convention of the Canadian Legion that he would introduce a bill creating a distinct Canadian flag. John Matheson, a wounded war hero, a United Empire Loyalist, and the Liberal member for Leeds, accompanied him and recalled how "completely relaxed and unafraid" Pearson seemed as they flew to Winnipeg. He also had, Matheson later wrote in his definitive history of Canada's flag, "the greatest difficulty in persuading the prime minister to bring along his medals".[86] He finally brought them, along with his own memories and a determination for the future. The audience waited expectantly as Mike, the only Canadian prime minister who had been on a battlefront, and one whose length of military service was more than double that of any other prime minister, rose to speak. When he went overseas in 1914, he recalled, he had as comrades "men whose names were: Cameron, Kimora, English, Gleidenstein, de Chapin, O'Shaughnessy". Yet all these men with strange surnames "didn't fall in or fall out as Irish Canadians, French Canadians, Dutch Canadians, Japanese Canadians".

> We wore the same uniform, with the same maple leaf badge, and we were proud to be known as Canadians, to serve as Canadians and to die, if it had to be, as Canadians.... What we need is that soldierly pride in Canada, that confident, passionate pride in Canada, that men had who wore the uniform with the maple leaf badge on it.... We are all or should be Canadians — and unhyphenated; with pride in our nation and its citizenship, pride in the symbols of that citizenship. The flag is one such symbol.

Some in the crowd hissed, others booed when he called for a flag as distinctive as the "maple leaf on the Legion badge". He continued his speech, which ended with light applause and a strong mood of disapproval. Much of the Conservative press criticized Pearson, but even it tended to give him high marks for courage. It was his finest hour that year, perhaps in his prime ministerial career.[87]

What began as epic in Winnipeg became parliamentary farce. The cabinet were uneasy when Pearson spoke to them about it on May 19. He told them that the "Legion campaign on behalf of the Red Ensign" meant that the government had to act. He then presented the various designs for the flag that had been proposed, indicating that one with three red maple leaves with two blue bands was his favourite. But the cabinet had little useful aesthetic comment, although the next cabinet meeting brought forward a heraldic expert who deprecated the blue bands, which Mike strongly favoured, and the suggested reduction of the three maple leaves to one, an act that he claimed was "heraldically incorrect and ... [made it] more difficult to justify historical continuity in the emblem". In the discussion that followed it was resolved that the flag should first be presented to Parliament rather than the Liberal caucus, because the flag should not become a "partisan" issue. Cabinet finally approved the design on May 26.[88] On June 15, the resolution for the distinct Canadian flag and for the use of the "Union Jack" for certain purposes came before the House. For the next six months, the MPs waved many flags and, by the end, most were bloody.

Pearson spoke first, calling for a new flag that would say proudly: "I stand for Canada." Then, the bitter flag debate began. Diefenbaker immediately accused Pearson of dividing the country and of choosing his own personal design as the flag for the nation. He declared himself for the Red Ensign and against the "Pearson pennant".[89]

The debate turned vicious in Parliament and the country, as partisan fevers flared. In that summer of 1964 flag designs were everywhere. In Toronto, one burlesque house featured artists who wore only three strategically placed maple leaves. Designs came from school children and Group of Seven painters, as well as historians and heraldic experts. Although polls indicated that the idea of a new flag had majority support, the opposition was intense. It became an increasingly common theme that the new flag was, in the words of the Vancouver *Province*, a symbol "of Ottawa's pandering to French Canada". The journalist-academic Pierre Trudeau replied that French Canada did not give a "tinker's damn" about the flag.[90]

Both Diefenbaker and Pearson were determined in their beliefs. Pearson refused to allow the House to rise for summer recess; Diefenbaker ignored Liberal scandals to continue his defence of the Red Ensign and his demand for a referendum. By August there were rumours of an election on the issue, but Pearson's promise of a free vote ended the rumours. It did not still the anger. The party leaders met to attempt to resolve the impasse, but the animosity between Pearson and Diefenbaker prevented agreement. Finally, on September 10, it was announced that the issue would be given to a fifteen-member committee. After much deliberation and clever manipulation of the Conservative committee members, who believed that the Liberals would be voting for the three-maple-leaf "Pearson pennant", the committee chose the single-maple-leaf design that became Canada's flag. The Conservatives believed they had been tricked, and they had been. The battle had not ended. Léon Balcer, the Conservatives' leading francophone, was outraged by Diefenbaker's attitude, and on December 11 called for closure. The government responded by following Balcer's advice, and on December 15 at 2:15 a.m., to competing singing of "O Canada" and "God Save the Queen", the flag was approved, after 270 speeches, some tears, and much rancour. On that last day Pearson begged for unity. Diefenbaker refused and retorted:

> The Right Hon. gentleman has done everything to divide this country!
> Mr. Pearson: Will the Right Hon. Gentleman contain himself for two or three minutes longer and then we will vote.
> Mr. Diefenbaker: When the Right Hon. gentleman starts giving me advice, I say to him, "You have done more to divide Canada than any other Prime Minister."[91]

John Diefenbaker went to his grave with a Red Ensign above his coffin; Pearson's had the new flag. Maryon told those who mourned him that the flag was the achievement he prized most.[92]

That view is reflected in John Matheson's fine history of how Canada got its own flag. There were, he wrote, "few of Pearson's followers who were not under the spell of his personality".

> He charmed, he excited, and he inspired his warriors the closer he brought them into battle. The fight for a flag became a crusade for national unity, for justice to all Canadians, for Canada's dignity.

The enemy was an old one in new garb: "racial arrogance, the small and mean heart!" The decision was made to attack, and "Pearson became David, capable of slaying Goliath". And eventually the red maple leaf became Canada's flag, sewn onto hitchhikers' backpacks, displayed on millions of lapels, and linking Canadian memories ever so faintly with the prime minister who carried it forth through long-forgotten parliamentary wars.[93]

John Matheson, in describing how the caucus rallied behind Pearson in the battle for the flag, recalled New Democrat Colin

Cameron's remark: "The trouble with the Liberal Party is that they are involved in a love affair with Mike Pearson." There was, Matheson suggests, "some truth in his words".94 And yet we have seen how bitter is the memory of some others, most notably Judy LaMarsh and Walter Gordon, and how critical Pearson's closest assistant, Tom Kent, is. There is, of course, the traditional explanation that no man is a hero to his valet, and Kent and Gordon were to Pearson, between 1962 and 1964, political and even (as with the bow ties) sartorial valets. Anyone reading the correspondence between Kent and Gordon, on the one hand, and Pearson, on the other, is struck by the change from what might best be described as an attitude of "affectionate respect" in the mid-1950s to a tone of somewhat aggrieved annoyance. The bluntness of the correspondence is unparalleled in the papers of the twentieth-century prime ministers who preceded Pearson.* Certainly, no letter like the one Tom Kent sent on June 21, 1964, was sent to an earlier prime minister by someone who continued to serve that prime minister, with the possible exception of communications from Sam Hughes to Borden.

Pearson had agreed to have a camera follow him through his day with the hope that such *cinema vérité* would enhance his image, as it had Kennedy's. It was, of course, a ludicrous idea, for Pearson was no Jack Kennedy and Maryon was not Jackie. The director was the distinguished American filmmaker D.A. Pennebaker, who, when asked later about the film, said "it's about the Prime Minister of Canada, who was a kind of a nice ex-history teacher, and who … had a wonderful guy named Jim Coutes [*sic*] who was really a funny person. I wish I'd made the film about [him]." So did Pearson. The National Film Board had commissioned Pennebaker, but the board did the editing. In Pennebaker's words, it was edited "for the sake of humour". According to Pennebaker, the NFB editor tried to make

---

* The papers of the prime ministers who followed Pearson are not yet available. Pearson is compared here with Laurier, Borden, Meighen, King, Bennett, St. Laurent, and Diefenbaker, in whose papers I have carried out enough research to make this judgement.

Pearson look "foolish".* Not surprisingly, he did,[95] and the film was held back from being shown on the CBC on "technical" grounds. Inevitably, a controversy erupted.

Kent responded to a parliamentary debate on the film with an extraordinary letter to Pearson:

> This is a painful letter. I can only ask that you nevertheless read it remembering that it is written by someone who for seven years has worked, for what he thought the public good, in the belief that you were the country's best hope of political leadership.
>
> After hearing what had happened in the House on Friday, I thought that I ought to resign at once. On second thoughts, I decided that I should try once more to talk to you first.
>
> My views are: (1) You have been less than frank about the film; (2) It was improper for you to express your opinion that the film should be shown.
>
> I would not express those views so bluntly if they were just mine. But it is impossible to avoid being aware — though, needless to say, I have not invited opinions — that these are the views of many people whose judgment you would normally respect.
>
> The question that affects the future is how you of all people — an honourable man if ever there was one — got into this sort of mess.
>
> The answer is, again, one which I would not give if it were a purely personal opinion. My job is to be blunt in expressing not my personal opinion, which doesn't matter as such, but my sense of a collective wisdom of those who wish you well and are capable of objective judgment.

---

* Pennebaker told the American interviewer that "It was a better film than I was afraid it was going to be, but it also was a much worse film. I mean, it was not a real film at all. It wasn't really about Pearson. It was about making the funnies, you know." Pennebaker was disturbed because "people open themselves up and there you have them.... But you can really murder people, you know." Interview with D.A. Pennebaker, 6-427 (Columbia University Oral History Collection).

The answer is that your government is weak and disorganised because it depends on you and you are making it impossible for yourself to be a good Prime Minister. You are making it impossible because you are refusing to make a few crucial decisions. In the absence of those crucial decisions, you are personally faced with such an impossible volume of other decisions, on such a hasty, unplanned basis, that inevitably many of them are not made or not made in time, while others (such as the decision ever to make this film with such access to confidential information) are made without consulting any senior person capable of thinking through the constitutional and political implications. The consequence of the work load and tension you are imposing on yourself is that you are destroying yourself in brave but futile attempts to cope with an impossible situation.

Kent then suggested that a strategy group be formed, that Pearson's office staff be reorganized, and that he discipline his ministers. "This simply means," he claimed, "that you should be franker in telling the person concerned what you think, instead of being nice to everyone and telling the truth to someone else." Specifically, he and Gordon wanted Mary Macdonald out of the position she held, where, in their view, she influenced Pearson too much. "What is needed," Kent declared, is "moral courage ... You are not being Prime Minister just to enjoy it. We are playing for big stakes — nothing less than the survival of the country." If Pearson would not "save the situation", he should regard the letter as a resignation. If there was "a worthwhile job to be done", Kent would stay, "even at this late stage".[96]

Kent clearly should not have stayed, nor should Pearson have kept him. Walter Gordon, who realized this fact, wrote an equally strong memorandum, calling for office reorganization but proposing that Kent be reassigned to study economic interrelationships, as Kent himself wanted to do. Gordon, a skilled management consultant, saw correctly that Kent's work had meant that he would "cross departmental lines and assume on occasion the prerogatives of a sort of Deputy Prime Minister".[97] That should not be allowed to happen and should end immediately. Gordon's advice was good, but it was not taken. Both Kent and Mary Macdonald stayed, as did Gordon, whom Pearson asked to manage the next election campaign. With a minority government and the bitter mood of Parliament, an election might come at any time.

It would have been so easy to let Kent go, but what Kent offered was, as Gordon said, "brilliance" and "resourcefulness", which were desperately needed in 1964 and 1965. Old assumptions were crumbling around sixty-seven-year-old Mike Pearson. A confirmed centralist in his youth, he presided over the most rapid and extensive decentralization in Canadian history between 1963 and 1965. A minister who had hovered above parliamentary politics in the 1950s, he was dragged into the cockpit of some of the most vicious parliamentary battles in Canadian history. A leader who enjoyed the lively debates and prickly personalities of his External Affairs colleagues in the 1940s and 1950s, he did not see the dangers of concentrating so many clever politicians with prickly personalities in one place at one time, as his government did. There was a frustration that André Laurendeau perceptively noted in midsummer 1964 when he met with Pearson. He had "all the right qualities". There was "a quick and sensitive intelligence, common sense, apparently solid will power, at least with respect to himself, the ability to take in information and consider a question in a new way ... and a certain intellectual daring". But, Laurendeau asked, "Can he achieve his vision in spite of his colleagues, friends and adversaries?"[98]

He could never be the Olympian leader occupying the lonely heights, as King and St. Laurent had done. He stayed in the marketplace below, which, in the 1960s, became more crowded and its occupants ruder. But it was there, in the *polis*, that his government gained its life. It was as difficult for the fastidious and rational Gordon and the cool Kent, whose intellectual tastes were Olympian, as it was for Pearson. They rubbed together. There were sparks. Some died quickly, some were dangerous, but many ignited creative responses to Canada's crises in the sixties.

CHAPTER NINE

OLD FRIENDS, NEW WAYS

Nous sommes honorés de recevoir aujourd'hui parmi nous un grand homme d'Etat. Nous sommes particulièrement heureux de reconnaître en lui la France, l'une de nos mère-patries.
—Speech (undelivered) by L.B. Pearson to welcome President Charles de Gaulle, July 27, 1967

Vive le Québec! Vive le Québec libre!
—Charles de Gaulle, Montreal, July 24, 1967[1]

JUST AFTER CHRISTMAS 1964, the Aurora *Banner* wrote about Christmas in Aurora long ago, when the Rev. Edwin Pearson preached the Christmas message in the Methodist church. Reading the *Banner*, Mike Pearson saw in his mind's eye a vision of rural Ontario in those days: "of snow fights and sliding down barrel staves in winter; of baseball, with father playing centre field and Mr. Sprague, the Baptist minister, in the infield, and an awed little boy watching from the bench." It was in a kindergarten class in Aurora that he had become "publicly rebellious for the first time by tagging along with the big boys when they marched away from school because they would not give us a holiday on the Queen's birthday". And he recalled, as if it were yesterday, "the day the train slowed up so that, from my father's shoulders, I could see the Duke and Duchess of York on the rear platform".[2]

A few months earlier in 1964 another queen, Elizabeth II, had come to Canada to be met not only, in Charlottetown, by small children on their fathers' shoulders, waving Union Jacks, but also, in Quebec City, by riot-helmeted police carrying menacing truncheons and sparse crowds in which many turned their backs as her cavalcade approached. "The Queen—Murder Plot Probe — We'll kill her on royal tour says Canadian killer gang", the London *Daily Mirror* proclaimed.[3] The Queen had come to Canada to celebrate the Charlottetown and Quebec conferences that, a century before, had begun to apply the mortar to the bricks that formed Confederation in 1867. November 22 in Dallas was a recent memory, and the Queen's visit was a gamble by Lesage and by Pearson, who reassured British officials that security would be tight. Mike even had what he correctly called a "Walter Mitty phantasy" of assuming his place in history by riding with the Queen as her car passed through its most dangerous path, from Wolfe's Cove to the Château Frontenac, and "throwing his body in front of her" when the shooting began.[4] Fortunately, there was no shooting (and he did not ride with the Queen). But instead of bringing Canadians together in honour of their first steps towards unity, the visit disunited them. Quebec cabinet minister René Lévesque boycotted the royal dinner, as rumours swirled that he was now a separatist. The Quebec Provincial Police made martyrs of the separatists. Pearson understood more clearly than before what forces and challenges Lesage faced — and knew more than ever that they were his challenges too.

The old colleagues met in Florida on their winter vacations in 1965. Pearson asked Lesage to join the federal cabinet to be the francophone bulwark that Favreau had failed to be and, very likely, his own successor. Lesage said he could not leave Quebec. When Pearson asked him why, he said he had a rampaging bear by the tail and simply could not let go. He could no longer promise that the Fulton-Favreau formula for amending the constitution would ever pass the Quebec legislature. Lesage left in the evening, as the sun set over Hobe Sound, but the southern stillness did not calm the new disquiet Mike felt.[5]

He believed that he too could not let go. Quebec's progress had led him to positions that had once been unthinkable for him. He had, like most English-Canadian nationalists in the 1930s, ridiculed talk of Confederation as a "compact" that gave provinces the constitutional right to assent to constitutional changes affecting the extension of federal legislative jurisdiction. To accept this interpretation would mean, he wrote in 1931, that "Canada's constitutional machinery would be as up-to-date and as appropriate to our present needs as a plough" to the western prairie. The "whole direction of political development", he declared, "is towards unity", but such a doctrine "would encourage dis-union".[6] In 1936 he wrote anonymously for a British periodical about the need for Canada's federal structure to be "overhauled" completely "by a redivision of legislative authority through constitutional amendment to give the central government the power it needs; by confining the interpretation of the Canadian constitution to Canadian judges and by giving the Canadian Parliament power to amend its own constitution according to a procedure which will facilitate necessary reform without encouraging careless tinkering; which will ensure adequate protection for every legitimate provincial, and, what is more important, every minority right, without weakly yielding to every provincial claim." Canada needed such a constitution to provide national leadership for economic management and social justice for Canadians, and also to create Canada's "own national and distinctive personality", which would "set it off" from the American challenge it faced. He quickly dismissed those who were faint at heart and who worried about the effect of such policies and changes on the "precarious creation" of Canada: Canadian unity was not fragile and Canada was not a "precarious creation".[7]

Mike shared these views with most English-Canadian intellectuals in the 1930s, such as the Conservative Donald Creighton, the socialist Frank Scott, and the Liberal Norman Rogers. In the 1940s, the war and reconstruction, with their great economic successes, seemed to justify the beliefs they had held. In 1960, when he and Walter Gordon agreed on a program that would draw Gordon into politics, Mike and Gordon readily accepted that there must be a "stronger central government" for precisely the same reasons as in the 1930s: to counter the American challenge and to create the infrastructure for a modern social and economic system.[8] The Liberals' policy platform in 1963 did promise a revision of the taxation arrangements with the provinces, but it assumed that the major social programs it proposed, such as the pension plan, university financing, and medicare, would take form in the fashion earlier ones had, with the federal government giving leadership and maintaining control. In the United States, the bursts of reform of Kennedy's New Frontier and Lyndon Johnson's Great Society resulted in centralization of power in Washington. In 1960 and even 1963, it seemed that would be the case in Canada; but it was not to be.

The Canadian version of the "Great Society" took form in the 1960s not through Ottawa's fiat, but through federal-provincial diplomacy, to use Richard Simeon's very useful phrase. Simeon, in his path-breaking study of the pension, taxation, and constitutional negotiations during the 1960s, described how the process of federal-provincial action intensified and became institutionalized during Pearson's prime-ministerial tenure. There had been only 7 federal-provincial meetings in 1939; there were 64 in 1957; but there were no fewer than 125 in 1965, with as many as 200 members at a typical federal-provincial conference in the 1960s.[9] It was a revolution in Canadian government. That the process became akin to diplomatic negotiation during this period is due, in part, to the fact that Pearson was prime minister. He took quickly to negotiation and brought his vast experience to the conference table. Even his sternest critic, Judy LaMarsh, later wrote that "chairmanship was Pearson's special forte and he was a brilliant one. He never let debate get out of hand." He eased irritations by applying dollops of humour, and "subtly stroked the premiers' egos". LaMarsh wished all the conferences could have been on television, as his last one in 1968 was, for "his excellence as a chairman" only became "apparent [then] to the public ... when his virtuoso demonstration earned him kudos from press and public alike; but this came as no surprise to any of us who had attended so many of these meetings."[10] Pearson found the setting congenial, as John Diefenbaker and Mackenzie King did not. There were more meetings; and, as Simeon and many others have pointed out, the *process* of Canadian government was fundamentally changed by the fact that John Diefenbaker was not prime minister and Mike Pearson was.[11]

John Diefenbaker had difficulties not only with the process Pearson followed, but also with his goals. He had rejected the notion of a bilingual and bicultural Canada in 1962, as did Donald Creighton, Pearson's old colleague in the University of Toronto history department. In Creighton's view, "biculturalism" was a historical "myth". Advocates of French-Canadian "nationalism" had used "every conceivable form of persuasion, compulsion, shock and menace to compel English Canadians to buy a particular view of Confederation and of French Canada's place in it". This noxious view had "not got very far when it was given magnificent official recognition and approval by Prime Minister Pearson, who obligingly established a Royal Commission on Bilingualism and Biculturalism". What mattered to Pearson was "Canadian cultural duality":

> It didn't matter very much whether Canadian Confederation provided government and promoted economic growth. It didn't matter very much whether Canada was united at home and respected abroad. All that really mattered was whether Confederation satisfied French-Canadian cultural needs and fulfilled French-Canadian cultural aspirations.

Creighton and Pearson, both sons of Ontario Methodist manses, both Toronto- and Oxford-trained as historians, both imperialists in their youth and centralists long after, now trod different paths. Creighton regarded the movements to "reconstitute" Canada into a "bicultural, bilingual state" or create a Quebec with "special status" as leading ineluctably to a separate Quebec, especially if the "decentralizing" policies of Pearson's government continued.[12]

Pearson, of course, disagreed. The process of federal-provincial diplomacy, so congenial to his taste, was inherently decentralizing because it brought provinces into the decision-making process directly. But Pearson went even farther. His own beliefs had been centralist, his internationalism dependent upon a strong central government that represented all Canadians, and his social-welfare plans reflective of the assumption that Ottawa would lead as in the past. But the policy of "cooperative federalism" that Pearson declared to be his approach in November 1963 explicitly accepted decentralization and some asymmetry as well.

Pearson was troubled, but Creighton was correct in his charge that what mattered most to Mike Pearson was "whether Confederation satisfied" French Canada. Unlike Creighton, he believed there would no longer be a federation if French Canada was not satisfied. And so his programs, from the flag to the pension plan, from bilingualism to equalization, gained their shape in large part from his belief that in the mid-1960s national unity mattered most.

And so there were concessions to Quebec, but Pearson thought that his major goal, the constitutional amending formula he had called for in the 1930s, was near and that it justified such concessions. Lesage had told him that the so-called Fulton-Favreau formula was acceptable in 1963 and 1964; but, as we have seen, in 1965 Lesage began to weaken in his support. René Lévesque became more vocal; and to many observers, ranging from Donald Creighton to Pierre Trudeau and some federal officials, the Pearson government's "concessions" had only whetted the appetite for independence while weakening the federal government.

When some of the federal officials later spoke with Richard Simeon about this period, they themselves said that "concessions" had been made to Quebec because Ottawa believed they were essential to maintain unity. Furthermore, these officials sensed that they were in a "weak" position and, by implication, that the government had been weak.[13] This criticism became explicit and widely known because it was shared and expressed by Pierre Trudeau, even as he was preparing to run as a Liberal candidate for Pearson in 1965.[14]

These interpretations bear the strong imprint of hindsight. Contemporary documentation does not indicate that federal officials, including Pearson, thought their position "weak" in 1963 and 1964 so much as strategic. The best analogy is with pre-war appeasement, which similarly seems, in retrospect, so embarrassingly weak. Just as Mike between 1935 and 1937 believed that Germany had legitimate grievances that merited discussion and concession, so in the early 1960s he believed that Quebec had enormous and legitimate grievances that had been exposed by the Quiet Revolution. The evidence before him in 1963 seemed to compel "appeasement". The revelation that, in 1961, French-speaking Quebeckers controlled only 15.4 per cent of the province's manufacturing sector and 47.1 per cent of its economy, even though they were roughly four-fifths of the population of Quebec, embarrassed Liberals like Mike Pearson. In the 1960s, when liberal Americans rediscovered poverty and racism, liberal Canadians agreed that Quebec had its own case.

This sympathy, combined with the trust Pearson placed in his former assistant, Jean Lesage, made his reaction to the concessions of the pension plan and the division of tax spoils inevitable. Moreover, Pearson thought that these concessions would assure Quebec's acceptance of a revised federal system. Such concessions seemed effective when Lesage supported the Fulton-Favreau formula in 1963 and 1964, particularly in a speech of October 14, 1964. But his support ended soon after because of "une forte réaction" in Quebec. (So, incidentally, did John Diefenbaker's support, although his reasons were quite different.) In 1966, however, Lesage rejected the formula, and it seemed to many that the concessions of 1963 and 1964 had accomplished little. Lévesque asked openly what was next. Bitterness simmered, as it always does when appeasement fails. In Ottawa, there were demands that concessions must halt; to Quebec nationalists like René Lévesque and Claude Morin the Quebec "advance" into "federal territory" had brought only token gains.[15] But in April 1965 these recriminations belonged to the future, which Mike Pearson could not have predicted. At the end of 1963, the young historian Jack Saywell had written on the opening page of the normally staid *Canadian Annual Review* that the new prime minister, Lester Pearson, might well have echoed Roosevelt's comment when someone said to him that he would be America's greatest president: "either the greatest or the last." Mike knew he was not yet the "greatest", but he believed that his work in 1963 and 1964 had assured that he would not be the last, and that, if his hopes were fulfilled, he might yet grasp history's brass ring.[16]

Mike was feisty and not at all defensive when he met Bruce Hutchison at 24 Sussex Drive on February 11, 1965, and boasted that "what we've accomplished in the past twelve months is to ease the process of change in Canadian federalism". He was, he told Hutchison, "now totally devoted to the issue of national unity. If it weren't for that I wouldn't be in politics." He was, moreover, saving Canada from that "clown" Diefenbaker. He dismissed Hutchison's question about a successor: "I plan to fight one more election [and] get some essential things done so that my successor* has something to build on. Then I'll get out."[17]

Mike wanted a majority government in 1965, but that meant an election. He disliked minority government, which never allowed one to stand "at ease". On the one hand, he believed that another electoral defeat would drive Diefenbaker from politics. On the other, he realized that Diefenbaker's presence as Conservative leader was his most precious electoral asset. On April 13, 1965, he wrote a memorandum on political strategy — an unusual topic for him — in which he assessed coolly the options his government faced. The government, he claimed, should be neither overly partisan nor defensive. It should let Diefenbaker, "a real asset to us, hang himself". The New Democrats, who were creeping up in the polls because of the "plague on both your houses" mood, should be frankly identified as "socialists" and their "assumption of smug superiority" mocked. More substantively, he argued for an emphasis

---

* He thought the next leader should be a francophone. Lesage would be the logical successor, and he would be good, except that he was "working too hard and playing too hard". The latter was a reference to his heavy drinking.

on the need for a majority government and on the way in which the New Democrats made "instability" inevitable. Most of all, the Liberals should talk about what they had achieved, especially in the area of national unity, where the government had "successfully brought the country through a crisis". There was a danger in talking about national unity, because "English Canada is liable to suspect that ... we are really talking about more for Quebec". So far, however, the resentment was isolated, and it could be diverted by "solid achievement" in other areas.[18] Most Canadians, he believed, respected what he had done.

Gordon, too, wanted an election. Reappointed as campaign chair, he had told Mike on March 31, 1965, that Oliver Quayle's polls were showing a Liberal surge. He was asking Quayle to take another survey that would give fuller national details. If the results were good, he thought there should be an election in June, before Diefenbaker had a chance to announce retirement.[19] The economy was especially strong, with forecasts for 1965 predicting real growth of almost 5 per cent, inflation of 1.9 per cent, and unemployment of 4 per cent. A tax cut, so dear to electors' hearts, was possible.[20]

When Quayle reported, he was upbeat, claiming that "everything is working out famously", although Pearson's "image" still was not so "positive" as one might hope: "while few think he is doing a bad job, most feel he is only doing a fair job." Canadians did not like his prissy voice and his lack of aggressiveness. Still, they liked the pension plan, his honesty, and the fact that he "tries hard". While Mike's star was slowly moving into the ascendant, Diefenbaker's seemed in a free fall: in 1963, 40 per cent of Canadians thought Diefenbaker would be "the best prime minister", but in January 1965 only 23 per cent did. Pearson had risen from 33 per cent to 46 per cent in the same period. Pearson was not doing exceptionally well, but Diefenbaker was doing considerably worse. The heavens seemed auspicious for the Liberals.[21]

But they dithered. Tom Kent wondered about what issues should be presented. The expected Dorion Report on the Rivard scandal was delayed, and when it finally appeared at the beginning of July it was worse than had been feared. Still, Gordon was predicting 155 seats after it appeared — a solid majority. But then came a postal strike, which annoyed Mike greatly. As the summer neared its end, he ruminated over matters at his Harrington Lake retreat, and wrote tendentious memoranda to himself. His major consideration seemed to be that parliamentary redistribution would require that he wait until 1967 if he did not call an election in fall 1965. That consideration was, of course, difficult to explain. The campaign issue should be majority government and the stability it promised. After a strange cabinet meeting, in which "a substantial majority" supported an election, Pearson paid a visit to Governor General Vanier and an election was called for November 8, 1965.[22]

Gordon had pushed Mike towards the decision, and when Mike seemed to hesitate, Gordon told him that "he would be accused of further vacillation and indecision and that such charges would be valid". Gordon "predicted" an overall majority again. Mike said "he would resign if we did not [win a majority] and that [Gordon] would have to go with him". Gordon said he would. Gordon had begun his conversation with the "tired" and "depressed" prime minister with an admission that he knew he had been "irritating" Mike "of late" and that he knew that "Big Business" was pressing Mike to get him "out of Finance". He added that Pearson should not fear the campaign because he could campaign as a prime minister and leave Ottawa "for only 2 or 3 days a week".[23]

The campaign thus began with a "tired" prime minister, who would campaign only a few days a week, whose campaign chair, by his own admission, "irritated" him, and whose strategy emphasized "majority government" as the major issue. The polls were strong: Quayle showed a 13-point Liberal lead just before the election was called; Gallup's first poll in early October, with the campaign three weeks old, reported a 20-point Liberal lead (48 to 28). The strategy of not confronting or even mentioning Diefenbaker seemed to be working. Two weeks into the campaign, Gordon had raised his prediction to 164 seats.[24]

In outlining the party's strategy, Tom Kent emphasized the

Liberal achievements. They were impressive, and remain so: the pension plan; the Tax Structure Committee that revised fiscal federalism; the creation of the Economic Council of Canada; the Canada Assistance Program, which helped those whom the Canada Pension Plan missed; youth allowances; student loans; more regional development funds; grants to assist people who moved to new jobs; and expanded federal funding for technical and vocational training. The first steps towards a national medicare scheme, a more liberal immigration policy, and unification of the armed forces had also been taken, and the Canada–United States Autopact had been signed. And, of course, there were the flag and bilingualism and biculturalism. Political scientist Neil Swainson later wrote that the late Diefenbaker years, "one of the most extraordinary periods of indeterminacy and hesitancy in Canadian policy-formation history, was ... followed by one marked by an equally extraordinary commitment to action".[25]

The accomplishments, however, were to be used only to refute charges of inaction and indecisiveness. The Liberal offence was to be implicitly a plea for stability, for a majority government that would end the "continual uncertainty" of the previous two years. There was an inherent paradox in this approach, because the Liberal "record" itself had caused "uncertainty" because of its "extraordinary commitment to action". By September, Pearson himself was reluctant to talk about his record on "national unity", of which he had been so proud only a few months earlier. The scandals with the many French names had changed his mind. The result was an anodyne campaign that quickly raised the journalists' ire. Analysing the campaign's first month, Peter Newman wrote: "the mood of the nation seems to oscillate between apathetic lethargy and active disdain with some traces of disgust for politicians in general. So far, much of this campaign has been conducted in a sort of abstract world of its own, as if it were outside the mainstream of what's happening in our time."[26] But once again Canadians began to notice John Diefenbaker; and, as before, the election was a tonic that gave life to his age-worn phrases and raised the bristles on his spine.

When the campaign began, Diefenbaker saw enemies every-where — and they were there. Most francophones followed Léon Balcer out of the party in disgust in the last stages of the flag debate. Rumours of discontent elsewhere in the Conservative Party flour-ished. When his campaign-chair-elect, Eddie Goodman, first called on Diefenbaker, however, the Chief was surprisingly confident. He had a "secret" document linking Lester Pearson directly to the Communists, which he would reveal, at the proper moment, and destroy Pearson. The astounded Goodman nevertheless accepted the position of campaign chair (subject to the condition that Lowell Murray not enter Conservative headquarters) and set Diefenbaker loose on even better material: the Rivard and furniture scandals.* Diefenbaker made the most of them.[27] On warm fall nights he began, with dark eyes twinkling and outraged voice quavering, to recall for his delighted crowds how it was "a night like this when Lucien Rivard went out to flood the rink". The tired creases on his face became marvellously transformed into a sly grin that hinted broadly that the Liberals were accomplices in Rivard's escape from

---

* Pearson and Diefenbaker were on the worst of terms. Pearson told Bruce Hutchison in February 1965 that after the scandals "broke", he called the RCMP and asked for the files on "every MP since 1956 — I just wanted to see just what had been going on". Among the files was one which "to my astonishment" linked "Diefenbaker personally with a major breach of national security". He wrote to Diefenbaker believing that "if he was aware that I knew about the affair he might take it a little easier on us. He rushed over and started to wave his fists at me and said that he had a scandal on me. That he knew all about my days as a Communist. I laughed in his face and said, 'Oh, you mean that testimony to the MacCarran Committee by that deranged woman in Washington.'" He said that he had told the Americans to publish it. Diefenbaker, Pearson said, left "deflated". Obviously, he was not fully deflated. The Pearson material had been passed on to Diefenbaker in the 1950s. J.G. Diefenbaker Papers, Box II 008386-92 (Diefenbaker Centre, Saskatoon); and Hutchison, "A Conversation with the Prime Minister", Feb. 11, 1965, Hutchison Papers (University of Calgary Library). Goodman had "little respect for Lester Pearson", but he saw quickly that "it was clear on reading that Bentley had absolutely no direct evidence to bring against Pearson". Edward Goodman *Life of the Party: The Memoirs of Eddie Goodman* (Toronto: McClelland and Stewart, 1988), 113.

prison that night. Nor was it missed that Rivard, Favreau, and Lamontagne had French names. Without polls, "imagemakers", or the electronic circus of modern campaigning, Diefenbaker became, in Peter Newman's laudatory words, "a politician without rival", who, in "an age of political image-making", was "the greatest pretender of all". He travelled 36,000 miles and visited 196 towns, villages, and hamlets. His train passed through prairie and southern-Ontario towns where tears and cheers came quickly as "Dief the Chief" arrived with hands aloft, standing with Olive on the caboose. Not all went well: he jaywalked in Toronto; Conservatives in Taber, Alberta, annoyed him by placing the maple-leaf flag on his car; and in Quebec, when told a young man was "mon fils", greeted the young man with: "Bonjour, Mon-seer Monfils." But these pratfalls became grist for the legend that the seventy-year-old Diefenbaker was becoming.[28] It was his last hurrah, and a vintage performance. For sixty-eight-year-old Mike Pearson, it was also his last campaign. Most Canadians knew this, but the nostalgia and warmth that Diefenbaker's appeal evoked had no parallel response in Pearson's case. The slickness of the Liberal campaign may have worked against it. The Liberals had great hopes for Quebec, where the party successfully recruited three prominent new candidates: journalist Gérard Pelletier, Jean Marchand, and Pierre Trudeau. Marchand was the prize: a labour leader, a fiery orator, and a splendid public personality. On the advice of René Lévesque, among others, he insisted that he would not go to Ottawa without his friends Trudeau and Pelletier. Those two were hard for many Liberals to swallow. Pelletier's sharp criticism of the Liberals for *La Presse* and for *Le Devoir** and Trudeau's vicious attacks on Pearson had not been forgotten. André Laurendeau wrote in his diary that Pelletier and Trudeau were regarded as "NDP material". Unlike many of his friends, however, he supported their decision as legitimate: "the idea of their being 'traitors' is an NDP reaction of disappointment

---

* Pelletier lost his editor's position at *La Presse* in 1965. He suspected that the Liberals were behind his dismissal.

or even a separatist reaction":

> From the beginning, I kept saying to myself that their success
> would justify their choice; and by success I meant their election, and
> a certain effectiveness in Ottawa. However, the fact remains that
> their decision dealt a major blow to "democratic socialism" in
> Quebec, and killed a lot of hopes....

A couple of months later, Laurendeau met Marchand in Ottawa,
and Marchand told him that Pelletier still had not been forgiven for
the critical editorials that had appeared only weeks before he stood
as a Liberal candidate. As for Trudeau, he was "astounding" English
Canada, and Marchand was ready to bet his shirt that "within a year
Pierre will be their big man in French Canada".[29]

In English Canada, the "big man" was Robert Winters, a
Pearson recruit whose Liberal candidacy greatly annoyed campaign
chair Walter Gordon. If the so-called three wise men from Quebec
were meant to counter the "left" in Quebec, Winters, it was hoped,
would assuage the "right", particularly the business community,
which was increasingly critical of Gordon.

In the last week of the campaign, the Liberal campaign faltered
badly. In Montreal, the final rally was poorly attended and featured
brawls between hecklers and boos so loud that the press could not
hear what Mike, red-faced in anger, said. When he spoke English,
the demonstrators chanted, "En français"; they did the same when
he spoke French. From Montreal, he went to Lindsay, Ontario, in
the Ontario heartland, to be met by some Trent University students
screaming, "Mr. Pearson, Crime Minister". Mike and Maryon
caught influenza that night and were a weary pair when they came
to the traditional "monster rally" in Toronto that would end the
campaign. The crowd came in the tens of thousands to the new
Yorkdale shopping centre — so much a symbol of new times; but
when Mike rose to speak the sound system failed. There was no
campaign speech that night. Dan Lang, who had arranged the
meeting, boldly told Mrs. Pearson that the evening had worked out

"so well that had the sound system been working" he would have pulled the plug. Keith Davey claims that he still can hear Maryon "shooting back her magnificent, 'Oh, you would have, would you!'"[30]

On election day, Mike and Maryon nursed their ailments at 24 Sussex Drive. They voted early in Ottawa East at St. Vincent de Paul parish hall, and that night went to the Château Laurier to watch the returns. Most journalists expected a Liberal majority, and the final Gallup suggested they were correct (44 per cent Liberal to 29 per cent Conservative; a 4 per cent Liberal drop, but still a majority). They were wrong: the Liberal vote actually dropped to 40 per cent, 1.6 per cent lower than in 1963. "Minority Mess", the *Toronto Daily Star*'s lead headline declared on the morning after. Once again, Mike Pearson was denied his majority, this time by only two seats.* Mike won his own riding, where television announcer Joel Aldred ran a lavish campaign, but the west went badly. On the prairies, the Liberals took only one seat. On election night Mike waited until 11:30 p.m. to go on television, and his grin seemed as frozen as Joel Aldred's when he sold Chevrolets. He took no questions after his speech, telling reporters: "It's been a hard two months — I think I'll go home and go to bed." And he did.[31]

His rest did not last long. His first reaction, he told a friend, was to summon the National Executive and announce his resignation. On Wednesday morning, the cabinet met, and Mike did offer his resignation, which was quickly and generally refused. He then agreed to stay. The next day, Thursday, November 11, he met Walter Gordon, who had said in cabinet that he bore the responsibility for what had happened. Few had dissented. During the campaign, the

---

* The final results were:

Liberals	131
Conservatives	97
NDP	21
Créditistes	9
Social Credit	5

press was full of rumours that Gordon would be moved from Finance; but at one public meeting during the campaign Pearson had introduced Gordon and said he would be Finance minister after the election. He regretted the words. When they met, Gordon handed him a letter resigning as Finance minister, and Mike accepted it. Gordon would take neither another portfolio nor an ambassadorship in Washington. Mike, Walter wrote later, "appeared to be unhappy about the ending of our political partnership but did not seem to realize it would mean the culmination of our long personal friendship". Indeed he did not, for in a memorandum on the resignation, Mike said that the severance would not "affect our personal friendship in any way". But it did, and Mike should have admitted to himself that the friendship had ended long ago.[32]

In fact, a season had passed in Liberal Party history, and Mike knew over the winter that he would have to build a new team. Keith Davey resigned as national director. Mike had told Gordon he wanted Tom Kent to go as well, and Kent eventually asked for a new job of deputy minister of manpower and immigration, knowing, in his own words, "it was best that our ways should part ...". Jim Coutts went to Harvard to study for an MBA degree, and Dick O'Hagan became the press officer at the Canadian embassy in Washington. The political team that Gordon had brought together around the novice politician of 1958 had been cut asunder by the election of 1965. At Davey's farewell dinner, Maryon sat beside Davey, who was lamenting Gordon's fate. She asked him, very rudely and too often, why he "worried so much about 'a little chartered accountant from Toronto'".[33]

She, of course, had worried about him too, and had known for some time that Mike and Walter were not working together effectively. Gordon's achievement was the reconstruction of the Liberal Party, a party that had made Lester Pearson prime minister. He had also brought into Liberal politics exceptionally able people who greatly strengthened the party, especially in urban English Canada. He was a generous man who responded warmly to young people with ideas and energy. In this respect, he was like Pearson himself.

He challenged Pearson to take action, and Tom Kent, who came to admire Gordon greatly, claims that Gordon was, between 1963 and 1965, "the government's main strength" and the major source of the impetus "to push through its principal measures of economic improvement and social reform".[34]

Those were his strengths; but after 1963 he and Pearson were uncomfortable together, and it gave the government a nervous tension and an impulsiveness that were damaging. Pearson did not have confidence in Gordon, and many of his cabinet colleagues knew it. Gordon knew it too, but was loath to admit it. Moreover, Pearson had grown to resent the attempts to shape him, market him, and "speak frankly" to him, and the result was a confused self-image and a government whose nerves jangled publicly. Before the Liberals took power in 1963, just after Keith Davey became the Liberals' national director, Davey tried out on Pearson his analysis of the Liberal Party: "There were the old guard and the new guard, the right wing and the left wing." Gordon was left-wing, new guard; Mitchell Sharp, right-wing, new guard; Paul Martin, left-wing, old guard; and Jack Pickersgill, right-wing, old guard. Pearson was amused, but told Davey he would have to get along with all the "divergent factors and forces".[35]

Davey, to his credit, largely did; but use of the nomenclature spread and gave labels to Liberals who resented such categorization. Gordon saw his colleagues through these lenses, which Tom Kent often borrowed when he advised Pearson on cabinet changes. Jack Pickersgill, a superb debater, an excellent House leader in 1963, a competent minister, and a popular MP, was their frequent target, as were other "old guard" and "right wing" ministers. The cabinet did not have the sense of being a "team", and at times the prime minister himself did not feel like its captain. As early as January 1964, Pearson had sensed the problem. The Liberals, he told the cabinet, had come to office emphasizing their "team", but there were too many times "when we haven't given the impression of acting as a team". "The responsibility for this," Pearson admitted, "is largely mine; to give the signals and see that they are obeyed." But the problem was also that others gave signals, and that some of them were not understood or were deliberately ignored. Too often, the base runners missed the signs, and the outfielders missed the cut-off man. As for Mike, he never seemed to be in a position where he was comfortable.[36]

There were other Canadians who did not feel part of the team. John Nichol from Vancouver reportedly joked that to Gordon and Davey Canadian duality meant the Toronto Maple Leafs and the Italians in Davenport Riding. More seriously, political scientist Joseph Wearing has suggested that the centralized campaign structure weakened the regional bases of the party and focused too much attention on the leader. Moreover, the centralized campaign concentrated on media centres, an approach that hurt the Liberals in the Maritimes and even in Ontario outside the large urban centres. The Liberals gained Toronto, which they had never done before, but they wooed that fickle mistress too ardently and ignored areas that might have proven more faithful in the longer term.[37] One thing was certain: after Davey and Gordon, Canada and Liberal politics would never be the same.

In February 1965, Robert Fowler, a frequent adviser of Pearson who had worked with Gordon in the reconstruction of the party in the late 1950s and early 1960s, wrote to Pearson urging him "to take a personal lead in international affairs". He recommended "an imaginative, self-confident action abroad" as the best way to improve his image at home.[38] Mike trod carefully in external affairs because of his own background in the area. Paul Martin was given a clear hand in 1963, and Pearson stood back lest he be perceived by Martin or others as interfering in the department he knew so well. In doing so, he was limiting his activity in the field where he had his greatest strength. By 1965, he was eager to become more involved in foreign affairs, and international events were beginning once again to have a major impact on Canadian politics. The challenges came from the United States, as they always had, and also from France, which was quite unexpected.

Mike Pearson had met Charles de Gaulle in wartime and had

been impressed. Unlike many Canadians, including some in Parliament and in the diplomatic corps, Pearson had always favoured de Gaulle and his Free French, thoroughly rejecting the Pétainiste alternative. His choice was wise, but it was not informed by much understanding of French politics or, for that matter, of France.[39] Nor is it likely that Pearson's respect for de Gaulle was reciprocated. Pearson, after all, moved most easily in the Anglo-American orbit; and for the most part France lay outside that orbit — originally by Anglo-American design, later by Gaullist choice. In so many ways, in his internationalism, his liberal-democratic instincts, his ambling intellect and deportment, and his unilingualism, Pearson represented much of what de Gaulle opposed after the generals restored him in 1958. This Pearson knew, and this, as prime minister of a nation 28 per cent French in language and origin, he especially feared.

Aware of the dangers and inspired by the new Quebec, Pearson in his 1963 election campaign promised that he would visit Paris as well as London and Washington soon after the election. This commitment was strengthened after his election victory, when the new cabinet decided that a priority in Canadian external relations must be closer ties with France. The campaign promise was kept, and on January 15, 1964, Pearson and Paul Martin arrived in Paris. Early suspicions that the welcome would be cool were quickly dispelled by de Gaulle's charm and eloquence. At an elegant state banquet where, in Pearson's words, the French "really laid it on", de Gaulle publicly assured the Canadians that he would permit nothing to undermine "les heureuses relations de la République française avec votre Etat fédéral".[40] To underscore this public declaration, the French and Canadian officials committed themselves to "regular consultations" and to the furthering of exchanges in the arts and sciences. Still, the acute diplomatic antennae of Pearson and Martin sensed a delicate and potentially dangerous situation. The private discussions, which were carried on in French, made Mike nervous. He and Martin then resolved to replace the retiring ambassador to Paris, Pierre Dupuy, with another French Canadian, rather than an anglophone as they had originally planned. Their choice was Jules Léger, a former under-secretary of state for external affairs.[41]

Léger took over an embassy smaller in size than Canada's mission in Bonn. This was, of course, extraordinary, and it was a symbol of the historic indifference shown towards Canada's other mother country. But by 1965 a combination of factors was changing this situation rapidly, making closer contact with France inevitable. In the mid-1960s, Gaullism was hard to avoid; in the international community it was a disruptive force with which all Western nations had to come to terms. More important in the Canadian case, however, was the internal pressure to improve ties with France and to make Canadian external policy a more accurate reflection of Canada's bicultural character. The goal was admirable, but its achievement became increasingly difficult as France's international activities and attitudes rapidly diverged from those of Canada.

This divergence, which took various forms, was perhaps a product of de Gaulle's failure to realize his dream of an independent Europe based upon Franco-German accord. After Konrad Adenauer's departure, de Gaulle found Adenauer's successor, Ludwig Erhard, unwilling to share his vision. He therefore entered what Lord Gladwyn has termed his "prophetic" period, calling for a fundamental realignment of the world power balance, courting the Third World and the Soviets, and evoking the image of a new Europe "from the Atlantic to the Urals".[42] The sheer audacity of the image delighted many intellectuals but dismayed most politicians, although some did sympathize with individual policies that together would frame *le grand dessin*. France's traditional allies, however, were not among the sympathizers. De Gaulle frustrated them, and they often felt "as if new and ingenious ways of causing displeasure kept on occurring to him".[43] Canada was particularly unsympathetic, because de Gaulle's concept of power blocs would condemn Canada to a North American fate, bereft of the old counterweights.

There were other troubles, too. Pearson later recalled two specific items not directly related to French Canada that bedevilled

Franco-Canadian relations. The first was Air Canada's decision to buy an American airliner rather than the French Caravelle. The second and more serious problem was French hostility towards NATO.[44] There were several additional irritants of the same type that Pearson failed to mention. These included the ill-fated French attempt to purchase uranium from Canada, French refusal to give logistical or other assistance for Canadian aid to francophone African nations, French economic policies designed to undermine the role of the dollar in international transactions, and, not least, de Gaulle's often strident criticism of the United States and the war in Vietnam. All these were important, but other Western nations endured similar pains. What was most significant for Canada was France's increasing willingness to interfere in what Ottawa thought were purely domestic affairs. This, in the end, was the intolerable act.

Interference began innocuously enough with interest in the so-called new Quebec. As early as his 1960 visit to Canada, de Gaulle had alerted André Malraux, his minister for culture, to watch for "interesting events" in French Canada. Malraux's sharp eye soon detected what he termed in October 1961 "un climat nouveau" in Quebec and in Franco-Québécois relations.[45] From the time when Malraux made this observation —the opening of the Quebec délégation général — Gaullist France wooed an increasingly receptive Quebec, and the seductiveness was not entirely one-sided. De Gaulle saw in French Canada a French people who were infused with the spirit that France twenty years after the Liberation so obviously lacked. Quebec was a modern nation, a part of the North American technological miracle, and yet it was French; the appeal was obvious.[46] But if France and Quebec were to work together, what part would Ottawa play? This was the central question for Lester Pearson between 1965 and 1967.

Marcel Cadieux faced this question more often and more directly than anyone else. The appointment to the post of under-secretary of the voluble Cadieux, a lawyer who lacked ambassadorial experience, was highly controversial among some francophone departmental officers, and a number left the department. There was, not surprisingly, an element of personal jealousy in this; but there was also a feeling that Cadieux was unsympathetic to Quebec's new nationalism and, in particular, to Quebec's assertiveness in its relationship with France. There can be no doubt that Cadieux was concerned: in February 1964 he had talked in Quebec City with Quebec officials, notably Claude Morin. What he heard appalled him, and he apparently became convinced that Morin was separatist in aim if not in professed intention,[47] a view he expressed to Mike.

The federal government could not delay, and Cadieux moved with characteristic aggressiveness to thrust a federal presence into Franco-Québécois dealings. Ottawa, Cadieux argued, must represent French Canada abroad, and Canada's international personality must be a fusion of Canada's bicultural character. If it was not, Cadieux believed that independence for Quebec was both inevitable and logical. Thus Cadieux could understand Quebec's and France's resentment of previous neglect, but he was not inclined to try to right historic wrongs with conciliation. He would push, and push hard, to assure that the federal government was not merely a puzzled bystander, a rejected suitor, during a Franco-Quebec romance.

While Jules Léger shared Cadieux's goals, his methods differed from Cadieux's as much as his personality. Where Cadieux saw black and white, Léger perceived varying shades of grey in the France-Quebec-Canada relationship. Although both a lawyer and a humanist, his manner and tastes were those of the academy, not the courtroom. Ideas sprang from his imagination like sparks off a flint, but his true inventiveness lay in finding compromise. Despite the existence of a situation where compromise rapidly became impossible, Léger persisted in seeking one. His task was personally difficult. When he presented his credentials in 1964, he offended de Gaulle. From that point, he was regularly snubbed and overlooked by those who curried the French president's favour. Yet with others, notably those in the French Foreign Office (the Quai d'Orsay), he worked

Pride before the fall. Finance minister Walter Gordon and Pearson
prepare to present the disastrous 1963 budget.
(Douglas Cameron/NAC/PA-117104)

Pearson and Charles de Gaulle at the Elysée Palace in 1964. Three years
later, the French president outraged Pearson with his cry of "Vive le
Québec libre!" (Canapress Photo Service/Wide World Photo)

Keith Davey (centre), national director of the Liberal Party, tries to make a point, as B.C. Liberal John Nichol (right) looks on. (Douglas Cameron/NAC/PA-117103)

Pearson's invaluable assistant, Tom Kent, who shaped ideas into a political platform. (NAC/PA-110218)

Pearson with Judy LaMarsh, the only woman he ever appointed to his cabinet. (Douglas Cameron/NAC/PA-117097)

Duncan Macpherson sums up national exasperation over the interminable flag squabbles; the "toddler" on the right in NDP leader Tommy Douglas. (Reprinted with permission — The Toronto Star Syndicate)

In their book *Now Show Me Your Belly-Button*, Reuben Shafer and Ken Borden poked fun at U.S. irritation over Canada's refusal to isolate Cuba. Left of President Johnson is B.C. premier W.A.C. ("Wacky") Bennett. (Canada Wide)

Johnson and Pearson at Camp David. Johnson had just excoriated Pearson for daring to criticize U.S. policy in a speech at Philadelphia's Temple University. (Canapress Photo Service/Wide World Photo)

Jean Marchand (left), Maryon's favourite politician, and Guy Favreau in Quebec City. These were Pearson's Quebec lieutenants. (Douglas Cameron/NAC/PA-117099)

to avoid incidents, to garner information, and to win favours. He was inclined to sympathize with French foreign policy in general (his outlook was more radical than Cadieux's); and, influenced by the Parisian milieu, Léger sought to ameliorate Franco-Canadian relations by making Canadian foreign policy more like French foreign policy.

Obviously, Martin and Pearson could not agree with Léger: denouncing the Vietnam War was hardly a reasonable way to deal with Franco-Canadian problems. Yet Martin was more inclined towards compromise than Cadieux, and more willing to give the French the benefit of the doubt and, in the case of NATO, a helping hand. He trusted de Gaulle's foreign minister, Maurice Couve de Murville, and did not hesitate to confront him directly with criticism. The slights and insults merely annoyed this shrewd veteran of Canadian politics and international diplomacy; the prime minister, however, took the French actions more seriously. Just as Pearson found it difficult to adjust to the political rhetoric of the mid-1960s, so too did he find de Gaulle's diplomatic discourtesy profoundly offensive. This feeling intensified as the French became less sensitive to Canadian concerns in 1966 and 1967 and as the Prime Minister's Office began to participate directly in Canada's dealings with France.

The interest of the Prime Minister's Office in this foreign policy area was justified by the impact of French activity on Canadian politics and the Canadian constitution. These potential conflicts were illustrated on February 27, 1965, when Claude Morin and Paul Gérin-Lajoie, representing Quebec, and Christian Fouchet and Jean Basdevant, representing France, signed a Quebec-France cultural "entente". The substance of this accord — French technical and educational assistance to Quebec — is of less significance than the signing itself.[48] Ottawa was concerned; first because of Quebec's eagerness to sign the agreement independently, and secondly because of the publicity Quebec and France created for the occasion. The rhetoric also was disturbing. It was all too similar to that of Canada four decades earlier while on the "road to autonomy"; and

Mike Pearson, more than anyone, knew how that rhetoric had prophesied reality. For these reasons, Ottawa, in Claude Morin's words, "maintained a prudent and discreet stance, yet took pains to minimize the event's significance". The document, therefore, was termed an "entente" rather than a treaty, and its signing was accompanied by an exchange of notes.[49] But this stilled neither suspicion nor expectation.

In the Commons, the Liberals faced demands for a fuller explanation of what had happened and of what the Quebec ministers and press were saying about the agreement, which *Le Magazine Maclean* described as "l'entrée de l'Etat du Québec sur la scène internationale".[50] Martin denied these claims, but privately told Pearson that co-operation should go as far as possible so long as the federal government's pre-eminent authority in international relations was maintained.[51]

Martin insisted with some confidence that the French would not dispute his interpretation of what was needed. Facing many difficulties with NATO, with the Americans, and with the Germans, French officials were disposed to avoid Franco-Canadian conflict at this time. For their part, the Canadians were wooing France. In November and December 1964, Martin appeared to support France's stand in opposition to the American-sponsored Multilateral Nuclear Force. Speaking to reporters after a private talk with Couve de Murville on December 13, 1964, Martin announced that "Canada could not accept any formula [e.g., the MLNF] that would be incompatible with French participation".[52] On February 10, 1965, Pearson seemed to echo de Gaulle when, in a speech to the Ottawa Canadian Club, he suggested that NATO principles should be re-examined and, further, that NATO should consider new arrangements whereby Europe took responsibility for security for one side of the Atlantic and North America for the other side. Coming from Pearson — or from any senior Canadian official — this was an astonishing statement: among those astonished were several NATO ambassadors and Paul Martin. They had to be reassured that Canada continued to oppose European and North American "continentalism". Thereafter Pearson remained silent and did not repeat his comments publicly.[53]

It is possible that Pearson's remarks and Martin's efforts at the NATO meeting did garner some credit for Canada with the French.* Although the French were clearly eager to sign the agreement with Quebec, they were careful to keep the Canadians informed and to avoid an "incident". In the spring of 1965, it was Quebec, not France, that took the initiative in their relationship. But the peace did not last long. The "accord cadre" between France and Canada was successfully negotiated during the summer of 1965, but Canadian-French relations soon began to worsen. Several factors led to the disappearance of the optimistic mood. First, it became clear that certain members of the Quai d'Orsay, and especially of the Elysée Palace, were encouraging Quebec to assume a more independent role in its dealings with France. The French motives were apparently mixed. Some officials had a romantic vision of an independent Quebec; others, more pragmatic, believed that French interest in Quebec created Canadian support for French positions in international affairs. Secondly, it became apparent that Canada could not mediate between France and the other members of NATO because France was unwilling to compromise on the question of nuclear sharing. After the NATO meetings in July 1965, the French and Canadian paths began to diverge more widely. The third cause of Franco-Canadian discord was the failure of the two countries to work out a satisfactory arrangement by which France could buy Canadian uranium, and this directly affected the member for Algoma East, where uranium was mined.

When Martin visited Paris in May 1965, the sale of uranium, which in French eyes had been promised by Pearson during his visit

---

* On one level, Canadian attention to things French was increasing. Between 1960 and 1964, Canadians had increased their consumption of French wines and spirits by 75 per cent. Sixty per cent of all French liqueurs sold in Canada were consumed in Ontario.

the previous year, had run into difficulties. These were well summarized by William Hunter:

> The French case is that to exact promises and claim the right of search is discriminatory and unacceptable, since no such conditions were imposed on Washington and London. Canada acknowledges that France is committed to a heavy atomic power programme and that Canadian fuel is needed for it, but reiterates that the sale can only be effected within the framework of international agreements. As a member of the International Atomic Energy Agency and a signatory of the test-ban treaty, Canada is supposed to discourage the proliferation of atomic weapons; failure to secure firm undertakings from France could conceivably lead to conflicts with this objective of policy.

By the time Hunter wrote, the conflict had already occurred. In May 1965, Mitchell Sharp led a Canadian ministerial delegation to Paris that was unable to obtain adequate guarantees from the French. Although the technical experts were able to agree on a system of control, "political" considerations made the French offer unacceptable to the Canadian cabinet.[54]

Pearson's dilemma was clear, and the cabinet did not speak with a single voice. On the one hand, he represented a constituency where much of Canada's uranium was produced and he was devoted to improvements of Canadian-French relations. On the other hand, he felt embarrassed by his acceptance of nuclear weapons in 1963 and was genuinely frightened by the proliferation of nuclear weapons in the world. Moreover, as we have seen, the left wing of his party was in the ascendant in 1965; with a minority government, Pearson could not afford to alienate that constituency, which was already troubled by Canada's role in Vietnam and was being wooed by the NDP.

On June 3, 1965, Pearson announced what he thought would be a compromise: all Canadian uranium sales, including those to Britain and France, would be subject to the same safeguards. This de facto removal of discrimination against the French did not help matters, for the French continued to reject the kind of international supervision that the new policy implied. Further difficulties arose over the proposed length of the contract, the price of the uranium, and the quantity to be supplied. The amount ordered by the French was generally agreed to be far more than was required for "peaceful use" in the foreseeable future. Negotiations thus collapsed in the fall of 1965, and the French — erroneously — blamed American pressure upon Canada for the failure. The timing could not have been worse.[55]

De Gaulle had also made up his mind about NATO and about the "vassalage" of Britain and Canada to the United States. Simultaneously quarrelling with his Common Market partners and creating a crisis within NATO, France in 1965 and early 1966 "drew closer to the Soviet Union ... relaxed its ties with its Western allies", and more actively championed Third World liberation movements. Canadians were mainly puzzled by de Gaulle's gestures. Some, notably members of the Canadian embassy in Paris, urged that Canada follow de Gaulle's path, at least to the point of criticizing Vietnam and attacking "superpower hegemony". The same note was sounded by the prominent academic Stephen Clarkson, who urged that Canada should follow France by using foreign policy to stimulate national pride and should declare "independence" from the United States. As Clarkson observed: "The more recalcitrant de Gaulle becomes, the more Americans treat him with understanding moderation." But moderation became more difficult when de Gaulle, in a news conference of February 21, 1966, demanded that Canadian forces leave French soil. Mike exploded in his diary: "De Gaulle makes his appeal to a past that has no validity, least of all to the French. *La Gloire*, 'The old guard dies but never surrenders' — all these things are relics of a nationalist society that is as anachronistic as the bow and arrow." There was little "understanding moderation" when Pearson asked "a high ranking French public servant" whether the Canadians were to take their hundred thousand dead to Germany along with their planes and soldiers.[56]

There were other factors that contributed to Canadian exasperation. One of them was French ambassador François Leduc, who, according to Paul Martin, "gave distressing proof of de Gaulle's delight in throwing the fat in the fire".[57] Leduc regularly failed to notify Ottawa of the visits of French officials to Quebec City, although both diplomatic protocol and a personal pledge from Leduc required that he should. Similarly, he failed to notify Ottawa when Quebec officials visited Paris, the most important omission being the Laporte–Gérin-Lajoie visit to Paris to sign the cultural accord of November 1965. When Canadian officials expressed displeasure, the effect on Leduc seemed negligible, although it was later learned that Leduc had tried to ameliorate the situation.

No Canadian was so disturbed about the differences between France and Canada as Governor General Georges Vanier. He thought that perhaps a visit to France and a discussion with his wartime colleague President de Gaulle would break down some of the barriers and clear up misunderstandings. Martin and Pearson agreed, and Martin raised the question of a Vanier visit with the French in January 1966. De Gaulle, however, was not receptive. In February, an official told the Canadian embassy in Paris that de Gaulle was "touched" to learn that his old friend General Vanier wanted to see him, but, alas, Vanier was not a head of state and therefore would not receive the head-of-state treatment that Canada deemed appropriate. This outraged Pearson: the French terms were unacceptable, and finally on July 27, 1966, the Canadian embassy was instructed to tell the French that de Gaulle's conditions were intolerable. The question of an official visit was therefore deferred — perhaps indefinitely.[58]

The general public was unaware of these conflicts between France and Canada, with the exception of the NATO crisis. Even seasoned observers of Canadian foreign policy tended to emphasize the growing links between Canada and France rather than their differences. This, of course, is what the government wanted; and it was not entirely misleading, for Canadian-French contact was much fuller than at any time since 1763. By mid-1966, senior officials could point to a surprising range of mutual interests and activities, including university and cultural exchanges, formal economic links, and even aerospace and defence co-operation.

There were other areas of co-operation and consultation, and the list of the activities was impressive. Yet senior officials were not greatly sanguine. However active Canada had been, it had not been so active as Quebec; and in those numerous areas where the federal government had shown little interest in the past, the Quebec government now played an active part. Moreover, the co-operation that had developed between France and Canada arose almost entirely from Canadian initiative. The French appeared to care only in such areas as atomic research, defence production, and space, fields where the Canadian government found full co-operation difficult. Only in the area of cultural affairs was it possible to speak of a "special relationship" between Canada and France.[59]

Both the Canadian embassy in Paris and senior officials in Ottawa were most concerned and eager to expand ties with France. But the Ottawa officials were not willing to adjust Canadian policies in other areas to improve the relationship with France. They were also less willing than Paris embassy officials to meet French insults with good cheer and to sympathize with Gaullist foreign policy. In any case, all federal officials agreed that they should do little until the impact of the June 1966 Quebec election could be assessed. The assessment took longer because the result was completely unexpected in Ottawa.

Since the November 1965 cultural agreement, the Quebec government had been quite aggressive in its dealings with France, and Mike was troubled. The Lesage government, desiring to make nationalism the essence of its election platform, claimed that in the future it need only *inform* Ottawa of its decision to enter into international agreements. It was a bold claim that was impossible for Mike to accept. Jean Chrétien, a young Quebec MP who was becoming a favourite of Pearson's, was told by Claude Morin that Quebec would "separate from Canada the same way that Canada separated from England" — a precedent here, a concession there, then "snap". Mike knew the pattern well, for he had presided at the creation of an autonomous Canada a generation earlier. He hoped for a clarification of Quebec aims when the hustings rhetoric finally subsided. But the clarification did not come: the new Union Nationale government under Daniel Johnson confused rather than clarified, leaving federal officials more uncertain than ever what course Quebec might take.[60]

The federal officials had also changed. With the 1965 election, new voices were heard in the Prime Minister's Office. The most prominent were those of Pierre Trudeau, Pearson's prickly and clever parliamentary secretary, and two new advisers, Marc Lalonde and Jean Beetz. Trudeau, a constitutional lawyer, was profoundly disturbed by the implications for Canadian federalism of Quebec's activities in international affairs. Alone he could have little influence; but with lawyers of like views, such as Lalonde, Beetz, and Allan Gotlieb, who became head of the legal division of External Affairs, Trudeau's opinions gained wider currency and influence. In terms of relations with France, this meant less tolerance of French indiscretions and interference; it also meant an intensification of efforts to link Canada with France culturally and economically and to make External Affairs better reflect the bicultural nation. Thus Quebec's argument that its external affairs activities were necessary because Canadian diplomacy had not reflected the needs and interests of Quebec was, in essence, accepted.[61]

In mid-1966, as Canadians waited to see if the Quiet Revolution had ended, Canada's relations with France were debated in the press, in Parliament, and in private gatherings.[62] Canada's policy reflected the debate: it was sometimes contradictory, at other times simply puzzling. Martin had come to believe that de Gaulle challenged Canada through Quebec in order to obtain Canadian support or acquiescence in the international arena. When the price was low, as in June 1966, Canada should pay it. Pearson generally agreed. Yet questions remained: when would the price be deemed too high? and when should de Gaulle's conduct be deemed so offensive that Canada should oppose France in the international arena? The problem was complicated by the celebrations being planned for centennial year — 1967 — and the need to invite Charles de Gaulle to Canada.

With the secrecy characteristic of all dealings with France, the Canadians extended an informal invitation to de Gaulle in early spring 1966. Very soon, news of the invitation leaked to Quebec authorities, who themselves became much interested in de Gaulle's presence and what it could mean for them. Not surprisingly, Pearson was "apprehensive" about a de Gaulle visit, but since invitations had to be sent to all heads of state, little could be done. The apprehension grew when the new Quebec premier, Daniel Johnson, informed Pearson on August 4 of his intention to send a personal invitation to de Gaulle and to the Pope. By September, when Pearson replied to Johnson's announcement, it had become clear that the change of government in Quebec would not lead to a loss of provincial interest in international ties.[63] The motives of the new government, however, seemed somewhat different from those of the Lesage Liberals. As Pierre-Louis Guertin has pointed out: "les initiatives internationales de Johnson ne procédaient pas, comme c'était le cas pour le gouvernement Lesage, d'un simple désir de pallier à la carence absolue du gouvernement canadien dans le domaine de la francophonie, mais d'une volonté d'affirmer la personnalité internationale du Québec." The difference was very much not to the liking of Ottawa officials, who soon became, in Guertin's words, "beaucoup plus agressif".[64] Slights became ever more a threat to sovereignty, and, in the fall of 1966, Ottawa became much less disposed to tolerate French discourtesy. At the same time, Canadian officials, most of whom still believed that France's principal interest in Canada was in relation to Canada's international influence, argued with French officials that, without Quebec in Canada, France would lose considerable advantage in its bargaining with the United States. What remained of "Canada" after separation would be a bitter Ulster, profoundly hostile to all things French. France's true interest, the Canadians argued, therefore lay in a united Canada.

De Gaulle would have none of this: he had become infatuated

with the idea of Quebec.* "For him," his finest biographer writes, "that preponderance of the Anglo-Saxon world over a fragment of the French people, that fossil that had survived in a pure state from the centuries of the Valois and the Bourbons, who spoke the language of Molière's peasants, was unbearable." From Paris came the surprising information that Lesage and de Gaulle had corresponded privately on matters concerning the economic and political future of Quebec. Ottawa was also not informed of the visits to Quebec of two French ministers, Maurice Couve de Murville and Christian Fouchet; nor did Leduc inform the federal government of his movements, despite solemn promises to do so. The greatest annoyance, however, came from de Gaulle's refusal, in November 1966, even to see Jean Marchand, although some Quebec ministers had been given elaborate welcomes on recent visits.[65]

Canadian officials in Paris and in Ottawa had placed great hope upon the planned visit of the convivial and charming Marchand, whose reputation in Ottawa was at its height. When Léger asked French minister of state Louis Joxe (who himself visited Canada for the opening of the Montreal Métro) whether de Gaulle could see Marchand, the answer was no: the President would see only foreign ministers. Since he had recently seen not only the Quebec education and cultural affairs minister but also the mayor of Montreal, and during that time had not spoken with a Canadian minister, the excuse was not convincing. Léger was especially offended when told that future visitors would have a better chance of seeing de Gaulle if they arranged the visit through Leduc in Ottawa. External officials were also angered, and shortly after the event — in early December — Martin told Pearson that Canada should consider the implications of Marchand's treatment for Canadian bilateral relations with France. In the meantime, he could raise the matter with Couve de

---

* So had some French officials. According to J.L. Granatstein and David Stafford, a "Quebec Mafia" appeared in the French bureaucracy in the 1950s whose aim was to assist Quebec separation. See J.L. Granatstein and David Stafford, *Spy Wars: Espionage and Canada from Gouzenko to Glasnost* (Toronto: Key Porter, 1990), 200 ff.

Murville at the NATO meetings in mid-December 1966 in Paris.

Couve de Murville was not so obliging as before: he offered neither excuse nor apology. It was then suggested that Pearson should personally confront de Gaulle with a demand for an explanation of his behaviour. Upon mature consideration, this plan was abandoned in favour of the traditional diplomatic protest. This protest was presented in Paris by J.G.H. Halstead, who called on both Quai d'Orsay and Elysée Palace officials. In Ottawa, both Martin and Cadieux called on Ambassador Leduc with the same message. For all, the results were disappointing.[66]

Leduc told Martin that de Gaulle had "something" against Ambassador Léger, and that the Canadians should not expect their ambassador to be invited to presidential functions. Halstead's report from Paris was equally discouraging. After speaking with several French officials, he had concluded that the French were generally hostile towards Canada. There could be no hope of improvement in Franco-Canadian relations so long as Charles de Gaulle remained. Direct confrontation of de Gaulle therefore seemed the best course.[67] To the Canadian government, however, such a Franco-Canadian confrontation was fraught with peril. In centennial year, with de Gaulle's visit only months away and Daniel Johnson's first visit to Paris a few weeks distant, confrontation was unthinkable. But what was to be done?

In the spring and early summer of 1967, frustration and bafflement were the most notable characteristics of those Canadians who had to worry about the French president's plans. Two events in particular seemed to confirm the impression that de Gaulle's actions towards Canada were malevolent. The first of these occurred when de Gaulle sent only formal condolences on the death of Governor General Vanier and an inappropriate representative, Claude Hettier de Boislambert, to the Vanier funeral in early March. Hettier apparently felt that the Canadians responded to his presence with some disdain and, through Leduc, he complained of unsuitable treatment. He specifically took offence at some remarks that Mme Vanier had made to him. Learning of Hettier's protest, Mme Vanier, in her last official act, called Leduc to Government House and handed him a blunt message for de Gaulle: "1940." There was no reply.[68]

This incident may have arisen from misunderstanding, but the failure of the French to send a representative to the ceremonies commemorating the fiftieth anniversary of the Battle of Vimy Ridge was, in Pearsonian understatement, "unfortunate to say the least". The troubles began when the Canadians informed the French that they were planning a special tribute to the men who had died taking Vimy Ridge. Prince Philip was invited, and it was hoped that de Gaulle might come as well, but de Gaulle was outraged when he learned that the Prince had been invited first. The Canadians had erred. Pearson contacted de Gaulle directly, indicating that Prince Philip would be representing the Queen of Canada, but the explanation was unacceptable to the French. The ceremony, de Gaulle explained, was to be a strictly Canadian ceremony. There would be no high-level French presence. Thus, on that spring day at Vimy only a very few local officials joined the Canadians in tribute to Canada's greatest military triumph.[69]

Mike had been in London in April 1917 when friends fought and died in France and London's news headlines proclaimed "Vimy: Canada's Easter Gift to France". He recalled how fervently Pauline Vanier had denounced Pétain and cheered de Gaulle in 1940. He was furious. At Martin's request, however, he played down the incident. The aftermath of the Vimy Ridge incident reveals the conflicting pressures upon Canadian officials. Martin argued that Canada had nothing to gain by stating that the French behaviour was offensive. He and his officials pointed out that Canada had been accomplishing much in developing exchanges and co-operation between France and Canada.[70] He had great hopes for a scheme for a francophone commonwealth that he intended to present to the French in June and that had been welcomed by francophone African nations. A public dispute would end these plans. Despite widespread misgivings and irritation, this attitude of keeping silent prevailed. Pearson was inclined to publicize the disagreements, but his PMO advisers and his foreign minister warned that such publicity would imperil not only Canada's expanding cultural and technical agreements with France but also Canada's national unity. The latter was the special concern of Pearson advisers Lalonde, Beetz, and Trudeau. Although they deeply resented France's behaviour and were annoyed with Martin's eagerness to compromise, they feared what de Gaulle might be able to do if truly angered. Despite misgivings and later denials of such misgivings, the record clearly shows that they agreed with the policy of silently waiting and hoping.[71]

Claude Morin underestimated the awareness at the federal level when he asserted that "Ottawa only realized later [that is, after 1967] that, in its direct relations with France, Quebec was now poised not only to hatch new exchange programs or even simply discuss political problems with French representatives but also to consult with Paris as if it were a virtually sovereign state". By March 1967, many saw that the Johnson government was following a path that might lead rapidly to a de facto sovereignty. The Union Nationale government seemed to Ottawa, as to one of its members, "[une] famille indisciplinée et divisée", but this very quality made its actions, especially the formation of a department of international affairs, all the more troubling. The utterances of Jean-Noel Tremblay and Marcel Masse, two younger ministers, were profoundly disturbing to the federalists. Tremblay complained publicly of France's continuing to treat Canada as a sovereign state, and Masse talked of Quebec's opening up to the world and independently signing treaties with foreign governments in Quebec's areas of jurisdiction. They were yet another element that contributed to Ottawa's hesitations in the spring of 1967.[72]

To Ottawa, then, the de Gaulle visit was unwanted but necessary. Its cancellation could provoke a series of events leading to catastrophe. But if there was hesitation and fear in Ottawa, there was growing enthusiasm for the visit in Paris and Quebec City. For de Gaulle, foreign policy had become ever more an obsession. "Domestic events," a biographer writes of the period, "occasionally forced themselves on the general's attention but only when they were so big that they could not be ignored." After de Gaulle's 1966 Russian trip, his foreign policy was marked by "the increasing virulence of his attitudes, their deepening unreality, and their unfailingly theatrical character".[73] In the view of Daniel Johnson's biographer: "En effet, de Gaulle s'apprête à jouer la pièce nommée Québec sur l'échiquier d'une grandiose stratégie qui consisterait à libérer les nations de leur sujétion au monde américain et, ce faisant, à inscrire le mot Québec dans le vocabulaire international."[74] For Daniel Johnson, too, foreign policy — if that term can be used — also became a means of binding together his ideologically disparate supporters and of gaining grudging concessions from the federal government.

Ironically, de Gaulle had not formally accepted the Canadian invitation or, for that matter, Premier Johnson's August 1966 invitation. After several attempts to clarify what de Gaulle intended to do, the Canadian embassy in Paris had told the French in late March that de Gaulle must let his intentions be known and that an itinerary must be arranged soon. This latter request stemmed from "alarming" rumours that de Gaulle intended to come in a warship and to visit Quebec first and alone. In fact, such plans had been tentatively worked out by the Quebec délégation générale and French officials. Both the method and the substance annoyed Ottawa. But the proposals pleased de Gaulle enormously. He would go, as Cartier had, to the land that had once been French.

In the first week of April, Martin told Pearson of de Gaulle's rumoured plans. Pearson declared that if de Gaulle would not come to Ottawa, there could be no visit. He further agreed with his advisers' demand that the federal government must control the whole visit and that the visit must begin in Ottawa unless very special circumstances dictated otherwise. Believing that de Gaulle was being "used" by the Union Nationale government,* Pearson urged that

---

* Johnson said to de Gaulle when he met him: "Mon Général, Quebec needs you. It is now or never." De Gaulle, much flattered, immediately liked Johnson, "though to the European French he may have seemed, with his rural manner and outlandish accent, somewhat exotic". To de Gaulle, this "exotic" creature who spoke the "patois of Molière" became the "authentic representative of a long-lost past". Jean Lacouture, *De Gaulle. The Ruler: 1945-1970* (London: Harper Collins, 1991), 450.

Johnson should be discouraged from pressing for a Quebec visit first. The federal government should draw up an itinerary for de Gaulle before it was faced with an unacceptable *fait accompli*. But if Quebec had uses for de Gaulle, so too did the federal government: de Gaulle should address Parliament in French to demonstrate that the federal government was a legitimate expression of French as well as English Canada. In short, the aims of Quebec and Ottawa had become mutually exclusive, and General de Gaulle, that most individualistic and unpredictable leader, was loath to let others decide what he should do.[75]

On April 5, 1967, Martin learned from Leduc that de Gaulle did indeed intend to come by warship to Quebec. Martin, who had always got on well with de Gaulle in past meetings, told Leduc that he believed that he should fly to Paris to clear matters with de Gaulle personally. At this point, the Prime Minister's Office began to take over complete responsibility for de Gaulle's visit from Lionel Chevrier, the commissioner for official visits during centennial year. When Leduc confirmed on April 12 that de Gaulle did intend to come first to Quebec, Ottawa moved to counteract this decision. A program for a visit was drawn up quickly to present to de Gaulle after he had given his acceptance (to have presented it before would have given him too much room to negotiate). In the meantime, Pearson would see Johnson to warn him of the grave consequences of a cancellation of the visit or of an incident.

Pearson's meeting with Johnson in a Montreal hotel room in April 1967 is reported in Pearson's memoirs:

> We both agreed that it was foolish to dispute Quebec's special relationship to and feeling for France, or the renewed desire of France to develop that relationship. We did, however, discuss the difficulties and dangers to Canadian unity that could derive from this situation, especially, as Mr. Johnson put it, from the tendency of "certain people" to sound off or become too sensitive. We discussed in this context the proposed centennial visit of de Gaulle.... At this encounter I let Mr. Johnson know that we did not desire confronta-

tion or conflict over Quebec's relations with France; neither did he. He also tried to reassure me about the purposes and programme of his own proposed visit to Paris, and told me he would do his best to keep our Ambassador, Mr. Léger, informed during the visit.

In his diary after the discussion, Pearson reflected what was the common Ottawa view of Johnson: "He is quite frank about his own more extreme nationalists and is prone to excuse his own lapses from common sense and moderation by the necessity of handling carefully his 'wilder men'." Pearson does not indicate that the discussion brought to the surface the fundamental disagreement on French aims.[76] Pearson believed that de Gaulle and France were ill-disposed towards Canada and anxious to exploit differences at every opportunity. Johnson, however, saw France as his natural ally in obtaining that equality within Confederation that he so much desired. Thus, this amiable meeting clarified little and settled nothing. Pearson's suggestion that Johnson join him in requesting that de Gaulle's visit begin in Ottawa was rejected, with courtesy but also with firmness. Johnson's rejection strengthened Martin's intention to meet de Gaulle; Konrad Adenauer's funeral provided a useful pretext.

Martin met de Gaulle on April 23, but the conversation was not fruitful. De Gaulle used the occasion to reflect upon the inevitable decline of the American empire. This fascinating though hardly original *tour d'horizon* permitted the General to evade Martin's question about his plans for the visit. Nevertheless, Martin was encouraged by the mood, and he gave an optimistic report on his discussion to his officials and to his prime minister. For the first time in several weeks, Ottawa exhaled.[77]

The relief was short. Within a few days, Quebec City and Ottawa were fighting over the draft press release on de Gaulle's visit. In angry communications, the Quebec officials indicated — and rightly so — that they alone possessed the French president's favour and that they had fuller knowledge of what he planned to do. The major quarrel arose over Ottawa's insistence that the phrase "with the agreement of the Federal Government" be included in the announcement of de Gaulle's itinerary in Quebec City. On behalf of Johnson, Claude Morin refused to accept that wording. Morin further warned that de Gaulle might provoke a diplomatic incident during Johnson's Paris visit in May if federal officials further interfered with Quebec's arrangements for the visit. Johnson finally intervened, indicating to Pearson that Quebec must play a role analogous to that of the federal government in the preparations for the visit. In this duplication of preparation lay the seeds of continuous dissension and, ultimately, the much-feared "diplomatic incident".[78]

Troubles began on May 5 when a Canadian official, General R.W. Moncel, sent the French a draft program that had General de Gaulle beginning his visit in Ottawa, then going to Montreal, and finally travelling to one or more provincial capitals. Later that same day, a French official called on Moncel and presented the French plans, in which de Gaulle would begin in Montreal, go next to Quebec, and then end his visit in Ottawa. Moncel warned that the date on which de Gaulle planned to be at Expo — July 26 — was Cuba's national day, and that sharing national days was impossible. The French official emphasized that Quebec wanted de Gaulle to visit Quebec City first and that Montreal was de Gaulle's proposed compromise. Moncel warned that any change in the program would require that he seek new instructions — instructions whose nature he could not predict. He ended with a suggestion: de Gaulle should fly to Ottawa on July 23 from St. Pierre et Miquelon, go to Expo for the French National Day on July 24, and then end the visit in Quebec.

The French, however, continued their insistence upon the Montreal–Quebec City–Ottawa order and also upon arrival by ship rather than plane. After some debate, the Canadians reluctantly agreed to the French proposal, provided that a strong federal presence in Montreal was accepted by the Quebec government.

De Gaulle, however, was soon subjected to other pressures. During his visit to France, Johnson urged that the visit must begin in Quebec City. French officials, fearing — probably correctly — that any decision would be offensive to someone, asked Canadian officials what they should do. External Affairs continued to insist on Montreal as the first step, but Lalonde and Beetz in the Prime Minister's Office saw this insistence as diplomatic pettifoggery. Why not Quebec City, if a federal presence were there? The important issue, they argued, was where the visit ended. De Gaulle would surely be less likely to be disruptive if he knew his final words were to be spoken in Ottawa. Their arguments were flawed, but Pearson agreed: Quebec should be informed that Ottawa was quite willing to have the visit begin in Quebec City even though it had already accepted the French proposal that had the visit beginning in Montreal. This seemed like shrewd conciliation, Pearsonian intuition penetrating the diplomatic haze. But conciliation in this case did not bring the desired result.[79]

Reports reached Ottawa of de Gaulle's behaviour during the Johnson visit and of Johnson's enthusiastic response to his "accueil éclatant" ("remarkable welcome"). Moreover, de Gaulle began to dispense with the caution that had marked his language, if not always his actions. He used the phrase "Etat du Québec", which, although not original, still assured excitement in the anglophone Canadian press. Canadian officials accordingly warned the French that the President must choose his words more carefully when in Canada lest he excite an acrimonious domestic debate. De Gaulle did not take instructions well, and protocol difficulties persisted. Who should sit beside de Gaulle in the open car in Quebec City? Who should be at the head table at the dinner? A meeting of de Gaulle and Martin on June 14 was cordial but failed to answer these questions.

Despite personal slights by de Gaulle, Léger continued to believe that, fundamentally, France had shown goodwill towards Canada during his tenure as ambassador. The evidence for his argument lay in the numerous exchanges, educational accords, and more regular consultations at all levels. The de Gaulle visit, if properly handled, promised to be the climax of this increasingly complex drama,

enacted until then by players of the second rank. And yet Canada
was ill prepared to prevent the visit from becoming a celebration of
the new Quebec rather than a conclusion to one act of the Canadian-French relationship and a prologue to another, more exciting
act. What, Léger asked, could Pearson and de Gaulle discuss? So
wide was the divergence of view between the two men that, less than
a month before the visit, he could not imagine a satisfactory agenda.
In Léger's view, Canada was all too close to the American viewpoint,
from which France dissented with increasing vigour. In the remaining few weeks, Canada must find some common grounds for discussion — perhaps joint production of an earth satellite — and Canada
might also consider changing some of its attitudes, which con-
formed to American viewpoints that France found obnoxious. The
situation, Léger warned, was much more serious than Ottawa realized. The France-Quebec relationship possessed all the temptation
of illicit romance and all the lure of long-dormant dreams. Bilingualism and biculturalism must have an external as well as an internal application; otherwise, the vision would be limited and, exciting
no one, it would fail.

This warning came as the Canadian State Visits Office, the Prime
Minister's Office, and External Affairs were recognizing that
Pearson's concession, allowing the visit to begin in Quebec City,
had not produced a spirit of compromise in the Quebec capital.[80]
The French were now disposed to let Ottawa and Quebec resolve
differences between themselves; by taking this stance they were, at
least tacitly, treating Ottawa and Quebec as equals in the planning of
the visit, a status for Quebec that Ottawa would not recognize.
Thus, attitudes hardened in Ottawa, especially those of the Quebec
ministers, who argued that the Canadian government must not
renegotiate what had already been agreed upon. As a result, de
Gaulle's itinerary continued to cause federal-provincial argument
until a few hours before his ship, the *Colbert*, reached Canadian soil.
Although the disagreement had many facets, one item stands out.
Quebec officials claimed that the Quebec City portion of the visit
was private, a response to a personal invitation from Johnson to de

Gaulle. Ottawa denied this, arguing that the presence of the governor general* in Quebec City made the capital different from other
provincial capitals visited by foreign dignitaries during centennial
year. Ottawa further claimed that Quebec had accepted a "strong
federal presence" in Quebec City when Ottawa agreed to arrival in
that city. Now, Quebec was reneging on this agreement.

On July 6, with the visit less than two weeks away, Marc Lalonde
met with Johnson, who was in Ottawa. An agitated Lalonde indicated that he had learned from Quebec official André Patry and
Leduc that French and Quebec officials had arranged for a reception
aboard the *Colbert* for 5:00 p.m. on July 23, the same time that the
governor general was to host a reception at the Quebec Citadel in
honour of President de Gaulle. Lalonde, reflecting Pearson's
instructions, told Johnson that this was pure mischief and it was
simply intolerable. To Lalonde's surprise, Johnson agreed: he
himself had told Paris that the Quebec government approved of a
French reception only in Montreal and a federal government reception in Quebec City. But the French would not give way, even when
confronted with a united Canada-Quebec stand. De Gaulle insisted
that he was obliged to return the hospitality of the people of Quebec
in Quebec City. He further indicated that he intended to hold a
reception in Ottawa as well, even though such a reception would be
a clear breach of the established practice (for centennial year) of no
reciprocal receptions. The Canadians demanded an explanation; the
French obliged.

On July 7, Leduc pointed out to Moncel that the numerous
Canadian-French crises had irritated de Gaulle, who believed that
his own behaviour had been thoroughly logical and courteous. De
Gaulle, Leduc explained, had responded to two separate invitations
— one from Quebec and another from the governor general. Moreover, the visit was for Expo, *not* for the centennial celebrations.

---

* The new governor general was Roland Michener, a former Conservative MP who
had been Pearson's Oxford classmate and frequent tennis partner. Diefenbaker
loathed him; Michener reciprocated his feelings.

Since he had already made a state visit to Canada and there had been no return visit by the head of state, he was under no obligation to visit Ottawa. This argument ignored, of course, the French resistance to Vanier's attempt to visit Paris and evaded the question of whom the French believed the Canadian head of state to be. Apparently, in French eyes, there was none. The logic, however, was confusing rather than Cartesian.

Leduc continued with an outline of what de Gaulle intended to do. In Quebec City, de Gaulle would meet with Governor General Michener on his arrival; after a brief morning visit to Michener at the Citadel, he would put himself fully in the hands of his provincial hosts. He would also extend hospitality in Quebec and Montreal to those Quebec officials who had invited him, and the presence of federal ministers would be embarrassing on these occasions. Finally, if the federal government continued to insist that he come to Ottawa — even though diplomatic protocol dictated that he should not — he would come. While in Ottawa he would hold a reception (the invitations were already printed), and if Pearson and Michener failed to appear at this reception, there would certainly be a diplomatic incident. The French had raised the stakes dramatically. For the Canadians, Ottawa was too much to bargain.

The game had been played secretly; the public knew nothing about the turmoil. This secrecy, however, seemed imperilled by declarations by Quebec officials, especially Marcel Masse, that Ottawa could no longer conduct international negotiations for Quebec in fields of provincial competence.[81] Masse's statement in late June was supported by his Liberal predecessor, Paul Gérin-Lajoie, who attacked the intransigence of the federal government towards Quebec's "opening" to the world. With the Quebec Liberal Party undergoing a tortuous searching of its federalist soul in opposition, for the federal government to take strong issue and force a Quebec common front against Ottawa was dangerous and unthinkable. Moreover, Johnson's behaviour was interpreted to mean that he had no desire to embarrass the federal government and that he feared division as well. When press leaks pointed to disagreements

over de Gaulle's itinerary, Johnson quickly, and without federal
encouragement, expressed support for an Ottawa statement indicating that de Gaulle would first meet with Michener in the Citadel.
Johnson also accepted that the Citadel could host a reception in the
late afternoon. The remainder of the program, however, was the
General's choice, not Quebec's or Ottawa's.[82]

As the diplomats and officials completed their private agreements, the francophone press in Quebec enthusiastically heralded
the visit. De Gaulle's infant playthings, his love of animals, Mme de
Gaulle's morning masses — all formed the background for the
appearance of this great man, so quintessentially French. Articles
expatiating on the President's career overflowed the first page into
the editorial sections, sometimes extending into the sports. For a
leader besieged by domestic critics for whom his idiosyncrasies had
become the source of ridicule rather than the stuff of charisma, this
acclaim surely must have been satisfying. In the Quebec Assembly,
deputies fought to have the General pass through their constituency, as if his path would leave his political genius as a residue.
Mayors clamoured to greet him, each offering more fleurs-de-lis
and tricolours than his neighbour, each sensing a unique occasion.[83]

And the occasion was uniquely de Gaulle's: the setting, the time,
and the itinerary were of his choosing. A sense of the past and a
dream of French renewal came inevitably with the *Colbert* to
Quebec on the morning of July 23, 1967. For the Québécois, the
world would now learn what they had never forgotten. "Le
monde," Johnson declared on July 21, "saura que nous existons."
("The world will know that we exist.") De Gaulle's presence stirred
an enthusiasm for France and the French that had long been
dormant. De Gaulle, through his visit, created the occasion and the
new sense of joy.[84]

At the moment of disembarkation, de Gaulle was met by a thunderous roar, Michener by scattered boos. Soon, Johnson took away
the General. They passed together through the streets of Old
Quebec, to the shrine at Ste. Anne de Beaupré, and then back to
Quebec, all in open cars, through seas of waving flags and ceaseless

chants of "de Gaulle, de Gaulle. Vive la France." Late on that Sunday afternoon, de Gaulle returned to the *Colbert* for his reception. The atmosphere was cordial for all: to Martin, de Gaulle said, "Well, Martin, this is going well."[85] But that evening at the Château Frontenac dinner hosted by Johnson, Martin was less pleased. There was the inevitable problem of the seating (Louis St. Laurent, for example, had to take his place at an inconspicuous table). But it was de Gaulle's response to Johnson's toast that most disturbed Martin. De Gaulle, Martin reported to Pearson, had taken sides in the Canadian constitutional debate. The best approach, in Martin's view, would be to ask de Gaulle what he meant in his more opaque references to Quebec's "evolving" ties with France. Martin's response indicated his fear of an incident as well as his typical caution in Franco-Canadian relations. The following day, however, there would be no federal officials to remind de Gaulle of his limits.[86]

Along the newly christened Chemin du Roy on July 24, de Gaulle received a regal welcome. He responded in kingly fashion. Grasping hands everywhere, his withered face transformed into childlike joy, de Gaulle sparked the crowd's soul. Like some grand progress of Henri IV, the long caravan snaked its way to Montreal, where half a million thronged the streets, pressing to witness the great moment.[87] At the Montreal Hôtel de Ville, Mayor Jean Drapeau and Johnson waited, a bit anxious about what they had heard. Pearson was in Ottawa, but in a railway car at Windsor station, Martin listened on the radio to the astonishing events. De Gaulle finally arrived and walked onto the balcony of the Hôtel de Ville. The impatient crowd stretched all the way to the Champs de Mars. Drapeau said there was no microphone, but then, miraculously, one appeared. De Gaulle hesitated; the crowd chanted. He spoke:[88]

C'est une immense émotion qui remplit mon coeur en voyant devant moi la ville française de Montréal. Au nom du vieux pays, au nom de la France, je vous salue de tout mon coeur. Je vais vous confier un secret que vous ne répéterez pas. Ce soir ici, et tout le long de ma route, je me trouvais dans une atmosphère du même genre que celle de la Libération. Outre cela, j'ai constaté quel immense effort de progrès, de développement, et par conséquent d'affranchissement vous accomplissez ici et c'est à Montréal qu'il faut que je le dise, parce que, s'il y a au monde une ville exemplaire par ses réussites modernes, c'est la vôtre. Je dis c'est la vôtre et je me permets d'ajouter c'est la nôtre....

Voilà ce que je suis venu vous dire ce soir en ajoutant que j'emporte de cette réunion inouïe de Montréal un souvenir inoubliable. La France entière sait, voit, entend, ce qui se passe ici et je puis vous dire qu'elle en vaudra mieux.*

Vive Montréal! Vive le Québec! Vive le Québec libre!

Vive le Canada français et vive la France!

"Vive le Québec libre!" Mike heard the words on the television broadcast and was startled. Martin gasped as the crowd roared. He tried to call Léger — no answer. When he finally reached him, no explanation. Find Couve de Murville, Martin demanded; but he could not be found. Martin left his guests and returned to Ottawa, where an angry Pearson had called a cabinet meeting.[89] By this time, Couve de Murville had got in touch with Martin and told him to remain cool and the incident would pass away: Franco-Canadian relations were too important to rupture for the sake of a few careless

---

* "An immense emotion fills my heart when I see before me the French city of Montreal. In the name of the old country, in the name of France, I greet you with all my heart. I'm going to tell you a secret that you will not repeat. This evening, here and all along my route, I found the same kind of atmosphere as that of the Liberation. Furthermore, I noted what an immense effort of progress, of development, and consequently of emancipation you are accomplishing here, and I must say this in Montreal, because if there is in the world a city that is exemplary in its modern successes, it is yours. I say it is yours, and I venture to add, it is ours.

"That's what I have come to say to you this evening, and I'll add that I will take away with me an unforgettable memory of this incredible meeting in Montreal. All France knows, sees, and hears what goes on here, and I can tell you, it will be the better for it."

words. Martin and Léger tended to agree, and in cabinet on July 25 Martin asked for time to allow de Gaulle to explain himself. But with de Gaulle expected in Ottawa very soon, time was too precious. Besides, reports had reached Ottawa during the day that de Gaulle was speaking openly about Quebec independence as he toured Expo and that French officials were taunting Lionel Chevrier, the federal representative accompanying de Gaulle at Expo. De Gaulle *had* explained himself. Faced with a wave of English-Canadian anger, that night Pearson read a statement that declared de Gaulle's remarks unacceptable. "The people of Canada," Pearson continued, "are free. Every province of Canada is free. Canadians do not need to be liberated." Creating a distinction between the French and de Gaulle, Pearson concluded:

> Canada has always had a special relationship with France, the motherland of so many of her citizens. We attach the greatest importance to our friendship with the French people. It has been, and remains, the strong purpose of the government of Canada to foster that friendship. I hope that my discussions later this week with General de Gaulle will demonstrate that this purpose is one which he shares.

Those discussions would not take place; that evening de Gaulle announced that he would fly to Paris the following day.[90]

De Gaulle's remarks and the events had stunned Canadians and others. Their sheer boldness took most off guard, and public opinion was perplexed. The press seemed to report what readers felt. Anglophone newspapers vehemently disapproved, often questioning the General's mental capacity and stability and minimizing the crowd's enthusiasm and numbers. Francophone reporters angrily dissented, and many of them signed a petition protesting anglophone coverage of the de Gaulle visit. French-language newspaper editorials tended to stress other aspects of the de Gaulle visit, but, with some exceptions, they were not critical of de Gaulle's remarks.[91] "Vive le Québec libre" was interpreted not as a separatist slogan, but as mere recognition of the fact of Quebec freedom.

Perhaps de Gaulle was excessive, Claude Ryan wrote in *Le Devoir*, but was not the English-Canadian reaction hysterical, a betrayal of fear, doubt, and animosity?[92] That Ryan's attitude reflected that of most French Canadians was borne out by polls taken after the general's departure. Only 20 per cent in one sample taken in Montreal, Quebec, and Trois-Rivières thought that de Gaulle wanted to encourage separation. Only 16.4 per cent thought the voyage had served no good purpose, while 69.3 per cent believed it had been worthwhile. When asked whether de Gaulle's remarks had constituted interference in Canada's internal affairs and whether Pearson's reproach was justified, 58.7 per cent said no. The strongest disagreement came from Trois-Rivières (80.4 per cent), where de Gaulle did not visit, but even in Montreal, with its substantial anglophone population and press, only 36.2 per cent believed de Gaulle had interfered and should have been reproached.[93]

In its response, however, Quebec was also unlike France. French newspapers did not share the viewpoint of their transatlantic linguistic counterparts. *Le Monde* admitted that French Canadians had not always played a full part in Canadian national life, but pointed to the Royal Commission on Bilingualism and Biculturalism as proof of the Pearson government's intention of improving matters. De Gaulle's intervention, which *Le Monde* felt was aimed at the dismemberment of Canada, could only reinforce the American hegemony de Gaulle so much detested. The conservative *Le Figaro* termed the incident disgraceful, and even the Communist *L'Humanité* criticized de Gaulle's "interference". De Gaulle knew what they would say, but had no regrets: "What I did I had to do."[94] And Mike Pearson did what he had to do.

When Mike met the cabinet on July 25, he told its members that de Gaulle's intentions were clear. Martin said there was no chance of any retraction and that the mood in Montreal was dangerous. Some hesitated to act, including Jean Marchand, but Pearson said he had no choice: English Canada would never accept the comparison between the Liberation and de Gaulle's visit. Long after the visit, it was learned that some French embassy officials had reported to

Paris that Pearson had always tried to be fair and understanding and recommended that his wounds should be salved. His wounds should be ignored, de Gaulle responded. Quebec's liberation, not Pearson's feelings, was what really mattered now.[95]

And so Mike bled awhile. But his wounds healed when he saw that de Gaulle's words and their electric effect in Quebec had awakened in all Canadians a new sense of the crisis their divided nation faced. René Lévesque later said that de Gaulle was the first outsider "who understood what was going on". But if he did, he did not advance his cause in the end, because, as Stephen Clarkson has observed, "it was federal Canada that turned out to be a winner" (if there are any winners in such games). The reaction to de Gaulle brought forth Pierre Trudeau, who countered the French challenge to Canada's nationhood and who tangled ferociously with those forces de Gaulle had summoned that summer night in Montreal. Mike knew he would not fight another day; but, by summer's end, he knew he had new generals who would.[96]

CHAPTER TEN

LAST INNINGS

As one who has known both the shelter of academic halls and the anonymous security of the civil service, I have at times had my own doubts about the wisdom of venturing forth, with wary shield and uncertain sword, among the lions in the open forum of party politics. But that's where the action is today. Without action we can't make progress no matter how brilliant our thoughts may be.

—Lester Pearson to the Canadian Political Science Association, June 8, 1967[1]

THE DE GAULLE AFFAIR left many wounded — most notably Paul Martin, whom the increasingly influential francophone ministers and Marc Lalonde in Pearson's office blamed for failing to recognize the dangers and for compromising too quickly. In June 1965 the Gallup poll asked Canadians whom they favoured as Pearson's successor. Forty-three per cent favoured Martin. Lesage stood at 16 per cent, but his support was very weak outside Quebec, and, in any event, he was no longer a factor once he lost the Quebec election in 1966. Walter Gordon was the third highest with 11 per cent, but he was a casualty of the 1965 election.[2] The poll revealed how little impression other cabinet ministers had made. Paul Hellyer had been an important Defence minister, but his program of defence unification, for which he was fully responsible, had entered rough political waters. In the first Pearson government, External

Affairs under Martin had had some major accomplishments, notably the extension of external aid, the signing of the Autopact, the negotiation of an "accord cadre" with France, and the creation of a peacekeeping force for Cyprus, which was very much the product of Martin's personal initiative. After 1965, however, troubles mounted, and the problem of succession became greater as Mike moved closer to his seventieth year just as the young were saying they trusted no one over thirty.

After the election, Pearson surveyed his disappointed troops and decided that some major changes had to be made. He wanted less "flamboyance" and more stability. Mitchell Sharp replaced Gordon at Finance, and Robert Winters took over at Trade and Commerce. These appointments seemed to tilt the cabinet to the "right", but Mike vigorously denied that such a tilt had occurred when Garth Stevenson, a student then and a distinguished political scientist later, accused him of it. He assured Stevenson that a Liberal Party led by him would always be on the "left".[3] Yet with Gordon gone, Kent no longer prodding Pearson, and a lot of unfinished business from the first term of government, the reform impetus lagged. Moreover, its costs, political and economic, caught up with the government in early 1966. Sharp faced a situation where inflationary pressures were rising and growth of expenditures and deficits had to be curtailed. The government received much blame for the problem, especially after Mike appointed his old friend Larry MacKenzie to arbitrate a St. Lawrence Seaway Workers' dispute. On June 9, 1966, MacKenzie announced an astounding arbitration award of 30 per cent (an earlier conciliation board had recommended only 14 per cent). The preparations for the Montreal Expo meant that the workers had a powerful threat. It was Pearson himself who finally decided that the award should stand, even though several of his ministers opposed it. Although he had erred in appointing MacKenzie, who was not a labour arbitrator, Pearson believed he had to respect the agreement. Sharp was troubled, particularly when he had to ask for a delay in the introduction of medicare because of the need for fiscal restraint. He did agree to the introduction of the Guaranteed Income Supplement to the old-age pension, however.[4]

Reformers remained, but they were younger and new. Most notable were the francophone ministers: Marchand at Citizenship and Immigration (later Manpower and Immigration); Jean-Luc Pépin at Mines and Technical Surveys (later Energy, Mines and Resources); and Maurice Sauvé at Forestry (later Forestry and Northern Development). Marchand took the lead in the reform of the labour market and, over the objections of some cabinet colleagues, pushed for the right of public servants to strike. Mike was doubtful, as were former civil servants Sharp and Drury, but the right was granted in 1967.[5] The "left Liberal" Allan MacEachen replaced "reformer" Judy LaMarsh at Health and Welfare. LaMarsh, who was bitter when Pearson removed her from Health and Welfare, told him she would go to the back benches. He had offered her the position of solicitor general, which she refused because she believed in the death penalty and, she later wrote, "Pearson would bring up the death-penalty question again and again, until he got it passed".[6] It would be, she rightly believed, impossible. But she had second thoughts about the back benches and came to Pearson and asked to become secretary of state, a position in which she organized Canada's centennial celebrations for 1967 and did so splendidly.*

Pearson had new ministers from Quebec, but one of his most dif-

---

*Her new responsibilities for official courtesies did not alter her combative ways. Here is an example of that style as she battled with Arthur Laing, the Indian Affairs and Northern Development minister:

> I have received from the Prime Minister a copy of your letter of March 20th, in which you once again interfere in my department. I should have thought that even one with your limited intelligence would have appreciated that suggestions with regard to the Centennial Train should be forwarded to this department. I have to advise you that there is a sub-committee dealing with the possibility of continuance of Centennial projects. Your suggestion has been made many times, and by much better qualified people.
>
> I wish, however, to point out to you that in your estimates' debate on Page 1348 of June 9th, you took completely unwarranted credit for "frontier

ficult tasks was the dropping of Lamontagne and Tremblay from the cabinet because of the furniture scandals. Since Tremblay had simply refused to pay for furniture that was not delivered, a perfectly sensible action, his guilt was by association, but he went quietly to the back benches. Lamontagne, however, was bitter when Pearson asked him to resign. He told Pearson that the decision to drop himself and Tremblay meant that he had decided "not to go on the attack, not to lead and deal with [the charges against Lamontagne and Tremblay] squarely".[7] But they both went, and it was a clear indication of Pearson's hope that the "new look" cabinet, as it was called, would efface the bad memories of Rivard, Banks, and the other thugs who had tainted his first government.

The "new look" went out of style quickly in 1966. When Favreau resigned in July 1965, Pearson had decided that the Justice ministry must be held by a francophone. Fulton-Favreau was not yet interred by Lesage, and Mike believed that only a francophone could keep it from the grave. He therefore appointed Lucien Cardin, a parliamentary brawler who had made a vicious and memorable attack on Diefenbaker in 1962. His words then had not been forgotten; his words and actions as minister would be watched carefully in the future by Diefenbaker, the greatest parliamentary debater of his time.

Just after the election, Cardin appeared on the CBC program "This Hour Has Seven Days" and was asked about a low-level Soviet agent and Canadian postal clerk named George Victor Spencer. Cardin said that although Spencer would not be charged for his alleged espionage activities, he would be under RCMP

---

packages". There can be no sense whatsoever in your statement, "in co-operation with the C.B.C. we ...".

I am, however, informed that the announcement which you made respecting the C.B.C. in the area which is most sensitive, and which is no way your responsibility, is quite false.

You seem to have enough difficulties with your own department, and I would suggest you should keep your nose out of mine.

LaMarsh to Laing, June 14, 1967, Pearson Papers, MG26 N5, v.45 (NAC).

surveillance for the remainder of his life, which would presumably not be long because Spencer had terminal cancer. Cardin's comments were, Jack Pickersgill later said, all Diefenbaker needed. The opposition began a relentless attack on Cardin for the assumption of guilt his statement implied. Diefenbaker railed against the denial of civil liberties, and the New Democrats urged an inquiry. Pearson promised to consider the request, especially since Spencer had been fired under a clause in the Civil Service Act that prohibited any appeal.[8] On February 23, 1966, however, Pearson told the House that he had examined the entire Spencer file and had decided that "an inquiry into this matter is not necessary and would not be useful".[9] Cardin had convinced Pearson that he must support Cardin's decision that there should be no inquiry.

Mike was troubled, however, and correctly so, for Spencer had not been given any chance to defend himself. Mike had often been the victim of flimsy charges, and had never forgotten what had happened to Herbert Norman, whose rights he believed had been abused. Diefenbaker and his colleagues sensed Pearson's uncertainty. In fact, they knew of it because a wiring error had, inadvertently and incredibly, linked the Liberal caucus room with the earpiece in the Conservative caucus room. Erik Nielsen, who used the overheard information most effectively, later admitted that "from late 1965 until well into 1966" he and other Conservatives "had a pipeline into the Liberal caucus". He recalled with some satisfaction how he "would look across from my position in the fourth row of the opposition benches and see the looks of consternation on the faces of cabinet ministers who could not understand how information only recently released within their caucus was being used to frame questions fired at a particular minister". No one got more fire than Cardin. In the caucus of March 2, however, he was ready to fight back. Pearson gave, in the description of Nielsen, who was listening in, "a rally-round-the-leadership" speech. Knowing that the Liberals were themselves troubled, the Tories stepped up the assault on March 4.[10]

The Tories got help from the NDP's David Lewis, who ingeniously called Spencer's lawyer and asked him whether Spencer wanted an inquiry. Spencer said he did. Lewis then moved to reduce Cardin's salary by $17,000, a motion that was, in effect, one of non-confidence. Mike knew that some Liberals were also unhappy with the situation and wanted an inquiry, as did most of the English press. Many Liberals were missing; a defeat loomed; and an election would follow. Pearson reacted quickly, calling in Cardin and saying that he had decided to have an inquiry. Cardin was unhappy but did not argue against the decision forcefully. Mike returned to the House at 3:50 p.m. and told Lewis that he was going to call Spencer and that Lewis and Diefenbaker should listen in to the conversation on another telephone. If Spencer wanted an inquiry, he could have one. Lewis withdrew the motion and refused to listen to any conversation with Spencer, but, as he said: "If I can't trust my country's Prime Minister to tell me the truth about a telephone conversation, we are really in bad shape." The "bad shape" would soon become worse.[11]

Lucien Cardin had said in anger on March 4 that Diefenbaker had no right to lecture anyone on security cases, "and I am not kidding". Diefenbaker did not back down and shouted at the Liberal front bench: "And again applause from the Prime Minister. I want that on the record." What followed is inexcusable;[12]

> Cardin: I understand the right hon. gentleman said he wants that on the record. Would he want me to go on and give more?
> Some hon. members: Go on. He wants it.
> Cardin: Very well.
> Some hon. members: Hear, hear.
> Cardin: I want the right hon. gentleman to tell the house about his participation in the Monseignor case when he was prime minister of the country.

Diefenbaker told nothing, and debate shifted, but the string had become untuned, and perhaps the worst cacophony in modern parliamentary history began.

While reporters scurried about trying to discover who "Monseignor" was, the Liberal government began to crumble because Cardin decided he should resign. Pearson, he charged, had "backed down" and not "backed" him. Following the resignation of Favreau and the dismissals of Lamontagne and Tremblay, Cardin's resignation was too bitter a pill for many Quebec members. The quick-tempered Jean Marchand, now the most important Quebec minister, was "furious like hell", and said if Cardin resigned he would follow. Two other ministers, Leo Cadieux and Jean-Pierre Côté, said they would also resign. On Friday, Mike believed he had averted defeat in the House by calling for an inquiry; now he faced personal defeat in his own caucus. He tried to persuade Cardin to stay. Lamontagne learned that Marchand was likely to resign and tried to stop him. The conversation, as recalled by Lamontagne, is revealing. Marchand told Lamontagne: "After what has been done to you and Tremblay and all the others I will not tolerate going through another period like this." Lamontagne responded: "there's no necessity for you to go. After all, you don't know Cardin very well. You'd never met him until you became a Member of Parliament [in November 1965]."[13] Cardin decided to stay on Tuesday evening, after he was consoled by Lamontagne and Gordon, who was invited by his seat-mate, Lamontagne, to become involved. Lamontagne finally told Mike on Wednesday, March 9, a caucus morning: "Everything is solved. You're safe now." Then, he claims, "Mike began to cry a little bit."[14] Well he might.

What went through Mike's mind that morning? Cardin had been chosen because he was francophone; the more competent George McIlraith and Larry Pennell, both from Ontario, had been ignored because Favreau could not be replaced by an anglophone. Mike had wooed Marchand, who had rejected him in 1963, and had even accepted Pelletier and Trudeau, though both had attacked him viciously in 1963 and, in Pelletier's case, even in 1965. Marchand, in Ottawa for only a couple of months, was about to resign in support of an incompetent minister whom he had met only three months before. Lamontagne and Gordon, the same adviser who had advised against a commitment to bilingualism and biculturalism only four years before, were now the mediators. Mike had pressed for compromise with Quebec, and old colleagues dismissed him as a hopeless compromiser. He had decided to commit the federal public service to bilingualism, even though he knew the decision was unpopular throughout English Canada. He had the greatest number of francophone ministers in Canadian history and had given them a power they had never possessed before. And yet the government that had done all these things was the one Cardin's actions threatened to destroy. The prime minister who had, at some political cost, brought "French power" to Ottawa was, the Quebec caucus complained, a leader who had let them down. Opposite Mike sat John Diefenbaker, who had fought him every step of the way and who had, in the recent election, delighted in his infamous list of French names and in telling English Canadians that Pearson always gave in to Quebec.

Mike may have thought such things; remarkably, however, there is no evidence to suggest that he did. He became angry with Cardin but not with his Quebec members. He resolved to remain, and in April 1966 announced the details of his program of bilingualism for the public service. He held no grudge against Marchand and soon began promoting him as his successor. When Liberal Barney Danson, later a Trudeau cabinet minister, wrote to him in late March 1966 telling him he should resign, he replied thoughtfully. No, he would not resign, even though it was "very irritating to be associated with Mr. Diefenbaker in joint responsibility" for the sorry state of Parliament. There were more important considerations, "especially the strengthening of unity inside our Party and, far more important, inside the country, between English-speaking and French-speaking Canadians. I hope I am not being egotistical in saying that I have been convinced that, were I to retire from politics at this time, it would have a harmful effect on this overriding issue."[15] The Pearson years had brought a revolution in government that had ended the isolation in which Quebec members and ministers worked in Ottawa. Under Pearson, French and English began to work — and quarrel — in the same forum. The propinquity bred some fears, occasional contempt, and much anger; but by the mid-1960s, French and English Canada could no longer lead separate lives together in the same party or the same country. The Liberals learned that lesson then, with much pain; for the Tories, the realization and the pain came later.

Mike stayed; but whatever the "overriding issue", Barney Danson was correct when he charged that there was "something terribly wrong" in Canadian politics, and that Mike was partly responsible. His battles with Diefenbaker had marred his judgement badly. He had asked the RCMP for the file on the Gerda Munsinger case and, inexcusably, had raised it with Diefenbaker in a fashion that was threatening. Even worse, Favreau had threatened Fulton directly with revelation if parliamentary criticism continued. Pearson had applauded, as Diefenbaker noted, when Cardin threatened to reveal the Munsinger name. He had permitted Favreau, Cardin, and others to talk about "using" the Munsinger file if the parliamentary struggle became rough. He was too pleased when the Tories "squirmed" after the Munsinger revelations. And he kept Cardin in his cabinet after Cardin's press conference of March 10, 1966. Cardin had told Pearson of the press conference only moments before, had ignored Pearson's plea that he say nothing about Munsinger, and had spilled out erroneous details about "Olga" Munsinger, a dead "Soviet spy" who had been "involved" with Tory ministers. Cardin revealed these details, he declared, because, in his own unfortunate words, "there is a working arrangement not only between the Prime Minister, myself and the members of the cabinet, but also all the MPs, and what we're going to do is fight and fight hard, and, if we have to, use the same methods that are being used and have been used against us for the past three years".[16] It was an appalling comment, one of the lowest moments in Canadian parliamentary history, and the nadir of Mike Pearson's public career.

Cardin did not even have his facts straight. "Olga" was really Gerda, who was soon found not dead but alive, garrulous and "working" in a Munich bar, by *Toronto Daily Star* reporter Robert

Reguly (who also found Hal Banks after Canadian officials declared him dead). Canadians were excited at having their own sex scandal to match Britain's delightful Profumo romp, which had titillated them the previous year. *Maclean's* ran a limerick contest,* and Gerda Munsinger was soon on the late news on the CBC — in those days, such matters were deemed too dangerous for the early news, since children might be watching. Munsinger quickly identified the Diefenbaker minister allegedly involved with her as Pierre Sévigny, Diefenbaker's associate defence minister. There was a sad irony in the fact that Cardin, who was enraged by the linkage between francophone ministers and scandals, should have created yet another one.[17]

New member Gérard Pelletier was profoundly troubled: Parliament was "an absurd nightmare, a Kafkaesque sort of labyrinth without any exit". Most Canadians, the Gallup poll revealed, wanted both Pearson and Diefenbaker to leave. Gerda played her part splendidly and told the German press she would tell all about her "fast-living reckless life" in Canada and "the men of society who wanted to have my love". There was, in fact, little more to tell. Nevertheless, a royal commission was established to investigate whether security had been breached. The Conservatives, understandably, objected to having an inquiry into long-past events conducted by a recently appointed Supreme Court judge, Wishart Spence, who was widely viewed as a Liberal. The commission did manage to entertain Canadians through the summer, and eventually found that Diefenbaker and his Justice minister, Davie Fulton, had not been sufficiently vigilant. (The finding notwithstanding, Canadian security hardly seemed at risk in the Montreal apartment where

---

*The winner:
> There was a young lady from Munich
> Whose bosom distended her tunic
> Her main undertaking
> Was cabinet making
> In fashions bilingue et unique.

"Gerda and Pierre" had trysted.) During the wild and bitter ex-changes in the Commons, Paul Martin, veteran of three decades of parliamentary battles, walked across to the Conservative front bench and said: "Think of this place; what are we doing to this place?" What they had done was not easily undone.[18] It was not until Diefenbaker and Pearson both departed that the noxious clouds of these tragic battles really lifted.

Several friends told Pearson, as he struggled through his troubles in early 1966, that he should look outward towards the international arena for the remainder of his prime-ministerial career. Pearson asked Martin whether he wanted a domestic portfolio, but Martin had strong leadership ambitions and believed that in External he "was isolated from the worst of the controversy". What had been true for Pearson in the 1950s was untrue for Martin in the mid-1960s, as foreign policy issues provoked bitterness. The Canadian-American relationship, which had seemed to heal so quickly after the election of 1963, became once again an open sore.

Mike Pearson had met Lyndon Johnson at John Kennedy's funeral, and the grief his nation shared he expressed to the new president. In those early days, Johnson would tell Canadian ambassador Charles Ritchie to send on his warmest greetings to Pearson. On one occasion, he even told Ritchie that Mike was the political leader he "felt closest to".[19] Their first meetings went well enough, although Johnson's rough Texas ways jarred Pearson, and Mike wondered about the President's grasp of world affairs. Still, the circumstances of the succession and his genuine support for Johnson against the increasingly right-wing Republican Party made him willing to forgive personality quirks. Johnson, in Mike's own words, revealed that he knew "nothing about Canada" when they met in Washington on January 21 and 22, 1964, but Mike realized, as few Canadians do, that American presidential ignorance can be bliss for Canadians. In any event, Secretary of State Dean Rusk was an old friend, an alumnus of Mike's old Oxford college, St. John's, and aware of Canadian needs and interests. Despite their similar backgrounds, however, Rusk was obsessed — the term does not seem too strong — with American interests in East Asia. It had troubled Mike's relationship with him earlier; it would do so again. In Washington, the Americans pressed the Canadians to strike a committee to examine the possibility of expanding the machinery of economic co-operation. There was some Canadian reluctance, but eventually this idea became reality with the appointment of Livingston Merchant, a former U.S. ambassador to Canada, and Arnold Heeney to undertake an examination of the U.S.-Canada relationship that had been so badly frayed during the Kennedy-Diefenbaker quarrels.[20]

Vietnam was scarcely mentioned in January 1964 when Pearson and Johnson met, but on May 28, 1964, in a New York hotel room, Johnson drew Pearson directly into the developing war. With the profanity and bluster that marked his ways, Johnson asked if the Americans could use Canadian diplomat Blair Seaborn as an intermediary who would tell the North Vietnamese leaders that the Americans had "carrots" for the North if it behaved, "sticks" if it did not. A report on the meeting released later in the Pentagon Papers said that "Pearson, after expressing willingness to lend Canadian good offices to [Seaborn's mission], indicated some concern about this [sic] nature of 'sticks'. He stipulated that he would have great reservations about the use of nuclear weapons, but indicated that the punitive striking of discriminate targets would be 'a different thing'."[21] Pearson has been strongly criticized for his apparent acceptance of bombing and his statement that, in the words of the American report, "he would personally understand" American recourse to such measures. In fact, he could not have had "advance" warning of an American bombing campaign, because such a campaign was not yet planned. Moreover, the note was based upon a conversation its author, who was not present, had had with McGeorge Bundy. Bundy's own memorandum, which was released in 1992, indicates that Mike was cautious indeed. He told Johnson that "any drastic escalation would give great problems both in Canada and internationally" and that it "would be one thing to attack a bridge or an oil tank, but quite another to shower bombs on a village full of women and children". The President, in Bundy's words, "expressed his clear agreement".

Pearson did agree to the use of Seaborn, a decision for which he has also received criticism. He did so because he believed Canada must be a sympathetic ally and because he regarded a negotiated settlement or peace as the best possible outcome of the mounting conflict. As political scientist Douglas Ross emphasizes, it was important, in Pearson's view, that Canada have information when the United States made decisions about war and peace. That was the lesson of the fifties for Pearson; he saw no reason to forget it in the 1960s.[22]

Seaborn travelled to Hanoi and carried the U.S. message, which was recast as a Canadian view of U.S. policy. He reported on his return that North Vietnam was "not now interested in negotiation". There were two more visits in 1964, and each time the North Vietnamese were unchanged in their attitude. On his last trip, Seaborn reported that North Vietnamese leaders "gave no indication of being worried" by the firm U.S. message. Johnson had already decided to begin continuous air strikes against the North. Seaborn's missions came to an end, and Pearson became worried.[23]

In the attempt to "save" South Vietnam, February 1965 seems in retrospect a fateful month. American involvement became deeper, sustained by thickening tentacles between Saigon and Washington. For many Americans, not only soldiers and their families, but also President Johnson and his advisers, the war became personal. Pearson and Martin knew this after their discussions with Johnson at the fabled LBJ Ranch in mid-January 1965. These discussions were a turning point in the Canadian perception of American involvement. Before they flew to Texas, the Canadians were puzzled and disturbed by the direction of American policy in Vietnam. They knew that the South Vietnamese were weaker than ever before and that the existence of the regime depended more and more on American support. What the United States intended to do was a mystery to them and to the Canadian officials who briefed them before departure. The Canadians were wary, not least because the U.S. ambassador to South Vietnam, Henry Cabot Lodge, had spoken of "internationalizing" the war when he had visited Ottawa in September 1964. In December, President Johnson himself had requested that some Canadian technical assistance be sent to Vietnam. Although Pearson and Martin both felt that they could not possibly comply with this request, they had not yet said no when their plane landed on the runway at the LBJ Ranch in Texas on January 15, 1965.

The meetings got off to a bad beginning when Johnson, wearing a cowboy suit, welcomed "Prime Minister Wilson" and his Canadian colleagues.* He immediately invited his visitors to tour the massive ranch. With Pearson attired in a black suit but minus the diplomat's homburg he had worn on arrival and Johnson in his cowboy suit, the presidential progress whirled over the desolate countryside, commanded by the President, full of Texas tales and profanity and, by journey's end, alcohol. The "press" was in the second car, the "ladies" in the third and last. There were pit stops where the President took the lead in urinating at the side of the road. Mike did not respond as LBJ told "Lester" that he should join them in "taking a leak". The dinner that followed featured steak and catfish on the same plate and Johnson as the central player who dominated conversation and interrupted anyone else who ventured a few words. Pearson later wrote: "General MacArthur would definitely not have approved, nor, I suspect, John Kennedy." Neither did Lester Pearson. Pearson saw that the style was not his own; more important, the substance also seemed flawed. Pearson and Johnson never found the easy familiarity that Kennedy and Pearson had had at Hyannis Port.[24]

Vietnam was apparently not discussed in detail in Texas. The reason for the trip was the Canada-U.S. Autopact, which was officially signed. The Canadians, however, knew that the Americans faced a critical decision about the war's future. The next month the

---

* When Johnson saw on television that he had made this gaffe, he apologized. Mike replied: "Think nothing of it, Senator Goldwater."

decision was made. On Sunday morning, February 7, the raid on Pleiku, an American advisers' base two hundred miles from Saigon, brought "a decisive change in Washington's attitude toward the conflict".[25] "Advisers" became soldiers; dependents went home; bombs rained on North Vietnam. Three days after Pleiku, Pearson warned his countrymen against either "automatic support or captious criticism" of the United States: "We must protect and advance our national interests, but we should never forget that the greatest of these is peace and security. The achievement of this aim — it is chastening to realize — does not depend on our policies so much as it does on those of our neighbour." The remainder of the speech deserves careful reading:

> This will mean, in practice, that our official doubts about certain U.S. foreign policies should be expressed in private, through the channels of diplomacy, rather than publicly by speeches to Canadian Clubs. It does not mean that we must always remain silent if there is strong disagreement on matters of great moment or principle. Not at all. Canadians in official positions have more than once spoken very frankly about policies and actions of our neighbour. Washington ruefully refers to it as arm-twisting from a close friend. But we must never do this merely for the purpose of rousing a chauvinistic cheer at home. Pulling the eagle's tail feathers is an easy, but a dangerous, way to get a certain temporary popularity, as well as a feeling of self-satisfaction at having annoyed the big bird.
>
> It's a form of indulgence that we should keep strictly under control — for national and international reasons.

Mike's speech betrayed his fears. On February 9, he made "some rather bleak comments" to André Laurendeau and Davidson Dunton "on the American chances in Vietnam". He feared "escalation" and expressed his belief that the South Vietnamese "were the first to want to get rid of the Americans, and that a compromise would have to be reached". He did not state such views publicly, and these were not the views expressed by Paul Martin, his foreign minister.[26]

On March 30, 1965, Johnson sent a note to Mike in which he congratulated Mike "on the occasion of your receiving the Temple University World Peace Award" and praised his "wisdom and courage". On April 2 Mike flew to Philadelphia to receive the award, determined to give a speech that would lead Johnson to question his wisdom. He had decided to suggest that Johnson should consider temporarily stopping the bombs. As in 1951, when General MacArthur seemed ready to expand the Korean War, Pearson decided he should come out of the shadows of "quiet diplomacy" and expose Canadian doubts to the glare of public revelation.

Martin told him not to do it; Canadian ambassador Charles Ritchie told Mike that he should give an advance copy of the speech to the White House. He rejected the advice. After he received the peace award, he began his speech with praise for the American motives in their Vietnam involvement. His government and the "great majority" of Canadians had supported U.S. "peace-keeping and peace-making policies in Vietnam". Then significantly: "We wish to be able to continue that support." A negotiated peace was the only exit, and that exit could not become overgrown with thickets of resistance coming from both sides. The bombing "beyond a certain point" might "only harden [North Vietnamese] determination to pursue, and even intensify, their present course of action". Perhaps now we had come to that "point". After two months of bombing, "the message should ... have been received 'loud and clear' in Hanoi". Admitting that he might not know many factors, Pearson suggested that there might be "a possibility" that

> a suspension of air strikes against North Vietnam *at the right time* [italics in original] might provide the Hanoi authorities with an opportunity, if they wish to take it, to inject some flexibility into their policy without appearing to do so as the direct result of military pressure. If such a suspension took place for a limited time, then the rate of incidents in South Vietnam would provide a fairly accurate way of measuring its usefulness and the desirability of con-

tinuing it. I am not, of course — I would not dare — proposing any compromise on points of principle, nor any weakening of resistance to aggression in South Vietnam. Indeed resistance may require increased military strength to be used against the armed and attacking Communists. I merely suggest that a measured and announced pause in one field of military action at the right time might facilitate the developments of diplomatic resources which cannot easily be applied to the problem under the existing circumstances. It could at least, at the very least, expose the intransigence of the North Vietnam government if they remained intransigent.

This proposal was much more than the "diffident aside" journalist Charles Taylor suggests; it challenged the clear direction of American policy at the time. LBJ noticed.[27]

The speech ended, the President invited Pearson to join him for lunch at his Camp David retreat. Mike knew what was coming. During the lunch, Johnson shouted on the telephone about Vietnam, ignoring Pearson. Not even the normal pleasantries could be exchanged, and Ritchie recalls the occasion as "very strained". After lunch, Pearson and Johnson left the other diners and went to chat on the terrace. Then Johnson "simply exploded". Pearson's speech was "bad", and for the next hour Johnson berated his visitor. "He strode the terrace, he sawed the air with his arms, with upraised fist he drove home the verbal hammer blows." If the language came from the locker room, the bullying was from the schoolyard. Pearson could scarcely say a word during the harangue. Johnson complained that Pearson

had joined the ranks of the domestic opponents of his Vietnam policy: [Senator Wayne] Morse, [Walter] Lippmann, the *New York Times*, ADA [Americans for Democratic Action], the ignorant Liberals, the "know nothing" do gooders, etc. By doing so, I had made it more difficult. He didn't expect that of me, etc.; that I would come into the United States and make a speech of this kind without consulting him or "Mac" Bundy or Dean Rusk or somebody.

As Johnson towered over Pearson and shouted him down, Pearson tried to explain his motives. A bombing pause "might be of help"; and, moreover, "public opinion in [Canada] was profoundly disturbed by the implications of certain aspects of U.S. policy and ... some of us were having difficulty with public opinion in our complete support of that policy". Johnson could not see why these difficulties occurred. There were three choices: the expansion of the war, perhaps even to Peking; withdrawal; and the policy that was being followed. "It's hard to sleep these days," Johnson complained. "I'm beginning to feel like a martyr; misunderstood, misjudged by friends at home and abroad. You don't come here and piss on my rug."[28]

Johnson's public face did not conceal his unhappiness when Pearson and he met the press. Asked what he thought of Pearson's speech, Johnson answered: "It is not a matter for me to pass judgment on what other governments do. It is his expression. He has expressed it very well."[29] If any doubted what Johnson meant, his aides explained it clearly to the press "off the record". Mike's face was ashen, Johnson's angry. Mike tried to conceal the battle scars, but they showed. Moreover, American "aides" took care to let Canadian reporters know that Johnson had "chewed out" Mike. Johnson's reaction is probably most easily explained. For Johnson's purposes, Mike's speech was badly timed. The months of February and March were critical in the decision to extend the Vietnam commitment. There had been much hesitancy in approving the bombing operation, Rolling Thunder. But, in General Maxwell Taylor's words, "having crossed the Rubicon on February 7 [the bombing decision], [Johnson] was now off for Rome on the double". In mid-March, Johnson demanded that the Joint Chiefs of Staff find ways to "kill more VC" and save the deteriorating position of the South Vietnamese government. In National Security Memorandum 328, the President personally approved the deployment of two battalions of Marines and several other measures recommended by the Joint Chiefs of Staff. This decision, the Pentagon Papers rightly declared, was pivotal: "It marks the acceptance by the President of the United States of the concept that U.S. troops would engage in offensive ground operations against Asian insurgents."[30]

Many, including Maxwell Taylor, doubted the wisdom of Johnson's decision, and he was in a foul mood. He expected more from the Canadians, for whom he had done recent "favours", such as the Autopact and an exemption to the interest-equalization tax. Moreover, Canada's own representative, Blair Seaborn, had told the Americans that the North Vietnamese were not interested in negotiations. The Canadian International Control Commission minority report had also pointed to the North Vietnamese aggression in the South. The stakes had become the prestige of America, not the survival of a decaying Saigon government. With the stakes so high, Canada had no right to tell America how to play its game.

Years later the State Department's William Bundy, who had become a major adviser to Johnson after late 1964, said that he could never understand Pearson's decision to make "that speech at that particular moment on American soil". The place and the time were, according to Bundy, "what really put Johnson over the boiling point". There is another factor. Rufus Smith, who was then on the staff of the American embassy in Ottawa, recalls that George Ball, the undersecretary of state, had been invited to speak on a controversial subject in Canada. Ball had refused because the Canadian government had suggested he should not give the speech. Pearson should have had the courtesy to ask the Americans if they minded. The American mood is illustrated in a 1965 article by William Bundy's father-in-law, Dean Acheson, a "hawk" on Vietnam. Acheson responded with characteristic irritation to a Pearson article on "Good Neighbourhood", entitling his response, "Canada: 'Stern Daughter of the Voice of God.'" In Acheson's view, Canada's moral earnestness was too forced; its moral superiority insufferable. Perhaps it was just as well that Americans knew so little of Canada. A future relationship of "understanding and respect" was not foreordained: "If it is to be achieved, Americans must not take Canadians for granted. But something more is needed. Canadians must not take Americans for granted either."

Lester Pearson had taken Lyndon Johnson for granted. He had learned the consequences.[31]

In fact, the Americans had taken Pearson for granted. Despite Seaborn's "valuable" work for the Americans and the public support Mike had expressed for the war's broader aims, the Americans had not told Ottawa what they intended to do. Canadians knew little more about Washington's intentions than about Moscow's. The signals changed hourly from storm to calm. It is in this changing climate that Pearson's actions are best understood.

Personal relations are also important. Lyndon Johnson was not Mike's idea of what a president should be. Norman Mailer's fictional answer to the question "Why are we in Vietnam?" was a Texan's hunting trip, and it is a metaphor Mike Pearson would have understood, after his LBJ Ranch encounter with Johnson's profanity, crude behaviour, and crass ambition. That ambition was well symbolized by the President's request that Martin and Pearson make their marks in LBJ Ranch cement, just like celebrities outside Grauman's Chinese Theater in Hollywood. If the Americans were in danger of losing their balance, Mike, in the interests of the United States itself and the Western alliance, thought he should help them stand upright. As Pearson later said to Bruce Hutchison, he simply decided "on a constructive intervention, a piece of friendly advice from a good neighbour". Besides, he told Hutchison, persons highly placed in the U.S. government had told him he should speak out.[32]

On March 30, three days before the speech, a prominent Washington journalist and old Pearson friend, Marquis Childs, had called on him and warned him that Johnson was about to "step up" the war. He was listening to the military and the "hawks". The "doves" like Hubert Humphrey were concerned, and they needed help. Childs's comments may not have influenced Mike's thinking so much as reflected it. So many of Mike's American friends — Walter Lippmann and James Reston, for example — shared his fears. Pearson wrote in his diary after his Camp David quarrel: "The crisis over Vietnam is going to be a great test for LBJ. I'm not now certain that he is going to be successful in meeting it." If he did not, it would be disastrous for the Americans, for the West, and for Canada. And it was.[33]

We must finally consider what influence public opinion had on Pearson. When he told Johnson that he was having "some difficulty with public opinion", what did he mean? In February 1965, the voices of dissent were weak, except on the left, and Johnson was surprisingly popular in Canada: in late April 1965, 29 per cent of Canadians thought him an "excellent" president and 43 per cent thought him "pretty good". More thought him excellent in April 1965 than in February 1964. But those who did not were more critical and had more influence on Mike. Geoffrey and Maryon, for example, both thought the American policy dangerous. So did Walter Gordon and many of the "left" candidates Pearson was trying to woo in Quebec. "Public opinion" in any traditional sense, therefore, explains little. Dean Acheson, in his attack on "the stern daughter" of the north, cleverly pointed to a Canadian public-opinion survey that showed Canadians and their politicians to be "far apart" in their attitudes on foreign policy. The "people" favoured a "harder line" on Communism than did the politicians. But Acheson knew that in Canada "politics" mattered more than "public opinion". The chattering classes, as the British called the media and intellectual élites, were making noises, and Mike heard them and knew others would soon.[34]

Martin had told Pearson he would resign if Mike made the speech. Rusk had warned Martin that the Americans were sensitive on the subject of Vietnam and that Canadians should keep silent if their soldiers were not bearing arms. Before the speech was delivered, Martin warned Pearson that, if he made it, he would "discount our influence in Washington and your own forever".[35] He did not resign, but his words were prophetic. For the remainder of Pearson's years in office, Canada was in the dark about Vietnam, and Martin's warning that Canada would lose influence proved correct. As Bill Bundy later remarked, the speech "did seriously impair the relationship". Canada was not informed of new American initiatives or of various peace "feelers". Sources became unofficial, and rumour became the common currency of Vietnam transactions. According to a prominent American official, Canada after the Temple speech was told less than the more "reliable allies" of the United States, such as Australia, New Zealand, and Britain. Fair enough. Most unfair, however, was the gathering of diplomats in Washington where Johnson drawled, "Here are the loyal Germans, always with us when it matters," then turned towards Ambassador Ritchie and said, "And then there are the Canadians." The international balance was shifting, and Pearson sensed that Canadian-American relations could not be those of the past. In 1963 most in English Canada supported Pearson and opposed Diefenbaker's anti-Americanism. Pierre Berton, as we have seen, complained about Canadian "fence straddling" and "welshing" in its relation with the United States. In the summer of 1965, in the Black Swan coffee house in Stratford, Ontario, a mate for coffee houses sprouting in Berkeley and Cambridge, Massachusetts, Berton demanded that we not support, much less fight, America's wars any more. Berton may have lacked consistency, but he admirably reflected trends. And Pearson, who had Berton with him on election night in 1965, recognized that he did.[36]

The Temple speech did not end Canadian involvement with Vietnam, although it meant that what followed was dénouement. Canada continued its International Control Commission membership, although the commission was ever more ineffective. It also contributed indirectly to American military efforts through the sale of military goods under the Defence Production Sharing Agreement. Nor did diplomatic efforts to produce negotiations cease. Indeed, Blair Seaborn returned to Hanoi at the end of May 1965. But Mike and Johnson would never be the same together; and when Ritchie left Washington, no warm greetings were sent to Mike.

After the speech, Mike sent a long letter to Johnson in which he expressed understanding of Johnson's difficulties. It was neither an apology nor a firm stand on his Temple position, although historians have seen it as evidence of both. Its importance lies in its statement that if the North Vietnamese did not respond to a bombing halt, the U.S. case for "planned and limited air retaliation" would be stronger. They did not respond, and Mike said nothing when the bombing resumed.[37] What little he did say caused some confusion. On July 20, Johnson sent a letter to the heads of state of several nations in which he asked for support of South Vietnam. In answer to a parliamentary question, Pearson implied that this meant that the United States had asked for token Canadian military assistance. Martin denied this. To clarify what was meant, Pearson asked Washington to release the exchange of letters. Jack Valenti, a White House aide, warned Johnson that Pearson was "getting beat over the head from the opposition who accused him of lying about what he told the President." To "cleanse" himself Pearson proposed the release of a paper explaining the Canadian position that would incorporate summaries of the letters. Johnson was unwilling to help out. He had clearly not forgiven Pearson, and the Washington *Daily News* reported that, in the Washington doghouses, Pearson occupied the "No. 1 kennel". In future, he would have to rescue himself when he was being beaten.[38]

This incident followed a major debate on Canadian-American relations that was provoked by the publication of the Merchant-Heeney report on July 12. The report arose out of the Johnson-Pearson discussions of January 1964, but the mood had changed by the next summer. The report's authors, Livingston Merchant and Arnold Heeney, favoured closer institutional links between the two countries: indeed their mandate "to make it easier to avoid divergencies in economic and other policies" made such a thrust inevitable. Thus, Merchant and Heeney identified "divergencies" and suggested methods of resolving them. They concluded: "It is in the abiding interest of both countries that, wherever possible, divergent views between two governments should be expressed and if possible resolved in private, through diplomatic channels." This statement brought down upon the distinguished authors' heads a fusillade of criticism in Canada. As the *Canadian Annual Review* observed, the "admonitions" of Merchant and Heeney, "though written well before the Prime Minister's speech in Philadelphia, were examined with the aftermath in mind". The opposition responded angrily, with Conservative Alvin Hamilton excoriating the report as a sell-out that allowed Canada a role in world affairs only as an American lap-dog. Journalist Charles Lynch used the report to criticize Pearson's approach to diplomacy. The report, Lynch wrote, was a bureaucrat's dream: "Keep it quiet, boys, work it out, we will all keep out of trouble and things will go smoothly." Heeney, in Lynch's view, "has many of the characteristics of Lester B. Pearson — in fact he is the kind of man Mr. Pearson might have become had Mr. Pearson stayed out of politics". The aggressive peacemaker of the 1950s, who had pulled the eagle's tail feathers when MacArthur threatened to take Korean conflict to a nuclear conclusion and had pushed the British towards sensible compromise during the Suez madness, now seemed curiously incapable of an imaginative and effective response to clear, present dangers. Pearson's domestic difficulties did much to transform the perception of his character and purposes, but so did his difficulties with the Americans. Heeney and Pearson, the professional diplomats who cherished the values of their craft, realized that the new day that had dawned in the mid-1960s did not respect those values. The public declaration and the angry voice were more commonly the currency of international affairs. The abrasive style of Johnson in the White House was matched by that of his opponents in the streets and even in the academy and the newsroom. Heeney wrote to Merchant, in "a philosophical and optimistic vein", that their report would "be around for quite a long time". Indeed it was: it haunted Mike and his memory.[39]

Johnson's rage at Camp David and the startling reaction to Merchant-Heeney made Mike more nervous than usual as he tested the international waters. His greatest success, however, came in the Commonwealth meetings where, after Rhodesia's unilateral declaration of independence, he proved a brilliant mediator between the British and black African Commonwealth members. Harold Wilson later said that only "Mike could have done it", and similar tributes were paid by Kenneth Kaunda. Mike's early interest in the new nations and their fate was reflected in his government's commitment to increase greatly Canada's external aid. Indeed, the targets that he set and that his party committed itself to (0.7 to 1 per cent of GNP) have never been met.* Others noticed what he said and, after 1965, Pearson was seen internationally as one of the best friends the Third World had in the industrialized West.[40]

If Pearson was wary about "solving" Vietnam, Paul Martin was enthusiastic about the task. He decided to send Chester Ronning to Hanoi and, he hoped, Peking, to put out "feelers" about the war and about the possibility that Canada would recognize the Communist regime. When U.S. ambassador Walt Butterworth heard about the plan, he exploded. Butterworth, whom a senior American official described as "abrasive, arrogant, and stubborn", rushed to see Pearson, whom he regarded as a friend. Butterworth reported to Rusk that "Pearson confirmed Ronning['s] mission was Martin's idea, that it entailed greater dangers than Martin had perhaps appreciated and that he had 'scared the hell out of Paul about it last night' … if anything went wrong, his government would disavow any involvement in the Ronning mission". In another telegram of the same day, Butterworth claimed that Martin had "volunteered" the remark that the Ronning visit reflected his concern for "the domestic political scene". He claimed that Martin believed "that at some point he should demonstrate to the Canadian people that Canada had not just been a U.S. satellite but had done what it could to bring about a solution".[41]

Butterworth's claim seems peculiar in view of the fact that Ronning's visit was to remain secret. Moreover, Martin denies

---

* Although Mike believed in development assistance, he became annoyed when Ayub Khan of Pakistan was blatant in his linkage between aid and behaviour. Pearson did not reply to Ayub's letter which said: "If therefore assistance is given in a large-hearted manner, there is no reason why the Commonwealth should not continue to remain a living organisation." If sufficient aid were not given, the Commonwealth would simply "wither away". Khan to Pearson, May 4, 1967, Pearson Papers, MG26 N3, v. 175 (NAC).

having said what Butterworth attributed to him. In any event, despite his well-known sympathies for Chinese Communism, Ronning was denied entry to Peking. He did visit Vietnam, where U.S. ambassador Lodge complained about him to Rusk. He received a cable from Rusk in reply, in which Rusk said that Pearson was "skeptical about the whole affair" but went along with Martin. He added a telling comment: "Quite frankly I attach no importance to his trip and expect nothing out of it...".[42] Nothing did come of the Ronning visits although, in Martin's later view, the Americans failed to take advantage of an "opening" that occurred when Ronning met North Vietnam premier Pham Van Dong in early March 1966.

Pearson was troubled. Of course there was value in talking to Hanoi, but Canada must never become, he told a foreign-service officer, a mouthpiece of Washington. And Washington was not being helpful. Billy Bundy visited Ottawa but made it clear, as he later said, that it "wasn't much of a time to be exploring new gambits". And perhaps Bundy was correct, however undiplomatic his attitude. By that time neither side wanted negotiations. North Vietnam would negotiate on winner's terms alone, and the United States could never imagine that it might be the loser.[43] Nevertheless, Ronning did return to Hanoi in late June. The United States postponed a planned bombing raid on Hanoi because, as Rusk told Defence Secretary Robert McNamara, "if [Ronning] has a negative report, as we expect, that provides a further base for the action we contemplate and would make a difference to people like [Harold] Wilson and Pearson". Of course, if there were some positive news, the President should be aware of that too. There was none, and on June 29, 1966, the bombs began to fall on Hanoi, just shortly after Ronning left. The Americans "leaked" news of Ronning's failure to justify renewed bombing.[44]

Mike was angry and distressed. He had wanted neither the Ronning visits nor the bombs. His relationship with Martin suffered accordingly. Vietnam, which had seemed so far away when he and Kennedy sat on the porch at Hyannis Port, now penetrated all aspects of North American politics, including his own caucus and cabinet. The May 1966 Gallup poll showed that Canadian support for American "handling" of Vietnam had decreased considerably: 34 per cent disapproved, 35 per cent approved, and 29 per cent had no opinion. In March, the Canadian Labour Congress had broken with the AFL-CIO position on Vietnam and had urged Canada to work for a negotiated solution. When Robert Kennedy criticized the Canadian stand on Vietnam in early July — "the hottest place in hell is reserved for those who in periods of crisis preserve their neutrality" — he received harsh rebukes for interference. Diefenbaker started to criticize American bombing, although he continued to argue that the United States must save South Vietnam from Communism. In fact, Diefenbaker's ambivalence was shared by the government. Although Pearson and Martin could never accept the NDP's argument that peace and "neutrality" would come to Vietnam with withdrawal, the simplicity of the argument was becoming attractive at a time when the hottest places were becoming more unbearable. The American journalist I.F. Stone wrote of Canada's critic, Bobby Kennedy: "While others dodge the draft, Bobby dodges the war." Neither he nor the Canadian government could do so much longer.[45]

The war came closer to Mike in 1966, as Canadians, like Americans, began to sing the songs of protest from wars long past to protest a war that seemed very new. These protests had resonance for Maryon, the former Student Christian Movement and Voice of Women activist. When asked whether he worried when anti-Vietnam protesters blocked the path of his car, Mike said he was indeed worried lest Maryon leave the car and join the protesters. From the United States came messengers bearing witness to the impact the war was having. The first "draft dodgers" were barely noticed, but they soon had an impact on campuses and on the young. They had come to Canada for many reasons, but their interest in things American remained. It remained as well for the many American academics who staffed the swelling Canadian universities. As they (and Mike) read their Sunday *New York Times*, they learned that Joan Baez, Walter Lippmann, and many others who meant a great deal to them thought Vietnam was the wrong war in the wrong place at the wrong time. What was happening seemed a parody of the hopes that had billowed on the New Frontier. And every day casualties mounted, as Vietnam became a symbol of the ceaseless whirl that marked those years in America. No one, it seemed, got much satisfaction as the war accompanied a new stridency in North American life.

Mike met Johnson again on August 21, 1966, at Campobello Island, where the two leaders went to dedicate a park to the American president modern Canadians loved most, Franklin Roosevelt. The visit took place as Canadian public opinion shifted to support for American withdrawal from Vietnam.* The Campobello meeting accomplished nothing and is ignored in Pearson's memoirs. (Pearson is entirely ignored in Johnson's memoirs, with nary an index reference.) Throughout the year, from the party's back benches, Walter Gordon had urged a more independent stand for Canada. In May he had published a book whose title was more a call to arms than the contents: *A Choice for Canada: Independence or Colonial Status.* Gordon's book — and, even more, his arguments — attracted young Liberals, including the new members Herb Gray, Donald Macdonald, and Edgar Benson from Ontario, and Pierre Trudeau, Jean Marchand, and Gérard Pelletier from Quebec. Gordon told Mike that he thought his chapters on foreign policy would upset Paul Martin. The Ronning visits had upset Mike, and he said to Gordon that it didn't matter. In his book, Gordon set out three choices for the Liberal Party: a "cautious and conservative approach", "a firm determination to keep Canada free and indepen-

---

* The poll indicated that 31 per cent of Canadians, 68 per cent of the French, 42 per cent of Britons, and only 18 per cent of Americans thought the United States should withdraw from Vietnam. Twenty-seven per cent of Canadians, 5 per cent of the French, 16 per cent of Britons, and fully 55 per cent of Americans believed that the United States should increase its attacks. The differences were the cause of the growing rifts in the Atlantic alliance. Canadian Institute of Public Opinion, August 1966.

dent", or a policy that would "waffle in between these two positions in the hope that by so doing, no one will be offended". To Gordon, the choice was clear. He watched carefully to make certain that his successor, Mitchell Sharp, with whom he increasingly clashed, did not weaken provisions limiting the foreign ownership of banks, notably the Mercantile Bank. He also prodded the government to end the tax exemptions on advertising in the Canadian editions of *Time* and *Reader's Digest*. For Gordon, the choice seemed obvious, but to Mike there were many dangers. The United States was passing through a dangerous time, and its eruptions could quickly flow over the border.[46]

Gordon had growing support in the party and, in bitter meetings with Pearson in 1966, he bluntly pointed it out. He told Pearson that he might consider the leadership and wrote in a memorandum that he thought he could win. Mike was worried and even suggested to Gordon that he should think of the leadership. Gordon spoke about organizing the caucus against Sharp's plan to raise interest rates, and Mike threatened to resign. Mike, Gordon wrote, "said he couldn't continue as P.M. if he was not able to support his Min. of Finance. I mentioned that I was hardly the person to be convinced by that remark." In October 1966, the Liberal Policy Conference in Ottawa rejected Gordon's nationalist stand, and Gordon himself was coolly received at this national convention. His leadership hopes were exposed as futile, as Mike had surely known they were when he suggested that Gordon consider the leadership a few months before. Only Donald Macdonald, who ironically would play such a large role in bringing free trade to Canada in the 1980s, vigorously defended Gordon at the conference, but to no avail. The conference supported free trade, and the western-Canadian delegates who backed Sharp against Gordon carried the day. Gordon was bitter and called a meeting of his riding association to announce his resignation. Macdonald, Marchand, Benson, LaMarsh, and others warned Pearson that the resignation would be disastrous. Those on the "left" would be convinced that the Liberal Party had no place for them at a moment when the NDP, which was rising in the polls, was beckoning. Mike had several difficult meetings with Gordon, who made it clear that his return would mean that "the Govt. was concerned about the Foreign Control issue and was prepared to do something about it" and that Mike "was ready to acknowledge the unhappiness of the 'progressive wing' of the Party". In his notes prior to his conversation of December 29 with Mike, Gordon wrote about the "backstabbing tactics" of Sharp and outlined a full program to regain control of the Canadian economy. He wanted a commitment that Sharp would not block him. On January 3, 1967, Gordon, Sharp, and Pearson met at 24 Sussex Drive, and the three agreed on a policy on limiting Citibank holdings in the Mercantile Bank (although the agreement came apart after), on a White Paper to be prepared on foreign ownership, and on the need to have Gordon in the cabinet to respond to nationalist pressures. Gordon returned to the cabinet as president of the privy council. The "progressive" and "nationalist" wing had its champion — but an angry one, who wrote on the eve of his appointment: "There is no doubt that (a) Sharp & especially Winters are strongly opposed to doing anything [about foreign ownership] (Sharp would go along with a whitewash approach); (b) that Mike will renege if he can; (c) that nobody really gives a damn." The problem, of course, is that they did.[47]

Gordon's return linked domestic economic nationalism with the growing opposition to the Vietnam War. *Maclean's* called for the Americans to "get out of Vietnam". *Le Magazine Maclean* was even harsher, with André Langevin calling Vietnam "une guerre inutile et insensée", in which "nous sommes complices". André Laurendeau worried more about the effect of speaking out against the United States, but reported that Ottawa officials privately said that the Americans should get out. When Senator William Fulbright came to Ottawa as an observer to the Commonwealth Parliamentary Conference, he publicly expressed sympathy for Pearson's anti-bombing stand at Temple. He privately wrote to Pearson after the visit: "There are more of us than you think who approve of you speaking up about the war — Not all Americans are idiots."[48]

Fulbright may have been sympathetic, but he carried no weight in the White House. Johnson called him Senator Halfbright. Johnson had no time for enemies, and now they appeared everywhere. The Canadians had offended him too much already. The Temple speech, the attempt to bring China into the United Nations, the Mercantile Bank issue, and Canadian grumblings about American policies were all noted by Johnson. In November 1966, Canada asked Johnson to visit in centennial year, and Johnson accepted a May visit. Then the troubles began. Johnson refused to be pinned down on the date, and he definitely refused to consider a change in the U.S. national day when the Canadians politely requested it. In early May, all the Canadians knew was that some American would come to celebrate their birthday. When the Canadians asked Butterworth why Johnson hesitated, he gave three reasons: Pearson had indicated he could not meet Johnson at Expo; there had been "leaks" to the press about the visit; and, most important, on May 13, 1967, Walter Gordon had publicly attacked American policy in Vietnam and had called for Canada to get out of NATO. Mike and Martin were furious as well, and Mike publicly repudiated Gordon. Gordon's speech, he said, went far beyond "anything we have discussed — let alone decided — in the Cabinet as to what we should do about NORAD, NATO and US policy in Vietnam". Walter remained in the cabinet but was largely silent. He was far from silent in the corridors as he began to concentrate his energies on a search for Mike's successor.* In September 1967, the Conservative leadership convention chose Robert Stanfield to succeed Diefenbaker. Diefenbaker did not go quietly into the politi-

---

* Gordon made early contact with Pierre Trudeau. He, along with his cabinet allies Edgar Benson and Larry Pennell, met Trudeau "in my suite at the Chateau" in mid-November. Gordon told them that the cabinet must be changed and Mitchell Sharp must be dropped, that Mike should leave immediately, and that Paul Martin should become leader until a convention was held in fall 1968. According to Gordon's account of the meeting, the others agreed with his views and with his lack of enthusiasm "for any of the leadership candidates". Walter Gordon, Memorandum, Nov. 17, 1967, Gordon Papers, MG32 B44, v.16 (NAC).

cal night, but fought a final battle he could not win. We do not know what Mike thought when he watched on television as Olive and John walked out of Maple Leaf Gardens after "the Chief" finished fifth on the third ballot, but he knew that a new Tory leader meant that his own end as leader was near. In November, Walter went to tell him that he must go, just as he had told him a decade earlier that he had to stand for the Liberal leadership. Mike resented Walter's rudeness in raising the matter in cabinet but, as in 1957, he listened to him.[49]

Lyndon Johnson finally came to Expo and Ottawa, but only after the Canadian embassy in Washington had reported that Johnson would not come but would be represented by the postmaster general. Then two days later, on May 24, 1967, Rusk called Mike personally to tell him that Johnson was arriving the next morning and was bringing a gift! The incredible visit, which lasted a few hours, was all made possible by the helicopter that whisked LBJ from Expo to Harrington Lake. The lunch was elegant — sweetbreads in mushrooms, and fresh strawberries, hardly the hominy grits Mike had had in Texas — but the conversation was crude. Pearson knew it was his last visit with Johnson and tried to take advantage of it. He told him that the bombing should be stopped unconditionally. Johnson told Pearson he would consider the advice, but when the two leaders met with others, Johnson, in Pearson's words, "was more vigorous in his defence of the existing bombing campaign and more reluctant to consider any proposals for change which were not linked with concessions of some kind by the North". In short, Johnson let Pearson know that he did not take him very seriously. Pearson, however, took Johnson very seriously indeed. The American frightened him: "the President's views on Vietnam gave no ground for optimism that any new move of any kind is likely to break the present deadlock." Johnson, to Mike, was "more of an enigma than ever, only he is now an older and more impatient and irascible enigma; feverish in his insistence on activity, verbal and physical; moving so much and so fast in the hope, perhaps, that movement is progress; that you can be jet-propelled to peace and all the good things for everybody which he has seen granted to Texans and which everybody in Vietnam and other far off places like Canada should also have." If we had come to share the American dream in the twentieth century, we would also share its nightmare.[50]

In the summer, demands became louder that Canada end its association with the war. Four hundred university professors called for an end to the sale of Canadian defence products to the United States, which had, in fact, risen dramatically as the U.S. involvement in Vietnam grew. Several of Mike's old colleagues and friends — Escott Reid, Douglas LePan, and Wynne Plumptre — made public a letter they had written to him that called for an end to bombing without conditions. Mike was friendly but ambiguous in reply, even though he had said as much to Johnson only a few days before. But the pressure to say something publicly was growing. A Gallup poll at the summer's end indicated that 41 per cent of Canadians now favoured withdrawal, and only 16 per cent supported continuation. But when Martin attended the NATO meeting in June, he found little support for his attempt to have NATO discuss Vietnam. Gordon, who was with Martin, was surprised at how wary the Europeans were of angering the American giant.[51]

In September, at the United Nations, Martin called for an unconditional halt to the bombing. His choice of forum was symbolic and, for Canada, appropriate. The United Nations had been ignored both by the United States and by the other side. This especially troubled Canadians, because the United Nations had been the instrument they had so shrewdly wielded in the heyday of Pearsonian diplomacy. The speech reminded Canadians of how much the institution had meant in the past, and how committed Mike and Martin remained to it. It was a tough decade for U.N. people, all the more so in 1967 when U.N. secretary general U Thant acceded to Nasser's demand for a withdrawal of UNEF. For Mike, the decision was astonishing, the Six Day War that followed a tragedy. In Egypt (by then the United Arab Republic), UNEF, for whose creation Mike had been so much honoured, became a bitter target — as did both Canada and Mike when they tried to argue against the withdrawal decision. Particularly harmful were the charges — which brought a protest from the Canadian ambassador to Cairo, John Starnes — that Canada was part of a British, French, and Israeli conspiracy against Egypt.[52] The only consolation was the outstanding work that George Ignatieff did on the Security Council after the war in preserving a U.N. presence in the troubled area.

In April 1967, political scientist Peyton Lyon had written: "Quiet diplomacy is the best diplomacy for a nation of Canada's modest means, but it does precious little for the national ego."[53] But the national ego needs boosting if it is not to wither. For some time, Canada's sense of effectiveness had suffered, and its belief that it mattered, so strong in the forties and fifties, had weakened. Now the United States, which had seemed so confident when the decade began, lurched towards its most agonizing period of self-doubt, and Canadians suddenly began to sense that they did matter. The lighting of the centennial flame in 1967 had somehow cleared away some of the dark clouds that had hovered above Canadian political and national life for so long. As the centennial winter became glorious summer, millions of Canadians went on pilgrimages within their own land and seemed to see it anew. The light was clearer and the landscape and streetscapes possessed a charm they had often overlooked as they gazed in wonder at the skyscrapers to the south. But now the clouds of a black political time hung over the southern neighbour. Canadians mattered, not as citizens of a superpower whose sway was enormous, but as a people who might yet find a better way. As the last flags went down on centennial year and Bobby Gimby's catchy theme song played into the night, Mike felt more content than he had in years. On December 14, 1967, ten years after he had won the Nobel Prize and decided to seek the Liberal leadership, he announced that he would resign as soon as the Liberals had chosen his replacement. His last words at the press conference where he made his announcement were simply: "Well, good-bye, *c'est la vie.*" The words were short, "la vie" had been so large.

CONCLUSION

Lester Bowles Pearson should be borne in spirit to the Pearly Gates by a large black limousine. If St. Peter challenges credentials, all is soon resolved by firm yet quiet negotiation: the gates swing open, the limousine glides through, from its rear seat a cheerful, rumpled figure waves a greeting and then returns to perusing memoranda to aid in facing Final Judgment.

      — James Eayrs, December 29, 1972

Don't be downhearted in the thick of battle. It is where all good men would wish to be.

      — Lester Pearson to the students of Victoria College[1]

LESTER PEARSON left the thick of battle when the flares still lit the heavens and the guns roared below. His ministers, like Caesar's generals, glared towards each other as they began to gather their forces to take his place. Pearson had told Jean Lesage in 1965 that he thought his successor should be a francophone, and that the party tradition of leadership alternation seemed to compel such a choice. He had not changed his mind in 1967.

According to the polls, Paul Martin remained the popular choice among Liberals, but Mike thought Martin's time, like his own, had passed. Martin bore the scars of too many political battles, and despite his French-Canadian father he would not be regarded as a francophone. Mike told him that he should not stand and that he could not win. He wounded Martin deeply, especially when it became known that he was encouraging others to consider the race. Another casualty of political wars, in this case an embarrassing small skirmish in early 1968, was Mitchell Sharp, Pearson's favourite among potential English-Canadian successors. In mid-February Mike and Maryon were vacationing in Jamaica with Senator Hartland Molson. A call came on the evening of February 19, just as the Pearsons were, most unusually, trouncing the Molsons at bridge: the Liberals had lost a vote, 84-82, on the third reading of a tax bill. Sharp had been in charge of the bill and the House, and that night he lost control of both. Mike himself lost his temper and upon his return roasted his colleagues, particularly Paul Martin and Bob Winters, for being away on the campaign trail. He then convinced Bob Stanfield that there should be a twenty-four-hour adjournment. Stanfield, an eminently reasonable man, agreed, and some say he then lost his chance to be prime minister of Canada. So did Mitchell Sharp. The crisis passed, and the Liberals looked more anxiously for a new leader.[2]

Mike turned first to Jean Marchand, who had become Maryon's "favourite politician" and whose popularity among the Quebec caucus was impressive. His liberal credentials glowed brightly after his reforms of Canadian immigration policy, which ended racial bias in immigration selection. But the charming and voluble Marchand knew his weaknesses better than Mike did and wisely refused to stand. He proposed Pierre Trudeau to Mike and asked that Mike meet with him and encourage him to run. Mike did so in January with Marchand present, but Trudeau appeared to be reluctant. Mike knew well how politically useful such reluctance could be and reassured Trudeau. Mike and Marchand were certain that Trudeau's fears that he was not well known and that Liberals would think he was too non-partisan were unjustified. Marchand gave Trudeau a key role at the Quebec Liberal convention in January, where his speech gained much attention and approval. Mike was even more effective in giving Trudeau a platform at the historic federal-provincial constitutional conference of February 5-7, 1968.

Despite his passion for a distinctive Canadian flag, Mike was a lifelong monarchist. Here he shares a private joke with Queen Elizabeth in Centennial year. (Canapress Photo Service/CP Photo)

Although Pearson and Diefenbaker respected the formalities at events like this 1967 garden party for the Queen, they never saw eye to eye. (Canapress Photo Service/CP Photo)

Pearson announced his retirement in December 1967, after the triumphs of Centennial year. The following April, Pierre Trudeau was chosen to replace him as Liberal leader. (Canada Wide)

Four decades of Liberal leaders. From left: Pierre Elliott Trudeau, John Turner, Jean Chrétien, and Lester Pearson. (Douglas Cameron/NAC/PA-117107)

Surrounded by his grandchildren at his summer residence at Harrington Lake, Mike celebrates his 70th birthday. From left, the children of Landon and Geoffrey: Michael, Anne, Katharine, Hilary, and Patricia. (Canapress Photo Service/CP Photo)

Mike and Maryon (Ashley & Crippen Portraits)

Pearson, Pierre Trudeau, and Quebec premier Daniel Johnson preparing for the duel of the 1968 Constitutional Conference. Paul Martin is behind Johnson. (Douglas Cameron/ NAC/PA-117460)

Lester Pearson died December 27, 1972, and lay in state in Parliament beneath the flag he had been so proud of. The much-disputed flag had become Canada's international symbol — but Pearson's diplomacy had already changed the way the world saw Canada. (Canapress Photo Service/CP Photo)

"Here the road forks," Mike declared as the conference opened. "If we choose wrongly, we will leave to our children and our children's children a country in fragments." In his opening remarks, Quebec premier Daniel Johnson demanded that the conference recognize that there were "two nations" in Canada and that Quebec be given a full panoply of powers to fulfil its "national" responsibilities. Trudeau as Justice minister responded that such special powers for Quebec would weaken the position of federal MPs and that two nations within Canada would inevitably become two nations separate and apart. His words and the way he said them caused English Canada to sit up and take notice, and from that moment the political heart of English Canada beat in ever more sympathetic rhythm to his words.[3]

And so the television cameras, in the words of Stephen Clarkson and Christina McCall, began to pursue Trudeau "as though he were a male Garbo" with all the allure of her mystery.[4] His high cheekbones and peculiar pallor intrigued viewers. By mid-February, Trudeau was the candidate to watch, and by the convention in early April, he led the field. Mike had played a large part in his success. The February conference focused Canadian attention upon the crisis of Quebec and brought forth a declaration, inconceivable a few years earlier, of the principles of language equality in Canada as recommended by the Royal Commission on Bilingualism and Biculturalism. The conference statement on language rights was a considerable achievement for Mike, whose "masterful chairmanship" was widely praised. But Trudeau stole the show, and Mike was an accessory in the theft.[5]

It was probably Pearson's help that made Trudeau the Liberal leader. Certainly a disappointed Paul Martin thought so, as did a bitter Judy LaMarsh.* Trudeau barely defeated Robert Winters, a late candidate who gathered conservative Liberal support almost as quickly as Trudeau won over those on the left. That Mike favoured

---

* LaMarsh sealed her political fate when a microphone overheard her urging Paul Hellyer to join Winters after the second ballot to get "that bastard" Trudeau.

his successor seems clear, but he also had many doubts about him. He could not penetrate the masks that Trudeau wore and confided in his friend Bruce Hutchison that he thought "ice-water" ran in Trudeau's veins. He told his sister-in-law, who contracted a severe case of Trudeaumania in spring 1968, that Trudeau was too much a centralist and too acid in his political ways. Trudeau in turn seemed dismissive of Pearson; he made it clear that he believed Pearson's internationalism was flawed, and that its distinctly Anglo-American flavour had a rancid taste in the mid-to-late 1960s. And, of course, Trudeau's combativeness offended one who instinctively preferred quiet words and ways.[6]

Trudeau's entry into politics gained its verve and strength from what Clarkson and McCall term his "magnificent obsession", his attempt to resolve through constitutional reform the contradictions of the Canadian nation. Pearson's obsessions were few and never magnificent, but in the winter of 1968 he had one. A francophone must succeed him, and in characteristic Pearsonian style — by a hint to "a few friends", by giving Trudeau a prominent place at his side at the historic February conference, and by constant references to Canada's national crisis — he made certain he got his way. On the common ground of fear for Canada's future, these two very different Canadians met. It is a pity, however, that they never knew each other better. If Pearson found Trudeau's masks impenetrable, Trudeau had no understanding of what had made Mike Pearson in the late 1940s and early 1950s as much fortune's darling as Trudeau became for Canadians a generation later.

After winning the Liberal leadership, Trudeau dissolved Parliament immediately and gave no time for tributes to his predecessor. It surely hurt Mike, although, typically, he did not complain. Douglas Fisher later recalled in 1973 "the atmosphere of indifference to Mr. Pearson when he retired in April 1968; there was a notable keenness by his successor to separate his government distinctly from the bad Pearson years — scandals, leaks, messy staggering parliaments and disorganized ventures."[7] It was, perhaps, a wise political move for Trudeau to dissociate himself from the Liberal past. Even

Mike admitted that Trudeau's attempt to impose the arcane methods of management science on the practice of government was worthwhile. Mike's time and his office had been "messy", and new elixirs such as systems analysis deserved to be tried.

What troubled him was Trudeau's cavalier dismissal of his foreign policy accomplishments and tradition. In Trudeau's publicly expressed view, Canada under Pearson had been a "helpful fixer", had had no foreign policy but only a defence policy, and had heeded too closely the commands of Washington. Trudeau's review of Canadian foreign policy seemed mainly a critical review of Mike's own record. Mike was especially hurt by the comment that Canada had only a defence policy. He decided to "have it out" with Trudeau but never did, and Trudeau never consulted him in a serious way about what Pearson thought about foreign affairs. Mike wrote scathing remarks on his copy of Trudeau's foreign policy review. He also wrote a memorandum about the review, which he gave to close friends but not to Trudeau, in which he condemned Trudeau's proposal that the primary test of Canada's foreign policy was whether an action promoted Canada's "national interest", narrowly defined. "Surely," he wrote, "a far better foreign policy is that which is based on a national interest which expresses itself in co-operation with others; in the building of international institutions and the development of international policies and agreements, leading to a world order which promotes freedom, well-being and security for all."[8]

Mike, it seems, was right. Trudeau admitted as much when he spent his last months in office touring world capitals as a "helpful fixer", offering to assist in repairing the growing gap between East and West. He took Geoffrey Pearson with him on his progress from capital to capital. He also named Toronto's airport after Lester Pearson, following the fashion set in Paris and New York with Charles de Gaulle and John F. Kennedy airports. Mike, who almost always got airsick, would surely have smiled.

He smiled often after April 1968, even though the times remained troubling. Whatever his doubts about his successor's foreign policy review, he admired Trudeau's purposeful leadership of cabinet and shared the occasional bemusement and amusement of Canadians generally at his antics. Trudeau, after all, had complained in 1963 that "les hipsters" of Camelot had influenced Mike and Canada too much. Now his court was resplendently "hip" itself, with Marshall McLuhan, Liona Boyd, and Barbra Streisand, the Trudeau parallel to Kennedy's Robert Frost, Pablo Casals, and Marilyn Monroe. And his sliding down bannisters recalled Arthur Schlesinger's plunges into the White House pool.* In the October Crisis of 1970, Trudeau, like Kennedy in the Cuban Missile Crisis, played tough and did not blink. Mike admired his strength, but privately told Geoffrey that the government "should disengage from the atmosphere of crisis quickly — in order to deal more effectively with the problem".[9]

He was encouraged by the constitutional conference of February 1971 and wrote to Trudeau ("Dear Pierre") to congratulate him on what had been done. He had been very worried, he told Trudeau, "that our concern with other matters of more immediate urgency might push into the background what I still consider to be the most important problem of all for national unity, namely bringing our Constitution in line with the realities of today". Trudeau in reply ("Dear Mr. Pearson") prophetically warned that "we have not yet wrestled this thing away from the jaws of adversity, and the months ahead ... are strewn with obstacles". He recalled Mike's remarks in the February 1968 federal-provincial conference that a martyr stalked such conferences "with her head under her arm; there are one or two others who would do well to put theirs back onto their shoulders and use it for thinking rather than lamenting".[10] Robert Bourassa, in Trudeau's view at least, kept his head tightly under his arm, and the path opened up first by Fulton-

---

* At Christmas Mike told Geoffrey, who had been born on December 25, that there was "another Xmas baby to join Geoffrey Pearson and [his former secretary] Annette Perron, to wit Justin Trudeau — called, no doubt, after that 'Justin' who is Twiggy's boyfriend!" Still, despite Trudeau's quirks and his "very low" political standing in December 1971, Mike predicted that "he will be back as P.M." in the election of 1972. L.B. Pearson to Geoffrey Pearson, Dec. 1971 (PPP).

Favreau reached a dead end with Bourassa's decision to reject the so-called Victoria Charter in June 1971. It was profoundly disappointing to Pearson and Trudeau.

Mike's disappointments were rare in the first years of his retirement. He and Maryon moved quickly from 24 Sussex Drive to a house in Rockcliffe, 541 Montagu Place, which Maryon had bought in 1966 in preparation for retirement. There the best moments came with the grandchildren, whom Mike adored. He missed Geoff's family, who were with Geoff in India, but his letters convey the tone of banter and affection that marked Mike's ways with his grandchildren. "I often lament," he wrote to the Pearsons in India in January 1970, "that I don't possess that command of the English language that Hilary seems to have inherited from her parents — even though she hasn't the gift of pungent and punchy expression that Michael has, or the ability to put 17 'o's' and 19 'x's' in a line that Patsy has, or the poetic fancy of Anne or the casual gossipy ease of Katharine".[11] In fact, Mike had all these qualities and demonstrated them in a remarkable flurry of writings that followed his retirement.

In 1968, on the BBC, he gave the celebrated Reith lectures, which took the form of reminiscences about his own work and the worlds he knew. He followed with the Smuts lecture on the Commonwealth at Cambridge University, but his major publication was in international development, an area that became his primary concern after April 1968.[12] Robert McNamara, president of the World Bank, had asked him on July 17, 1968, to head a study of "how to mobilize effective opinion in the 'North'" behind an adequate development program. Mike met with McNamara in Washington in mid-August and accepted the task, which came with "a full professor's salary" and "the cost of your own and your wife's first class air travel". The commission had seven other members, five of them from the "North" but none from Africa, South Asia, or the Middle East. There were complaints about this lack of representation, even in the United Nations, but Mike told George Ignatieff, then the Canadian ambassador to the United Nations, that his commission's task was to convince the First World, especially the American

Congress, of the argument for development assistance. That could be done most convincingly by voices from the First World, not the Third.[13]

The commission's final report bore the mark of its times and its origins. It extrapolated from the rapid growth figures in the so-called developing world in the 1950s and 1960s and suggested that self-sustained growth could be assured if generous dollops of international assistance were forthcoming from the rich "North".* There was too much optimism about progress, too many false assumptions about the efficiency and viability of state structures in the Third World, and too much emphasis on supply and not enough on demand. There was, Jim Eayrs later wrote, "too much wishful thinking. Pearson, like the rest of the coterie of development ideologues who met in spa, castle or luxury hotel to discuss in comfort and at far remove [from] the wretched of the earth, simply did not know what matters most to the people of the developing countries."[14]

But really who did? The Pearson report, whatever its flaws, strengthened McNamara's hand as he transformed the World Bank's assistance program into a concentration upon projects closer to the people. The Pearson report, like its successors the Brandt and Brundtland reports, was primarily educational in purpose, alerting those who had so much that they must care for those who had little. Edward Hamilton was the executive secretary to the commission, and he recalled how Mike's major contribution to the commission's work was his "humanity". His mere presence, Hamilton later wrote, "induced a breathtaking reduction in the pettiness, the self-serving, the back-biting, the callousness, and the small-mindedness to which

---

* The choice of Pearson to chair the commission was the result of his own obvious commitment to development assistance. Canadian development assistance rose by approximately 280% between 1964 and 1967. In 1967 Mike committed Canada to development assistance equal to 1% of GNP (from 0.29% in 1967). This target has never been met. See R. Carty, "Going for Gain: Foreign Aid and CIDA", in R. Swift and R. Clarke, eds., *Ties That Bind: Canada and the Third World* (Toronto: Alger Press, 1981), 149-213.

all of us are subject". If it was necessary to group progress that he "appear slow, indecisive, untutored, or even inarticulate", he would do so. When some objected at regional hearings that there were too many rich commission members, Pearson would break the tension and embarrass some pretentious assistants by announcing that "although the hearings had left him confused, he was confused on a much higher level". Such self-inflicted levity deflated many rhetorical balloons and kept the focus on the commission's broader purposes. Pearson, Hamilton wrote, "led us by drawing out the best in us. He showed us that it was possible to be serious without taking oneself seriously". He was, Hamilton reflected, "the loveliest human being I have ever known".[15]

Philip Ziegler said that when he wrote the biography of Lord Mountbatten he kept above his desk the motto, "But he was a great man", which he stared at whenever he had doubts. Like Mountbatten but for different reasons, Pearson often infuriates a biographer, and Ziegler's motto and Hamilton's words are worth recalling. Pearson did tell people all too often only what they wanted to hear — as with Walter Gordon, to whom he preposterously suggested that the leadership was within reach; or with Sam Bronfman, so desperately seeking gentility, to whom Pearson hinted that a post even "more prestigious" than the Senate was awaiting him, a post that turned out to be membership for the rough-edged whisky-baron on the lowly board of the Canada Council.[16] Mike reminds one of John Updike's liberal parson who can't bring himself to tell dying parishioners that there probably is no heaven. Small wonder that the Liberals embraced Trudeau, who demanded a return to first principles and a relentless pursuit of truth, however painful it might be. Those who sought truth so vigorously or believed that they had found it did not take to Mike Pearson. It is not surprising that Malcolm Muggeridge, so certain that he knew Truth, declared Pearson "outrageously stupid".[17]

There was a restlessness to Pearson's mind and schedule that suggests that he never wanted to take the time to examine first principles, even at the end. After he finished the Pearson commission, he began to work on his memoirs, taught at Carleton University, and defied his doctor's warnings that he must rest. Written with the assistance of John Munro and Alex Inglis, his prime ministerial memoirs are the best any Canadian prime minister has produced. The first volume, which was largely his own, is memorable for its wonderful anecdotes and personal charm. He finally mastered the medium of television in 1969 when the CBC brought him and Diefenbaker together to tell the story of Canada's tenth decade. Diefenbaker told his tale with a sharp edge; Mike coated his with lavish servings of humour and generosity and, though the victory was late in coming, finally beat the Chief decisively. At Carleton, he taught a three-hour seminar on Canadian foreign relations. Pearson always had time for students and for their opinions. Once he brought his granddaughter Hilary with him, and Blair Neatby, the distinguished historian, remarked how excited Mike was, and how he exuded a genuine enthusiasm for the young. He went to the university but did not mount the steps of the ivory tower.[18]

In mid-summer 1970 Mike learned that his "eye-trouble" was a cancerous tumour. He told his family that it finally proved "what some people have long felt, that you never knew what was going on in my head". He got a glass eye and learned, he claimed, the true meaning of "eyewash".[19] The doctor told him the prognosis was good, but Mike knew his time might be short. When he retired, Maryon as usual had the best line: "I married him for better or worse, not for lunch." But there were few lunches — far too few — for both Mike and Maryon, who became closer in the later 1960s, their letters childlike in affection. She feared desperately the day she would lose him. He kept his schedule crowded, left his door open for students, and signed the many copies of his books and articles that Norman Hillmer, his Carleton assistant and autograph collector, brought to him. In the fall of 1972 the first volume of *Mike* appeared, to critical and popular acclaim. It rose quickly to the top of the bestseller list, in part because Pearson went on a punishing promotional tour in October. Shortly after, his health began to fail and word passed among friends that they should see Mike soon.

George Ignatieff and John Turner told Walter Gordon about Mike's condition, and on November 28, 1972, Gordon went to Ottawa to see Mike. They had not spoken more than a few words in passing since Gordon left politics in 1968. Mike greeted Gordon at the door with a joke about finally losing twenty-five pounds. He told Gordon he was spending each free moment on his memoirs, but he would not be able to finish. He was, he said, sorry about two things in his prime-ministerial period: the Favreau tragedy and the way Gordon and he "had drifted apart". Walter said little and soon left.[20]

He saw Keith Davey a couple of weeks later and told him that their beloved Toronto Maple Leafs would not make the play-offs this year. Davey disagreed, but Mike added: "It's a little worse than that: it's a crisis you're going to have to face alone."[21] Maryon thought they should not go to Florida as they usually did in December, but Trudeau finally had Mike to lunch and offered him a government plane.* He flew to Florida, but his condition worsened, and just before Christmas he took his last flight home. The cancer had spread to his liver, and there was no hope. On December 27, 1972, he fell into a coma; the next day he died.

His coffin was draped with the maple leaf flag as he lay in state in Parliament's Hall of Honour, and 12,000 people queued outside on a bitterly cold Ottawa Saturday, December 30, to pay their last respects. The funeral took place the next day in Christ Church Anglican Cathedral, which stands on a hill above the Ottawa River. Beyond it one sees the Gatineau Hills rise in Quebec. The service was bilingual and ecumenical. Britain, which Mike had loved so much, sent her prime minister, Edward Heath. However, Richard Nixon's representative, Vice-president Spiro Agnew, did not arrive because the blizzard that day prevented his plane from landing. The Very Rev. A.B. Moore, past moderator of the United Church, whose traditions had shaped so much of Mike Pearson's character, ended his address with the quotation with which Mike had ended his own address when he became chancellor of Victoria College.

---

* Trudeau had also named the new External Affairs building after him.

Mike had quoted a few lines from the Chinese poet Li Po: "After the guest is gone, watch him make his way into the distance. If he leaves just at daybreak, that is very agreeable, particularly if he plays upon the flute as he goes." And thus, Reverend Moore concluded, Mike Pearson "makes his way into the distance. The dawning of a new day in which he believed is still not with us, but he is playing his flute as he goes and we hear the sad and joyful music of humanity and follow."

Mike Pearson rests beside Hume Wrong and Norman Robertson in a grave with a modest tombstone in a graveyard on a Gatineau hill in Quebec. The town below was then Wakefield. It is now "La Pêche". The change of name reminds one that his remains may some day rest in another country, but his life made it less likely that they will. The "new day" in which he believed has not yet dawned, but his own day now seems to have been a decisive one in his nation's history.

Pearson became prime minister at a moment when the Canada he had known was changing utterly. What was born in his time was a new relationship between French and English in Canada, both language and people. Prior to the 1960s, they had lived their separate lives together, their paths seldom crossing. What better evidence of these solitudes is there than the life of Canada's greatest diplomat, who felt more distant from Quebec City than from London, Washington, and even Paris? In the 1960s the two solitudes rubbed against each other, creating new sores but also the need to find salves to heal the abrasions. The alternative was to move apart, and many thought that should be done. It was not, and what occurred was a revolution in Canadian government, one that threatened to topple its foundations. The Liberal government that took power in 1963 was taken at the flood. In the torrent that followed, Mike Pearson barely kept his ship afloat, much less on course, as he guided it through swift rapids and perilous narrows. The journey was rough, but its direction was always forward. He could have turned back, but he determined that justice and fairness required him to stay the course and accompany Quebec on its own passage lest it move out of sight. Bilingualism, biculturalism, more franco-phone ministers who mattered more than they ever had before, meant a sea change in the life of Canada.

That change was made even more meaningful because Mike Pearson's government introduced a flurry of legislation that created a broad range of social programs. Until the Pearson government, Roosevelt's New Deal had made the United States North America's kinder and gentler place for the poor, the old, and the young. Pearson's government changed this perception. In a short period in the 1960s, Canada established programs that not only provided security but also came to define for Canadians what their country was.

Pearson knew little French, but he introduced bilingualism. He was most comfortable in common rooms, millionaires' villas, and London men's clubs, but he presided over the introduction of the greatest number of social programs in Canadian history. He was ill at ease with his only female cabinet minister, but he appointed the Royal Commission on the Status of Women, an inquiry of historic and international importance. He refused to cling to what he knew, and the ambiguity and uncertainty that marked his career and his personality were the counterpart of a remarkable generosity, an openness to the new and to the "other" that is rare in our times, and especially in our politicians. Unlike Mackenzie King, from whom he learned so much, he never led us back to where we had been before. His life changed that of his nation. What he said of Hammarskjöld can be said of him: "that when this man disappeared, people began to realize that he stood for something so much greater than the pomp and power that we have so much of." It is not that he haunts us, but the sound of the flute he played as he left echoes still, and so many of his paths we still follow.

APPENDIX

Liberal

April 22, 1963 to April 20, 1968

Prime Minister

The Right Honourable Lester Bowles Pearson

The Ministry

Ministry of Agriculture
Harry William Hays   Apr. 22, 1963 - Dec. 17, 1965
John James Greene   Dec. 18, 1965 - Apr. 20, 1968

Minister of Citizenship and Immigration
Guy Favreau   Apr. 22, 1963 - Feb. 2, 1964
René Tremblay   Feb. 3, 1964 - Feb. 14, 1965
John Robert Nicholson   Feb. 15, 1965 - Dec. 17, 1965
Jean Marchand   Dec. 18, 1965 - Sept.30, 1966

Minister of Consumer and Corporate Affairs
John Napier Turner   Dec. 21, 1967 - Apr. 20, 1968

Minister of Defence Production
Charles Mills Drury   Apr. 22, 1963 - Apr. 20, 1968

Minister of Energy, Mines and Resources
Jean-Luc Pepin   Oct. 1, 1966 - Apr. 20, 1968

Secretary of State for External Affairs
Paul Joseph James Martin   Apr. 22, 1963 - Apr. 20, 1968

Minister of Finance and Receiver General
Walter Lockhart Gordon — Apr. 22, 1963 - Nov. 10, 1965
Mitchell William Sharp *(Acting Minister)* — Nov. 11, 1965 - Dec. 17, 1965
Mitchell William Sharp — Dec. 18, 1965 - Apr. 20, 1968

Minister of Fisheries
Hédard Robichaud — Apr. 22, 1963 - Apr. 20, 1968

Minister of Forestry
John Robert Nicholson — Apr. 22, 1963 - Feb. 2, 1964
Maurice Sauvé — Feb. 3, 1964 - Sept.30, 1966

Minister of Forestry and Rural Development
Maurice Sauvé — Oct. 1, 1966 - Apr. 20, 1968

Minister of Indian Affairs and Northern Development
Arthur Laing — Oct. 1, 1966 - Apr. 20, 1968

Minister of Industry
Charles Mills Drury — July 25, 1963 - Apr. 20, 1968

Minister of Justice and Attorney General
Lionel Chevrier — Apr. 22, 1963 - Feb. 2, 1964
Guy Favreau — Feb. 3, 1964 - June 29, 1965
George James McIlraith *(Acting Minister)* — June 30, 1965 - July 6, 1965
Louis Joseph Lucien Cardin — July 7, 1965 - Apr. 3, 1967
Pierre Elliott Trudeau — Apr. 4, 1967 - Apr. 20, 1968

Minister of Labour
Allan Joseph MacEachen — Apr. 22, 1963 - Dec. 17, 1965
John Robert Nicholson — Dec. 18, 1965 - Apr. 20, 1968

Minister of Manpower and Immigration
Jean Marchand — Oct. 1, 1966 - Apr. 20, 1968

Minister of Mines and Technical Surveys
William Moore Benidickson — Apr. 22, 1963 - July 6, 1965
John Watson MacNaught — July 7, 1965 - Dec. 17, 1965
Jean-Luc Pepin — Dec. 18, 1965 - Sept.30, 1966

Minister of National Defence
Paul Theodore Hellyer — Apr. 22, 1963 - Sept 18, 1967
Léo Alphonse Joseph Cadieux — Sept.19, 1967 - Apr. 20, 1968

Associate Minister of National Defence
Louis Joseph Lucien Cardin — Apr. 22, 1963 - Feb. 14, 1965

Léo Alphonse Joseph Cadieux Feb. 15, 1965 - Sept.18, 1967
Vacant Sept.19, 1967 - Apr. 20, 1968

Minister of National Health and Welfare
Julia Verlyn LaMarsh Apr. 22, 1963 - Dec. 17, 1965
Allan Joseph MacEachen Dec. 18, 1965 - Apr. 20, 1968

Minister of National Revenue
John Richard Garland Apr. 22, 1963 - Mar. 14, 1964
Vacant Mar. 15, 1964 - Mar. 18, 1964
George James McIlraith *(Acting Minister)* Mar. 19, 1964 - June 28, 1964
Edgar John Benson June 29, 1964 - Jan. 17, 1968
Joseph Jacques Jean Chrétien Jan. 18, 1968 - Apr. 20, 1968

Minister of Northern Affairs and National Resources
Arthur Laing Apr. 22, 1963 - Sept.30, 1966

Postmaster General
Azellus Denis Apr. 22, 1963 - Feb. 2, 1964
John Robert Nicholson Feb. 3, 1964 - Feb. 14, 1965
René Tremblay Feb. 15, 1965 - Dec. 17, 1965
Joseph Julien Jean-Pierre Côté Dec. 18, 1965 - Apr. 20, 1968

President of the Privy Council
Maurice Lamontagne Apr. 22, 1963 - Feb. 2, 1964
George James McIlraith Feb. 3, 1964 - July 6, 1965
Guy Favreau July 7, 1965 - Apr. 3, 1967
Walter Lockhart Gordon Apr. 4, 1967 - Mar. 10, 1968
Pierre Elliot Trudeau *(Acting Minister)* Mar. 11, 1968 - Apr. 20, 1968

Minister of Public Works
Jean-Paul Deschatelets Apr. 22, 1963 - Feb. 11, 1965
Vacant Feb. 12, 1965 - Feb. 14, 1965
Louis Joseph Lucien Cardin Feb. 15, 1965 - July 6, 1965
George James McIlraith July 7, 1965 - Apr. 20, 1968

Registrar General of Canada
Guy Favreau Oct. 1, 1966 - Apr. 3, 1967
John Napier Turner Apr. 4, 1967 - Dec. 20, 1967

Secretary of State of Canada
John Whitney Pickersgill Apr. 22, 1963 - Feb. 2, 1964
Maurice Lamontagne Feb. 3, 1964 - Dec. 17, 1965
Julia Verlyn LaMarsh Dec. 18, 1965 - Apr. 9, 1968

John Joseph Connolly *(Acting Minister)*   Apr. 10, 1968 - Apr. 20, 1968

Solicitor General of Canada
John Watson MacNaught   Apr. 22, 1963 - July 6, 1965
Lawrence Pennell   July 7, 1965 - Apr. 19, 1968

Minister of Trade and Commerce
Mitchell William Sharp   Apr. 22, 1963 - Jan. 3, 1966
Robert Henry Winters   Jan. 4, 1966 - Mar. 29, 1968
Jean-Luc Pepin *(Acting Minister)*   Mar. 30, 1968 - Apr. 20, 1968

Minister of Transport
George James McIlraith   Apr. 22, 1963 - Feb. 2, 1964
John Whitney Pickersgill   Feb. 3, 1964 - Sept.18, 1967
Paul Theodore Hellyer   Sept.19, 1967 - Apr. 20, 1968

President of the Treasury Board
Edgar John Benson   Oct. 1, 1966 - Apr. 20, 1968

Minister of Veterans Affairs
Roger Joseph Teillet   Apr. 22, 1963 - Apr. 20, 1968

Minister without Portfolio
William Ross Macdonald *(Senator)*   Apr. 22, 1963 - Feb. 2, 1964
John Watson MacNaught   Apr. 22, 1963 - July 6, 1965
René Tremblay   Apr. 22, 1963 - Feb. 2, 1964
John Joseph Connolly *(Senator)*   Feb. 3, 1964 - Apr. 20, 1968
Yvon Dupuis   Feb. 3, 1964 - Jan. 21, 1965
Lawrence Pennell   July 7, 1965 - Sept.30, 1966
Jean-Luc Pepin   July 7, 1965 - Dec. 17, 1965
John Napier Turner   Dec. 18, 1965 - Apr. 3, 1967
Walter Lockhart Gordon   Jan. 9, 1967 - Apr. 3, 1967
Joseph Jacques Jean Chrétien   Apr. 4, 1967 - Jan. 17, 1968
Charles Ronald McKay Granger   Sept.25, 1967 - Apr. 20, 1968
Bryce Stuart Mackasey   Feb. 9, 1968 - Apr. 20, 1968

NOTES

For a detailed listing of papers and other sources, see "A Note on Sources", in *Shadow of Heaven: The Life of Lester Pearson. Volume One: 1897-1948.* (Toronto: Lester & Orpen Dennys, 1989). The Pearson Papers are referred to by their National Archives numbering: MG26 N. The papers are indexed under "N" categories, which are also given. PPP indicates papers in the possession of the Pearson family. NAC means the papers are found in the National Archives of Canada, in Ottawa. NA identifies papers in the National Archives in Washington. PRO identifies papers in the Public Record Office, Kew, England.

CHAPTER 1: THE GOOD YEAR

1 L.B. Pearson, *Mike: The Memoirs of the Right Honourable Lester B. Pearson. Volume II: 1948-1957* (Toronto: University of Toronto Press, 1973), 37.

2 Ottawa's weather is described in *The Canadian Almanac and Directory for 1950* (Toronto: Copp Clark, 1949). Also, *Ottawa Citizen*, Apr.-July 1949.

3 Arthur Spencer, "How Mrs. Mike sees Diplomatic Ottawa", Oct. 1952, in L.B. Pearson Papers, MG26 N8, v. 10 (NAC).

4 *Ninth Census of Canada, 1951. Volume 1 Population* (Ottawa: King's Printer, 1953), 9-16. Numbers are approximations. Actual figures are 1931, 126,872 and 1951, 202,045.

5 Spencer, "How Mrs. Mike sees Diplomatic Ottawa".

6 See, for example, *Ottawa Journal*, Sept. 13, 1948.

7 Interview with Paul Martin.

8 The Gallup editor is quoted in Joseph Goulden, *The Best Years* (New York: Atheneum, 1976), 9. Also, Benjamin Spock, *Common Sense Book of Baby and Child Care* (New York: Bantam, 1946), and Alfred Kinsey, *Sexual Behavior in the Human Male* (Philadelphia: W.B. Saunders, 1948).

9 *Globe and Mail,* Oct. 27, 1948; and *Mike, II:* 17-18. The anecdote and others are found in Heather Robertson, *More Than a Rose: Prime Ministers' Wives and Other Women* (Toronto: Seal Books, 1991), 264-84.

10 Spencer, "How Mrs. Mike sees Diplomatic Ottawa".

11 *Ibid.* The story has been confirmed by his colleague Paul Martin.

12 "How Mrs. Mike sees Diplomatic Ottawa"; Clipping File, Maryon Pearson, MG26 N11, v. 11 (NAC); confidential interviews; Susan Riley, *Political Wives: Wifestyles of the Rich and Infamous* (Toronto: McClelland and Stewart, 1989); Maryon Pearson to Kenneth Kirkwood, May 21, 1924 (private collection); and David McLellan and David Acheson, eds., *Among Friends: Personal Letters of Dean Acheson* (New York: Dodd Mead, 1980), 250.

13 John Patrick Diggins, *The Proud Decades: America in War and Peace* (Norton: New York and London, 1988), 214. Maryon retained her doubts about working mothers well into the 1960s when many other women lost theirs. See stories from *Trinidad Sunday Guardian,* Dec. 19, 1965, and Toronto *Telegram,* Oct. 2, 1965, in Clipping File, MG26 N11, v. 11 (NAC).

14 Robertson, *More Than a Rose,* 276-8; Douglas Fullerton, *Graham Towers and His Times* (Toronto: McClelland and Stewart, 1986), 107-15; Bruce Hutchison, *The Unfinished Country* (Vancouver: Douglas and McIntyre, 1985), 69; and confidential interviews. Maryon's appointment books are found in MG26 N8, v. 10. Nell Martin, the wife of Paul Martin, described Beaverbrook's techniques to me. On Diana Cooper, see Philip Ziegler, *Diana Cooper: The Biography of Lady Diana Cooper* (Harmondsworth, Eng.: Penguin, 1983).

15 F.R. Scott, "Saturday Sundae", in F.R. Scott and A.J.M. Smith, eds., *The Blasted Pine: An Anthology of Satire, Invective and Disrespectful Verse* (Toronto: Macmillan, 1957), 52. The poem was first published in 1945.

16 A.D.P. Heeney Diary, Heeney Papers, MG30 E144, v.2 (NAC).

17 A.D.P. Heeney, *The Things That Are Caesar's: The Memoirs of a Canadian Public Servant* (Toronto: University of Toronto Press, 1972), ch. 8. Pearson himself does not mention Heeney's appointment in his memoirs. For an exceedingly complimentary appraisal of Heeney, see J.L. Granatstein, *The Ottawa Men: The Civil Service Mandarins 1935-1967* (Toronto: Oxford University Press, 1982). Pearson's private high opinion of Heeney is seen in Pearson to Robertson, Jan. 22, 1949, MG26 N1, v. 13 (NAC).

18 "Tommy" Stone to Dean Acheson, Jan. 8, 1949, MG26 N1, v. 1 (NAC).

19 L.B. Pearson, "Memorandum for File", no date (Jan. 1949), MG26 N1, v. 1 (NAC). See Dean Acheson, *Present at the Creation: My Years in the State Department* (New York: Norton, 1969), 250-2. In fact, Acheson had not been fully candid in his testimony about Hiss and his brother Donald, who had been his law partner. See Allen Weinstein, *Perjury: The Hiss-Chambers Case* (New

York: Vintage, 1979), 384-6. Hume Wrong told Pearson that his friend Acheson "enjoyed his performance" before the committee. Wrong to Pearson, MG26 N1, v. 1 (NAC).

20 External to Canadian Embassy, Jan. 21, 1949; and Wrong to Pearson, Jan. 22, 1949, MG26 N1, v. 1 (NAC).

21 Interviews with Bruce Hutchison and William Bundy (Acheson's son-in-law).

22 *Mike, II:* 41; and Escott Reid, *Time of Fears and Hope: The Making of the North Atlantic Treaty* (Toronto: McClelland and Stewart, 1977), 31-4. Another major study of NATO from a Canadian point of view is James Eayrs, *In Defence of Canada: Growing Up Allied* (Toronto: University of Toronto Press, 1980).

23 King on Churchill is found in J.W. Pickersgill and D.F. Forster, eds., *The Mackenzie King Record. Volume IV, 1947-1948* (Toronto: University of Toronto Press, 1970), 117. See also *Mike, II:* 41ff.

24 *King Record IV,* 176.

25 Pearson to Canadian Embassy, Prague, Mar. 5, 1948, External Affairs Records, file 50165-40. I owe this reference to Fred McEvoy, "The Last Bridge between East and West: Canada's Diplomatic Relations with Czechoslovakia — 1945-48" (unpublished paper). Pearson's critics among scholars include Denis Smith, *Diplomacy of Fear: Canada and the Cold War 1941-1948* (Toronto: University of Toronto Press, 1988), especially 223-36, and R.D. Cuff and J.L. Granatstein, *Canadian-American Relations in Wartime: From the Great War to the Cold War* (Toronto: Hakkert, 1975), especially the final chapter.

26 On Maclean's presence, its effect, and the talks, see Eayrs, *Growing Up Allied,* 71-84.

27 L.B. Pearson, "Memorandum for the Prime Minister", Mar. 17, 1948, with notation "Brought to Washington by General Foulkes, March 30th. H.W.", Escott Reid Papers, MG30 E101, v.4, file 25 (NAC). The other memoranda dealing with these talks are in the same file. See the American accounts in *Foreign Relations of the United States, 1948. III, Western Europe* (Washington: Government Printing Office, 1974), 88ff. The membership of the national delegations varied, with Wrong, for example, missing the first two meetings and others.

28 Robertson to Secretary of State for External Affairs, Apr. 2, 1948. External Affairs Records, file 264(s); and Alex Danchev, "Taking the Pledge: Oliver Franks and the Negotiation of the North Atlantic Treaty", *Diplomatic History* (Spring 1991), 199-219.

29 Pearson, "Memorandum for the Prime Minister", Mar. 27, 1948.

30 Smith, *Diplomacy of Fear,* 268, n. 77.

31 Arthur Schlesinger, *The Vital Center: The Politics of Freedom* (Boston: Little Brown, 1949). See also Alonzo Hamby, *Beyond the New Deal: Harry S. Truman*

and American Liberalism (New York: Columbia University Press, 1973), ch. 12. L.B. Pearson, *Words and Occasions* (Toronto: University of Toronto Press, 1970), 90.

32 Barbara Ward, *The West at Bay* (London: Allen and Unwin, 1948), 221. Ward wrote the book between Jan. 20 and March 15. It is a remarkable testimony to her intellectual energy and breadth.

33 Kennan to Marshall and Lovett, June 10, 1948, State Department Records, RG59, Policy Planning Staff Records, Box 13, National Archives, Washington (NA). The British shared some of the Americans' worries about Canadian insistence on multilateralism. See A. Clutterbuck to Philip Noel- Baker, Oct. 1, 1948, DO351 G2050/54, Public Records Office (PRO). For Kennan on NATO, see David Moyers, *George Kennan and the Dilemmas of U.S. Foreign Policy* (New York: Oxford University Press, 1988), 153-5; and Eayrs, *Growing Up Allied,* 79-82, which has an excellent discussion of the attempt to woo Kennan. For Pearson's argument for multilateralism, see L.B. Pearson, "Memorandum for the Prime Minister", Apr. 12, 1948, Reid Papers, MG30 E101, v. 4 (NAC).

34 See Eayrs, *ibid;* and Melvyn Leffler, "Was the Cold War Necessary?", *Diplomatic History* (Spring 1991), 265-75.

35 Quoted in Walter Isaacson and Evan Thomas, *The Wise Men: Six Friends and the World They Made* (New York: Simon and Schuster, 1986), 450. Only 20% opposed military assistance to Western Europe, according to a confidential State Department poll. Wrong to Pearson, Apr. 16, 1948, Reid Papers, MG30 E101, v. 4 (NAC).

36 Pearson to Robertson, Apr. 22, 1948, Pearson Papers, MG26 N1, v. 13 (NAC); Pearson to Wrong, Mar. 31, 1948, External Affairs Records, file 2885; and Pearson to Wrong, May 7, 1948, *ibid.*

37 Wrong to Pearson, Sept. 2, 1948, King Papers, MG26 J4, file 2315 (NAC); and Pearson to Wrong, Sept. 3, 1948, *ibid.*

38 *Mike, II:* 49-51. Theodore Achilles, Draft Memoirs, 420-30 (in the possession of Professor Lawrence Kaplan, Lyman Lemnitzer Center, Kent State University).

39 Pearson to St. Laurent, Nov. 25, 1948, MG26 N1, v. 3 (NAC); and H.E. Russell, American Consul General, Toronto, to Secretary of State, Jan. 18, 1949, State Department Records 742.00/1-1849 (NA).

40 Pearson to St. Laurent, *ibid.*

41 Pearson to Robertson, Jan. 22, 1949, MG26 N1, v. 13 (NAC).

42 Full accounts of the conflict can be found in Eayrs, *Growing Up Allied,* 97ff, and Reid, *Time of Fear and Hope,* 137-218.

43 Gladwyn Jebb (Lord Gladwyn), review of *Time of Fear and Hope, International Journal,* XXXIII (Winter 1977-8), 261.

44 Acheson, *Present at the Creation*, 277; House of Commons, *Debates*, Feb. 4, 1949; and Eayrs, *Growing Up Allied*, 120ff.

45 "Progress Report on Questions Raised at February 12 Conference between the President and the Canadian Prime Minister", Mar. 24, 1949, State Department Records 711.42/3-2449 (NA). For the Canadian reactions, see Eayrs, *Growing Up Allied*, 124.

46 Acheson, *Present at the Creation*, 277; *Mike, II:* 57-8; *Foreign Relations of the United States 1949. Volume IV. Western Europe* (Washington: Government Printing Office, 1975), 85-6; Reid, *Time of Fear and Hope*, ch. 15; Eayrs, *Growing Up Allied*, 122-8; Achilles, Draft Memoirs; and interview of Gerald Wright and Tom Hockin with John Hickerson, Oct. 27, 1969, York University Oral History Project, York Archives.

47 Acheson, *Present at the Creation*, 284.

48 L.B. Pearson, "On Signing the North Atlantic Treaty", in *Words and Occasions,* 89.

49 Isaacson and Thomas, *The Wise Men*, 489. His statements at the time can be found in Department of State *Bulletin,* Apr. 17, 1949, 471ff. The text of the treaty is found in *Foreign Relations of the United States 1949*, IV: 281ff.

50 On the zeal of External Affairs' official, see David MacKenzie, *Inside the Atlantic Triangle: Canada and the Entrance of Newfoundland into Confederation, 1939-1949* (Toronto: University of Toronto Press), 172-6.

51 J.W. Pickersgill, *My Years with Louis St. Laurent* (Toronto: University of Toronto Press, 1975), 86; *Mike, II:* 13-14; and House of Commons, *Debates,* Feb. 4, 1949.

52 *Mike, II:* 13-15 and Pearson, *Words and Occasions,* 87; and *Toronto Daily Star,* June 28, 1949.

53 Heeney to Pearson, June 18, 1949, MG26 N1, v. 5 (NAC).

54 Heeney to Robertson, Feb. 16, 1949, Heeney Papers, v. 5 (NAC).

55 *Mike, II:* 16. On Reid's failure to be promoted to the under-secretary's position see Granatstein, *The Ottawa Men*, 251-2.

56 Heeney to Pearson, June 29, 1949, being an account of events since Attlee told St. Laurent of currency crisis, St. Laurent Papers, MG26L, box 175 (NAC).

57 Bruce Hutchison, "Memorandum", Oct. 5, 1949, Crerar Papers, v. 105 (Queen's University Archives).

58 *Mike, II:* 106.

59 House of Commons, *Debates,* Nov. 16, 1949, 1835.

60 *Ibid.* The American concern is in Laurence Steinhardt (American Ambassador) to State Department, Nov. 18, 1949, State Department Records 711.42/11-1849 (NA). The British comments are in High Commissioner to Secretary of State

for Commonwealth Relations, received 5 Dec. 1949, DO 35/3509/113382 (PRO).

CHAPTER 2: BECOMING ADULT

1 U.K. High Commission to Commonwealth Relations Office, Apr. 2, 1951. Minute by R.H. Scott, FO371/92799/FK1071/400 (PRO).

2 Quoted in Max Hastings, *The Korean War* (London: Pan, 1988), 281, 287, 290-1. Canadian accounts of Canada's involvement are Denis Stairs, *The Diplomacy of Constraint: Canada, the Korean War and the United States* (Toronto: University of Toronto press, 1974), an excellent diplomatic history, and H.F. Wood, *Strange Battleground: Official History of the Canadian Army in Korea* (Ottawa: Queen's Printer, 1964). Two recent works, one by an academic, the other by a good popular historian, are of interest: Rosemary Foot, *The Wrong War* (Ithaca: Cornell University Press, 1985) and Joseph Goulden, *Korea: The Untold Story* (Englewood Cliffs, N.J.: McGraw-Hill, 1982). A more controversial work is Bruce Cumings, *The Origins of the Korean War. Volume II: The Roaring Cataract* (Princeton: Princeton University Press, 1990).

3 Greg Donaghy, draft paper on Korea (provided by Greg Donaghy), and L.B. Pearson, *Mike: The Memoirs of the Right Honourable Lester B. Pearson. Volume II: 1948-1957* (Toronto: University of Toronto Press, 1973), 145ff.

4 LBP to Wrong, Mar. 24, 1950, MG26 N1, v. 1 (NAC).

5 See H.J. Morgan, *Canadian Men and Women of the Time* (Toronto: Briggs, 1912), 128. Interview with Newton Rowell Bowles (son of the missionary Newton Bowles).

6 See my "Lester Pearson and China", in Paul Evans and Bernard Frolic, eds., *Reluctant Adversaries: Canada and the People's Republic of China* (Toronto: University of Toronto Press, 1991), 133-47.

7 Pearson Diary, MG26 N8, v. 2, entry for Jan. 13, 1936.

8 Pearson to Norman Robertson, Aug. 12, 1942, King Papers, MG26 J1, v. 331 (NAC).

9 See Pearson to James Endicott, Nov. 21, 1946, External Affairs Records, file 11578-B-40. Also, Kim Nossal, "Business As Usual: Canadian Relations with China in the 1940s", Canadian Historical Association, *Historical Papers 1978*, 139-47; and Steven Endicott, *Rebel Out of China* (Toronto: University of Toronto Press, 1980), 217-18. Nossal's article is based on his thesis, "Strange Bedfellows: Canada and China in War and Revolution" (Ph.D. thesis, University of Toronto, 1979). A recent thesis on the subject is Ernest Levos, "The War for Men's Minds: The Canadian Perspective of Foreign Policy in Asia, 1945-1957" (Ph.D. thesis, University of Alberta, 1990).

10 The debate is found in External Affairs Records, file 11044-B5-40.

11 House of Commons, *Debates*, Nov. 17, 1949. See also, *ibid.*, Mar. 7, 1950. The recognition question is covered in Donald Page, "Admission to the U.N.: Canadian Perspectives and Initiatives", Paper presented to Canada-China Relations Since 1949 Conference. Montebello, 1985.

12 Macdonald to LBP, Jan. 6, 1950, MG26 N1, v. 8 (NAC); and Macdonald to Maryon Pearson, Jan. 6, 1950, *ibid*. On the pipe band, see the *Globe and Mail*, Jan. 3, 1950, and *External Affairs* 2:1 (1953), 28-9.

13 LBP to Heeney, Jan. 17, 1950, MG26 N1, v. 22 (NAC). Pearson reported to the House on Colombo on Feb. 22, 1950, House of Commons, *Debates*, Feb. 22, 1950. An Indian view of Pearson is found in Rajeshwar Dayal, "The Power of Wisdom", *International Journal* (Winter 1973-4), 10-21.

14 "Commonwealth Meeting on Foreign Affairs, January 1950". Meeting of Jan. 9 at 11 a.m., CAB 133/78 (PRO).

15 Interview with Escott Reid, *Mike, II:* 118-19; D. LePan, "Around the World in 1500 Words", Escott Reid Papers, MG3E1010; and D. LePan, *Bright Glass of Memory* (Toronto: McGraw-Hill Ryerson, 1979).

16 Thomas Schoenbaum, *Waging Peace and War: Dean Rusk in the Truman, Kennedy and Johnson Years* (New York: Simon and Schuster, 1988), 195.

17 McNaughton's role and his unhappiness with Pearson's performance in South Asia are found in John Swettenham, *McNaughton: Volume 3, 1944-1946* (Toronto: Ryerson, 1969), 154-62. The British attitude is seen in R.H. Scott to Permanent Under Secretary, Jan. 17, 1950, FO 371/821206/FL/ 015/ 23 (PRO). See also, *Mike, II:* 115-17. The Canadians were already sceptical before the Nehru-Pearson conversation. Heeney to LBP, Jan. 20, 1950, MG26 N1, v. 5 (NAC).

18 "Statement by Mr. Pearson, European Economic Cooperation", Jan. 13, 1950; MG26 N1, v. 22 (NAC); and Alan Bullock, *Ernest Bevin. Foreign Secretary 1945-1951* (New York: Norton, 1983), 746.

19 Bullock, *Bevin*, 288, 749-50.

20 Interviews with Lord Sherfield (Roger Makins), and Escott Reid. Bevin to Maryon Pearson, n.d. (1950), Pearson Papers Personal (PPP); and Bullock, *Bevin*, 749.

21 *Mike, II:* 116.

22 Escott Reid, *Radical Mandarin: The Memoirs of Escott Reid* (Toronto: University of Toronto Press, 1989), 249-50. The Commonwealth's popularity grew throughout the 1950s and early 1960s. Even Suez scarcely affected this trend. See Mildred Schwartz, *Public Opinion and Canadian Identity* (Scarborough, Ont.: Fitzhenry and Whiteside, 1967), 74-5.

23 Mike did not tell the British liaison officer in Tokyo, Sir Alvary Gascoigne, any details of his visit with the prime minister, nor was Gascoigne curious. Nevertheless, he reported in detail Pearson's full comments about his MacArthur meetings. Gascoigne to Bevin, Feb. 6, 1950, FO 371/83840/ FJ1022/3 (PRO). The controversy among historians developed after the publication of Michael Schaller, *The American Occupation of Japan: The Origins of the Cold War in Asia* (New York: Oxford University Press, 1985).

24 *Mike, II:* 145-6. Interview with Escott Reid.

25 *Mike, II:* 145-7; Gascoigne to M.E. Dening, Feb. 1, 1950, FO 371/83814/ FJ10111/12 (PRO); David McClellan, *Dean Acheson: The State Department Years* (New York: Dodd Mead, 1976), 209-11; *The Times,* Feb. 3, 1950; and Mary Macdonald to LBP, Feb. 3, 1950, in which Macdonald says that the Canadian press was reporting that Mike had said in Tokyo that Canada would recognize Communist China, MG26 N1, v. 8 (NAC). On Acheson's speech, see Walter Isaacson and Evan Thomas, *The Wise Men: Six Friends and the World They Made* (New York: Simon and Schuster, 1986), 477-8.

26 McClellan, *Acheson,* 220-1.

27 Wrong to Pearson, Feb. 7, 1950, External Affairs Records, RG25, vol. 84/ 85/150/50, file 4901-40 (NAC); and Wrong, "Note for file", Mar. 6, 1950, *ibid.*

28 LBP, "Memorandum for the Prime Minister", Jan. 17, 1948, King Papers, MG26 J4, v. 334 (NAC); Hume Wrong, "Influences Shaping the Policy of the United States towards the Soviet Union", Dec. 4, 1947, *ibid.;* LBP to Wrong, Mar. 24, 1950, MG26 N1, v. 1 (NAC); and LBP, "Address to an Ottawa Study Club", June 1, 1934, MG26 N1, v. 10 (NAC).

29 Isaacson and Thomas, *The Wise Men,* 495-503; and John Gaddis, *Strategies of Containment* (New York: Oxford, 1982), 98-126. Nitze refused my request for an interview. His thoughts may be found in Paul Nitze, *From Hiroshima to Glasnost: At the Center of Decision* (New York: Grove Weidenfeld, 1989).

30 Wrong to LBP, Feb. 23, 1950, and Mar. 15, 1950, Wrong Papers, MG30 101, v. 42 (NAC); and LBP to Wrong, Mar. 24, 1950, MG26 N1, v. 1 (NAC).

31 LBP, "Memorandum from Mr. Pearson to the Prime Minister concerning talks with Mr. Jessup, Mr. Rusk, and Mr. Gross", Apr. 4, 1950, MG26 N1, v. 65. Cabinet Conclusions, RG2, v. 20, Mar. 10, 1950 (NAC).

32 Schoenbaum, *Waging Peace and War,* 224. Rusk himself does not seem to accept Schoenbaum's arguments in his recent memoir. See Daniel Papp, ed., *As I Saw It by Dean Rusk As Told to Richard Rusk* (New York: Norton, 1990), 422-4.

33 There is a full account of the meeting in Goulden, *Korea,* 65-9. Also John Hickerson oral history interview, Harry Truman Library, Independence, Missouri.

34 Stairs, *Diplomacy of Constraint,* 41. Stairs's excellent work is based upon numerous interviews with Pearson and others. Pearson personally supplied him with much information.

35 Hickerson oral history interview.

36 House of Commons, *Debates,* June 28, 1950.

37 James Barros, *Trygve Lie and the Cold War: The U.N. Secretary-General Promotes Peace 1946-1953* (DeKalb, Ill.: Northern Illinois University Press, 1989), 353.

38 *Ibid.,* 273-300.

39 Reid, *Radical Mandarin,* 260.

40 House of Commons, *Debates,* June 29, 1950; Stairs, *Diplomacy of Constraint,* 55-60, 83-4; Peter Stursberg, *Lester Pearson and the American Dilemma* (Toronto: Doubleday, 1980), 88-9; interviews with J.W. Pickersgill and Paul Martin; and Cabinet Conclusions, July 27, 1950, RG2, Series 16, v. 20 (NAC). The cabinet conclusions do not reflect the agreement in principle to commit ground forces. See also, Paul Martin, *A Very Public Life: Volume II. So Many Worlds* (Toronto: Deneau, 1985), 93-4.

41 See Mildred Schwartz, *Public Opinion and Canadian Identity* (Scarborough, Ont.: Fitzhenry and Whiteside, 1967), 80-1. Claxton's comment can be found in R.D. Cuff and J.L. Granatstein, "Looking Back at the Cold War, 1945-1954", *Canadian Forum.* (July-August 1972), 11.

42 LBP, "Memorandum for the Prime Minister: Discussions on Korea", Aug. 1, 1950, MG26 N1, v. 35 (NAC). The American reaction is in Dean Acheson, "Memorandum of Conversation", July 29, 1950, State Department Records 794A.00/7-2950 (NA).

43 Dean Rusk's view of Acheson is described in Schoenbaum, *Waging Peace and War,* 193. In the memorandum cited in the above note, Pearson described Acheson's low opinion of Nehru.

44 See Goulden, *Korea,* 151-5, for an account of this incident. For the Chinese reaction, see K.M. Pannikkar, *In Two Chinas: Memoirs of a Diplomat* (London: Allen and Unwin, 1955), ch. 3.

45 LBP to Wrong, Aug. 7, 1950, MG26 N1, v. 35 (NAC). On the American side, see Bonbright to Acheson, Aug. 21, 1950, State Department Records 611.42/ 8-2150 (NA).

46 LBP to Acheson, Aug. 15, 1950, *ibid.;* and Acheson to LBP, Sept. 8, 1950, *ibid.* See also Stairs, *Diplomacy of Constraint,* 96-8; and, for American concerns that Acheson did not express Mike in his letter, see Dean Acheson, *Present at the Creation: My Years in the State Department* (New York: Norton, 1969), 422-4.

47 See the full account in *Mike, II:* 160ff.

48 See Goulden, *Korea,* chs. 9 and 11, for an excellent and useful account of this period. Mike communicated directly with Nehru and sought to have him involved. Saul Rae to Sir Saville Garner, Dec. 3, 1950, FO 371/84106/ FK1022/360 (PRO).

49 Reid, *Radical Mandarin,* 260.

50 See *Mike, II:* 269-70.

51 LBP to A.R.M. Lower, Oct. 12, 1950, MG26 N1, v. 7 (NAC). Carl Berger, *The Writing of Canadian History: Aspects of English-Canadian Historical Writing: 1900 to 1970* (Toronto: Oxford, 1976), 203. Berger suggests that Lower "expressed" no reservations about the degree to which Canada was integrated into American defense planning (204). The exchange with Pearson indicates that, privately at least, he had reservations.

52 Stairs, *Diplomacy of Constraint,* xi.

53 *Mike, II:* 170. Pearson's diary describing the commission's work is found in *Mike, II:* 279-314. The original, which is very slightly different, is in MG26 N8, v. 1 (NAC).

54 Diary, Jan. 28, 1951.

55 "Record of Conversation between Sir R. Makins and Mr. Heeney at Ottawa on 11th December, 1950", PREM 8/1200/119358 (PRO); *Mike, II:* 169-71.

56 Paper No. 31 (50) final, Nov. 21, 1950, St. Laurent Papers, box 174 (NAC). On the spies see Christopher Andrew and Oleg Gordievsky, *KGB: The Inside Story* (New York: Harper Collins, 1990), 394-5. On NATO and the build-up, Samuel Wells, "The First Cold War Buildup: Europe in United States Strategy and Policy, 1950-1953", in Olav Riste, ed., *Western Security: The Formative Years. European and Atlantic Defense* (Oslo and New York: Universitetsforlaget and Columbia University Press, 1985), 181-97. Claxton's announcement is in House of Commons, *Debates,* Feb. 14, 1953. The later assessment of Soviet military success is in Defence Liaison (2) to LBP, June 1, 1951, St. Laurent Papers, box 175 (NAC).

57 LBP to Geoffrey Pearson (GP), Jan. 15, 1951 (PPP).

58 LBP to GP, Jan. 27, 1951 (PPP).

59 This letter is quoted fully in *Mike, II:* 171-5.

60 The Wrong report is also in *ibid.,* 177-9. Rusk's views are described in Rusk, *As I Saw It,* 174ff.

61 LBP to GP, Mar. 19, 1951 (PPP).

62 R.J. Rogers, "The Effect of the Far Eastern Crisis on Relations between Canada and the United States", Mar. 30, 1951, External Affairs Records, file 1415-40, v. 3; and A.F.W. Plumptre, "Relations with the United States", Mar. 31, 1951, *ibid.,* v. 2.

63 This account is based upon the information in the forthcoming External Affairs history. The most recent assessment of the evidence is J.L. Granatstein and David Stafford, *Spy Wars: Espionage and Canada from Gouzenko to Glasnost* (Toronto: Key Porter, 1990), 88ff.

64 LBP to GP, Mar. 19, 1951 (PPP).

65 Minute (illegible signature) on despatch from High Commissioner, Ottawa, to Commonwealth Relations Office, April 2, 1951, FO 371/92779/ FK 1071/400 (PRO); Howard Sykes to C.D. Howe, Mar. 2, 1951, Howe Papers, v. 178, file 90-29; Howe to Sykes, Apr. 8, 1951, *ibid.*

66 *Mike, II:* 180-1; and LBP to GP, Apr. 17, 1951 (PPP); Department of External Affairs, *Statements and Speeches,* No. 51/14.

67 Stanley Woodward to Acheson, Apr. 10, 1951, State Department Records 642.00/4-105 (NA); and Cecil Gross to State Dept., Apr. 17, 1951, State Department Records 611.42/4-1751 (NA).

68 Sykes to Howe, Apr. 13, 1951, Howe Papers, v. 178, file 90-29; and Howe to Sykes, Apr. 16, 1951, *ibid.* (NAC).

69 See, for example, "Memorandum of Conversation", Hume Wrong, Dean Acheson, and George Perkins, State Department Records 611.42/9-750 (NA).

70 "Memorandum of Conversation", Hume Wrong and W. Willoughby, State Department Records 611.42/4-1751 (NA); and Wade to State Department, May 1, 1951, State Department Records 611.42/5-1451 (NA).

71 Wrong quoted in J.L. Granatstein, *The Ottawa Men: The Civil Service Mandarins 1935-1957* (Toronto: Oxford, 1982), 117-18; LBP to GP, Nov. 1950 (PPP); and Department of External Affairs, *Statements and Speeches,* Apr. 10, 1951.

72 Quoted in William Pfaff, *Barbarian Sentiments: How the American Century Ends* (New York: Hill and Wang, 1990), 22.

73 *Mike, II:* 184-5; Acheson, *Present at the Creation,* 700-5; and John Milloy, "The Korean Ceasefire", Oxford special paper, 1991.

CHAPTER 3: THE PEACEMAKER

1 John R. Seeley, R. Alexander Sim, and E.W. Loosley, *Crestwood Heights: A Study of the Culture of Urban Life* (Toronto: University of Toronto Press, 1956), 6.

2 John Holmes, *The Shaping of Peace: Canada and the Search for World Order, 1943-1957,* Vol. 1 (Toronto: University of Toronto Press, 1979), 97.

3 Walter Gordon, "LBP", Dec. 5, 1965, Gordon Papers, MG22B44, v. 16 (NAC). Interview with Mary Macdonald.

4 Bill Stephenson, "The Haughtiest Suburb of Them All", *Maclean's* (Sept. 15,

1954), 29, 69. Interviews with Geoffrey Pearson, Patricia Hannah, and Mary Macdonald.

5 LBP to Geoffrey Pearson (GP), Oct. 21, 1951 (PPP).

6 LBP to GP, Oct. 1951 (PPP). There is, in the parents' attitude, an attempt to represent "rational" argument. Peter Laslett comments that the contemporary United States, "which has a claim to be the best instructed population of its size that has ever existed", exhibits patterns of behaviour in familial situations that "can scarcely have arisen from . . . rational comportment and calculation". See his appropriately entitled "The Family as Knot of Individual Interests", in Robert McC. Netting, Richard Wilk, and Eric J. Arnold, eds., *Households: Comparative and Historical Studies of the Domestic Group* (Berkeley: University of California Press, 1984), 362.

7 Theodore Caplow and Howard M. Bahr, *Middletown Families: Fifty Years of Change and Continuity* (Minneapolis: University of Minnesota Press, 1982), 284.

8 LBP to GP, June 11, 1952 (PPP).

9 Arnold Heeney Diary, Sept. 24-25, 1955, Heeney Papers, MG30 E144, v. 2 (NAC).

10 L.B. Pearson, *Mike: The Memoirs of the Right Honourable Lester B. Pearson. Volume II: 1948-1957* (Toronto: University of Toronto Press, 1973), 18.

11 Patricia Hannah, "My Father", interview with Patricia Hannah, 95; and LBP to GP [Nov. 1950] (PPP).

12 Hannah, "My Father", 95. Veronica Strong-Boag points out that many Canadian magazines "pictured" men who did domestic duties as somewhat less masculine. "'Women with a Choice': Canada's Wage-earning Wives and the Construction of the Middle Class". Paper presented to Canadian Historical Association, May 1992. The interview with Maryon is found in MG26 N8, v. 11 (NAC).

13 LBP to GP, Sept. 16, 1951, and Hannah, "My Father", 29.

14 Quoted in Hannah, "My Father", 28.

15 On the notion of chivalry and its residue, I am much influenced by Paul Fussell's splendid "The Fate of Chivalry and the Assault upon Mother", in Paul Fussell, *Thank God for the Atom Bomb and Other Essays* (New York: Ballantine, 1988), 186-210. Quotation from Maryon Pearson to Kenneth Kirkwood, May 21, 1924 (Kirkwood Papers Private).

16 Pearson Diary, Mar. 27, 1953, MG26 N8, v. 5 (NAC); and LBP to St. Laurent, Dec. 29, 1952, MG26 N1, v. 64 (NAC). Letter not sent but discussed. Also, Grant Dexter, "Memo — Maxie, July 19, 1952", Grant Dexter Papers, TC643 (Queen's University Archives).

17 Michael Barkway, "Lester Pearson, Reluctant Politician", *Saturday Night* (Apr. 26, 1952), 14. On Pearson's view of the NATO position, see Grant Dexter, Memorandum, Jan. 23, 1952, Dexter Papers, TC641 (Queen's University Archives). Mary Macdonald, a strong Roman Catholic, liked Barkway's article but did not like the "confining" term "Methodist conscience". Macdonald to LBP, Apr. 21, 1952, MG26 N1, v. 8 (NAC).

18 Peter Dempson, "Pearson Slips in Leadership Race", Toronto *Telegram,* Sept. 23, 1953. Also, "Maxie" — telephone conversation between Grant Dexter and Max Freedman, July 19, 1952, Dexter Papers, TC643 (Queen's University Archives).

19 Bruce Hutchison to Grant Dexter, Jan. 23, 1952, Dexter Papers, TC641 (Queen's University Archives). See the excellent study dealing with the role of the journalists in promoting Liberalism and Mike Pearson, Patrick Brennan, "'A Responsible Civilized Relationship': Reporting the Nation's Business", unpublished manuscript.

20 Barkway, "Lester Pearson", 13-14. Most of this political gossip derives from the Hutchison–Dexter–Max Freedman correspondence in the Dexter Papers (Queen's University Archives) and the Hutchison Papers at the University of Calgary. I have also interviewed Hutchison, Abbott, Paul Martin, Walter Harris, and Jack Pickersgill. There are few differences among them, although Pickersgill is understandably not so convinced that his power diminished when he left the Prime Minister's Office. Pearson learned of Abbott's impending departure on Feb. 6, 1953. See Pearson Diary, Feb. 6, 1953, MG26 N8, v. 5 (NAC).

21 Pearson Diary, Jan. 13 and Feb. 4, 1953, *ibid.*

22 LBP to GP, Mar. 18, 1952; and LBP to Peter Waite, Mar. 22, 1952, MG26 N1, v. 16 (NAC).

23 Donald Creighton, *The Forked Road: Canada 1939-1957* (Toronto: McClelland and Stewart, 1976), 235.

24 Pearson Diary, Jan. 20, 1953, MG26 N8, v. 5 (NAC).

25 Dalton Camp, *Gentlemen, Players and Politicians* (Toronto: McClelland and Stewart 1970), 137; and Reginald Whitaker, *The Government Party: Organizing and Financing the Liberal Party of Canada 1930-1958* (Toronto: University of Toronto Press, 1977), 201.

26 *Mike, II:* 18-19.

27 Whitaker, *Government Party,* 181.

28 Pearson Diary, Feb. 6, 1953, MG26 N8, v. 5 (NAC). Interview with Paul Martin.

29 Wilgress to Heeney, Mar. 7, 1953, Heeney Papers, MG30 E144, v. 1 (NAC).

30 Pearson Diary, Feb. 6, 1953, MG26 N8, v. 5 (NAC). The Gordon proposal is

described in Denis Smith, *Gentle Patriot: A Political Biography of Walter Gordon* (Edmonton: Hurtig, 1973), 29. St. Laurent told Pearson on Feb. 6 that both Gordon and Towers were good appointments.

31 Grant Dexter Memorandum, Mar. 1952, Dexter Papers, TC641 (Queen's University Archives).

32 *Ibid.;* and Dexter Memorandum, May 1954, *ibid.*, TC744.

33 LBP to T.A. Stone, Jan. 23, 1954, MG26 N1, v. 15 (NAC); LBP to N.A. Robertson, *ibid.*, v. 83; and LBP to N.A. Robertson, *ibid.*, v. 17. Interview with George Glazebrook.

34 Wrong to "Marga", June 6, 1929, Mrs. C.H.A. Armstrong Papers (privately held).

35 "Mac" to Polly Armstrong, Mar. 16, 1954, ibid.; and LBP to Polly Armstrong, Mar. 1954, *ibid.*

36 See J.L. Granatstein, *A Man of Influence: Norman Robertson and Canadian Statecraft, 1929-1968* (Ottawa: Deneau, 1981), 293-6. Robertson had apparently been willing to take the job.

37 Lesage was Pearson's parliamentary assistant in 1951 and was on the U.N. delegation in 1952. Léger's comments were made in a "Round Table" discussion on the subject of Norman Robertson. (External Affairs Records, Historical Section, Transcript.) See ch. 5, n. 6. Interview with Geoffrey Pearson. On Pearson's French, see the comments of his first French speech writer, Maurice Lamontagne, in Peter Stursberg, *Lester Pearson and the Dream of Unity* (Toronto: Doubleday, 1978), 48. On Léger's role, see LBP to St. Laurent, n.d., St. Laurent Papers, MG26L, v. 174 (NAC).

38 Dulles's views are set out in "Policy for Security and Peace", *Foreign Affairs* (Apr. 1954), 357-9. On the change in American policy, see John Gaddis, *Strategies of Containment: A Critical Appraisal of Postwar American National Security Policy* (New York: Oxford University Press, 1982), 136-48. On the Canadian response, see Douglas Ross, *In the Interests of Peace: Canada and Vietnam* (Toronto: University of Toronto Press, 1984), 44-6.

39 L.B. Pearson, "Korea and the Atomic Bomb", reprinted in full in James Eayrs, *In Defence of Canada: Growing Up Allied* (Toronto: University of Toronto Press, 1980), 374-5.

40 A.D.P. Heeney Diary, July 7, 1955, Heeney Papers, MG30 E144, v. 2 (NAC).

41 See Escott Reid, *Envoy to Nehru* (New Delhi: Oxford University Press, 1981) for a detailed account of this relationship.

42 The RCMP advice is found in J.R. Lemieux to G.P. deT. Glazebrook, Oct. 30, 1953, MG26 N1, v. 33 (NAC). The comments and press clippings are in *ibid.*, v. 33. See also *New York Times*, Nov. 25, 1953; LBP to St. Laurent, Nov. 16, 1953, St. Laurent Papers, MG26L, v. 174 (NAC); and B.S. Keirstead, *Canada in World Affairs, 1951-1953* (Toronto: Oxford, 1956), 118-21. The Bentley com-

ments are discussed in Volume 1, 302-08. The McCormick comment on Pearson appeared in his "diary" in the *Chicago Tribune* on Mar. 24, 1953. He declared that he "considered communist infestation even more prevalent than we have suspected in our state department, in the left wing of the British Labor party, and in Canada where Lester Pearson is the most dangerous man in the English speaking world".

43 LBP to A.B. Moore, Nov. 16, 1953, MG26 N1, v. 66 (NAC). Interview with the Very Rev. A.B. Moore.

44 David Lewis to LBP, Nov. 27, 1953, MG26 N1, v. 33 (NAC). On the press, see Keirstead, *Canada in World Affairs,* 119-20.

45 LBP to St. Laurent, Nov. 16, 1953, St. Laurent Papers, MG26L, v. 174 (NAC). No American account exists. See *Foreign Relations of the United States 1953-4,* Vol. VI (Washington: Government Printing Office, 1986), 2115-16.

46 Keirstead, *Canada in World Affairs,* 118.

47 Lewis to LBP, Nov. 27, 1953, MG26 N1, v. 33 (NAC).

48 LBP to St. Laurent, Nov. 16, 1953, St. Laurent Papers, MG26L, v. 174 (NAC).

49 Heeney to Pearson, Dec. 9, 1954, MG26 N1, v. 5 (NAC).

50 Department of External Affairs, *Statements and Speeches,* 53/50.

51 See Ross, *In the Interests of Peace,* 45. Also, interview with Arnold Smith; and Evelyn Shuckburgh, *Descent to Suez: Diaries 1951-56* (London: Weidenfeld and Nicolson, 1986), 160.

52 See the excellent account in McGeorge Bundy, *Danger and Survival: Choices about the Bomb in the First Fifty Years* (New York: Random House, 1988), 263-70. On Dulles's rhetoric, see John Gaddis's analysis in Richard Immerman, ed., *John Foster Dulles and the Diplomacy of the Cold War* (Princeton: Princeton University Press, 1990), 44-77.

53 Ross, *In the Interests of Peace;* and James Eayrs, *In Defence of Canada. Indo China: Roots of Complicity* (Toronto: University of Toronto Press, 1983).

54 Shuckburgh, *Descent,* 157; Eden tried to enlist Pearson's assistance in persuading Churchill not to go to Moscow. See LBP to Robertson, July 7, 1954 (not sent), MG26 N1, v. 86 (NAC). The Churchill-Eisenhower correspondence can be read in *Foreign Relations of the United States. Volume VI,* 964-7.

55 Shuckburgh, *Descent,* 187; Smith to Dulles, May 30, 1954. State Department Records 741.13/5/3054 (NA). An excellent account of the Anglo-American relationship in this period is found in David Dimbleby and David Reynolds, *An Ocean Apart: The Relationship between Britain and America in the Twentieth Century* (New York: Random House, 1988), 212ff. The oil question and British financial difficulties also troubled the relationship.

56 Shuckburgh, *Descent,* 183.

57 Pearson to Reid, June 1, 1954, MG26 N1, v. 12 (NAC). Holmes's and Ronning's accounts can be found in the former's "Geneva-1954", *International Journal*

(Summer 1967), 46; and the latter's *A Memoir of China in Revolution* (New York and Toronto: Pantheon, 1974), 214-35. The Chou En-lai discussions are described in L.B. Pearson, *Mike: The Memoirs of the Right Honourable Lester B. Pearson. Volume III: 1957-1968* (Toronto: University of Toronto Press, 1975), 120-1.

58 Grant Dexter, "Memo on E.D.C.", Sept. 17, 1954, Dexter Papers, TC744 (Queen's University Archives).

59 See Ross, *In the Interests of Peace,* 88-9.

60 L.B. Pearson, *Democracy in World Politics* (Toronto: Saunders, 1955), 115. On Niebuhr, see John Patrick Diggins, *The Proud Decades: America in War and Peace* (New York and London: Norton, 1988), 172-3.

61 Shuckburgh, *Descent,* 184.

62 See Bundy, *Danger and Survival,* 295. On Soviet military thought, David Holloway, *The Soviet Union and the Arms Race,* 2nd ed. (New Haven: Yale University Press, 1984), 31ff. Also Nikita Khrushchev, *Khrushchev Remembers* (Boston: Little Brown, 1970), 392.

63 The diary of Sinclair's trip is held in the Archives of the University of British Columbia. It yields few nuggets. Also Joseph Levitt, "Lester Pearson and Peaceful Coexistence with the Soviet Union" (unpublished paper). An analysis of Pearson's attitude is found in Micheline Rondeau-Parent, "Lester B. Pearson and the Soviet Union: An Analysis (1948-1967)" (MA thesis, Carleton University, 1978).

64 Pearson to Watkins, Nov. 26, 1954, MG26 N1, v. 16 (NAC). Also, Albert Parry, "Russia's New Look at Canada, Theme and Variations", in J.L. Black and Norman Hillmer, eds., *Nearly Neighbours: Canada and the Soviet Union* (Kingston: R.P. Frye, 1989), 77-9 See also, Rondeau-Parent, "Pearson and the Soviet Union".

65 George Ignatieff, *The Making of a Peacemonger: The Memoirs of George Ignatieff* (Markham, Ont.: Penguin Books, 1987), 128.

66 A.R. Crépault, "Memorandum for the Minister", Sept. 23, 1955, Ignatieff Papers, Trinity College Library (TCL), Box 7.

67 George Ignatieff, "Memorandum for the Minister", Sept. 28, 1955, Ignatieff Papers, *ibid.*

68 "Talk by Comrade Socherhatov", Oct. 10, 1955, Ignatieff Papers, *ibid.*

69 "The Honourable L.B. Pearson's Diary of His Visit to the Soviet Union, South and Southeast Asia and the Middle East, September 30 to November 15, 1955", MG26 N8, Diary 1953, v. 1 (NAC).

70 *Ibid.*

71 For full accounts, see Ignatieff, *Making of a Peacemonger,* 140-7, and *Mike, II:* 204-11. There are shorter accounts in René Lévesque, *Memoirs* (Toronto:

McClelland and Stewart, 1986); and John Watkins, *Moscow Despatches: Inside Cold War Russia*, eds. Dean Beeby and William Kaplan (Toronto: Lorimer, 1987), 122-7. Pearson's secretary said that Lévesque's comments were "good": Mary Macdonald to Pearson, Oct. 12, 1955, MG26 N1, v. 8 (NAC).

72 Based on the account in *Mike, II:* 204-8; and George Ignatieff, "Ministers visit to the U.S.S.R., Oct. 5-12, 1955", Oct. 28, 1955, Ignatieff Papers (TCL), Box 7.

73 *Mike, II:* 211, and Ignatieff, *ibid.*

74 Watkins to Pearson, Feb. 3, 1956, MG26 N1, v. 16 (NAC). Also H.A. Caccia to Under Secretary, Oct. 20, 1955, FO 371/16698/NS1063169 (PRO).

75 House of Commons, *Debates,* Jan. 31, 1956.

76 Pearson to Watkins, Feb. 27, 1956, MG26 N1, v. 16 (NAC).

77 In an interview with Edgar McInnes of the Canadian Institute of International Affairs, Pearson responded to the question of positive results: "that is very hard to tell . . . ". He added that "I got their point of view on all these controversial questions and that was, I suppose, helpful and in return I did my best to give them our point of view. Whether that was of assistance to them I don't know." McInnes interview, MG26 N1, v. 16 (NAC).

CHAPTER 4: SUEZ

1 L.B. Pearson Diary, Nov. 28, 1915, MG26 N8, v. 1 (NAC); and Foreign Office to U.K. Permanent Delegation NATO, May 3, 1956, PREM 11/1342 (PRO).

2 L.B. Pearson, *Democracy in World Politics* (Toronto: Saunders, 1955), 82-3.

3 *Ibid.,* 114.

4 L.B. Pearson, "Christian Foundations for World Order", Dec. 2, 1954, in L.B. Pearson, *Words and Occasions* (Toronto: University of Toronto Press, 1970), 128. Part of this speech was repeated in *Democracy in World Politics.* Arnold Smith drafted both, *Democracy in World Politics* almost in its entirety. Interview with Arnold Smith.

5 See Peter Gellman, "Lester B. Pearson, the Foundation of Canadian Foreign Policy, and the Quest for World Order" (Ph.D. thesis, University of Virginia, 1986).

6 Quoted in Escott Reid, *Time of Fear and Hope: The Making of the North Atlantic Treaty, 1947-1949* (Toronto: McClelland and Stewart, 1977), 168.

7 Quoted in Pierre Mélandri, "France and the United States", in L. Kaplan, S.V. Papacosma, Mark Rubin, and Ruth Young, eds., *NATO after Forty Years* (Washington, Del.: Scholarly Resources, 1990), 58.

8 Interview with L.B. Pearson by Thomas Hockin and Gerald Wright, May 7, 1970, York University Oral History Collection (original corrected by Pearson).

9 Pearson to Vanier, Nov. 6, 1950, RG26, file 50154-40 (NAC). See the excellent account of the German question in James Eayrs, *In Defence of Canada: Growing Up Allied* (Toronto: University of Toronto Press, 1980), 7, in which the Davis incident is described in detail, 331-3.

10 LBP to Geoffrey Pearson (GP) [1951] (PPP).

11 L.B. Pearson, "Memorandum", July 1951, MG26 N1, v. 84 (NAC), and L.B. Pearson, *Mike: The Memoirs of the Right Honourable Lester B. Pearson. Volume II: 1948-1957* (Toronto: University of Toronto Press, 1973), 63-74.

12 *Mike, II:* 62-76.

13 Theodore Achilles, draft memoirs (courtesy of Professor Lawrence Kaplan); and Hockin-Wright interview with Pearson.

14 *Mike, II:* 78.

15 A.E. Ritchie, "Memorandum for the Under-Secretary" (drafted by J.H. Warren), Feb. 10, 1953, MG26 N1, v. 84 (NAC).

16 Quoted in Stephen Ambrose, *Eisenhower. Volume Two. The President* (New York: Simon and Schuster, 1984), 177. On the general question of NATO and "outside area" questions, two recent books are most valuable: Elizabeth Sherwood, *Allies in Crisis: Meeting Global Challenges to Western Security* (New Haven and London: Yale University Press, 1990), chs. 2-4; and Douglas Stuart and William Tow, *The Limits of Alliance: NATO Out-of-Area Problems since 1949* (Baltimore and London: Johns Hopkins University Press, 1990), chs. 1-5, 8-10, 15-17. There is also valuable background in Olav Riste, ed., *Western Security: The Formative Years* (New York and Oslo: Columbia University Press, 1985).

17 Dean Acheson, *Present at the Creation: My Years in the State Department* (New York: Norton, 1969), 385. The "Durham miners" most concerned Herbert Morrison. See Alistair Horne, *Macmillan, 1894-1956. Volume I* (London: Macmillan, 1988), 319.

18 *Mike, II:* 84. On this general question, see the excellent article by Alan Henrikson, "The North American Perspective: A Continent Apart or a Continent Joined", in Kaplan et al., eds., *NATO after Forty Years*, 3-32.

19 LBP to Hubert Guérin, Dec. 30, 1953, MG26 N1, v. 84 (NAC).

20 Pearson Diary, Sept. 27, 1954, MG26 N1, v. 84 (NAC). David Carlton, *Anthony Eden* (London: Allen and Unwin, 1981), 360-1; and Geoffrey Warner, "The Anglo-American Special Relationship", in Kaplan et al., eds., *NATO after Forty Years*, 38-9. Note the differences in the description of Mendès-France in *Mike, II:* 89. He is no longer "dark". See also Clive Baxter, "Will NATO fade under Russia's soft look?" *Financial Post* (Oct. 15, 1955). The following sections rely greatly upon Joseph Sinasac, "The Three Wise Men: The Effects of the 1956 Committee of Three on NATO" (MA thesis, University of Waterloo, 1989); and John Milloy, "The Formation and Work of the 1956 Committee of

Three on Non-Military Cooperation in NATO" (Research Paper, Oxford University, 1991).

21 LBP, "Memorandum for the Prime Minister", Feb. 25, 1955, MG26 N1, v. 47 (NAC); and LBP, "After Geneva: A Greater Task for NATO", *Foreign Affairs* (Oct. 1955), 14-23.

22 Sinasac, "Three Wise Men", 55.

23 John Foster Dulles, "Developing NATO in Peace", in Department of State *Bulletin* (Apr. 30, 1956), 706-10. Milloy, "The Formation and Work of the 1956 Committee of Three".

24 LBP, "Appreciation of NATO Ministerial Meeting, May 4 to 5", May 11, 1956, MG26 N1, v. 47 (NAC).

25 LBP to W.M. Newton, May 28, 1956, MG26 N1, v. 56 (NAC). Sinasac, "Three Wise Men", *passim.*

26 NATO Committee of Three. "Preliminary Views of Mr. Dulles (Revised by Mr. Pearson)", MG26 N1, v. 47 (NAC); and *Mike, II:* 93.

27 LBP, "Memorandum", July 9, 1956, MG26 N1, v. 19 (NAC).

28 Quoted in Horne, *Macmillan, I:* 396.

29 The questionnaire, the reports from individual nations, and documents leading to the report's preparation are in the External Affairs Records. The Canadian pre-eminence in the report's preparation is revealed there and in the Pearson papers. See RG25, 90-91/008 50105-F40, Box 248 (NAC); and MG26 N1, volumes 45-7 (NAC). For a fuller discussion, see Sinasac, "Three Wise Men", 65ff. Denmark was one small country that did not support fuller consultation and co-operation.

30 LBP to Richard Casey, May 28, 1956, MG26 N1, v. 2 (NAC).

31 Sir John Wheeler-Bennett, *Knaves, Fools and Heroes* (London: Macmillan, 1974), 13; and Carlton, *Eden,* 71.

32 *Mike, II:* 90

33 LBP, "Diary: Commonwealth Prime Ministers' Conference, London, January-February, 1955", MG26 N1, v. 86 (NAC).

34 Heeney Diary, MG30 E144, v. 2, file memoirs 1955 (NAC).

35 LBP to "Landon and Geoffrey", Mar. 15 [1955] (PPP).

36 LBP to GP, Feb. 25, 1956 (PPP).

37 *Mike, II:* 69. The American account of the White Sulphur Springs meeting indicates that Mike took issue with the American appreciation of the China issue. R.K. Sherwood to "Waddell", n.d., State Department Records RG59, v. 2481, 611.42/2956 (NA). Some historians have argued that Dulles was more flexible than Mike believed. See Robert Divine, "John Foster Dulles: What You See Is What You Get", *Diplomatic History* (Spring 1991), 277-85.

38 Quoted in Walter Isaacson and Evan Thomas, *The Wise Men: Six Friends and the World They Made* (New York: Simon and Schuster, 1986), 581.

39 See Ambrose, *Eisenhower: The President*, 270-2; 322ff.

40 An excellent account of this arms request is given in Michael B. Oren, "Canada, the Great Powers, and the Middle Eastern Arms Race, 1950-1956", *International History Review* (May 1990), 280-300.

41 *Ibid.*, 294ff; and Cabinet Conclusions, July 12, 1956, RG2, v. 16 (NAC). There are numerous recent accounts, on which the following section draws as well as on records in the Israeli State Archives, the Public Record Office, and the National Archives in Washington and in Ottawa. The best accounts of the Canadian role are in: *Mike, II:* ch. 10; J.L. Granatstein, *A Man of Influence: Norman A. Robertson and Canadian Statecraft* (Ottawa: Deneau, 1981), ch. 10; Michael Fry, "Canada, the North Atlantic Triangle, and the United Nations", in W. Roger Louis and Roger Owen, eds., *Suez 1956* (Oxford: Oxford University Press, 1989), 285-316; and three dated but nonetheless valuable accounts: James Eayrs, *Canada in World Affairs. October 1955 to June 1957* (Toronto: Oxford University Press, 1959); John Holmes, *The Shaping of Peace: Canada and the Search for World Order, 1943-1957,* vol. 2 (Toronto: University of Toronto Press, 1979), 348-93; and Terence Robertson, *Crisis: The Inside Story of the Suez Conspiracy* (Toronto and Montreal: McClelland and Stewart, 1964). The last of these had access to most of Pearson's own papers dealing with the crisis. The definitive account of the crisis is found in Keith Kyle, *Suez* (London: Weidenfeld and Nicolson, 1991).

42 *Mike, II:* 218.

43 LBP, "Israel-Arab Relations", Feb. 23, 1955, MG26 N1, v. 37 (NAC).

44 LBP, "Memorandum for the Under-Secretary", July 1, 1955, MG26 N1, v. 37 (NAC).

45 LBP, "Memorandum of a Conversation with Colonel Gamal Abdul [*sic*] Nasser . . . ", Nov. 11, 1955, MG26 N1, v. 37; and "Diary", MG26 N1, v. 68 (NAC). See also *Mike, II:* 220-3.

46 These are described in Shimon Shamir, "The Collapse of Project Alpha", in Louis and Owens, eds., *Suez 1956,* 76-8.

47 LBP to T.W.L. MacDermot, Dec. 12, 1955, MG26 N1, v. 8 (NAC); and Maudling to Lloyd, Dec. 6, 1955, PREM 11/1022/119429 (PRO).

48 R.A.D. Ford, "Conversation between the Minister and the Ambassador of Israel", Dec. 23, 1955, MG26 N1, v. 37 (NAC).

49 Maudling to Lloyd, Dec. 6, 1955.

50 Ford, "Conversation", Dec. 23, 1955; Pearson-Comay Talks, Dec. 23, 1955, Israeli State Archives 2414/19.

51 Fry, "Canada, the North Atlantic Triangle, and the U.N.", 286.

52 LBP to GP, Feb. 25, 1956 (PPP).

53 LBP to T.W.L. MacDermot, March 3, 1956, MG26 N1, v. 8 (NAC).

54 LBP to St. Laurent, May 10, 1956, MG26 N1, v. 37 (NAC).

55 Evelyn Shuckburgh, *Descent to Suez: Diaries 1951-1956* (London: Weidenfeld and Nicolson, 1986), 345; and LBP to St. Laurent, May 9, 1956, St. Laurent Papers, MG26L, v. 220, file U-20 (NAC). On the Baghdad Pact, see Kyle, *Suez,* 111ff.

56 Brian Urquhart, *Hammarskjöld* (New York: Harper and Row, 1972), 153.

57 Pearson to Hammarskjöld, May 19, 1956, MG26 N1, v. 37 (NAC). See Geoffrey Pearson's comments in Peter Stursberg, *Lester Pearson and the American Dilemma* (Toronto: Doubleday, 1980), 149.

58 The best account is in Robert Bowie, "Eisenhower, Dulles, and the Suez Crisis", in Louis and Owens, eds., *Suez 1956,* 190-6.

59 Quoted in Horne, *Macmillan, I:* 395.

60 Commonwealth Relations Office to U.K. High Commissioner in Canada [July 27, 1956], PREM 1094/1/9429 (PRO); and LBP to Robertson, July 28, 1956, MG26 N1, v. 37 (NAC). See also, Fry, "Canada, the North Atlantic Triangle and the U.N.", 288ff, and Granatstein, *Man of Influence,* 298ff.

61 WC[?] to H. Smedley, July 30, 1956, PREM 11/1094/1/9429 (PRO).

62 U.K. High Commissioner to Commonwealth Relations Office, July 30, 1956, PREM 11/1094/1/9429 (PRO); and U.K. High Commissioner to Commonwealth Relations Office, *ibid.*

63 Commonwealth Relations Office to High Commissioner, Ottawa, Aug. 1, 1956, *ibid.*

64 *Ibid.*

65 Granatstein, *Man of Influence,* 299. See also Pearson's comments to Dulles in Kyle, *Suez,* 101.

66 Commonwealth Relations Office, "The Use of Force over Suez", Aug. 9, 1956, PREM 11/1094/1/9429 (PRO).

67 "Record of Conversation between the Secretary of State for Commonwealth Relations and the Canadian High Commissioner — 15th August 1956", *ibid.;* Ambrose, *Eisenhower: The President,* 332ff; and Home to Eden, Aug. 17, 1956, PREM 11/1094/1/9429 (PRO).

68 LBP to External Affairs, Sept. 5, 1956, MG26 N1, v. 37 (NAC); and Anthony Eden, *Full Circle: The Memoirs of Sir Anthony Eden* (Boston: Houghton Mifflin, 1960), 458.

69 LBP to External, Sept. 17, 1956, MG26 N1, v. 37 (NAC).

70 Cabinet Conclusions, Sept. 27, 1956, RG2, v. 5775 (NAC).

71 Meir to LBP, Oct. 12, 1956, quoted in Oren, "Canada and the Arms Race", 299.

The Egyptians did not protest the sale vehemently. Herbert Norman to LBP, Oct. 6, 1956, RG25, file 50372-40, v. 8 (NAC).

72 See LBP to Robertson, MG26 N1, v. 37 (NAC).

73 House of Commons, *Debates*, Oct. 15, 1956.

74 Quoted in Fry, "Canada, the North Atlantic Triangle, and the U.N.", 306.

75 Robert Rhodes James, *Anthony Eden: A Biography* (New York: McGraw-Hill, 1987), 527; and Kyle, *Suez*, 319-20.

76 Roy Fullick and Geoffrey Powell, *Suez: The Double War* (London: Leo Cooper, 1990), 88-90; see also the discussion and documents in David Carlton, *Britain and the Suez Crisis* (Oxford: Basil Blackwell, 1988).

77 LBP to Embassy, Paris, Oct. 30, 1956, MG26 N1, v. 38 (NAC); LBP to Embassy, Washington, *ibid.*, v. 37. The superb account by Michael Fry ("Canada, the North Atlantic Triangle, and the U.N.") suggests (306) that Robertson had one hour's notice. This does not seem to be true.

78 *Mike, II:* 237-8; and Eden to U.K. high commissioners in Canada/New Zealand/South Africa, Oct. 30, 1956, PREM 11/1096/1/9516 (PRO). The telegram was sent at 20:00 London time, which would be 3:00 p.m. Ottawa time, one and a half hours before Eden spoke. The message reached St. Laurent at 5:00 p.m. St. Laurent to Eden, Oct. 31, 1956, MG26 N1, v. 37 (NAC).

79 *Mike, II:* 238.

80 St. Laurent to Eden, Oct. 31, 1956, MG26 N1, v. 37 (NAC). This copy indicates that St. Laurent made almost no changes.

81 Grant Dexter, "Historic Step at United Nations", *Winnipeg Free Press,* Nov. 13, 1958. Dexter was Pearson's confidant, and the story is almost certainly correct.

82 *New York Times,* May 31, 1956. Holmes is quoted in Stursberg, *Lester Pearson and the American Dilemma,* 143.

83 Robertson to LBP, Nov. 1, 1956, MG26 N5, v. 85 (NAC). See also, Granatstein, *Man of Influence,* 302-5; and Robertson, *Crisis,* 183-5.

84 There are discrepancies between the account by Urquhart, Hammarskjöld's biographer, who claims that Pearson told Hammarskjöld *before* the Assembly meeting on Nov. 1 (Urquhart, *Hammarskjöld,* 176) and Pearson's account, which suggests that it was raised on Nov. 2 (*Mike, II:* 247). The account of Eden's idea of the U.N. force in David Carlton's recent *Britain and the Suez Crisis,* 72, suggests that the U.N. force came up first on Nov. 2 and that Eden was reluctant. This does not accord with the Robertson-Kirkpatrick discussions on the morning of Nov. 1 described above.

85 Geoffrey Murray, "Glimpses of Suez 1956", *International Journal* (Winter 1973-4), 46-8; and Urquhart, *Hammarskjöld,* 176.

86 Department of External Affairs, *The Crisis in the Middle East* (Ottawa: Queen's Printer, 1957), 10; and Dulles-Lodge conversation, Nov. 2, 1956, Dulles Papers, Box 5 (Eisenhower Library, Abilene, Kansas). Holmes, *The Shaping of Peace,* 359.

87 Cabinet Conclusions, Nov. 3, 1956, RG2, v. 5775 (NAC); *Mike, II:* 248-9; Eayrs, *Canada in World Affairs,* 260; Urquhart, *Hammarskjöld,* 176; and A.D.P. Heeney, Memorandum for File, Nov. 3, 1956, MG26 N5, v. 85 (NAC).

88 Heeney, *ibid;* and *Mike, II:* 250.

89 See the very full and accurate account in Robertson, *Crisis,* 206.

90 Urquhart, *Hammarskjöld,* 177.

91 Interview with John Holmes. Holmes, "Memorandum for the Minister", Dec. 6, 1956, MG26 N5, v. 85 (NAC).

92 The account of the UNEF formation in *Mike* draws directly from the documents. Indeed, much of it was written at the time by Mike or John Holmes. *Mike, II:* 250-73. Also, interview with Sir Brian Urquhart. See also, Stursburg, *Lester Pearson and the American Dilemma,* 153ff. Pearson's arguments in New York are found in BEU DAG 1/2.3, Box 85, file 491 (United Nations Archives, New York).

93 *Mike, II:* 275-6, and interview with Mary Macdonald. *Ottawa Journal,* Oct. 15, 1957. A good summary of Pearson and Suez based on secondary works and some primary documents is Helen Adams, "Canada and the Suez Crisis 1956" (MA thesis, Acadia University, 1988).

94 *Globe and Mail,* Nov. 5, 1956.

95 House of Commons, *Debates,* Nov. 26-7, 1956.

96 *Mike, II:* 274. See the full letter justifying the stand.

97 Charles Ritchie, *Diplomatic Passport* (Toronto: Macmillan, 1981), 120, 122.

98 Horne, *Macmillan, I,* 446.

99 Carlton, *Britain and the Suez Crisis,* 73.

100 William P. Bundy (Acheson's son-in-law), in Stursberg, *Pearson and the American Dilemma,* 159.

101 *Ibid.,* 157.

102 Carlton, *Britain and the Suez Crisis,* 110.

103 Gunnar Jahn, quoted in L.B. Pearson, *The Four Faces of Peace,* ed., S.G. Pierson, ed. (New York: Dodd Mead, 1964), 3.

104 *Mike, II:* 277. Ralph Bunche, a Nobel winner, and Mahmoud Fawzi agreed that Pearson had been central in resolving the crisis. See RJB file, Nov. 6, 1956, BEU DAG V.2.3, Box 331, file 2579 (United Nations Archives, New York).

CHAPTER 5: GRITTERDÄMMERUNG

1 Bruce Hutchison, *Canada: Tomorrow's Giant* (Don Mills, Ont.: Longman, 1957), 5.

2 *Ibid.,* foreword (n.p.).

3 Bruce Hutchison, *The Unfinished Country: To Canada with "Love and Some Misgivings"* (Vancouver and Toronto: Douglas and McIntyre, 1985), 86. On the role of the journalists, see Patrick Brennan, "'A Responsible Civilized Relationship': Reporting the Nation's Business", unpublished manuscript.

4 Dalton Camp, *Gentlemen, Players and Politicians* (Toronto: McClelland and Stewart, 1970), 137-8; and Reginald Whitaker, *The Government Party: Organizing and Financing the Liberal Party of Canada, 1930-1958* (Toronto: University of Toronto Press, 1977), 402.

5 Hutchison, *Canada,* 129-30, 141-2.

6 Gotlieb and Cadieux comments are found in the transcript of the Norman Robertson "Round Table" discussion, Feb. 18, 1978 (External Affairs Records, Historical Section). See ch. 3, n. 37. M. Cadieux spoke of this question with some passion in a conversation with me in 1978. On the general question of External and bilingualism see Gilles Lalande, *The Department of External Affairs and Biculturalism* (Ottawa: Information Canada, 1970).

7 On the resignations, see J.W. Pickersgill, *My Years with Louis St. Laurent* (Toronto: University of Toronto Press, 1975), 214-19. I asked Abbott about Pickersgill's account shortly after publication. Abbott claimed that Pickersgill was incorrect in his suggestion that he had asked for the Supreme Court vacancy. He claimed that St. Laurent offered it to him after he asked for a Senate seat. R.S. Bothwell and J.R. English interview with D.C. Abbott, Nov. 5, 1975.

8 J.L. Granatstein, *A Man of Influence: Norman A. Robertson and Canadian Statecraft, 1929-1968* (Ottawa: Deneau, 1981), 322.

9 See Douglas Fullerton, *Graham Tower and His Times* (Toronto: McClelland and Stewart, 1986), 270-3.

10 Interview with Mary Macdonald.

11 LBP to Geoffrey Pearson (GP), Feb. 25, 1956 (PPP).

12 Paul-Henri Spaak, *The Continuing Battle: Memoirs of a European, 1936-1966* (Boston: Little Brown, 1971), 260; Heeney to Pearson, Dec. 7, 1956, MG26 N1, v. 84 (NAC); Ritchie to Pearson, Oct. 29, 1956, *ibid.;* Heeney Diary, June 3-5, 1956, MG30 E194 (NAC).

13 Mary Macdonald to LBP, Jan. 29, 1955, MG26 N1, v. 18; and M. Macdonald to LBP, Sept. 11, 1956, *ibid.*

14 L.B. Pearson, *Mike: The Memoirs of the Right Honourable Lester B. Pearson.*

Volume II: 1948-1957 (Toronto: University of Toronto Press, 1973), 15; and Macdonald to LBP, Sept. 11, 1956.

15 Hutchison to Dexter, Apr. 7, 1955, Hutchison Papers (University of Calgary).

16 Heeney Diary, Mar. 17, 1955, MG30 E114 (NAC). Robert Bothwell and William Kilbourn in *C.D. Howe: A Biography* (Toronto: McClelland and Stewart, 1979), 293-4, claim Robert Winters was Howe's favourite, but Winters was probably regarded as too young.

17 Brennan, "A Responsible Civilized Relationship", 329.

18 *Ibid.*, 328.

19 Ferguson to LBP, Feb. 23, 1956 (PPP).

20 Charles Ritchie, *Diplomatic Passport: More Undiplomatic Diaries, 1946-1962* (Toronto: Macmillan, 1981), 107-8.

21 This account draws on William Kilbourn, *Pipeline: TransCanada and the Great Debate* (Toronto: Clarke Irwin, 1970), 110-33; and Bothwell and Kilbourn, *C.D. Howe,* ch. 18; Knowles's comment is in Peter Stursberg, *Lester Pearson and the Dream of Unity* (Toronto: Doubleday, 1978), 38-9. The Hansard record and Pearson's comment are in L.B. Pearson, *Mike: The Memoirs of the Right Honourable Lester B. Pearson, Volume III: 1957-1968* (Toronto: University of Toronto Press, 1975), 7-12.

22 Howe to H.R. MacMillan, June 7, 1956, Howe Papers, v. 185 (NAC).

23 Heeney Diary, Dec. 7, 1954; Mar. 17, 1955; Dec. 6, 1955; and Feb. 28-9, 1956, MG30 E144 (NAC). The fact that Heeney is constantly concerned about his own future perhaps explains why Pearson's future is also a topic.

24 *Ibid.*, June 3-5, 1956.

25 *Ibid.*, June 9-11, 1956.

26 Howe to Jimmy Gardiner, May 24, 1958, Howe Papers, v. 107 (NAC).

27 Quoted in Peter Newman, *Renegade in Power: The Diefenbaker Years* (Toronto: McClelland and Stewart, 1964), 34.

28 *Financial Post,* Dec. 29, 1956.

29 See, for example, Paul Martin, *A Very Public Life: Volume II: So Many Worlds* (Toronto: Deneau, 1985), 259. Also, interview with Paul Martin. Harris was regarded as the favourite of Jack Pickersgill. On the budget and "six-buck Harris", see Pickersgill, *My Years with St. Laurent,* 319. On Harris as a potential successor, see Stursberg, *Lester Pearson and the Dream of Unity,* 42,49.

30 Montreal *Gazette,* Jan. 11, 1957. House of Commons, *Debates,* Jan. 9, 1957.

31 Interviews with Walter Harris, Douglas Abbott, and Paul Martin. J.L. Granatstein, for example, has spoken of Pearson's ambition in his *The Ottawa Men: The Civil Service Mandarins* (Toronto: Oxford, 1982), 84. It is also a subtext in *A Man of Influence.* Harris (interview of Oct. 22, 1975) said that

Pearson told him in the late 1940s that he would be the next leader. Harris did not think Pearson was familiar enough with politics to be leader. Abbott made his comment to Robert Bothwell and myself on November 5, 1975.

32 *Mike, III:* 27-8.

33 Christina McCall-Newman, *Grits: An Intimate Portrait of the Liberal Party* (Toronto: Macmillan, 1982), 32. It is a constant theme of the Hutchison-Dexter correspondence. See Brennan, "A Responsible Civilized Relationship", 400ff.

34 *Mike, III:* 13-14.

35 Whitaker, *Government Party,* 414.

36 Heeney Diary, June 9-11, 1956, v. 2, MG30 E114 (NAC); and LBP to GP, Feb. 7, 1956 (PPP).

37 Stephen Leacock, "Greater Canada: An Appeal", *University Magazine* (Apr. 1917), 136. On Ed Pearson and the Wrong-Pearson attitudes see vol. 1, chs. 2, 6-8.

38 Eugene Forsey's comments are found in his *Freedom and Order* (Toronto: McClelland and Stewart, 1974), 91.

39 *Mike, III:* 4; and interviews with George Ignatieff and confidential interview.

40 Victor Mackie quoted in Stursberg, *Lester Pearson and the Dream of Unity,* 35. Paul Hellyer's opinion is found in his *Damn the Torpedoes: My Fight to Unify Canada's Armed Forces* (Toronto: McClelland and Stewart, 1990), 15.

41 *Mike, II:* 19-20. See also Pearson's *Democracy in World Politics* (Toronto: Saunders, 1955), esp. v-vi.

42 Heeney Diary, Apr. 16, 1957, v. 2, MG30 E114 (NAC).

43 The Norman case is the subject of two major books, which use the same documents to reach dramatically opposed conclusions. James Barros, in *No Sense of Evil: Espionage, The Case of Herbert Norman* (Toronto: Deneau, 1986), builds a strong case that Norman was an "agent of influence". Roger Bowen, in *Innocence Is Not Enough: The Life and Death of Herbert Norman* (Vancouver: Douglas and McIntyre, 1986), argues that Norman was the victim of a witch hunt. J.L. Granatstein's and David Stafford's *Spy Wars: Espionage and Canada from Gouzenko to Glasnost* (Toronto: Key Porter, 1990) is ambivalent and treats the charges against Norman as "not proven". When the Norman case was taken up in the House of Commons, External Affairs and International Trade Canada commissioned Peyton Lyon to examine the documents to determine whether Barros's charges against Norman were valid. Lyon concluded they were not. See *The Loyalties of E. Herbert Norman* (Ottawa: External Affairs and International Trade Canada, 1990). Arthur Kilgour, who was in Cairo with Norman, offered an odd interpretation of Norman's suicide that does not reflect well on Norman (*Globe and Mail,* Apr. 3, 1990). The best review of the controversy is by Norman Hillmer in the *Canadian Historical Review* (Dec. 1988), 563-4. Reg

Whitaker's attack on Barros is found in "Return to the Crucible", *Canadian Forum* (Nov. 1986), 11-28.

44 *Toronto Daily Star,* Apr. 4, 1957.

45 On the IPR, see Barros, *No Sense of Evil,* 22-8; and, more sympathetically, John Thomas, *The Institute of Pacific Relations: Asian Scholars and American Politics* (Seattle: University of Washington Press, 1974). Also, J.K. Fairbank, *Chinabound: A Fifty Year Memoir* (New York: Harper Colophon, 1983), 320-4.

46 Herbert Norman, *Japan's Emergence as a Modern State: Political and Economic Problems of the Meiji Period* (New York: Institute of Pacific Relations, 1940).

47 Quoted in Christopher Andrew and Oleg Gordievsky, *KGB: The Inside Story* (New York: Harper Collins, 1990), 210. On the "Cambridge 5", see also Goronwy Rees, *A Chapter of Accidents* (London: Chatto and Windus, 1971); Victor Kiernan, "Herbert Norman's Cambridge", in Roger Bowen, ed., *E.H. Norman: His Life and Scholarship* (Toronto: University of Toronto Press, 1984); Robert Cecil, "The Cambridge Comintern", in Christopher Andrew and David Dilks, eds., *The Missing Dimension: Governments and Intelligence Communities in the Twentieth Century* (London: Macmillan, 1984); and Michael Straight, *After Long Silence* (London: Collins, 1983) for reflections on Cambridge by three who were there.

48 Straight, *After Long Silence,* 60-1.

49 Rees, *Chapter of Accidents,* 110-11; Norman to Howard Norman, quoted in Bowen, *Innocence Is Not Enough,* 65.

50 See Barros, *No Sense of Evil,* 32-6; H.S. Ferns, *Reading from Left to Right* (Toronto: University of Toronto Press, 1983), 218-19; and Granatstein, *Ottawa Men,* 259.

51 See vol. 1, 245-6. The "History of Examination Unit" with documents was released to me by the Department of National Defence. It reveals that Norman thrived on intelligence work and was anxious for assignments in that area.

52 See Barros, *No Sense of Evil,* 37. I could not locate this letter, which Professor Barros found in CIA files in Canadian records.

53 L.B. Pearson Diary, Feb. 13, 1943, MG26 N8, v. 8 (NAC); *ibid.,* May 26-30, 1943.

54 Pearson to Robertson, Oct. 24, 1944, External Affairs Records, RG25 A12, v. 2120 (NAC); and Barros, *No Sense of Evil,* 198.

55 See Barros, *No Sense of Evil,* 159-62. June Callwood's *Emma* (Toronto: Stoddart, 1984) expresses doubt about the story (99).

56 *Mike, III:* 166. The Malania story is told in Denis Smith, *The Diplomacy of Fear: Canada and the Cold War, 1941-1948* (Toronto: University of Toronto Press, 1988), 115-16. On Kiernan, see his article "Herbert Norman's Cambridge", in Bowen, ed., *His Life and Scholarship,* 25-46.

57 Smith, *ibid.* On Hiss, see Allan Weinstein, *Perjury: The Hiss-Chambers Case* (New York: Random House, 1979), 366.

58 Quoted in Andrew and Gordievsky, *KGB*, 214. Recent evidence on the extent of Maclean's commitment reveals a deeper and more damaging role in the 1930s. See *The Guardian,* June 25, 1992.

59 *Mike, III:* 166.

60 Ottawa *Citizen,* May 3, 1950.

61 Fairbank, *Chinabound,* 333.

62 Review of Robert Newman's *Owen Lattimore and the "Loss" of China, The Economist* (May 23, 1992), 95.

63 The subject is covered well in Bowen, *Innocence Is Not Enough,* ch. 6.

64 *Ibid.,* 216-17.

65 On Irene Norman, see *ibid.,* 225. Barros discusses the interrogation in *No Sense of Evil,* 67-79.

66 Barros, *ibid.,* 70; and Bowen, *Innocence Is Not Enough,* 225, 229-30.

67 Quoted in Bowen, *ibid.,* 211. Interview with G.P. Glazebrook.

68 Department of External Affairs, *Statements and Speeches* 51/14. See also, ch. 2.

69 See, for example, *Globe and Mail,* Aug. 11, 1951. Also, State Department Records 742.001/8-1451 (NA) for the Canadian protest and reaction.

70 See vol. 1, 303ff.

71 The investigation is described in Bowen, *Innocence Is Not Enough,* ch. 8; and Barros, *No Sense of Evil,* 88 ff.

72 *Ibid.;* interviews with G.P. Glazebrook and T.J. Guernsey; and Pearson to Norman, Mar. 3, 1952, External Affairs Records, RG32 C2, v. 339 (NAC).

73 See *Mike, III:* 167; *Toronto Daily Star,* Nov. 23, 1953; and Pearson FBI file, Access no. 262554E.

74 Both Welch and Reston are quoted in Edwin Bayley, *Joe McCarthy and the Press* (Madison: University of Wisconsin Press, 1981), 208.

75 On these postings, see Bowen, *Innocence Is Not Enough,* 272-3.

76 *Ibid.,* 293ff.

77 *Globe and Mail,* Mar. 16, 1957.

78 "Middle East Crisis: Diary of Developments in New York, March 16-17 [1957]", MG26 N1, v. 63 (NAC).

79 *Globe and Mail,* Apr. 11, 1957.

80 Heeney Diary, Apr. 16, 1951, Heeney Papers, MG30 E44, v. 2 (NAC).

81 L.B. Nichols to Tolson, Apr. 12, 1957, FBI Pearson file; and A. Belmont to L. Boardman, Apr. 12, 1957, *ibid.*

82 *Globe and Mail,* Apr. 13, 1957, and Apr. 18, 1957. Pearson responded to articles by Arthur Blakely in the Montreal *Gazette* that complained about the vagueness of the statement on the 12th.

83 Heeney Diary, Apr. 16 and 23, 1957, MG30 E44, v. 2 (NAC).

84 "The Prime Minister", Apr. 15, 1957, MG26 N1, v. 84 (NAC).

85 LBP to Casey, Apr. 18, 1957, MG26 N1, v. 84 (NAC).

86 "The Prime Minister", Apr. 15, 1957.

87 Not only Barros but also his critic Reg Whitaker holds this viewpoint.

88 The External Affairs draft history has as its chapter title "One of Us" (unpublished ms.).

89 LBP to Crerar, May 18, 1956, MG26 N1, v. 3 (NAC). Noel Annan, *Our Age: Portrait of a Generation* (London: Weidenfeld and Nicolson, 1990).

90 Annan, *ibid,* 425. On the homosexual issue, see *Globe and Mail,* Apr. 24, 1992. On Bryce, see the interview with him, *Toronto Star,* Apr. 5, 1981.

CHAPTER 6: THE DUEL

1 Peter Stursberg, *Lester Pearson and the Dream of Unity* (Toronto: Doubleday, 1978), 40.

2 John Meisel, *The Canadian General Election of 1957* (Toronto: University of Toronto Press, 1962), 190; and Peter Regenstreif, *The Diefenbaker Interlude: Parties and Voting in Canada* (Don Mills, Ont.: Longman, 1965), 10.

3 Dale Thomson, *Louis St. Laurent: Canadian* (Toronto: Macmillan, 1967), 502-3.

4 *Globe and Mail,* June 3, 1957.

5 *Ibid.*

6 J.W. Pickersgill, *My Years with Louis St. Laurent* (Toronto: University of Toronto Press, 1975), 324.

7 *Winnipeg Free Press,* June 3, 1957; Meisel, *Election of 1957;* and *Le Devoir,* June 4, 1957.

8 *Globe and Mail,* June 3, 1957. Others despaired about the state of the Liberal machine. See Grant Dexter to T.A. Crerar, May 23, 1957, Crerar Papers, v. 105 (Queen's University Archives).

9 See Thomson, *Louis St. Laurent,* 506-7. For Pearson's view of Victoria, see L.B. Pearson, *Mike: The Memoirs of the Right Honourable Lester B. Pearson. Volume III: 1957-1968* (Toronto: University of Toronto Press, 1975), 16-17.

10 Thomson, *ibid.,* 516; *Mike, III:* 18-19; and *Globe and Mail,* June 8, 1957.

11 *Maclean's,* June 22, 1957.

12 Peter Newman, *Renegade in Power: The Diefenbaker Years* (Toronto: McClelland and Stewart, 1963), 34.

13 Meisel, *Election of 1957*, 157.

14 Norman Ward and David Smith, *Jimmy Gardiner: Relentless Liberal* (Toronto: University of Toronto Press, 1990), 314.

15 See *Mike, III:* ch. 1. Also, interviews with Paul Martin, J.W. Pickersgill, and Douglas Abbott.

16 House of Commons, *Debates*, Nov. 26, 1956.

17 Meisel, *Election of 1957*, 56-9, 254-5; and House of Commons, *Debates*, Nov. 29, 1956. The evidence suggests a marked shift of English-Canadian Protestants towards the Conservatives.

18 Quoted in Meisel, *Election of 1957*, 58.

19 House of Commons, *Debates*, Feb. 11, 1957. See also Denis Smith, *Gentle Patriot: A Political Biography of Walter Gordon* (Edmonton: Hurtig, 1973), ch. 2; and Walter Gordon, *A Political Memoir* (Toronto: McClelland and Stewart, 1977), ch. 4.

20 P.W. Kriebel to State Dept., Mar. 13, 1957, State Department Records 742.00/3-1357 (NA). Also, Ambassador Livingston Merchant to Dulles, Jan. 18, 1957, State Department Records 611.42/1-1857 (NA).

21 LBP to Richard Casey, Apr. 18, 1957, MG26 N1, v. 2 (NAC); and Heeney Diary, Mar. 25, 1956 and Apr. 23, 1957, MG30 E144, v. 2 (NAC).

22 Polling indicates that it was the better-educated anglophones who defected first. See Regenstreif, *The Diefenbaker Interlude*, 47. On the correlation of Conservatism with English Canadianism, see Janine Brodie and Jane Jenson, *Crisis, Challenge and Change: Party and Politics in Canada* (Toronto: Methuen, 1980), 248.

23 Livingston Merchant to Julian Nugent, June 18, 1957, State Department Records 742.00/6-1157 (NA).

24 On this important subject, see Joseph Jockel's definitive *No Boundaries Upstairs: Canada, the United States and the Origins of the North American Air Defence, 1945-1958* (Vancouver: University of British Columbia Press, 1987).

25 Merchant to Acheson, May 11, 1961, Acheson Papers, Series I, Box 22, file 282 (Yale University Archives). Interviews with Bruce Hutchison and William P. Bundy.

26 Acheson to LBP, June 12, 1957, Acheson Papers, Series I, Box 24, file 310 (Yale University Archives); and LBP to Acheson, June 17, 1957, *ibid.*

27 Meisel, *Election of 1957*, 251-2; and Brodie and Jenson, *Crisis, Challenge and Change*, 248-9.

28 LBP to Curtis, June 17, 1957, MG26 N1, v. 29 (NAC).

29 Not all ministers agreed. Jimmy Gardiner and Paul Martin strongly dissented. See Martin's comments in Stursberg, *Lester Pearson and the Dream of Unity*, 40-1. On Gardiner, see Ward and Smith, *Jimmy Gardiner*, 317.

30 Dexter to Tom Kent, Oct. 9, 1957, Dexter Papers, v. 7 (Queen's University Archives).

31 Hutchison to LBP, Aug. [?], 1957, MG26 N1, v. 36 (NAC).

32 *Mike, III:* 24-5.

33 *Ibid*. Interview with Lionel Chevrier. St. Laurent's biographer and former secretary, Dale Thomson, seems to confirm Chevrier's account. See Thomson, *Louis St. Laurent*, 524. Pickersgill was not informed of the decision until it happened and was hurt by the action of the prime minister he most admired. J.W. Pickersgill, *The Road Back, by a Liberal in Opposition* (Toronto: University of Toronto Press, 1986), 13. See Lionel Chevrier, "The Practical Diplomacy of Lester Pearson", *International Journal* (Winter 1973-74), 127-8.

34 *Toronto Daily Star*, Sept. 7, 9, 1957. Pearson actually had a column in the *Star* the same day. Also, *Globe and Mail*, Sept. 7, 1957.

35 Pickersgill, *The Road Back*, 15; and *Globe and Mail*, Sept. 3, 1957.

36 *Toronto Daily Star*, Sept. 12, 1957.

37 Robert Bothwell and William Kilbourn, *C.D. Howe: A Biography* (Toronto: McClelland and Stewart, 1979), 336; interview with Paul Martin.

38 *Globe and Mail*, Oct. 24, 1957; Halifax *Chronicle-Herald*, Nov. 14, 1957; and House of Commons, *Debates*, Oct. 23, 1957. Also, Grant Dexter to Tom Kent, Oct. 9, 1957, Dexter Papers, TC746 (Queen's University Archives).

39 Paul Hellyer agrees that the Nobel Prize assured Pearson's victory, but press comment and private correspondence at the time do not support his interpretation that Harris was the front runner at that point.

40 *Globe and Mail*, Dec. 19, 20, 1957; and Gordon to LBP, Dec. 14, 1957, MG26 N1, v. 36 (NAC).

41 *Toronto Daily Star*, Dec. 20, 1957.

42 Gordon to Pearson, Dec. 14, 1957, MG26 N1, v. 36 (NAC). See also, Paul Martin, *A Very Public Life, Volume II. So Many Worlds* (Toronto: Deneau, 1985), 310ff.

43 *Toronto Daily Star*, Jan. 7, 1958; and Pickersgill, *The Road Back*, 16.

44 Martin, *A Very Public Life, II*, 314-15.

45 Stursberg, *Lester Pearson and the Dream of Unity*, 48-9. *Globe and Mail*, Jan. 14, 1958.

46 *Winnipeg Free Press*, Jan. 14, 1957.

47 *Winnipeg Free Press*, Jan. 17, 1958.

48 *Ibid.; Globe and Mail*, Jan. 17, 1958; and *Mike, III:* 30-1.

49 Bruce Hutchison, *The Far Side of the Street* (Toronto: Macmillan, 1976), 242; and *Globe and Mail*, Jan. 17, 1958. See also, Tom Kent's account in *A Public Purpose: An Experience of Liberal Opposition and Canadian Government* (Kingston and Montreal: McGill-Queen's University Press, 1988), 58ff.

50 Hutchison's description of Pickersgill's explanation of the motion is in *The Far Side of the Street*, 243. Dexter was aware how dangerous an election would be. See Grant Dexter to Tom Kent, Oct. 9 and 23, 1957, Dexter Papers, TC746 (Queen's University Archives). The Liberals were clearly unprepared. Dexter said of Pickersgill: "Jack is running wild, reaching out for all kinds of responsibility he has no right to and no fitness to discharge." See also Pickersgill, *The Road Back*, 16-17.

51 House of Commons, *Debates*, Jan. 20, 1958; and *Mike, III:* 33.

52 House of Commons, *Debates*, Jan. 20, 1958; J.L. Granatstein, *Canada 1957-1967: The Years of Uncertainty and Innovation* (Toronto: McClelland and Stewart, 1986), 34-5; Mitchell Sharp, Memoirs, unpublished ms.; and on the provenance of the document, Patrick Nicholson, *Vision and Indecision* (Toronto: Longmans, 1968), chs. 4 and 5.

53 *Winnipeg Free Press*, Feb. 3, 1958.

54 Stursberg, *Lester Pearson and the Dream of Unity*, 52-3.

55 See Regenstreif, *The Diefenbaker Interlude*, 33.

56 *Ibid.;* and *Globe and Mail*, Feb. 18, 1958.

57 Interviews with Herbert Moody and Tom Kent; *Winnipeg Free Press*, Mar. 5, 1958.

58 Stursberg, *Lester Pearson and the Dream of Unity*, 54.

59 *Ibid.;* and Newman, *Renegade in Power*, 75.

60 *Globe and Mail*, Mar. 25, 1958; *ibid.*, Mar. 15, 1958; *Kitchener-Waterloo Record*, Mar. 6, 1958; *Mike, III:* 35.

61 Hutchison to Acheson, Mar. 22, 1963, Acheson Papers, Series 1, Box 16 (Yale University Archives).

62 Interview with Bruce Hutchison. See also, Patrick Brennan's unpublished manuscript "A Responsible, Civilized Relationship". Hutchison's recollections of Pearson are also found in his fine memoir, *The Far Side of the Street (passim)*, and in his *The Unfinished Country* (Vancouver: Douglas and McIntyre, 1985), 242-8.

63 Hutchison, *Unfinished Country*, 242.

64 Dexter to Kent, Oct. 9 and 23, 1957, Dexter Papers, TC746 (Queen's University Archives).

65 Hutchison to Dexter, April 1958, Hutchison Papers (University of Calgary Archives).

66 Gordon to LBP, Jan. 21, 1949, Gordon Papers, MG32 B44, v.1 (NAC); and LBP to Gordon, Jan. 17, 1949, *ibid.*

67 McCarthy to LBP, Apr. 30, 1957, MG26 N1, v.36 (NAC); and LBP to McCarthy, May 8, 1957, *ibid.*

68 Pearson/Chester correspondence (private collection, Patricia Pearson Hannah).

69 Christina McCall-Newman, *Grits: An Intimate Portrait of the Liberal Party* (Toronto: Macmillan, 1982), 24.

70 See ch. 8. Also, confidential interview.

71 I am most grateful to my former student Frank Clarke, whose important work on Gordon's royal commission is the source of these details.

72 Macdonald to LBP, Apr. 22, 1953, MG26 N1, v. 8 (NAC); and Macdonald to LBP, Aug. 16, 1956, *ibid.*

73 McCall-Newman, *Grits,* 73.

74 Dexter to Tom Kent, Oct. 9 and 23, 1957, Dexter Papers, TC746 (Queen's University Archives).

75 Hutchison to Dexter, "Spring 1958", Hutchison Papers (University of Calgary Archives); and Hutchison to Dexter, "April 1958", *ibid.* Kent issued a pamphlet criticizing Gordon in 1958 and his call for restrictions on foreign investment.

76 Underhill to LBP, Jan. 20, 1958, Underhill Papers, v. 13 (NAC).

77 LBP to Underhill, Feb. 11, 1958, *ibid.*

78 McCall-Newman, *Grits,* 35.

79 *Ibid.,* 34. Keith Davey, *The Rainmaker: A Passion for Politics* (Toronto: Stoddart, 1986), 23; Gordon Dryden to Hugh Mackenzie, Oct. 17, 1957, MG26 N1, v. 36 (NAC).

80 See Pickersgill, *The Road Back;* Kent, *A Public Purpose;* and Gordon, *A Political Memoir.*

81 Dexter to Tom Kent, May 8, 1958, Dexter Papers, TC747 (Queen's University Archives); and Hutchison to Dexter, Nov. 1, 1958, Hutchison Papers (University of Calgary Archives).

CHAPTER 7: THE LIBERAL HOUR

1 Peter Newman, *The Distemper of Our Times: Canadian Politics in Transition* (Toronto: McClelland and Stewart, 1990; original ed., 1968), 27. This valuable journalistic study was based on excellent Liberal contacts, particularly Maurice Sauvé, whom his colleagues suspected of "leaking" to Newman. Walter Gordon also seems to have spoken quite freely with Newman.

2 These letters are found in MG26 N1, v. 8 (NAC).

3 Norman to LBP, Mar. 29, 1957, quoted in full in Roger Bowen, *Innocence Is Not Enough: The Life and Death of Herbert Norman* (Toronto: Douglas and McIntyre, 1986), 337-8.

4 Interview with Professor Denis Smith.

5 Interviews with Mary Macdonald, Patricia Pearson Hannah, and Landon Pearson. Maryon Pearson to "Issy" Chester, no date [Nov. 1965] (correspondence in possession of Patricia Pearson Hannah). Pearson's favourable comments are found in L.B. Pearson, *Mike: Memoirs of the Right Honourable Lester B. Pearson. Volume III: 1957-1968* (Toronto: University of Toronto Press, 1975), 42-4.

6 Pearson, *Mike, III:* 45.

7 Grattan O'Leary, *Recollection of People, Press, and Politics* (Toronto: Macmillan, 1977), 137.

8 Peter Stursberg, *Diefenbaker: Leadership Gained, 1956-1962* (Toronto: University of Toronto Press, 1975), 26.

9 Garrett Wilson and Kevin Wilson, *Diefenbaker for the Defence* (Toronto: Lorimer, 1988), 66-7.

10 *Ibid.;* and Basil Robinson, *Diefenbaker's World: A Populist in Foreign Affairs* (Toronto: University of Toronto Press, 1989), 314. I interviewed John Diefenbaker twice in 1978 for another project and observed personally his tendency not to listen to questions. He was very witty with a quick mind, but was unable to focus on the questions I asked. He was especially friendly because my grandmother had asked me to get an autographed photograph. She had it above her bed until the day she died and, until that day, pointed it out to every visitor.

11 On Macdonnell, see Diefenbaker's comments in *One Canada: The Memoirs of the Rt. Hon. John G. Diefenbaker: The Years of Achievement, 1957-1962* (Toronto: Macmillan, 1976). Fleming's anger is directed against Diefenbaker in his memoirs, *So Very Near: The Political Memoirs of the Honourable Donald M. Fleming. Volume 2: The Summit Years* (Toronto: McClelland and Stewart, 1985). See also J.L. Granatstein, *Canada 1957-1967: The Years of Uncertainty and Innovation* (Toronto: McClelland and Stewart, 1986), 67-8.

12 Quoted in Granatstein, *ibid.,* 39.

13 Newman, *Distemper of Our Times,* 102-3; J.W. Pickersgill, *The Road Back, by a Liberal in Opposition* (Toronto: University of Toronto Press, 1986), 96-9; Robert Bothwell, Ian Drummond, and John English, *Canada since 1945: Power, Politics, and Provincialism* (Toronto: University of Toronto Press, 1981), 260; Joseph Wearing, *The L-Shaped Party: The Liberal Party of Canada, 1958-1980* (Toronto: McGraw-Hill Ryerson, 1981), 19-20; and Pearson, *Mike, III:* 52.

14 *Toronto Daily Star,* Sept. 14, 1960; and R. MacIntosh, "The Kingston Conference", Kent Papers, Box 6/8 (Queen's University Archives). Interviews with Mary Macdonald and Michael Mackenzie.

15 Grant Dexter to Victor Sifton, Nov. 18, 1968, Dexter Papers, TC747 (Queen's University Archives).

16 LBP to Hutchison, Sept. 14, 1960; and Hutchison to Dexter, Jan. 2, 1961, Hutchison Papers (University of Calgary Library).

17 Robert Bothwell and William Kilbourn, *C.D. Howe: A Biography* (Toronto: McClelland and Stewart, 1979), 346. See the correspondence with Mitchell Sharp in Howe Papers, v. 197 (NAC).

18 Gordon to Kent, Jan. 16, 1961, Kent Papers, Box 6/8 (Queen's University Archives). Tom Kent, *A Public Purpose: An Experience of Liberal Opposition and Canadian Government* (Kingston and Montreal: McGill-Queen's University Press, 1988), 82-94.

19 Hutchison to Dexter, Jan. 17, 1961, Hutchison Papers (University of Calgary Library). Interview with Bruce Hutchison.

20 The relevant documents are found, in their entirety, in Denis Smith, *Gentle Patriot: A Political Biography of Walter Gordon* (Edmonton: Hurtig, 1973), 64-70. Gordon's own memory of the arrangement is found in a memorandum of Dec. 5, 1965, in Walter Gordon Papers, MG32 B44, v. 16 (NAC).

21 Interviews with Mary Macdonald, J.W. Pickersgill, Paul Martin, and Fraser Bruce.

22 LBP to Landon and Geoffrey Pearson, Mar. 31, 1959 (PPP).

23 Pearson, *Mike, III:* 53-4.

24 Keith Davey, *The Rainmaker: A Passion for Politics* (Toronto: Stoddart, 1986), 35-6. Also, Wearing, *The L-Shaped Party,* 19-30; and Smith, *Gentle Patriot,* 65-92.

25 Ramsay Cook, "Not Right, Not Left, But Forward", *Canadian Forum* (Feb. 1962), 241-2. See also J.T. Saywell, ed., *The Canadian Annual Review for 1961* (Toronto: University of Toronto Press, 1962), 74-8.

26 Kent to Pearson, June 13, 1960, MG26 N2, v. 127 (NAC). See Kent's own reflections on this document in *A Public Purpose,* 76-7.

27 See *Kent, A Public Purpose,* 100.

28 Hutchison to Dexter, Feb. 8, 1961, Hutchison Papers (University of Calgary Library).

29 LBP to Geoffrey Pearson (GP), May 25, 1960 (PPP).

30 LBP to GP, Feb. 11, 1961 (PPP).

31 LBP to GP, Sept. 11, 1961 (PPP).

32 See, for example LBP to James Duncan, Aug. 29, 1962, MG26 N2, v. 53 (NAC); House of Commons, *Debates,* Feb. 28, 1961; "Trade", MG26 N2, v. 96 (NAC); and Peter Stursberg, *Lester Pearson and the Dream of Unity* (Toronto: Doubleday, 1978), 65-6.

33 Walter Laqueur, *Europe in Our Time: A History, 1945-1992* (New York: Viking,

1992), 323ff. See also an important forthcoming study by Bruce Muirhead (McGill-Queen's University Press), which illustrates how reluctant Europe was to enter into trading arrangements with Canada in the 1950s.

34 Gordon's annoyance with the delay in making contact is recorded in his memorandum of Dec. 5, 1965, Gordon Papers, MG32 B44, v. 16 (NAC). In this memorandum, Gordon indicates he was "ignored by Mike" for three or four months. Smith, in *Gentle Patriot* (81), says it was "more than two months". Gordon indicated to Tom Kent that "Mike" had visited with him on Mar. 10, 1961. That suggests that he was "ignored" for a shorter time. Gordon to Kent, Mar. 14, 1961, Kent Papers, Box 6/8 (Queen's University Archives). See also Pearson, *Mike, III:* 54ff.

35 On Turner, see the file "John de B. Payne" in Liberal Party of Canada Papers, v. 742 (NAC). Also, see Wearing, *The L-Shaped Party,* 27-8.

36 Wearing, *ibid.,* 25-6; and Davey, *The Rainmaker,* ch. 3.

37 See Granatstein, *Canada 1957-1967,* 74ff.; and House of Commons, *Debates,* June 14, 1961. The account here follows Granatstein's excellent, detailed treatment of the topic.

38 House of Commons, *Debates,* Jan. 20, 1961; David Smith and David Slater, "The Economic Proposals of the Governor of the Bank of Canada", *Queen's Quarterly* (Spring 1961), 196-211; and Bothwell et al., *Canada since 1945,* 222.

39 House of Commons, *Debates,* July 7, 1961.

40 Saywell, ed., *Canadian Annual Review for 1961,* 19.

41 Walter Gordon, *A Political Memoir* (Toronto: McClelland and Stewart, 1977), 98-9; Stursberg, *Lester Pearson and the Dream of Unity,* 67ff.; Smith, *Gentle Patriot,* 86-8; Wearing, *The L-Shaped Party,* 33-5; Davey, *The Rainmaker,* 45-8; and "Pre-campaign Strategy", Liberal Party of Canada Papers, v. 692 (NAC).

42 Stursberg, *Lester Pearson and the Dream of Unity,* 69-70; and Davey, *The Rainmaker,* 47-8.

43 Stursberg, *Lester Pearson and the Dream of Unity,* 68.

44 Smith, *Gentle Patriot,* 88.

45 T.W. Kent, "Opinion Survey, Sept.-Oct. 1961", Kent Papers, Box 7/8 (Queen's University Archives); and Saywell, ed., *Canadian Annual Review for 1961,* 71.

46 Peter Regenstreif, *The Diefenbaker Interlude: Parties and Voting in Canada* (Don Mills, Ont.: Longman, 1965), 72-6. See also Regenstreif, "Group Perceptions and the Vote: Some Avenues of Opinion Formation in the 1962 Campaign", in John Meisel, ed., *Papers on the 1962 Election* (Toronto: University of Toronto Press, 1964), 235-52.

47 Regenstreif, *The Diefenbaker Interlude,* 72-6.

48 Cook, "Not Right, Not Left", *passim;* and Bothwell et al., *Canada since 1945,* ch. 25.

49 See Granatstein, *Canada 1957-1967*, 89.

50 House of Commons, *Debates*, Feb. 22, 1962.

51 *Globe and Mail*, Apr. 26, 1962. He had told Geoffrey earlier that he had given some "slam-bang" speeches and said he was trying to cling "to my higher plane but my grip is slipping". LBP to GP, Jan. 29, 1962 (PPP).

52 Connally told Bruce Hutchison that Kent had been appointed without his knowledge and that he threatened resignation. He blamed Gordon. Hutchison to Dexter, Oct. 1, 1961, Hutchison Papers (University of Calgary Library).

53 *Mike, III:* 58-9; and Gordon to Candidates, June 7, 1962, Liberal Party of Canada Papers, v. 689 (NAC); and Gordon, *A Political Memoir*, 97-9.

54 LBP to GP, June 26, 1962 (PPP). Quoted in full in Pearson, *Mike, III:* 65.

55 Pearson, *Mike, III:* 64.

56 Ibid., 61-3; Smith, *Gentle Patriot*, 107ff.; Rasminsky memorandum on *Gentle Patriot* account of crisis (given to me by Mr. Rasminsky); Fleming, *So Very Near*, ch. 93; and Granatstein, *Canada 1957-1967*, 98-100, which shows that the plan was drafted by officials on June 12. See also the comments criticizing *Gentle Patriot*'s presentation of Gordon's interpretation in A.F.W. Plumptre, *Three Decades of Decision: Canada and the World Monetary System, 1944-1975* (Toronto: McClelland and Stewart, 1977), 170, 180 n. 27.

57 Regenstreif, *The Diefenbaker Interlude*, 37, 157. Catholic support for Liberals was, of course, traditional.

58 Theodore Draper, *Present History* (New York: Vintage, 1984), 112. The defence crisis is covered in Granatstein, *Canada 1957-1967*.

59 John F. Kennedy, "The Terrain of Today's Statecraft", *Saturday Review of Literature* (Aug. 1, 1959), 19-20. See also L.B. Pearson, *Diplomacy in the Nuclear Age* (Cambridge, Mass.: Harvard University Press, 1959).

60 James Eayrs, *Northern Approaches: Canada and the Search for Peace* (Toronto: Macmillan, 1961), 40-56.

61 *Calgary Herald*, Sept. 26, 1961; and *Vancouver Sun*, Sept. 20, 1961. Interview with Jo Davis, founder of the Voice of Women.

62 LBP to Mrs. Walter Lee, Apr. 5, 1962, MG26 N2, v. 50 (NAC); LBP to F.M. Kelly, Oct. 24, 1961, *ibid.;* LBP to GP, Feb. 11, 1961 (PPP). GP to LBP, Feb. 4, 1961; and Paul Hellyer to LBP, Aug. 3, 1961, MG26 N2, v. 55 (NAC).

63 Michael Beschloss, *The Crisis Years: Kennedy and Khruschev, 1960-1963* (New York: Edward Burlingame Books, 1991), 4-5.

64 See Knowlton Nash, *Kennedy and Diefenbaker: Fear and Loathing across the Undefended Border* (Toronto: McClelland and Stewart, 1990), 128. Interview with Willis Armstrong.

65 See Nash, *ibid.,* 161-2.

66 Robinson, *Diefenbaker's World*, 285.

67 Interview with Mary Macdonald.

68 Granatstein, *Canada 1957-1967;* LBP to GP, Oct. 1962 (PPP).

69 Cees Wiebes and Bert Zeeman, "Political Consultation during International Crises: Small Powers in NATO", in Lawrence Kaplan, S.V. Papacsma, Mark Rubin, and Ruth Young, eds., *NATO after Forty Years* (Wilmington, Del.: Scholarly Resources, 1990), 94-5.

70 Hellyer to LBP, Nov. 25, 1962, MG26 N2, v. 55 (NAC). Hellyer's account is found in his memoirs, *Damn the Torpedoes: My Fight to Unify Canada's Armed Forces* (Toronto: McClelland and Stewart, 1990), 24-5.

71 *Toronto Daily Star,* Jan. 7, 1962 (Gallup poll). Liberals led Conservatives by 47% to 32% in the January Gallup poll.

72 LBP to Douglas LePan, Feb. 28, 1962, MG26 N2, v. 49 (NAC); and LBP to Geoffrey Andrew, Dec. 7, 1961, *ibid.,* v. 50.

73 LBP to George Brown, Nov. 19, 1962, *ibid.,* (NAC).

74 John Gellner to Paul Hellyer, Dec. 21, 1962, *ibid.,* v. 49 (NAC).

75 These letters are in *ibid.*

76 "On Canadian Defence Policy", Jan. 12, 1963, in Lester Pearson, *Words and Occasions* (Toronto: University of Toronto Press, 1970), 194-206.

77 Lloyd Axworthy to Pearson, n.d., MG26 N2, v. 50 (NAC); and Bothwell et al., *Canada since 1945,* 266.

78 The best account is in Nash, *Kennedy and Diefenbaker,* 239ff. House of Commons, *Debates,* Jan. 31, 1963.

79 John Saywell, ed., *The Canadian Annual Review for 1963* (Toronto: University of Toronto Press, 1964), 13.

CHAPTER 8: MR. PRIME MINISTER

1 David S. McLellan and David C. Acheson, *Among Friends: Personal Letters of Dean Acheson* (New York: Dodd Mead, 1980), 250. Letter was written on July 15, 1963.

2 George Grant, *Lament for a Nation: The Defeat of Canadian Nationalism* (Toronto: McClelland and Stewart, 1991; orig. ed. 1965). See also his *Technology and Empire: Perspectives on North America* (Toronto: House of Anansi, 1969), 68-9, where Grant denies that *Lament* was simply nostalgia, as many had claimed.

3 Butterworth to Lippmann, May 20, 1963, Lippmann Papers, v. 59 (Yale University Archives).

4 House of Commons, *Debates,* Feb. 5, 1963. See also Knowlton Nash, *Kennedy and Diefenbaker: Fear and Loathing across the Border* (Toronto: McClelland and Stewart, 1991), 302ff.

5 Grant, *Technology and Empire*, 68-9.

6 Margaret Conrad, *George Nowlan: Maritime Conservation in National Politics* (Toronto: University of Toronto Press, 1986), 168-290.

7 Walter Gordon, *Troubled Canada: The Need for Domestic Policies* (Toronto: McClelland and Stewart, 1961), 97.

8 The briefing book for President Eisenhower for July 1958 describes Diefenbaker as "basically friendly" and one who favours closer defence ties. Pearson is said to understand the U.S. point of view, "but he has not hesitated to criticize U.S. policy when it conflicted with Canadian objectives". Briefing Book for President Eisenhower's Visit to Canada, July 1958. Eisenhower Papers, WHCF, Box 28 (Eisenhower Library, Abilene, Kansas); and *New York Times*, Apr. 10, 1963.

9 Newfoundland voted 65.8% for the Liberals. Only 16% of francophones supported Diefenbaker, whereas 39.5% voted Liberal and 22% Social Credit. In Alberta and Saskatchewan, Diefenbaker received, respectively, 45.4% and 53.8% of the vote. In those provinces, the Liberals received only 22% and 24.1% of the popular vote. John Saywell, ed., *Canadian Annual Review for 1963* (Toronto: University of Toronto Press, 1964), 34-51; and Peter Regenstreif, *The Diefenbaker Interlude: Parties and Voting in Canada* (Don Mills, Ont.: Longman, 1965), 38.

10 Pierre Berton, "The Real Issues in the Election", *Maclean's* (Apr. 6, 1963), 62.

11 Douglas Owram, "Home and Family at Mid-Century". Paper presented at Canadian Historical Association Annual Meeting, 1992.

12 Charles Ritchie, *Storm Signals: More Undiplomatic Diaries, 1962-1971* (Toronto: Macmillan, 1983), 46. The information on voting patterns is found in Regenstreif, *The Diefenbaker Interlude, passim*.

13 House of Commons, *Debates*, Dec. 17, 1962; Peter Stursberg, *Lester Pearson and the Dream of Unity* (Toronto: Doubleday, 1978), 7-17, 93; *Le Devoir*, Dec. 18, 1962; and interviews with J.W. Pickersgill and Tom Kent. On Lamontagne, see André Laurendeau, *The Diary of André Laurendeau* (Toronto: Lorimer, 1991), 18-29.

14 LBP to Geoffrey, Feb. 22, 1963 (PPP).

15 See Saywell, ed., *Canadian Annual Review for 1963*, 16-35, for a good survey of the campaign. The public-opinion polls on the nuclear question are found in Peyton Lyon, *Canada in World Affairs: 1961-1963* (Toronto: Oxford University Press, 1968), 536ff.

16 Peter Stursberg, *Diefenbaker: Leadership Lost, 1962-1967* (Toronto: University of Toronto Press, 1976), 92; and Tom Kent, *A Public Purpose: An Experience of Liberal Opposition and Canadian Government* (Kingston: McGill-Queen's University Press, 1988), 171.

17 Kent, *ibid.*, 200. Pearson asked Keith Davey to take Kent off the leader's tour.

See Keith Davey, *The Rainmaker: A Passion for Politics* (Toronto: Stoddart, 1986), 69.

18 Walter Gordon, "Memorandum for Mr. Pearson", May 7, 1963, Gordon Papers, MG32 B44, v. 7 (NAC).

19 Denis Smith, *Gentle Patriot: A Political Biography of Walter Gordon* (Edmonton: Hurtig, 1973), 119. See also the comments of Pearson's nephew, Christopher Young, who indicates that "privately" Pearson would "give a wry grin" and admit that the Gallup figures influenced his decision. See Stursberg, *Lester Pearson and the Dream of Unity*, 87. On Kent's interpretation, see *A Public Purpose*, 192.

20 *Toronto Daily Star,* Mar. 11, 1963; Davey, *The Rainmaker,* 69-70; and "Election 1963", Liberal Party of Canada Papers, v. 694 (NAC). On the nuclear-weapons poll, see Lyon, *Canada in World Affairs,* 540-1.

21 Stursberg, *Lester Pearson and the Dream of Unity;* interview with Richard O'Hagan; and *Ottawa Journal,* Mar. 21, 1963.

22 "Backstage with Peter Newman", *Maclean's,* Apr. 6, 1953.

23 *Newsweek,* Feb. 18, 1963, 13-15; *Globe and Mail,* Mar. 9, 1963; Saywell, ed., *Canadian Annual Review for 1963,* 23.

24 There are several versions of this story and a related story concerning Walter Gordon. Pearson himself does not suggest in his memoirs that Kennedy offered to help. Bruce Hutchison revealed the story he heard from Pearson a few days after it occurred and indicated that the president did want to help. The fullest account is Knowlton Nash's *Kennedy and Diefenbaker.* L.B. Pearson, *Mike: The Memoirs of the Right Honourable Lester B. Pearson. Volume III: 1957-1968* (Toronto: University of Toronto Press, 1975); Bruce Hutchison, *The Far Side of the Street* (Toronto: Macmillan, 1976), 260-1; Peter Stursberg, *Lester Pearson and the American Dilemma* (Toronto: Doubleday, 1980), 186-7; and Nash, *Kennedy and Diefenbaker,* 278-9. Also, interviews with Rufus Smith, Bruce Hutchison, Knowlton Nash, Richard O'Hagan, and Willis Armstrong.

25 Interviews with Bruce Hutchison and Mary Macdonald.

26 Pearson, *Mike, III;* 82; and Vancouver *Province,* Apr. 2, 1963.

27 LBP to Geoffrey Pearson (GP), Feb. 22, 1963 (PPP).

28 Saywell, ed., *Canadian Annual Review for 1963,* 36; Regenstreif, *The Diefenbaker Interlude;* and Ottawa *Citizen,* Apr. 9, 1963. Popular vote totals were Liberal, 41.8%; Conservative, 32.4%, New Democrat, 13%; and Social Credit, 12%.

29 Pearson, *Mike, III:* 91. Gordon claims that Pearson said the Department of Industry would have been a new department and one whose organization would take much time. Walter Gordon, *A Political Memoir* (Toronto: McClelland and Stewart, 1977), 130.

30 Interview with Pauline Jewett.

31 McLeod's comments are in the *Toronto Daily Star,* Apr. 23, 1963; Meisel's in the *Canadian Forum* (May 1963). See also Peter Newman, *The Distemper of Our Times: Canadian Politics in Transition, 1963-1968* (Toronto: McClelland and Stewart, 1990; original ed., 1968), 31-3.

32 Lester and Maryon Pearson to Landon and Geoffrey Pearson, May 26, 1963 (PPP).

33 Quoted in Alistair Horne, *Macmillan 1957-1986: Volume II of the Official Biography* (London: Macmillan, 1989), 356, 394. Interview with Lord Trend. See also Basil Robinson, *Diefenbaker's World: A Populist in Foreign Affairs* (Toronto: University of Toronto Press, 1989), 267.

34 The Pearson description of the conversation is published in *Mike, III:* 98-100.

35 McGeorge Bundy Memorandum, Apr. 18, 1963, National Security Files, box 340 (John F. Kennedy Library). Nash, *Kennedy and Diefenbaker, passim;* and interview with Knowlton Nash.

36 Michael Beschloss, *The Crisis Years: Kennedy and Khrushchev, 1960-1963* (New York: Edward Burlingame Books, 1991), 297-8, 618-38; and, on Reston's importance, Taylor Branch, *Parting the Waters: American and the King Years, 1954-1963* (New York, Touchstone, 1988), 812.

37 *Mike, III:* 101; and Ritchie, *Storm Signals,* 48-9.

38 Newman, *Distemper of Our Times,* 34-5; Smith, *Gentle Patriot,* 378 n. 22; and interviews with Tom Kent, George Davidson, and other confidential sources. In *A Public Purpose,* 223, Kent strongly disagrees with the Newman account.

39 Denis Smith, *Gentle Patriot,* 136-7. The account in Smith is the best. Compare it with Gordon's own in his *A Political Memoir,* ch. 8; and with Pearson's in *Mike, III:* 103 ff. There are also excellent accounts in Kent, *A Public Purpose,* 235ff.; Newman, *Distemper of Our Times,* 39-44; and A.F.W. Plumptre, *Three Decades of Decision: Canada and the World Monetary System, 1944-1975* (Toronto: McClelland and Stewart, 1977), 202-4, 234-5. Newman was an Ottawa reporter at the time; Plumptre a Finance Department official. See also Gordon's memorandum of Dec. 5, 1965, MG32 B44 (NAC).

40 Smith, *Gentle Patriot,* 149. Pearson claims that he arranged the meeting, not Gordon. See *Mike, III:* 105. Rasminsky's *aide-memoire* for the occasion is found in "Some Comments on the Budget", Rasminsky Papers, LR76-549 (Bank of Canada Archives).

41 House of Commons, *Debates,* June 13, 1963. The full details are in an excellent article by Donald Forster in Saywell, ed., *Canadian Annual Review for 1963,* 195 ff.

42 Newman, *Distemper of Our Times,* 48. Confirmed by confidential source.

43 Robert Bothwell, Ian Drummond, and John English, *Canada since 1945: Power, Politics, and Provincialism* (Toronto: University of Toronto Press, 1981), 326-7. On the origins of Fisher's question, see Stursberg, *Lester Pearson and the Dream of Unity*, 126-7.

44 *Globe and Mail*, June 18-21, 1963; *Winnipeg Free Press*, June 20, 1963; Newman, *Distemper of Our Times*, 49-51; and Smith, *Gentle Patriot*, 161-3.

45 Gordon Memorandum, Dec. 5, 1965; Pearson, *Mike, III:* 107-8; and Stursberg, *Lester Pearson and the Dream of Unity*, 132-3.

46 Stursberg, *ibid.;* Mitchell Sharp, Memoirs (unpublished ms.); interviews with Mitchell Sharp and Mary Macdonald; and Heeney Diary, Aug. 23, 1963, Heeney Papers, MG30 E144, v. 2 (NAC).

47 Kent, *A Public Purpose*, 239-41; Sharp, Memoirs; and Gordon Memorandum, Dec. 5, 1965.

48 Heeney Diary, Aug. 23, 1963, Heeney Papers, MG30 E144, v. 2 (NAC); and House of Commons, *Debates*, May 29, 1963.

49 Smith, *Gentle Patriot*, 148; and Underhill to Pearson, Apr. 29, 1963, Underhill Papers, v. 13 (NAC); and Pearson to Underhill, May 6, 1963, *ibid.*

50 Lesage to Pearson, Oct. 13, 1953, MG26 N1, v. 7 (NAC).

51 Quoted in John Saywell, ed., *The Canadian Annual Review for 1961* (Toronto: University of Toronto Press, 1962), 48.

52 For Laurendeau's rather amusing description of his appointment, see his *Diary of André Laurendeau*, 18-29.

53 *Ibid.*, 21-2; and *Montreal Star*, Apr. 22, 1963.

54 *Diary of André Laurendeau*, 112-14.

55 Ramsay Cook, *The Maple Leaf Forever* (Toronto: Macmillan, 1971), 19.

56 Pearson, *Mike, III:* 38-9. See Newman for a strong criticism of Chevrier from Maurice Sauvé's viewpoint, *Distemper of Our Times*, 244ff.

57 André Laurendeau wrote of Pearson's cabinet: "nous gagnons en nombre, mais guère en qualité et en influence" ("we are gaining in number, but hardly in quality and influence"), *Le Devoir*, Apr. 23, 1963. This section draws greatly upon my article, "The 'French Lieutenant' in Ottawa", in Kenneth Carty and Peter Ward, eds., *National Politics and Community in Canada* (Vancouver: University of British Columbia Press, 1986), 184-200.

58 Jim Davey to Pearson, May 11, 1963, MG26 N3, v. 74 (NAC); and Gordon Memorandum, Dec. 5, 1965.

59 Newman's account indicates that a triumvirate was proposed by Pearson. Other information suggests that Sauvé proposed the triumvirate when his own hopes for the lieutenancy faltered. See Newman, *Distemper of Our Times*, 246-

50. Contrast with the interview with Lamontagne in Stursberg, *Lester Pearson and the Dream of Unity*, 211-12. Confidential sources indicate that Lamontagne's account is accurate.

60 Pearson, *Mike, III:* 214.

61 Connally to Pearson, Oct. 15, 1964, and Pearson to Connally, Oct. 19, 1964, MG26 N3, vol. 74 (NAC).

62 O'Hagan to Pearson, Oct. 5, 1964, *ibid.* (NAC).

63 House of Commons, *Debates*, Nov. 26, 1964, 10562.

64 Stursberg, *Lester Pearson and the Dream of Unity*, 221; and Kent, *A Public Purpose*, 328ff.

65 Gordon, *A Political Memoir*, 198.

66 *Preliminary Report of the Royal Commission on Bilingualism and Biculturalism* (Ottawa: Queen's Printer, 1965), 13; Pearson, *Mike, III:* 213-15; and Kent, *A Public Purpose*, 320-1.

67 Lower to Pearson, Dec. 22, 1964, MG26 N3, v. 3 (NAC).

68 The *Globe and Mail*, July 8, 1965, denounced Pearson for retaining Favreau, "a man who has demonstrated lack of judgement".

69 Cited in Blair Fraser, "Favreau, Pearson and a Sick Feeling Inside", *Maclean's*, 78: 1 (Jan. 2, 1965), 2.

70 Stursberg, *Lester Pearson and the Dream of Unity*, 223; and interview with Marc Lalonde.

71 Newman, *Distemper of Our Times*, 264. In his memoirs, Pearson describes this affair as "one of the most sordid and vindictive episodes in the history of the House of Commons". *Mike, III;* 151.

72 Quoted in Bothwell et al., *Canada since 1945*, 291.

73 *Mike, III:* 248-9.

74 This account is based upon Bothwell et al., *Canada since 1945*, 292-3; Judy LaMarsh, *Memoirs of a Bird in a Gilded Cage* (Toronto: Pocket Books, 1970), ch. 5; Stursberg, *Lester Pearson and the Dream of Unity*, ch. 7; Kent, *A Public Purpose*, 255-92; Dale Thomson, *Jean Lesage and the Quiet Revolution* (Toronto: Macmillan, 1984), 373-93; and Claude Morin, *Le pouvoir Québécois en négociation* (Montreal: Boréal Express, 1972), 19-47.

75 LaMarsh, *Bird in a Gilded Cage*, 130.

76 *La Presse*, Apr. 3, 1964.

77 Kent, "Memorandum for the Prime Minister", Apr. 6, 1964, Kent Papers, Box 3 (Queen's University Archives).

78 House of Commons, *Debates*, Apr. 6, 1964.

79 Kent, *A Public Purpose,* 281-2.

80 LaMarsh, *Bird in a Gilded Cage,* 94-5. LaMarsh was also angered by Pearson's later refusal to appoint her to the Ontario Bench.

81 LBP to GP, Feb. 7, 1964 (PPP).

82 Richard Gwyn, *The Shape of Scandal: A Study of a Government in Crisis* (Toronto: Clarke Irwin, 1965), 244.

83 "Transcript of Special Meeting of the Council held on Friday, 17th January, 1964", MG26 N3, v. 80 (NAC).

84 Hamilton *Spectator,* May 5, 1964, quoted in John Matheson, *Canada's Flag: A Search for a Country* (Boston: G.K. Hall, 1980), 70.

85 House of Commons, *Debates,* May 17, 1963.

86 Matheson, *Canada's Flag,* 72.

87 The speech is in L.B. Pearson, *Words and Occasions* (Toronto: University of Toronto Press, 1970), 228-32; and Toronto *Telegram,* May 20, 1963.

88 Cabinet Conclusions, May 19, 21, and 26, 1964 (Privy Council Office).

89 House of Commons, *Debates,* June 15, 1964. Diefenbaker had argued in 1957 that the flag was too difficult to handle. Cabinet Conclusions, Nov. 15, 1957 (Privy Council Office).

90 *Time* (Dec. 11, 1964), 7; Catherine Barclay, "Canada's Own and Only Canada's", unpublished paper, courtesy of the author; Newman, *Distemper of Our Times,* 258; and Guy Lamarche, "Le drapeau ne fait pas le pays", *Le Magazine Maclean* (Sept. 1964), 28ff.

91 House of Commons, *Debates,* Dec. 14, 1964; and Matheson, *Canada's Flag,* 163-70.

92 Notes for a talk, Dec. 1972 (PPP).

93 Matheson, *Canada's Flag,* 69.

94 *Ibid.*

95 Interview with D.A. Pennebaker (Columbia Oral History Collection).

96 Kent to Pearson, June 21, 1964, Kent Papers, Box 3 (Queen's University Archives). On the film, see Richard O'Hagan, "Memorandum", May 20, 1966, MG26 N5, v. 24 (NAC); Toronto *Telegram,* May 19, 1964; and House of Commons, *Debates,* May 21, 1964, and June 19, 1964.

97 Gordon, *A Political Memoir,* 188. Gordon discusses his memorandum and its effect in detail (197-9).

98 *Diary of André Laurendeau,* July 5, 1964.

CHAPTER 9: OLD FRIENDS, NEW WAYS

1 L.B. Pearson, *Words and Occasions* (Toronto: University of Toronto Press, 1970), 277-8; and *La Presse,* July 25, 1967.

2 LBP to James Johnston, Aurora *Banner,* Jan. 27, 1965 (PPP).

3 John Saywell, ed., *The Canadian Annual Review for 1964* (Toronto: University of Toronto Press, 1965), 46-7; L.B. Pearson, *Mike: The Memoirs of the Right Honourable Lester B. Pearson. Volume I: 1897-1948* (Toronto: University of Toronto Press, 1972), 295-8; and Dale Thomson, *Jean Lesage and the Quiet Revolution* (Toronto: Macmillan, 1984), 347-8.

4 *Mike, I:* 296.

5 *Ibid.,* 244-5; and interview with Tom Kent.

6 L.B. Pearson, "The Contract Theory of Provincial Rights", Apr. 4, 1931, MG26 N9, v.1 (NAC); and "The Privy Council and Canadian Federalism" [1936], *ibid.*

7 "The Privy Council", *ibid.;* and L.B. Pearson, "Review of André Siegfried", *ibid.*

8 See above, ch. 7. On the intellectuals and government, see Douglas Owram, *The Government Generation: Canadian Intellectuals and the State* (Toronto: University of Toronto Press, 1986).

9 Richard Simeon, *Federal-Provincial Diplomacy: The Making of Recent Policy in Canada* (Toronto: University of Toronto Press, 1972), 124-6.

10 Judy LaMarsh, *Memoirs of a Bird in a Gilded Cage* (Toronto: Pocket Books, 1970), 117.

11 See Simeon, *Federal-Provincial Diplomacy,* esp. chs. 6 and 12.

12 Donald Creighton, "The Myth of Biculturalism", in Donald Creighton, *Towards the Discovery of Canada* (Toronto: Macmillan, 1972), 256-7.

13 Simeon, *Federal-Provincial Diplomacy,* 170-1, 210-11. Pearson's defence of his "cooperative federalism" is in House of Commons, *Debates,* Apr. 6, 1965.

14 See P.E. Trudeau and Gérard Pelletier, "Pelletier et Trudeau s'expliquent", *Cité libre* (Oct. 1985), 3-5.

15 Claude Morin, *Le pouvoir Québécois en négociation* (Montreal: Boréal Express, 1972), 137; and his *Quebec versus Ottawa: The Struggle for Self-Government 1960-1972* (Toronto: University of Toronto Press, 1976), 71. See the assessment in J.L. Granatstein, *Canada 1957-1967: The Years of Uncertainty and Innovation* (Toronto: McClelland and Stewart, 1986), 262-6.

16 John Saywell, ed., *The Canadian Annual Review for 1963* (Toronto: University of Toronto Press, 1964), 3.

17 Bruce Hutchison, "A Conversation with the Prime Minister", Feb. 11, 1965, Hutchison Papers (University of Calgary Library).

18 L.B. Pearson, Memorandum, Apr. 13, 1965, MG26 N5, v. 45 (NAC). See L.B. Pearson, *Mike: The Memoirs of the Right Honourable Lester B. Pearson. Volume III: 1957-1968* (Toronto: University of Toronto Press, 1975), 199-200.

19 Gordon to Pearson, Mar. 31, 1965. *Ibid.*

20 R.B. Bryce to Gordon, Feb. 2, 1965, Gordon Papers, v. 37 (NAC); "Outlook for 1954", *ibid.;* and "Minutes of Meeting: National Campaign Committee", Jan. 5, 1965, Kent Papers, Box 418 (Queen's University Archives).

21 The Quayle analysis is found in Kent Papers, *ibid.* The leadership polls are taken by the Canadian Institute of Public Opinion, Jan. 20, Feb. 27, and Mar. 3, 1965 (University of Waterloo Library Collection).

22 L.B. Pearson, "The Points we have to meet", Sept. 2, 1965, MG26 N5, v. 45 (NAC); Tom Kent, "Strategy", Sept. 3, 1965, *ibid.;* Mitchell Sharp, Memoirs (unpublished ms.), *Mike, III:* 203-4; and Walter Gordon, "Memo of Conversation with Mike", Sept. 12, 1965, Gordon Papers, v. 35 (NAC). See also Keith Davey, *The Rainmaker: A Passion for Politics* (Toronto: Stoddart, 1986), 99-100.

23 Gordon, "Conversation with Mike", *ibid.* See also Walter Gordon, *A Political Memoir* (Toronto: McClelland and Stewart, 1977), ch. 12; and Tom Kent, *A Public Purpose: An Experience of Liberal Opposition and Canadian Government* (Kingston: McGill-Queen's, 1988), 384ff.

24 Peter Newman, *The Distemper of Our Times: Canadian Politics in Transition* (Toronto: McClelland and Stewart, 1990; original ed. 1968), 478. Newman effectively demolishes the argument that redistribution prevented any election until 1967 (470-1).

25 Neil Swainson, *Conflict over the Columbia: The Canadian Background to an Historic Treaty* (Montreal: McGill-Queen's University Press, 1974), 251; and Tom Kent, "Strategy", Kent Papers, Box 5 (Queen's University Archives).

26 *Toronto Daily Star,* Oct. 7, 1965; and Pearson, "The Points we have to meet". See also Granatstein, *Canada 1957-1967,* 286ff.

27 E.A. Goodman, *Life of the Party: The Memoirs of Eddie Goodman* (Toronto: Key Porter Books, 1988), 112-13; and Peter Stursberg, *Diefenbaker: Leadership Lost* (Toronto: University of Toronto Press, 1976), 137-9.

28 *Toronto Daily Star,* Oct. 1 and 14, 1965; and Newman, *Distemper of Our Times,* 480-1.

29 *The Diary of André Laurendeau* (Toronto: Lorimer, 1991), 152-4: and *Globe and Mail,* Nov. 6, 1965. See also, Stephen Clarkson and Christina McCall, *Trudeau and Our Times. Volume I: The Magnificent Obsession* (Toronto: McClelland and Stewart, 1990), 91-3.

30 *Globe and Mail,* Nov. 4, 1965; Montreal *Gazette,* Nov. 4, 1965; and Davey, *The Rainmaker,* 103.

31 *Globe and Mail,* Nov. 9, 1965.

32 Gordon, *A Political Memoir,* 232-3; *Mike, II:* 208-12; Pearson to Duke Pearson, Nov. 15, 1965, MG26 N5, v. 45 (NAC); Pearson to T.W. L. MacDermot, Nov. 29, 1965, MG26 N4, v. 59; Davey, *The Rainmaker,* 109-10; Pearson, "Election Analysis", Dec. 10, 1965, MG26 N5, v. 45 (NAC).

33 Davey, *The Rainmaker,* 111; and Kent, *A Public Purpose,* 392.

34 Kent, *ibid.,* 390.

35 Davey, *The Rainmaker,* 31.

36 Pearson to cabinet, Jan. 9, 1964, Kent Papers, Box 3 (Queen's University Archives). Interviews with Paul Martin and anonymous sources.

37 Nichol is quoted in Newman, *Distemper of Our Times,* 469; and Joseph Wearing, *The L-Shaped Party: The Liberal Party of Canada, 1958-1980* (Toronto: McGraw-Hill Ryerson, 1981), 168-73.

38 Robert Fowler to Pearson, Feb. 9, 1965, MG26 N3, v. 78 (NAC).

39 *Mike, I:* 177, 200. On this subject see also Dale Thomson, *Vive le Québec libre* (Toronto: Deneau, 1988); Stephen Clarkson, "Vive le Québec libre or Putting the Leader Back In", in David Sugarman and Reg Whitaker, eds., *Federalism and Political Community: Essays in Honour of Donald Smiley* (Peterborough, Ont.: Broadview, 1989), 55-69.

40 *Mike, II:* 261. One should note, however, that Paris came after trips to Washington and London. According to some sources, the French resented this. Interviews with Arnold Smith and Marcel Cadieux. De Gaulle quoted in Saywell, ed., *Canadian Annual Review 1964,* 189.

41 On the early difficulties that Léger had, see Charlotte Girard, *Canada in World Affairs, 1963-1965* (Toronto: Canadian Institute of International Affairs, 1983); and Paul Martin, *A Very Public Life. Volume II: So Many Worlds* (Toronto: Deneau, 1985), 578-80. This section is based on documents that I have not been permitted to quote directly.

42 Lord Gladwyn, *De Gaulle's Europe or Why the General Says No* (London: Secker and Warburg, 1969), 88-100. This view was shared by Jules Léger, who became Canada's ambassador to France in 1964. According to Léger, "Le monde irréel dans lequel il vit est de plus en plus éloigné du monde réel" ("The unreal world he lives in is farther and farther from the real world"). Léger to Cadieux, Nov. 25, 1965, Léger Papers, v. 1, Cadieux file 2 (NAC).

43 Brian Crozier, *De Gaulle: The Statesman* (London: Eyre Methuen, 1973), 572. See also, Jean Lacouture, *De Gaulle. The Ruler: 1945-1970* (London: Harper Collins, 1991), 448-9.

44 *Mike, III:* 259 ff. See also Martin, *A Very Public Life, II,* 574-5, 579-80.

45 This description comes from Christopher Malone's fine "La politique qué-

bécoise en matière de relations internationales: changement et continuité (1960-1972)" (MA thesis, University of Ottawa, 1974), 3-12. Several articles in Paul Painchaud, ed., *Le Canada et le Québec sur la scène internationale* (Quebec: Laval, 1977) are also useful for context.

46 Maurice Couve de Murville, *Une Politique étrangère 1958-1969* (Paris: Plon, 1971), 453-4. A good reconstruction of the mood is found in André Fontaine, "La France et le Québec", *Etudes internationales*, 8 (June 1977), 393-402. On de Gaulle's attitude in general, see Jacques Filion, "De Gaulle, la France et le Québec", *Revue de l'Université d'Ottawa*, 45 (July-Sept. 1975), 295-319; and Lacouture, *De Gaulle*, 449.

47 Interview with Marcel Cadieux. See also Granatstein, *Canada 1957-1967*, ch. 10, for an extensive discussion of Cadieux and Jules Léger; and J.L. Granatstein and Robert Bothwell, *Pirouette: Pierre Trudeau and Canadian Foreign Policy* (Toronto: University of Toronto Press, 1990), 121ff. The Cadieux-Léger correspondence in Léger Papers, v.1 (NAC) is the source for these generalizations.

48 See C. Malone, "La politique québécoise", 112; John Saywell, ed., *Canadian Annual Review 1965* (Toronto: University of Toronto Press, 1966), 250-1; *La Presse*, Mar. 6, 1965; and Peter Newman, "Is De Gaulle Seeking Quebec Link?", *Toronto Daily Star*, May 12, 1965.

49 Newman, *ibid.*, and Morin, *Quebec versus Ottawa*, 35; Paul Martin, *Federalism and International Relations* (Ottawa: Information Canada, 1968), 27; and his *A Very Public Life, II*, 580-1.

50 *Le Magazine Maclean* (Jan. 1965), 2. Gérin-Lajoie's speeches caused much concern, especially his speech to the Montreal Consular Corps (Apr. 14, 1965) on Quebec's international personality. *Le Devoir*, Apr. 14, 1965. Also Pierre Godin, *Daniel Johnson: 1964-1968. La difficile recherche de l'égalité* (Montreal: Editions de l'Homme, 1980), 183.

51 Martin, *A Very Public Life, II*, 480-1 and Martin to Pearson, Apr. 26, 1965, MG26 N3, v. 62 (NAC). This position was changed later. See Martin's *Federalism and International Relations*, 27. The fullest study of Quebec's legal and political position in international affairs is Louis Sabourin, "Canadian Federalism and International Organizations: A Focus on Quebec" (Ph.D. thesis, Columbia University, 1971), esp. ch. 7.

52 Quoted in Peyton Lyon, "Entente Difficile", *Commentator* (Feb. 1965), 7. A young parliamentary secretary, Jean-Luc Pépin, gave an important speech on Mar. 26, 1965, that expressed the high priority given to France in Canada's diplomatic relations. France, Pépin declared, was the fourth pillar of Canadian foreign policy. "Our Relations with France: One of the Pillars of our Foreign Policy", External Affairs, *Speeches and Statements*, No. 65-10, 1965.

53 Interviews with Paul Martin and Marcel Cadieux. Confidential sources.

54 See Saywell, ed., *Canadian Annual Review 1965,* 256-8; William Hunter, "Uranium Exports for Peace and Prosperity", *Canadian Forum* (July 1965), 73-4, 76; Bernard Kaplan, "Franco-Canadian Courtship", *Montreal Star,* May 12, 1965; Bertrand Goldschmidt, *Les Rivalités atomiques* (Paris: Fayard, 1967), 262, 278; and Martin, *A Very Public Life, II,* 581-2. The background in the 1950s is described in Robert Bothwell, *Eldorado: Canada's National Uranium Company* (Toronto: University of Toronto Press, 1984), 407-10.

55 House of Commons, *Debates,* June 3, 1965; and Goldschmidt, *Les Rivalités,* 278. The argument that the Canadian sale was prevented by American pressure is not supported by evidence I have accumulated. See, however, Mark Malone, "La francophonie 1965-71: un cadre institutionnel, reflet des réalités francophones" (Paris: Fondation Nationale des Science Politiques, 1971), 61. See also, Thomson, *Vive le Québec libre,* 160-1. I would like to thank Professor Robert Bothwell for assistance with this section.

56 Edward A. Kolodziej, *French International Policy under de Gaulle and Pompidou: The Politics of Grandeur* (Ithaca and London: Cornell University Press, 1974), 54; Stephen Clarkson, "Gaullism: Prospect for Canada?" *Canadian Forum* (June 1966), 52; and *Mike, II:* 264. The French action was not unexpected, as *Mike* claims it was.

57 Martin, *A Very Public Life, II,* 581.

58 *Ibid.,* 584-5. Also, Thomson, *Vive le Québec libre,* 173-5.

59 Paul Martin, "Memo for Prime Minister", Jan. 24, 1967; Martin Papers, v. 357 (NAC).

60 See André Patry, *Le Québec dans le Monde* (Montreal: Leméac, 1980), 76-84; Chrétien as quoted in Ron Graham, *One-Eyed Kings: Promise and Illusion in Canadian Politics* (Toronto: Collins, 1986), 66; on the election, see John Saywell, ed., *Canadian Annual Review for 1966* (Toronto: University of Toronto Press, 1967), 57-64.

61 Interviews with Marc Lalonde and Allan Gotlieb.

62 André Patry thus writes of the immediate aftermath of the Johnson election: "sur la scène internationale, l'avancement du Québec semble paralysé." *Le Québec dans le Monde,* 85.

63 On the Quebec invitations, see Godin, *Johnson, II,* 188ff.

64 *Mike, II:* 265; and P.-L. Guertin, *Et de Gaulle vint . . .* (Montreal: Langevin, 1970), 28-9. Christopher Malone claims that Johnson advisers Guy Bertrand, André Patry, and Charles Pelletier wanted to take Quebec towards sovereignty through a series of "coups" without provoking a major confrontation. C. Malone, "La politique québécoise", 173. See also Lacouture, *De Gaulle,* 450.

65 A circular note requiring all embassies to conduct all official business with the

provinces through the federal government was sent out in early December 1966. Lacouture, *De Gaulle,* 450. On Marchand, see Godin, *Johnson,* II, 209. Also, Martin to cabinet, Mar. 11, 1966, MG26 N4, v. 265 (NAC).

66 Martin, *A Very Public Life, II,* 588, and confidential sources.

67 There was another incident at this time surrounding a proposed French loan to Quebec. Leduc had told Martin that the loan was fully a Quebec initiative. Later, Candian officials learned that in fact the French were the first promoters of the loan. On the other hand, Leduc complained about insults that Pierre Trudeau directed towards him at a cocktail party. On Halstead, see Martin, *A Very Public Life, II,* 588ff. The original memorandum to Pearson was written by Halstead and Gotlieb and sent to Pearson on Dec. 8, 1966. MG26 N4, v. 266 (NAC).

68 Martin, *A Very Public Life, II,* 591; and conversation with Pauline Vanier.

69 *Mike, III:* 274; C.I.I.A. *Monthly Report* (Apr. 1967), 44; *Le Monde,* Apr. 12, 1967; Lacouture, *De Gaulle,* 449-50; and Martin to Pearson, Apr. 7, 1967, MG26 N4, v. 226 (NAC).

70 See the evasive replies to questions in the House. House of Commons, *Debates,* Apr. 6 and 12, 1967.

71 See M. Malone, "La francophone 1965-71", 194ff., and 345; and Godin, *Johnson,* II, 186. The file on which this section draws is MG26 N4, v. 258.

72 Morin, *Quebec versus Ottawa,* 37; Jérôme Proulx, *Le Panier de crabes* (Montreal: Editions parti pris, 1971), 102; and C. Malone, "La politique québécoise", 125-9. See also Jean Giroux, "Quebec doit s'ouvrier sur le monde", *L'Action Catholique* (Mar. 16, 1967), 23-5; Quebec, *Journal des Débats,* Apr. 13, 1967; and Patry, *Le Québec dans le Monde,* 85ff.

73 Crozier, *De Gaulle,* 578.

74 Godin, *Johnson,* II, 213.

75 Lacouture, *De Gaulle,* 450. The other information is from the Paul Martin Papers, v. 357 (NAC). See also, Patry, *Le Québec dans le Monde,* 97-100; and Thomson, *Vive le Québec libre,* 183-5.

76 *Mike, III:* 245-6; Godin, *Johnson,* II, 198; Cadieux to Martin, Mar. 21, 1967, MG26 N4, v. 258 (NAC); and Martin to Pearson, Apr. 3, 1967, *ibid.*

77 A partial account is found in Martin, *A Very Public Life, II,* 593.

78 Patry, *Le Québec dans le Monde,* 98-9; Johnson to Pearson, May 7, 1967, MG26 N4, v. 245 (NAC); and Marc Lalonde, "Memo for file", Apr. 26, 1967, *ibid.,* v. 258.

79 Marc Lalonde to Pearson, May 24, 1967, MG26 N4, v. 258 (NAC) and confidential sources.

80 In other respects, however, Johnson seemed more conciliatory. It was at this

time that he agreed to take part in Ontario premier John Robarts' Confederation of Tomorrow Conference. Godin, *Johnson*, II, 308-10. The section above is based mainly on confidential sources and MG26 N4, v. 258 (NAC).

81 Masse's speech to the Jean Baptiste Society, June 22, 1967, is quoted in C. Malone, "La politique québécoise", 127-8.

82 Peter Desbarats, *René: A Canadian in Search of a Country* (Toronto: MacClelland and Stewart, 1976), ch. 18; and Thomson, *Vive le Québec libre,* 200ff.

83 *La Presse,* July 11, 1967. See Guertin, *Et de Gaulle vint . . . ,* 34 Guertin indicates that France and Quebec presented identical itineraries. This is untrue, since the French originally called for the visit to begin in Montreal. Quebec City was Quebec's choice, which was agreed to by the federal government. Also, Lalonde to Hodgson, June 9, 1967, MG26 N4, v. 258 (NAC); and Godin, *Johnson,* II, 213-14; Proulx identifies Maurice Bellemare as one of the most eager deputies. *Panier de crabes,* 53.

84 Johnson as quoted in Guertin, *Et de Gaulle vint . . . ,* 41.

85 Newman has a slightly different version in which de Gaulle asked Martin, "How do you think it went?' Mr. Martin confirmed that the version in the text is correct. In any case, it is unlikely that de Gaulle would have asked such a question. See *Distemper of Our Times,* 427. See also the account in Godin, *Johnson,* II, ch. 6, and Martin, *A Very Public Life, II,* 594ff.

86 The texts of de Gaulle's speeches on arrival and at the Château Frontenac dinner are found in Charles de Gaulle, *Discours et Messages: vers le terme Janvier 1966-Avril 1969* (Paris: Plon, 1970), 186-90. The troubling passages in the Château speech were probably the second and seventh paragraphs, in which de Gaulle spoke of Quebec's ties with France. Martin to Pearson, July 24, 1967, MG26 N4, v. 257 (NAC).

87 Estimate from *Le Devoir,* July 25, 1967. See also *Le Monde,* July 25, 1967, and Godin, *Johnson,* II, 223.

88 De Gaulle, *Discours et Messages,* 191-2; and Lacouture, *De Gaulle,* 253-4.

89 *Mike, III:* 167-9. On the incident, see Guertin, *Et de Gaulle vint . . . ,* 50-8; Newman, *Distemper of Our Times,* 427-9; C.I.I.A., *Monthly Report* (July-Aug. 1967), 90-2; John Saywell, ed., *Canadian Annual Review for 1967* (Toronto: University of Toronto Press, 1968), 49-60; Couve de Murville, *Une politique étrangère,* 456; Gérard Bergeron, *Du Duplessisme à Trudeau et Bourassa* (Montreal: Editions parti pris, 1971), 437-73; D.J. Riseborough, ed., *Canada and the French* (New York: Facts on File, 1975), 109-20; Godin, *Johnson,* II, ch. 6; Martin, *A Very Public Life, II,* 595-7; Patry, *Le Québec dans le Monde,* 101-3; and Thomson, *Vive le Québec libre,* 209-14.

90 Quoted in Riseborough, *ibid.,* 112. Interviews with Paul Martin and Lionel Chevrier.

91 The text of this petition is in Guertin, *Et de Gaulle vint . . .* , 74-7; see also *Le Soleil,* July 25, 1967.

92 *Le Devoir,* July 25, 1967.

93 Bergeron, *Du Duplessisme,* 437-81; and Saywell, ed., *Canadian Annual Review 1967,* 55.

94 *Le Monde,* July 28, 1967; *Le Figaro,* July 27, 1967; and *L'Humanité,* July 27, 1967. The last of these did support Quebec self-determination; it merely opposed de Gaulle's methods. On de Gaulle's reaction, see Lacouture, *De Gaulle,* 460.

95 Cabinet minutes, July 25, 1967 (Privy Council Office); *Mike, III:* 267; and Pierre-Louis Mallen, *Vive le Québec libre* (Paris: Plon, 1978), 242-3. Maurice Sauvé's account of the cabinet meeting in Lacouture, *De Gaulle,* 457, seems highly inaccurate.

96 *Globe and Mail,* Nov. 2, 1977; and Clarkson, "Vive le Québec libre", 67.

CHAPTER 10: LAST INNINGS

1 L.B. Pearson, *Words and Occasions* (Toronto: University of Toronto Press, 1970), 272.

2 Canadian Institute of Public Opinion, Gallup Poll, June 23, 1965 (University of Waterloo Collection).

3 Pearson to Garth Stevenson, Nov. 1966 (courtesy of Professor Stevenson).

4 Mitchell Sharp, Memoirs (unpublished ms.) Interview with J.W. Pickersgill. See also, Peter Stursberg, *Lester Pearson and the Dream of Unity* (Toronto: Doubleday, 1978), 361ff., for a good discussion of the seaway controversy.

5 See J.L. Granatstein, *Canada 1957-1967: The Years of Uncertainty and Innovation* (Toronto: McClelland and Stewart, 1986), 11-12.

6 Judy LaMarsh, *Memoirs of a Bird in a Gilded Cage* (Toronto: Pocket Books, 1970), 240; see also Stursburg, *Lester Pearson and the Dream of Unity,* 287.

7 Stursberg, *ibid.,* 282.

8 L.B. Pearson, *Mike: The Memoirs of the Right Honourable Lester B. Pearson. Volume III: 1957-1968* (Toronto: University of Toronto Press, 1975), 175-6; Stursberg, *Lester Pearson and the Dream of Unity,* 292-301; Walter Gordon, *A Political Memoir* (Toronto: McClelland and Stewart, 1977), 236-40; and John Saywell, ed., *Canadian Annual Review for 1966* (Toronto: University of Toronto Press, 1967), 9-23.

9 House of Commons, *Debates,* Feb. 23, 1966.

10 Erik Nielsen, *The House Is Not a Home: An Autobiography* (Toronto: Macmillan, 1989), 152-3.

11 Stursberg, *Lester Pearson and the Dream of Unity,* 294; *Mike, III:* 277-8; and House of Commons, *Debates,* Mar. 4, 1966.

12 House of Commons, *Debates,* Mar. 4, 1966.

13 Sturberg, *Lester Pearson and the Dream of Unity,* 298.

14 *Ibid,* 301.

15 Pearson to Barney Danson, Apr. 12, 1966, MG26 N5, v. 45 (NAC).

16 Saywell, ed., *Canadian Annual Review 1966,* 14; on his mood, see *Mike, III:* 184; and Walter Gordon, "Memorandum", Mar. 15, 1966, Gordon Papers, MG32 B44, v. 16 (NAC).

17 Saywell, ed., *Canadian Annual Review 1966,* 13-16; *Toronto Daily Star,* Mar. 15, 1966.

18 *Montreal Star,* Mar. 15, 1966; Saywell, ed., *Canadian Annual Review 1966,* 14-16, 20-3; and J.L. Granatstein and David Stafford, *Spy Wars: Espionage and Canada from Gouzenko to Glasnost* (Toronto: Key Porter, 1990), 125-9.

19 Charles Ritchie, *Storm Signals: More Undiplomatic Diaries, 1962-1971* (Toronto: Macmillan, 1983).

20 See *Mike, III:* 119-24, for more details of the visit, including most of the diary account of the visit. On Merchant-Heeney, see "Note on Interdepartmental Meetings re U.S.-Canada Proposed Statement of Economic Principles", Heeney Papers, MG30 E144, v. 4 (NAC).

21 *United States–Vietnam Relations 1945-1967, I.* "Negotiations 1965-1966", in *Canadian Forum* (Sept. 1973), 10.

22 Douglas Ross, *In the Interests of Peace: Canada and Vietnam 1954-1973* (Toronto: University of Toronto Press.) 267-70; Charles Taylor, *Snow Job: Canada, the United States and Vietnam (1954 to 1973)* (Toronto: Anansi, 1974), 51ff.; Department of External Affairs history, unpublished manuscript; and McGeorge Bundy, "Memorandum for the Record of a Conversation between President Johnson and Prime Minister Pearson,... May 28, 1964" in *Foreign Relations of the United States, 1964-1968. Volume I: Vietnam 1964* (Washington: Government Printing Office), 394-96.

23 Forrestal to Rusk, Aug. 19, 1964; Report of Conversation with Prime Minister Pham Van Dong, Aug. 17, 1964; Saigon to Sec. of State, Aug. 18, 1964; all in *United States–Vietnam Relations 1945-1967, I.* Also, C. Taylor, *Snow Job,* ch. 2; and interview with William, Bundy. On Johnson's decision, see L.B. Johnson, *The Vantage Point: Perspectives of the Presidency, 1963-1969* (New York: Holt, Rinehart and Winston, 1971), 126. A recent account is Larry Berman, *Lyndon Johnson's War* (New York: Norton, 1989).

24 Rufus Smith, a senior State Department official concerned with Canada, recalled that Johnson could never call Pearson "Mike", despite pleas from his aides that he do so. The suspicion seems to have been mutual. Interview with Rufus Smith. The Pearson account is in *Mike, III:* 125ff. This section is based upon confidential documents that I am not permitted to quote directly or cite.

25 Allan E. Goodman, *The Lost Peace: America's Search for a Negotiated Settlement of the Vietnam War* (Palo Alto, Calif.: Hoover Institution, 1978), 21.

26 "Extracts from an Address by the Right Honorable Lester B. Pearson, Prime Minister of Canada, to the Canadian Club of Ottawa, February 10, 1965", External Affairs, *Statements and Speeches,* 65/3; and André Laurendeau, *The Diary of André Laurendeau* (Toronto: Lorimer, 1991), 128.

27 Johnson to Pearson, Mar. 30, 1965 (drafted by McGeorge Bundy), Johnson Papers (Johnson Library, Austin, Texas). Quoted in C.I.I.A., *Monthly Report* 4:4 (Apr. 1965), 30-2. This was not issued as one of the External Affairs *Statements and Speeches*. C. Taylor, *Snow Job,* 38. Taylor calls Pearson's later statement that this was a bold initiative on American soil "somewhat pathetic". He claims that Pearson had been "almost obsequious" in his deference to American war aims. He quotes Pearson's statement that "The Government and great majority of the people of my country have supported whole-heartedly U.S. peacekeeping and peacemaking policies in Vietnam", but he fails to quote the following sentence, which limits this statment: "We wish to be able to continue that support." Taylor also chides Pearson because he referred to North Vietnamese "aggression" six times. Pearson would not deny that. This reflects Taylor's judgement that "the real threat to peace and security in Southeast Asia came from Washington, rather than Hanoi or Peking". This judgement Pearson would debate today if he could. So, probably, would Peking. On the arguments for the bombing, see Brian Van De Mark, *Into the Quagmire: Lyndon Johnson and the Escalation of the Vietnam War* (New York: Oxford University Press, 1991), chs. 4 and 6.

28 *Mike, III:* 139-41. This is from the Pearson Diary. Charles Ritchie's later comments suggest that the quarrel began before Pearson and Johnson went to the terrace. See Peter Stursberg, *Lester Pearson and the American Dilemma* (Toronto: Doubleday, 1980), 220-1; Charles Ritchie, "The Day the President of the United States Struck Fear and Trembling into the Heart of Our PM", *Maclean's* (Jan. 1974), 35-40; and Ritchie, *Storm Signals,* 81-3.

29 C.I.I.A., *Monthly Report,* 4:4, 32.

30 Maxwell Taylor, *Swords and Plowshares,* (New York, 1972), 341.

31 *The Pentagon Papers: The Defense Department History of United States Decision-making on Vietnam* (Boston: Beacon Press, n.d.), 447. See also Guenter Lewy, *America in Vietnam* (New York: Oxford University Press, 1978), 46-7; and Leslie Gelb with Richard K. Betts, *The Irony of Vietnam: The System Worked* (Washington: Brookings Institution, 1979), 120 ff.; Bundy, as quoted in Stursberg, *Lester Pearson and the American Dilemma,* 221; also, interview with William Bundy; interview with Rufus Smith; Dean Acheson, "Canada: 'Stern Daughter of the Voice of God'", in Livingston T. Merchant, ed., *Neighbors Taken for Granted: Canada and the United States* (New York: Praeger, 1966), 134-47.

32 Bruce Hutchison, *The Far Side of the Street* (Toronto: Macmillan, 1976), 354; see also Bundy's comments in Stursberg, *Lester Pearson and the American Dilemma*, 222. See American criticism of Johnson in Van De Mark, *Into the Quagmire*, 117-19.

33 John Hadwen, "Memorandum", MG26 N3, v. 281 (NAC); *Mike, III:* 141; and confidential sources.

34 The poll on Canadian opinions of Johnson was sent to the President with the observation that a greater loss of support had been expected because of Vietnam. Johnson Papers (Johnson Library). For the 1965 poll, see "Our Quiet War over Peace: Politicians vs. the People", *Maclean's* (Jan. 23, 1965), 18.

35 Stursberg, *Lester Pearson and the American Dilemma*, 210-11, 218. Interview with Paul Martin.

36 *Maclean's*, Apr. 13, 1963. Interviews with Charles Ritchie, Rufus Smith, and William Bundy. External Affairs history, draft ch. 9; and Ross, *In the Interests of Peace*, chs. 9-10.

37 *Mike, III:* 142-3; and on the early evidence of the Seaborn visits, Geoffrey Stevens, "Quiet Canadian and a Tale of Two Cities", *Globe Magazine* (July 31, 1965), 2.

38 Valenti to Johnson, Aug. 14, 1965, Johnson Papers (Johnson Library); and Washington *Daily News*, Aug. 23, 1965.

39 John Saywell, ed., *Canadian Annual Review for 1965* (Toronto: University of Toronto Press, 1966); A.D.P. Heeney, *The Things That Are Caesar's: Memoirs of a Canadian Public Servant* (Toronto: University of Toronto Press, 1972), 196; Ottawa *Citizen*, July 14, 1965. C.I.I.A., *Monthly Report* (July-Aug. 1965), 79-81 and (Sept. 1965) 93, in which the more favourable American reaction is described.

40 On these negotiations, see the article by Frank Hayes, "Canada, the Commonwealth and the Rhodesia Issue", in Kim Nossal, ed., *An Acceptance of Paradox: Essays on Canadian Diplomacy in Honour of John W. Holmes* (Toronto: Canadian Institute of International Affairs, 1982), 141-73. On external aid, the finest study remains Keith Spicer, *A Samaritan State? External Aid in Canada's Foreign Policy* (Toronto: University of Toronto Press, 1966).

41 John Macy, "Memorandum for the President", Aug. 24, 1966, Johnson Papers (Johnson Library); and Butterworth to Secretary of State, Jan. 28 and Jan. 31, 1966 (two telegrams). *United States–Vietnam Relations 1945-1967, I.*

42 Interview with Paul Martin; C. Taylor, *Snow Job*, 96-9; Chester Ronning, *From the Boxer Rebellion to the People's Republic: A Memoir of China in Revolution* (New York: Pantheon, 1974); Chester Cooper, *The Lost Crusade: America in Vietnam* (New York: Dodd Mead, 1970); and State Department (Rusk) to American Embassy (Lodge), Feb. 25, 1966. *United States– Vietnam Relations 1945-1967, I.*

43 External Affairs, unpublished history, ch. 9; Stursberg, *Lester Pearson and the American Dilemma*, 271, 277-8; Goodman, *The Lost Peace*, esp. chs. 1 and 5; Henry Kissinger, "The Vietnam Negotiations", *Foreign Affairs* (Jan. 1969), 215-16; and Paul Martin, *A Very Public Life. Volume II: So Many Worlds* (Toronto: Deneau, 1985), 442.

44 Rusk to McNamara, June 8, 1966. *United States–Vietnam Relations 1945-1967, I;* Memorandum of Conversation, June 21, 1966. Participants: Canada—Paul Martin, Chester Ronning, Ralph Collins, Klaus Goldschlag, Thomas Delworth; United States—William Bundy, Joseph Scott, Paul Kreisberg, *ibid.;* Ronning, *Memoir of China*, 267-8; C. Taylor, *Snow Job*, 110-11; and Stursberg, *Lester Pearson and the American Dilemma*, 280-3. The Ronning visits are ignored in Van De Mark, *Into the Quagmire.*

45 House of Commons, *Debates*, July 8, 1966; "The Canadian Labour Congress and Vietnam", *Canadian Dimension* (Mar.-Apr. 1966), 5; *Le Devoir*, July 12, 1966; and *I.F. Stone's Weekly*, Oct. 24, 1966, quoted in Arthur Schlesinger, *Robert F. Kennedy and His Times* (Boston: Houghton Mifflin, 1978), 798.

46 The choices are described in a May 1966 speech to the Ontario provincial Liberals. See Gordon, *A Political Memoir*. Also, his *A Choice for Canada: Independence or Colonial Status* (Toronto: McClelland and Stewart, 1966). Gordon's bitter attitude towards Sharp is clear in several of his 1966 memoranda, notably those of June 14, June 27, and Dec. 29, 1966. Gordon Papers, MG32 B44, v. 16 (NAC).

47 *Mike, III:* 226-32; Walter Gordon, memoranda of Dec. 29, 1966, and Jan. 18, 1967, Gordon Papers, MG32 B44, v. 16 (NAC).

48 André Langevin, "Une guerre inutile et insensée", *Le Magazine Maclean* (Feb. 1966), 4; André Laurendeau, "Le Vietnam: saurons-nous dire Non aux Americains?", *ibid.* (Oct. 1966), 76. See also *Canadian Dimension* (May-June 1967) for even more critical articles. Also Fulbright to Pearson, Oct. 5, 1966 (PPP).

49 Pearson's letter to Gordon is in *Mike, III:* 232-4. Gordon's memorandum on the rebuke (May 23, 1967), which is defiant, is found in Gordon Papers, MG32 B44, v. 16 (NAC).

50 *Mike, III:* 144-7. Raymond Heard, "Meeting a Pseudo Event", *Montreal Star,* May 31, 1967. Johnson's indecision is seen in J.S. Hodgson to Pearson, May 18, 1967, MG26 N3, v. 264 (NAC).

51 *Globe and Mail,* June 26, 1967; C. Taylor, *Snow Job,* 122-4; Canadian Institute of Public Opinion, Poll 325, Sept. 1967; and Gordon, *A Political Memoir,* 286-7.

52 Starnes to External, June 11, 1967, MG26 N3, v. 245 (NAC).

53 Peyton Lyon, "The Dilemma of Canadian Foreign Policy", *Canadian Commentator* (Apr. 1967), 6.

CONCLUSION

1 James Eayrs, "We Are Conscious of — and Grateful for — a Job Well Done", *Toronto Star,* Dec. 29, 1972; and L.B. Pearson as quoted in address by the Very Reverend A.B. Moore, Christ Church Cathedral, Dec. 31, 1972.

2 L.B. Pearson, *Mike: The Memoirs of the Right Honourable Lester B. Pearson. Volume III: 1957-1968* (Toronto: University of Toronto Press, 1975), 313ff.; and interviews with Paul Martin and Mitchell Sharp; Mitchell Sharp, *Memoirs* (unpublished manuscript).

3 *Globe and Mail,* Feb. 5, 1968; and John Saywell, ed., *Canadian Annual Review for 1968* (Toronto: University of Toronto Press, 1969), 78-9.

4 Stephen Clarkson and Christina McCall, *Trudeau and Our Times. Volume I. The Magnificent Obsession* (Toronto: McClelland and Stewart, 1990), 111.

5 John Saywell, ed., *Canadian Annual Review for 1964* (Toronto: University of Toronto Press, 1965), 82; and Judy LaMarsh, *Memoirs of a Bird in a Gilded Cage* (Toronto: Pocket Books, 1970), 117. LaMarsh complains bitterly that Pearson let Trudeau "get away" with attacking Johnson.

6 Interviews with Bruce Hutchison and Herbert and Lorraine Moody.

7 Douglas Fisher, "The Quick, Unusual Hallowing of Lester Pearson", *Executive* (July 1973), 8.

8 "Report on Foreign Policy for Canadians" (PPP).

9 L.B. Pearson to Geoffrey Pearson, Dec. 9, 1970 (PPP).

10 Pearson to Trudeau, Feb. 11, 1971, MG26 N5, v.26 (NAC); and Trudeau to Pearson, Feb. 26, 1971, *ibid.*

11 L.B. Pearson to Landon and Geoffrey Pearson, Jan. 1970 (PPP).

12 The titles are, respectively, *Peace in the Family of Man* (London: BBC, 1969); *The Commonwealth 1970* (Cambridge: Cambridge University Press, 1971); and *Partners in Development: Report of the Commission on International Development* (New York: Praeger, 1969).

13 William Clark to L.B. Pearson, Aug. 14, 1968, MG26 N5, v. 1 (NAC); George Ignatieff to Pearson, Dec. 16, 1968, *ibid.;* and Ignatieff to Pearson, Dec. 23, 1968, *ibid.* The members of the commission were: Sir Edward Boyle (U.K.); Roberto de Oliveira Campos (Brazil); Douglas Dillon (U.S.); Wilfried Guth (West Germany); Arthur Lewis (Jamaica); Robert Marjolin (France); and Saburo Okita (Japan).

14 Brian Orend, "Lemonaid: An Analysis of Canadian Bilateral Aid in the 1960s", unpublished paper; and James Eayrs, "Sunny Side Up", *Weekend Magazine* (Dec. 17, 1977), 6.

15 Edward Hamilton, "Thoughts on the Chairman", *International Journal* (Winter 1973-4), 136-42.

16 See Michael Marrus, *Mr. Sam: The Life and Times of Samuel Bronfman* (Toronto: Viking, 1991), 411.

17 Robert Stall, "What Do You Think of Canada, Mr. Muggeridge?", *Weekend Magazine* (Mar. 23, 1974), 6.

18 See Peyton Lyon and Bruce Thordarson, "Professor Pearson: A Sketch", in Michael Fry, ed., *"Freedom and Change": Essays in Honour of Lester B. Pearson* (Toronto: McClelland and Stewart, 1975), 1-8.

19 L.B. Pearson to Landon and Geoffrey Pearson, Aug. 6, 1970 (PPP).

20 The visit is described in fuller detail in Denis Smith, *Gentle Patriot: A Political Biography of Walter Gordon* (Edmonton: Hurtig, 1973), 362-3.

21 Quoted in Peter Stursberg, *Lester Pearson and the American Dilemma* (Toronto: Doubleday, 1980), 320-1.

ACKNOWLEDGEMENTS

I am deeply indebted to several people who have assisted me with this book. The Pearson family has been remarkably kind and helpful, as I rummaged through their attics searching out their past. My chair at Waterloo, David Davies, has always supported me, and my colleagues create an excellent atmosphere for scholarship. Irene Majer, my good friend and secretary, has been indispensable in helping with my administrative duties at Waterloo. Gail Heideman typed the entire manuscript from my appalling handwriting without complaint; I could not have finished the book without her. As with Volume One, Irene Sage Knell has assisted with research and organization of my scattered notes and files; she has now left Waterloo to undertake doctoral work in international relations, and I know her contribution to that field will be outstanding, as was her contribution here. Many students at Waterloo helped with the research and patiently listened as I went on and on about Pearson. For their tolerance and help, I would like to thank Stephen Azzi, Frank Clarke, Greg Donaghy, Stefan Fritz, Mary Kate Kirvan, Jasmine Mangalaseril, Brian Orend, Galen Perras, Angie Sauer, and Joe Sinasac. Each summer Niveditha Logsetty has returned from Toronto to help me, and her warm presence has been a tonic for all of us each June. John Milloy of Oxford and William Christian of Guelph have provided me with some valuable references. Among the numerous academics from whom I have received information or guidance, I would like to thank Chris Armstrong, David Bercuson, Andy

Cooper, Jack Granatstein, Pat Harrigan, Norman Hillmer, Ken McLaughlin, Wendy Mitchinson, and Denis Smith. I have conducted many interviews and would like to thank all who have given their time to me.

The research and writing of the Pearson biography has been generously supported by the Social Sciences and Humanities Research Council. Without its support I could not have completed this project, and I am sincerely thankful. I also received a Killam Senior Fellowship and would like to thank the Canada Council for that assistance.

As a member of the editorial board of the Department of External Affairs historical project, I was able to read the forthcoming volume of the departmental history. It has influenced my interpretation of events in the 1960s, although I am not permitted to quote or cite directly from it. I also had access to relevant External Affairs records for a different project in the 1970s, where the same conditions applied. I would like to thank the department and John Hilliker, the outstanding head of the historical section, for their assistance. The National Archives, particularly Maureen Hoogenraad and Ian McClymont, have been most helpful.

It is a great disappointment that the publisher of Volume One, Lester & Orpen Dennys, is not here to publish Volume Two. The loss of the jewel of Canadian publishing saddens me and all who care not only about books but also about Canada. Nevertheless, it pleases me greatly to be able to work again with Louise Dennys, under the Knopf Canada imprint. Her enthusiasm for the book has been exceptional. At Knopf Canada, Louise Dennys has assembled a splendid team to bring rough words to final print. Those converting my words into clearer English include Margaret Allen, Susan Burns, Gena Gorrell, and Catherine Yolles. I thank them for their tolerance and cheerful ways. My agent, Linda McKnight, smoothed the path to publication.

Finally I would like to thank Hilde and Jonathan for once again enduring my frequent mental and physical absences as I worked on Lester Pearson. I thank them for being understanding with me.

INDEX

References to *PS1* through *PS4* are to
the four photo sections.